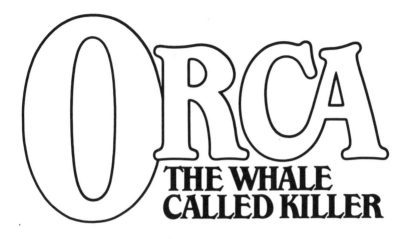

ORCA
THE WHALE CALLED KILLER

BY ERICH HOYT

ROBERT HALE • LONDON

To Robert Emmett Hoyt and Betty Shutrump Hoyt
with love and gratitude

Revised and reprinted 1990

ISBN 0-7090-4231-0

Robert Hale Limited
Clerkenwell House
Clerkenwell Green
London EC1R 0HT

Published simultaneously in Canada by
Camden House Publishing
(a division of Telemedia Publishing Inc.)

Drawings and maps by Kiyoshi Nagahama

Cover photographs © Peter Thomas

Printed in Canada

A portion of the royalties from this book will go to support international conservation work.

ACKNOWLEDGMENTS

I would like to thank the following for answering questions posed through correspondence and, in many cases, detailed interviews: Michael A. Bigg and Graeme Ellis (Marine Mammals, Pacific Biological Station, Nanaimo, British Columbia); John K.B. Ford and H. Dean Fisher (University of British Columbia, Vancouver); Kenneth S. Norris (University of California, Santa Cruz); Victor B. Scheffer (Bellevue, Washington); Edward Mitchell and Anne Evely (Arctic Biological Station, Ste. Anne de Bellevue, Quebec); Kenneth C. Balcomb and Richard W. Osborne (Friday Harbor, Washington); W.H. Dudok van Heel (formerly of Dolfinarium Harderwijk, Holland); Bob Wright and Alan Hoey (Sealand of the Pacific, Victoria, British Columbia); Murray A. Newman (Vancouver Aquarium, Vancouver, British Columbia); Brad Andrews and Tom Otten (formerly of Marineland, Rancho Palos Verdes, California); Lanny H. Cornell (formerly of Sea World, San Diego, California); Stephen Leatherwood (San Diego, California); Jón Gunnarsson (Sædyrasafnid, Iceland); Sam H. Ridgway (Naval Ocean Systems Center, San Diego, California); A.G. Greenwood (International Zoo Veterinary Group, England); Teruo Tobayama (Kamogawa Sea World, Japan); Masaharu Nishiwaki (formerly of University of the Ryukyus, Japan); Frank Brocato (San Diego, California); Robert B. Brumstead (National Marine Fisheries Service, Washington, D.C.); Don White (Vancouver, British Columbia); and Bill Cameron (Pender Harbour, British Columbia).

Thanks are also due my agent, Katinka Matson, and my editors, Marian Skedgell, Susan Brody, Susan Dickinson and Alice Z. Lawrence. Haruko Sato, Françoise Roux, Inke Kase, Jean-Pierre Sylvestre, Jerye Mooney, Lon Appleby, Sean Whyte, Vivia Boe and Jim Borrowman cheerfully assisted in various aspects of the research. John Oliphant provided advice and inspiration. Victor Scheffer, Niko Tinbergen, Graeme Ellis, Michael Bigg, Ronn Storro-Patterson and Jim Borrowman read the manuscript and made suggestions for which I am grateful. Of course, they are not responsible for any mistakes that remain. I especially want to thank my father, Robert Hoyt, for his imaginative editing and comments at every stage of the book.

CONTENTS

FOREWORD

By Sir Peter Scott

Erich Hoyt's book is a splendid introduction to one of the most fascinating and charismatic animals in the world. He blends the story of his exciting adventures working with orcas off the coast of British Columbia with plenty of facts about their behaviour and natural history, which makes a most readable mixture.

Whales and dolphins are all highly intelligent, but orcas are perhaps the most intelligent. Hence, the interactions between people and orcas are extraordinary. Humans and orcas, for example, are curious about one another: they investigate each other, they sing to each other, and they copy each other's tunes. One difference is that while both are among the top predators, orcas never kill men, but men still kill orcas.

As Erich Hoyt acknowledges, the public attitude toward orcas has changed over the last 20 years, partly because the whales have been widely exhibited in aquariums. Familiarity has bred affection, and fear has been replaced with respect. However, I am uneasy about keeping these powerful animals in concrete swimming pools – and making a lot of money out of doing so. The aquarium owners justify this by saying they are teaching people about whales and dolphins, but the price for the orcas is particularly high. It must be preferable for people to see whales and dolphins swimming freely in the sea, and I hope that more and more people will be able to do so from boats whose skippers know how to get close to these exciting animals without disturbing them. Erich Hoyt's book shows in vivid detail how much more can be learned this way.

On August 29, 1989, only days after writing this foreword for the third edition, Sir Peter Scott died at his home in England at age 79. As a founder of the World Wildlife Fund and the Wildfowl and Wetlands Trust and, more recently, as president of the Whale and Dolphin Conservation Society, Sir Peter devoted his life to conservation, using his talents as an ecologist, ornithologist, painter, writer and broadcaster. He was the first Briton to be knighted for services to conservation. The fruits of his efforts remain — all around us and in the way we think. He has sharpened our awareness of the urgency to act on behalf of the Earth.

PROLOGUE

I knew almost nothing about killer whales in June 1973 when I joined a sailing expedition along Canada's Pacific coast. We were to make a documentary film about killer whales. At that time, they had never been filmed in their natural habitat and had only rarely been observed at close range. Our three-month voyage, sponsored by the University of Victoria and funded by the Canadian government, sailed east, then north from Victoria, combing British Columbia's rainy and remote coastal inlets.

As sound man, my job was to record the whales' underwater "voices" with hydrophones (underwater microphones). Later, there would be the usual duties of recording a sound track — complete with narration, sound effects and music — to match the film. I had brought along my electronic music synthesizer, which, when connected to an underwater speaker mounted on the hull, would broadcast sounds to the whales. Although I had written jazz and electronic film scores, devising music to entertain whales was something new. Killer whales in captivity are known to be curious about man-made sounds. Maybe wild whales would be too. It was far beyond our modest budget to try to lure these big carnivores with bucket loads of live or freshly killed fish, but perhaps music piped into their underwater world would draw them in close enough for our cameras. It seemed very chancy, even to me.

Back then, I could not anticipate the depth of my involvement with the whales. I could not have imagined that 10 summers later, I would still be making an annual pilgrimage to visit them.

My first task, after I had decided to join the expedition, was to learn everything I could about the killer whale, *Orcinus orca*, or orca. To my surprise, I found no books devoted to the subject. The articles that I uncovered dealt mainly with how little was known about the species. Yet I did learn a few basic facts:

• Killer whales are the top predator in the sea, possessing 10 to 13 interlocking pairs of conical teeth in each jaw — usually 48 in all.

• The male orca attains a mature length of about 23 feet; the mature female averages less than 20 feet. The species record is 31 1/2 feet — small compared with the 50-to-90-foot lengths of the great whales.

• They are among the ocean's fastest creatures, capable of speeds of up to 30 miles per hour.

• They have no enemies (except man).

Killer whales also have a number of attributes common to other whales and dolphins:

• They are social mammals that eat, sleep, play and travel together in family groups, called pods.

• They have large, complex brains, but no one knows what they use them for.

• They possess all the human senses except smell but are essentially sonic creatures that apparently use sound to navigate, hunt and communicate with each other.

For the most part, I found that scientific studies on *Orcinus orca* in its natural habitat had been confined to examination of stomach contents and to accounts of the animal's attacking behaviour. In storybook tales, orcas are the monsters of the deep, always chewing up boats and sending terrified sailors to hasty funerals at sea. Anything that lived in, visited or fell into the sea — according to these grim stories — was food for orca. There was a grain of truth to many of the stories.

Probably the first published account of orca comes from the Roman scholar Pliny the Elder, who wrote in the first century A.D. in Volume IX of his *Natural History*: "A killer whale cannot be properly depicted or described except as an enormous mass of flesh armed with savage teeth." He called orca "the enemy of other whales" and described scenes in which orcas would "burst into [the other whales'] retreats . . . bite and mangle the females and their calves . . . and charge and pierce them like warships ramming."

The Latin word *orcinus* means "of or belonging to the realms of the dead," and *orca* denotes "a kind of whale." Hence, "killer whale." To the Romans, *orca* represented a single species — the killer whale. During the Middle Ages, orca degenerated to a "sea monster of indeterminate species." The real orca's reputation worsened. In 1598, the English poet Josuah Sylvester wrote: "Insatiable orque [orca], that even at one repast almost all creatures in the world would waste!"

Pliny's view of orca as a savage killer was based on secondhand information, although he had apparently once seen an orca in the harbour at Ostia, near Rome. Emperor Claudius, who was supervising the building of a new pier at the time, led his Praetorian guards in an attack on the hapless creature, spearing it "for to show a pleasing sight to the people of Rome." Pliny's description of orcas killing other whales in the first century resembles modern accounts of killer whales feeding. But Pliny viewed predatory behaviour as a cruel act of violence, as did many of his untrained successors. These accounts gave orca

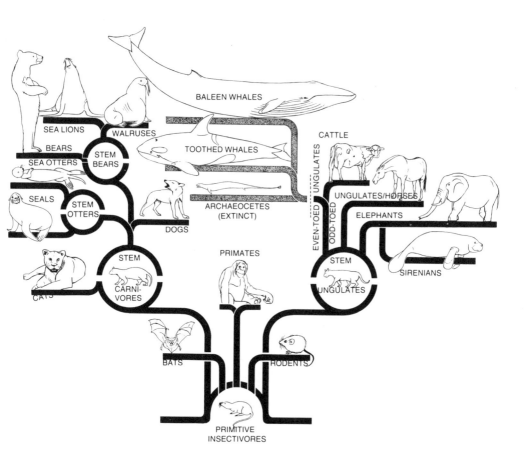

Whales in the family of mammals — possible relationships

its "killer" reputation, similar to that historically given to other large predators, like the wolf.

Killer whales also eat dolphins. The earlier Greeks, including Aristotle, immortalized the dolphin in their stories of dolphins saving drowning humans and playing with children. They knew that the dolphin was "intelligent" and recognized its altruistic nature. To see a dolphin was an omen of good fortune; to kill one, a curse. The dolphin-loving Greeks — and, to a lesser extent, Pliny and the Romans — did not take kindly to the dolphin-killing orca. Paradoxically, the killer whale is classified today as a dolphin. All dolphins are toothed whales, Odontoceti, and the killer whale is the largest member of the family of oceanic dolphins, Delphinidae.

For the 2,000-odd years since Pliny, orcas have probably suffered more abuse than any ocean creature, with the exception of the shark. Orcas have been called voracious and wasteful predators. They have been called man-killers, though there is no documented case of an orca ever killing a man. (There *are* a number of known "man-grabbing" varieties of sharks.) Killer whales have been hated and feared and commonly shot by fishermen, sailors and even governments throughout the world's oceans. The mere sight of a killer whale sends shivers down the spines of stranded mariners. One famous account comes from Lieutenant Henry R. "Birdie" Bowers, who accompanied Robert Scott to the South Pole on his 1911 expedition. One morning, Bowers awoke to find himself with two other men, three ponies and all their equipment adrift on a piece of ice. Hundreds of killer whales surfaced, perhaps attracted to the spot by Bowers' predicament. "Their huge black-and-yellow heads, with sickening pig eyes," wrote Bowers, "[were] only a few feet from us." Yet he and his crew escaped unharmed.

A number of accounts supposedly substantiate orca's bad name. Typical is an oft-misquoted 1862 report by Danish zoologist Daniel F. Eschricht, who found pieces of 13 porpoises and 14 seals in the stomach of a 23-foot-long mature male orca from the Kattegat near Denmark. This, probably more than any other research, firmly established orca's modern-day reputation.

Other controversial accounts are of orcas feeding on large whales. Indeed, this explains the origin of the creature's name: Killer whale derives from whale-killer, coined by 18th-century Spanish whalers who witnessed orcas tearing lips and tongues from great whales several times their size. Writing in 1874, whaler/naturalist Captain Charles M. Scammon likened an orca attack upon their gigantic prey to "a pack of hounds holding the stricken deer at bay. They cluster about the animal's head, some of their number breaching over it, while others seize it by the lips and haul the bleeding monster underwater; and when captured . . . they eat out its tongue."

Whalers and scientists seem to agree on the methodical pack-hunting manoeuvres displayed by orcas when attacking large whales. Yet accounts vary on the outcome. In many chronicles, the killers take the lips and tongue immediately. Then, in some cases, they abandon the animal "to bleed to death." In other accounts, killer whales strip the animal's skin or sample hunks of blubber. Scientists examining orca stomach contents aboard whaling ships have discovered remains of nearly every kind of whale, including the sperm whale, which has formidable jaws of its own and can be twice orca's size. And they have witnessed orcas subduing and feeding upon the blue whale — the largest-known creature ever to live on the planet.

These documented accounts leave little doubt that orcas are big eaters. In captivity, orcas consume at least 3 percent of their body weight in fish each day. While not a large percentage compared with other mammals, it is a lot of food given orca's size. At the Seattle Public Aquarium, Namu, the 3 1/2-ton male, devoured up to 375 pounds a day, 5 percent of his body weight. Active animals in the wild may eat more. Yet orca's voraciousness is often exaggerated, and the tales of its feeding habits tend to become bloodier in the retelling.

During the 19th and early 20th centuries, whalers and the scientists who sometimes accompanied them on their long voyages began to learn about the biology and social behaviour of the whales that they hunted, the great whales — the sperm, right, grey, blue, sei and humpback — but the orca was mostly avoided or ignored. To the whalers, orca was considered a nuisance, sometimes taking harvestable whales or following the boats and feeding off the large whales in tow. The orca was fired on and sometimes killed but rarely

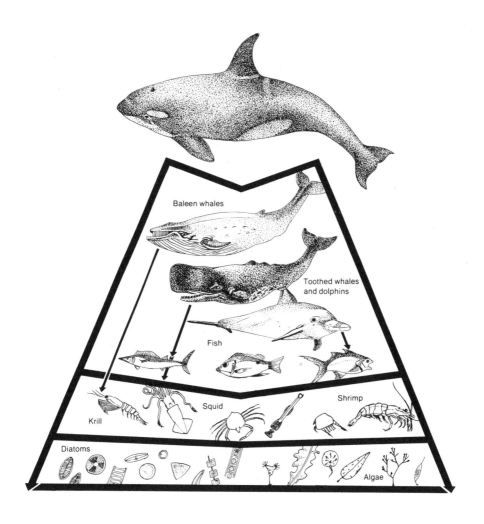

The top predator in the sea

---

taken, since the species was considered too small to be of economic importance. In the 1950s — partly because of diminishing great whale stocks — fisheries specializing in the taking of killer whales, minke whales and other small whales and dolphins were developed off the coasts of Japan and Norway as well as in the Antarctic, by the Soviet Union. These small-whale fisheries have produced almost no scientific studies, except for stomach-content examinations, which have extended the known diet of the killer whale to many new species.

In 1964, 38-year-old Samuel Burich, a sculptor, was commissioned by the Vancouver Aquarium to go out and kill a killer whale and to fashion a life-sized model for the aquarium's new British Columbia Hall. He and assistant Joe Bauer set up a harpoon gun on Saturna Island in British Columbia's Gulf

Islands. After a two-month vigil, with only occasional sightings of orcas, they watched a pod of about 13 approach the island shore. Burich fired one harpoon into the back of a youngster in the group, injuring but not killing it. Immediately, two pod members came to the aid of the stunned whale, pushing it to the surface to breathe. Then the whale seemed to come to life and struggled to free itself — jumping and smashing its tail and, according to observers, uttering "shrill whistles so intense that they could easily be heard above the surface of the water 300 feet away." Burich set off in a small boat to finish the job. He fired several rifle shells at the whale — he later told reporters that he thought "at least two" had hit the animal. But the orca did not die.

The aquarium director, Murray A. Newman, soon arrived from Vancouver by floatplane and decided to try to save the 15-foot-long 1-ton whale. Using the line attached to the harpoon in its back, Burich and Bauer towed the whale to Vancouver. No one could have predicted the 16-hour odyssey across the Strait of Georgia through choppy seas and blinding squalls. Burich did what he could to make the journey easy for the whale; he spliced a rubber tire in the line as a shock absorber and timed the whale's spouts, stopping whenever it seemed to tire or started blowing too fast. The two men, if not the whale itself, were exhausted by the time they reached Vancouver.

Thousands of people lining the shores watched as the "legendary" killer whale was led to a makeshift pen at Burrard Drydocks. A team of scientists was waiting, and many others arrived during the following weeks to observe the first specimen to be kept captive. They were especially surprised by the whale's docility. Newman commented at the time that this orca's tameness was "probably rare." The whale seemed to be suffering shock from its capture and internment, and some felt that this accounted for its subdued behaviour. For a long time, Moby Doll, as she was named, would not eat. She was offered everything from live salmon to horse hearts, but the whale only circled the pool night and day in the same counterclockwise pattern.

On the fifty-fifth day of captivity, Moby Doll broke her fast, began eating up to 200 pounds of fish a day and, almost immediately, became more active. Yet she still did not look healthy. Moby Doll had developed a skin disease from the low salinity of the harbour water and seemed to be suffering from exhaustion. A month after she had started eating, she died.

Moby Doll's death was headlined in newspapers around the world. *The Times* of London gave her obituary a two-column heading, the same size given to the outbreak of World War II. *Reader's Digest, Life* and many others published articles. Bearded captor Burich became a kind of Captain Ahab in reverse. "I worry about this sentimentalizing," Newman told a *Vancouver Province* reporter. "It was a nice whale, but it was still a predatory, carnivorous creature. It could swallow you alive."

The widespread publicity about Moby Doll — some of it, the first positive press ever about killer whales — marked the beginning of an important change in public attitude toward the species. An editorial in the *Victoria Times* the day the creature died contended that the young killer whale had "died a miserable death — unable to reach the clean salt water that was its natural habitat."

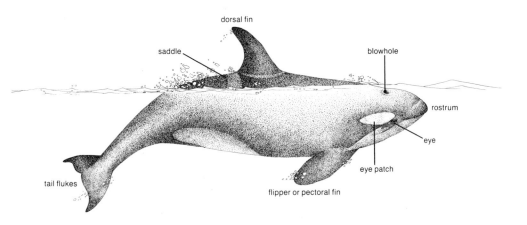

The parts of a killer whale

The autopsy added an amusing postscript: Moby Doll turned out to be Moby Dick — male, not female — something of an embarrassment to Newman and to the many biologists who had seen the animal. It seems that the harbour water was too murky to observe the animal's underside markings.

In 1961 and 1962, employees of Marineland of the Pacific, south of Los Angeles, had twice attempted to capture a killer whale. The first attempt followed the discovery of a single orca feeding alone in nearby Newport Harbor. For most of November 18, 1961, Marineland's head collector, Frank Brocato, and his assistant, Boots Calandrino, worked to corral the mature animal, and by late afternoon, they finally did bag it. They hoisted the whale up onto a flatbed truck and drove to Marineland. When the orca, a female, was introduced into the tank, she smashed head-on into the wall.

"We'd suspected the animal was in trouble because of its erratic behaviour in the harbour," Brocato told me over the telephone some 15 years later. "But the next day, she went crazy. She started swimming at high speed around the tank, striking her body repeatedly. Finally, she convulsed and died."

The autopsy revealed that the mature female had been suffering from acute gastroenteritis and pneumonia. The doctors felt that the great stress experienced during capture had contributed to her strange behaviour and sudden death. Examining her teeth, biologist David E. Sergeant of Canada's Arctic Biological Station estimated the animal's age at 25 years — probably middle to old age for an orca. The teeth showed "extreme wear" and would have limited her diet to smaller foods, according to biologist David K. Caldwell and David H. Brown, then Marineland director, who coauthored a paper correlating tooth wear with described feeding behaviour of the killer whale. "Because she was alone, instead of a member of a normal hunting pack," they wrote, "the animal was forced into an abnormal feeding pattern. . . . Thus . . . while still able to survive, [she] had had to undergo a marked change of social status, as well as a change in feeding behaviour."

In 1962, Brocato and Calandrino brought their 40-foot collecting boat, the *Geronimo*, to Puget Sound, Washington, again in search of a killer whale for Marineland. Kenneth S. Norris, ex-curator of Marineland and professor of natural history at the University of California (Santa Cruz), wrote to me in July 1978 describing the event:

"I knew they [Brocato and Calandrino] were filled with the uncertainty of trying to catch one of these fabled beasts. We all were. There were no stories of their gentle treatment of trainers to modify the stories of ferocity that were then their sole reputation. Some months earlier, together, we had looked down on a group of killers off Santa Barbara, California, that were ripping apart a dead 30-to-35-foot basking shark. The whales swam around our vessel and directly under us, one with about 60 pounds of basking shark crosswise in its jaws. The water was slick and pink with the liver oil and blood. It was an awesome sight and not one to fill a person with tranquillity about killer whales. So I knew they planned to arm themselves for self-protection in case the whales might attack. There were reports of such attacks, including one of a killer that had jumped on the stern of a jack-pole tuna boat, doing quite a bit of damage in the bait-tank area. I was all for the guns, as I didn't know what might happen either."

It was a misty September day when — after a month of searching — Brocato, Calandrino and crewman Mark Munoz encountered a mature male and female orca in Haro Strait, off San Juan Island. The female, who seemed to be chasing something, headed straight for the boat. At that moment, Brocato saw a harbour porpoise cross the bow and skirt the ship, which Norris said is "very unusual [behaviour] for these shy animals." The porpoise was followed by the female orca, hot in pursuit. The little porpoise, as Norris described it, "used the boat as a shield." The two animals, predator and prey, circled the boat.

"I realized there was a good chance to use the lasso," said Brocato, remembering the incident. "So I put my partner out on the bowsprit and told him to watch for that porpoise . . . because the orca might be right behind it. And it was. He slipped on the lasso. We had her. But then everything started to go wrong."

The cow cut sharply and dived under the boat, and before Brocato could stop the screw, its last few turns caught the heavy nylon line and wound it around the propeller shaft, immobilizing the boat. The line was too deep to reach, explained Norris, and "there was no desire to enter the water to cut it."

The female ran to the end of her 250-foot-long tether and surfaced at the edge of the mist. Then Brocato heard screaming — high-pitched piercing cries — coming from the female. On reflection, Brocato realized that it was probably a distress call because the big male appeared out of the mist a few minutes later, and together, the two animals started swimming at great speed toward the boat. They charged several times, turning away only at the last instant but thumping the boat with a sound thwack of the flukes as they passed.

"These blows convinced Frank he was in danger," wrote Norris. Also, the boat was drifting with the tides, and something had to be done. Brocato grabbed his 375-magnum rifle and started shooting. He put one bullet into the male, who then disappeared. But it took 10 shots to kill the female. It was all over in a few minutes. That night, Brocato towed the carcass to nearby Bellingham to have the animal weighed and measured. He also wanted to know the animal's stomach contents. The female's last meal had been a good one: 25 salmon, totalling about 150 pounds. Brocato took the teeth as souvenirs, and the animal was rendered for dog food.

Primarily because of lack of knowledge, it was several years before the first killer whale survived more than a year in captivity. Today, there are trainers who swim with killer whales and even put their heads into the animals' mouths. Scientists have had an opportunity to observe and to study the captive whales, and many advances have come in the new field of orca husbandry. But captive behavioural studies for such a large social mammal are naturally of limited value. At most, only two to three animals can be kept in the very small pool of an aquarium.

The most important result of the captive-orca era has been the almost overnight change in public opinion: People today no longer fear and hate the species; they have fallen in love with them. Aquarium director Newman says that captive killer whales act as goodwill ambassadors for their species. Hyak, who has lived at the Vancouver Aquarium since 1968, has become a star with tremendous drawing power, as have Orky and Corky, a mated pair at Marineland in California. The Sea World chain of aquariums in the United States features orcas that perform under the stage name of Shamu. Orcas have become big box office.

Some killer whale stars have had to put up with almost intolerable hokum. A few years ago, at Sea Worlds in San Diego, Ohio and Florida, orcas were trained to perform Bicentennial patriotic skits, which included donning George Washington wigs and reenacting scenes from American history. As if that were not indignity enough, some of those whales were Canadians — captured in Canadian waters. One night in a Los Angeles motel room, I turned on the television and saw an ex-Canadian killer whale wearing giant sunglasses and selling used cars for Ralph Williams, who cackled: "Orky sez you'll get a whale of a deal."

This new "manufactured" killer whale is a lovable "sea panda" that kisses its trainer and mischievously spits into the crowd during the hourly shows. That is as far from the real orca as the earlier storybook killer. Captive orcas at Sea World and Marineland have held trainers underwater, nearly drowning them. There have been a number of bitings. These incidents generally occur after an individual whale has been in captivity for several years. Due to a change in routine or sometimes due to boredom, the whale suddenly becomes frustrated or disturbed. Fortunately, there is usually some warning to the trainer. To date, no captive has killed its trainer.

Orcas live in every ocean of the world, the largest numbers in colder seas near the North and South Poles. Probably never numerous compared with other whale species, orcas number in the thousands, perhaps in the tens of thousands; these figures are fractional compared with original populations of some of the great whales. The Northwest Coast population of orcas — those living in British Columbia, Washington's Puget Sound and the Alaska panhandle waters — has long been believed to be one of the world's densest. Certainly, it has been the most accessible for aquarium captors. Most of the whales for the world's aquariums have come from the Northwest. And 95 percent of those have come from Puget Sound and southern Vancouver Island waters, a relatively tiny area of the Northwest. Between 1962 and 1973, there were an estimated 262 orcas captured, 247 from this area. Of the total, 11 reportedly died in capture, mostly by drowning in the nets; 53 were kept, of which about 16 died during the first year; the others escaped or were released.

By the early 1970s, killer whales began to avoid Puget Sound and southern Vancouver Island locales where pod members had been captured. One captor, Bert Gooldrup, reported that killer whales had simply stopped coming to Pender Harbour, the main centre for B.C. capture operations. Bob Wright, from Victoria's Sealand of the Pacific, felt that pods had become more cautious about entering Pedder Bay, on southern Vancouver Island, where he had captured whales for his aquarium and for sale to others.

For our film expedition, we decided to sail north to Johnstone Strait and Blackfish Sound, an unexploited region off northeastern Vancouver Island. We had heard that whales came there during the summer months. Ferry captains en route to Alaska and Prince Rupert, British Columbia, had logged more sightings of killer whales in Johnstone Strait than in any other area. Salmon fishermen reported many sightings too. Johnstone Strait was a busy place for these fishermen — many of them Kwakiutl Indians from nearby Alert Bay — who netted the bulk of their yearly salmon catch there. Presumably, the salmon attracted the killer whales. It seemed a good place to start.

Our boat was the *Four Winds*, a 32-foot wooden sailing yawl owned by skipper Bruce Bott who, for financial reasons as much as aesthetics, insisted that it remain as engineless as the day it was launched in 1906. It had to be stocked with supplies for the long voyage and outfitted with camera, sound and diving equipment. The University of Victoria biology department generously provided tape recorders as well as tape, amplifiers, a portable generator and numerous other items. Naturalist Grace Bell of Victoria, who had spent her professional life recording the birds and insects of British Columbia, sold me her valuable Nagra recorder for a ridiculously low price. The Canadian Navy lent us hydrophones and offered the services of their technicians for sound analyses. Electronics experts Jim Grieve and Rex Doane helped me design a working underwater sound system. Funding for the expedition came from the Leon and Thea Koerner Foundation in Vancouver and from the Canadian federal government. Letters of support from zoologist J. Bristol Foster, then director of the Provincial Museum in Victoria, and biologist George Mackie, chairman of the biology department, University of Victoria, helped ensure funding.

At the outset, we were only dimly aware of the problems that we would encounter. We would be studying a creature which spent 95 percent of its time underwater and which was always on the move. Of the dangers, we knew nothing, and a captive orca was not a good model on which to base a judgment. We would be cautious with the wild killer whales, although we believed that they presented no danger to man. Still, we would be dealing with the creature entirely on its terms, in its environment, and we would be facing all the hazards that accompanied sailing the Northwest Coast — unpredictable weather, strong winds and tides. Four of us, all in our mid-twenties, would live aboard the sailboat: Bruce Bott, skipper and diver; Michael O'Neill and Peter Vatcher, cameramen; and myself. In addition, James Hunter, a photographer, and Graeme Ellis, a diver and former killer whale trainer from Victoria, would rendezvous with us in their inflatable Zodiac, from which they would take still photographs. Together, we planned to track the whales, concentrating our energies, if possible, on one or two pods.

Although that summer 1973 expedition was only the first of many to Johnstone Strait whale country, it stands out in my memory. It was a period of discovery and excitement, when I met for the first time the true king of the sea, the whale called killer.

Part One
FIRST SUMMER

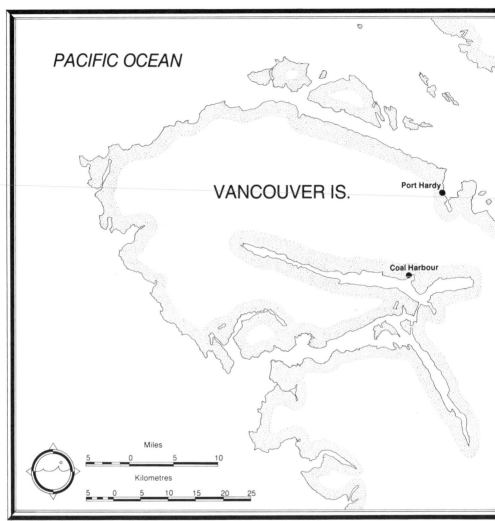

PACIFIC OCEAN

VANCOUVER IS.

Port Hardy

Coal Harbour

Miles
5   0   5   10

Kilometres
5   0   5   10   15   20   25

Northern Vancouver Island

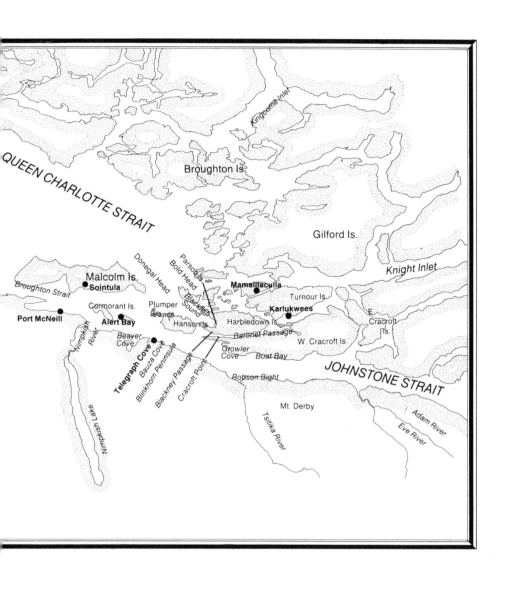

QUEEN CHARLOTTE STRAIT

Broughton Is.

Kingcome Inlet

Gilford Is.

Knight Inlet

Malcolm Is.
Sointula

Broughton Strait

Donegal Head

Parsons
Bold Head

Mamalilacula

Turnour Is.

E.
Cracroft
Is.

Cormorant Is.
Plumper
Islands

Blackfish
Sound

Karlukwees

Port McNeill

Alert Bay

Hanson Is.

Harbledown Is.

W. Cracroft Is.

Baronet Passage

Nimpkish River

Beaver
Cove

Telegraph Cove

Bauza Cove

Blinkhorn Peninsula

Blackney Passage

Cracroft Point

Growler
Cove

Boat Bay

JOHNSTONE STRAIT

Robson Bight

Nimpkish Lake

Mt. Derby

Tsitika River

Adam River

Eve River

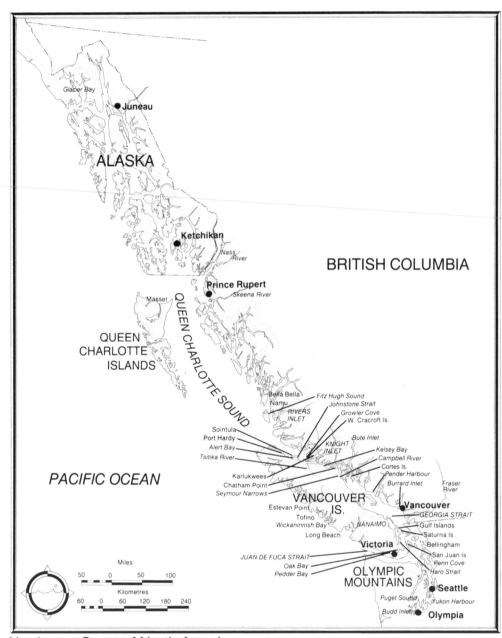

Northwest Coast of North America

KILLER WHALE COUNTRY

JULY 1973. JOURNAL ENTRY EN ROUTE TO JOHNSTONE STRAIT. It's raining . . . again. Seventh day in a row. The farther north we sail, the more it seems to rain, and the taller, thicker and greener grow these trees — the coniferous forest — which cover the mountains on both sides of the channel. I watch the mist as we pass, thick cloud banks sweeping across the mainland fiords, sometimes obscuring the many islands and island passages. I'm beginning to like this moody clime. The rain is gentle — unlike the raw thunderstorms I grew up with in Virginia, Ohio and Ontario. But it does persist. The deck of the boat has developed a number of leaks, and our bunks are constantly wet. I half expect Spanish moss — witches' hair — to start sprouting from the mast and stays.

When one explores new country, especially when the mode of travel is slow — on foot, on horseback or, as in our case, by sail — one experiences the country fully, digesting everything, delighting in the smallest things. I had never explored the coastal region of the Northwest, that vast, mostly uninhabited area which stretches from Washington's Puget Sound through British Columbia to the Alaska panhandle. It is an area unique on the North American continent because of its geography and climate. The coastline here is rocky and irregular, cut by long, deep fiords and dotted with thousands of islands and islets. This sawtooth irregularity gives the B.C. coast an 11,623-mile coastline, a length equal to halfway around the Earth at the equator. Northwest Coast climate is mild year-round; its shores are moderated by the warm Japan current and protected from frigid Arctic air masses by several mountain chains that form a thick spine along the west side of the continent. Northwest Coast rain is caused by the condensation of warm ocean winds striking the mountains' snow-capped peaks. This abundant moisture feeds wide and powerful river systems that cut through the coastal mountains and spill into the sea — rivers which supply a bounty of fresh, clean water and waterpower to the area. The moisture also feeds those vast tracts of evergreens — some of the largest, tallest, densest stands of timber left on the continent. While they are important for lumber, the trees also produce a steady supply of new oxygen, without which the atmosphere's oxygen would slowly disappear. I've heard biologists remark jokingly that if it weren't for all the trees in Canada and Alaska, Americans would suffocate.

We left warm and windy Victoria, at the southern tip of Vancouver Island, on June 27, sailing east to Washington's San Juan Islands and then north through the Strait of Georgia. We followed the route of Captain George Vancouver, who discovered and claimed most of the Inside Passage for England in 1792 and, in the process, determined that the land to the west, some 285 miles long, was an island, the largest off the continent's west coast. The journey to Johnstone Strait and northern Vancouver Island would take us a week to 10 days, and there was a chance that we might encounter whales anywhere along the way. We sailed almost round the clock for the first few days but made little progress, being dependent on a fickle wind. The warm island paradises off the southeastern Vancouver Island coast — islands covered with a colourful mixture of deciduous trees and conifers — gradually gave way to the rainier evergreen north country, with its rocky, sparser dimensions.

At Campbell River, halfway up Vancouver Island, we bartered with an old retired tugboat skipper for a tow through tricky Seymour Narrows. He exchanged a few words for the tow but accepted no money. One of the coast's hardy individualists, he was on an errand to deliver groceries to an isolated settlement in Bute Inlet.

"I like it up here . . . nice and cool. Gets too hot when the sun shines," he said with a smile. We were wearing sweaters and overcoats. He wore only a sleeveless undershirt while he towed us, in the rain, through the tide rips and little whirlpools of Seymour Narrows. "It's tricky to sail." (After waiting several days for the right conditions before looking for a tow, we knew what he was talking about.) "Got to have steady wind, best behind you and with slack tide." He talked about the more than 150 shipwrecks and some 177 lives lost in the narrows since 1875. On April 5, 1958, the largest nonatomic explosion ever contrived by man blew up Ripple Rock, a twin-headed reef that was the main navigational nemesis. "Before that, it was really dangerous here."

I asked if he ever saw killer whales.

"Blackfish?" he asked, using the B.C. fishermen's name for them. "Oh sure, I see 'em. One group — maybe a dozen of 'em — went through here 'bout a week ago, heading north. They were in an awful hurry to get somewhere. Didn't even wait for the tide to change in their favour."

Soon through the narrows, we thanked the old man and watched as he motored off, sweating in the rain.

JULY 5. Skipper Bott is a fixture at the helm, and he cuts something of a comic figure with his long navy peacoat, the white sailor pants and an old telescope (picked up in a secondhand store before we left) with which he scans the seas for orcas. Bott, the purist, is the only one of us with the patience to focus its ancient optics and to try to hold it steady in the swells. Only occasionally does he relinquish his post, usually to Vatcher, our jack-of-all-trades, always ready with a helping hand. O'Neill, our other cameraman, is easy to get along with but has little interest in anything but his cameras. He talks nonstop about the dangers of salt air as he cleans and recleans his equipment.

On July 6, we rounded Chatham Point on Vancouver Island, abruptly turning west by northwest and entering Johnstone Strait. On this same date in 1792, James Johnstone of the Royal Navy began to chart the area. Johnstone, master of the armed tender *Chatham*, had been sent ahead by Captain Vancouver to locate a safe passage. Several days later, Vancouver sailed into view (accompanied by "numerous whales enjoying the season . . . playing about the ship in every direction"), named the waters after his excellent navigator, Johnstone, and noted in his journal that they met a fresh westerly wind, strong flood tides, which fought the ship's progress, and a rising swell, "indicating that the ocean . . . was not quite so remote as it had been estimated . . . and that a passage leading [to the ocean] had been discovered."

Johnstone Strait is a deep channel, one to three miles wide, that separates northern Vancouver Island from mainland British Columbia and from hundreds of nearby islands. It is one sure 55-mile-long passage surrounded by a maze of others; well travelled by tugs, fishing boats and Alaska-bound ocean liners, it is part of the protected Inside Passage of the Northwest Coast.

But Johnstone Strait can be rough and choppy, as Captain Vancouver noted and as we were to discover. Westerlies funnelled down its length, gathering momentum and building seas that smashed against our bow. We were tacking into 15-to-25-knot westerlies most of the way, and to make headway, we had to time our departure to the 3-to-4-knot ebb tides.

As we sailed through, I reflected on how little the land had probably changed since Vancouver's time. From a distance, the terrain appears wild and unsettled: The shore on both sides is high and rugged, especially the Vancouver Island side, a continuous mountain range rising almost abruptly from the sea to the snow-capped peaks, up to 5,000 feet high.

Yet through the mist, we could glimpse evidences of modern man: the logging camps every 15 miles or so along the Vancouver Island coast; the logging roads winding up the mountains; the bald patches of some mountains where the big logging companies have clear-cut; the stray logs and "deadheads" in the water for which you must constantly be on the alert. Once, while anchored in an open bay, we were awakened in the middle of the night by a herd of stray timber crashing against our wooden hull. We pushed the logs away with the whisker pole, but they kept coming. We slept little that night. In the morning, they were gone, carried away on the shifting tide.

The forest industry — mostly logging and pulp mills — forms the backbone of northern Vancouver Island's economy. Far more important economically than commercial fishing, the five major logging companies (MacMillan Bloedel, Rayonier Canada and Canadian Forest Products are the largest; Crown Zellerbach and Tahsis Company are somewhat smaller) hold tree-farm licences, timber leases and pulp leases that cover much of northern Vancouver Island. The trees are cut at remote mountain camps, and the logs are trucked down winding logging roads to seaside centres like Beaver Cove. Here, the logs are graded, sorted and dumped into the water. A few are placed on huge self-loading, self-propelled log barges, but most are simply rafted and sent south to the sawmills of southern Vancouver Island and the lower mainland. The only sawmill on northern Vancouver Island is one at Telegraph Cove, at the western end of Johnstone Strait. It was here that we stopped to buy groceries and to make a telephone call one evening. We had anchored in nearby Bauza Cove just as the wind died. Hiking half an hour through the bush, we followed the old telegraph trail to Telegraph Cove, sometimes sidestepping the original line, which was falling down and overgrown in places. In 1911, a telegraph station had been established at the mouth of this cove, as the northern terminus on Vancouver Island. Although the station was moved across the strait to Alert Bay on Cormorant Island a few years later, Telegraph Cove survived as a mill town when the Wastell family of Alert Bay set up a sawmill to make boxes for salted salmon being shipped to Japan. It was good business for a decade, but the advent of the cardboard box forced the mill to diversify or die. In the decades since, the mill has grown some but not by much. Today, it employs 10 men who operate with the same old belt-driven saws and equipment used in the early part of the century. Yet the old-fashioned mill manages to survive in the age of automated electronic mills. The secret, explained the town's 73-year-old founder and mill owner, Fred Wastell, is that Telegraph Cove does not try to compete with "the big guys." The small mill does the odd orders for odd timbers cut to odd sizes. Big mills are not set up to handle things like railroad ties, oversized beams, bridge timbers and fence-posts — the mill's specialties. They also do small orders for local north coast communities, which Wastell still delivers on his boat, the *Gikumi*.

We walked slowly, testing our sea legs, as we explored the pocket-sized town, neatly tucked into the rocks and steep-treed hillside. About a dozen old wood-frame houses — painted white, green and brown, with marigolds and begonias spilling out of window boxes — are situated on either side of a board-walk that curves around the log-filled cove. We passed the mill at one end of the boardwalk, then, at the first house, we introduced ourselves. We were invited in, served tea and crumpets and welcomed as "old friends."

Our hosts, Bud Law and his wife, Renie, moved from Vancouver to work in the mill only a few years before. "About 50 people live here, mostly families, and most have lived here for years," Law said. His work as a travelling sales-man for a Vancouver insurance firm brought him to Telegraph Cove once a year. He began to feel that it was the best part of his job. Law grew friendly with the local people, and when he learned of a job opening in the cove, he grabbed it. "I wouldn't trade our life here for any city."

The people who have chosen to live in Telegraph Cove — some immigrants, some refugees from the city — allow no sentimentalizing about the place. They reject the word quaint to describe the town and their life style. Erik Vinderskov, a Dane who brought his German wife, Eva, here 20 years ago, explained: "People come up here to visit, or they see photos, and they get that nice shine in their eyes and say, 'That's what I always wanted — to get away from the smog and the noise and the rat race.' But few people nowadays really can stand the isolation. On a sunny day, it may look beautiful, but by February, sometimes we haven't seen the sun in five months. You've got to be attuned with nature; otherwise, there's no sense living here."

Wastell, the town's oldest resident, lives with his wife in a rambling house built high on a cliff overlooking Johnstone Strait. Talking to Wastell, I couldn't help comparing Telegraph Cove to the incorporated company towns on northern Vancouver Island. I pointed to the difference between quiet, aesthetic Telegraph Cove and a rough-and-tumble loggers' town like nearby Port McNeill, which looks like an instant town bulldozed out of the earth. Port McNeill's subdivision and trailer park on a steep hillside seemed ill conceived, a quick and ugly solution to a housing problem. But Wastell pointed out that Port McNeill was actually planned, while Telegraph Cove just evolved. The difference is primarily due to the bulldozer, today's efficient method of claiming the wilderness. Wastell and his generation of 50 years ago didn't have bulldozers, so they built around the big trees. And in Telegraph Cove, they built the boardwalk, a wooden road, because of the cove's geography and because they had no concrete. It had nothing to do with aesthetics. The old way probably looked as "violent" to the landscape then as the new way does today. Telegraph Cove has had years of weathering, that long process during which the work of man slowly begins to harmonize with nature. The paint on the houses may be fresh, but the wooden houses, the cedar-shake roofs, the boardwalk and the mill have aged and blended with the surrounding trees and hills.

Whales? The people at Telegraph Cove had many stories about them. On our first visit, we told Law about the film we were making. Law spends his Saturdays sport fishing, and he'd seen more than a dozen killer whales the previous month in Baronet Passage, a narrow, hazardous tide-swept channel that spills into Johnstone Strait. He'd tried to film them with his 8mm movie camera. "It's impossible," he said. "You never know where they're going to come up. But about six weeks ago, I did get some close-up footage of one of the largest groups of Steller sea lions ever seen around here, about a hundred of 'em. They were diving off the rocks, splashing for the camera."

I asked if he had ever seen killer whales eat sea lions. He shook his head. "They're chasin' salmon. Where the best fishing is — that's where you'll find the blackfish." He thought more whales would be coming to Johnstone Strait as the fishing boats moved in for the salmon. "It'll be like a city out there — nets everywhere. They'll be fishing a few days a week starting in July going through September."

The previous fall, Law told us, whales had swum inside the mouth of Telegraph Cove. Wastell mentioned incidents from other years. "Usually, only one or two of 'em come. They rest their white chins on the rocks. Seem to be looking at us. Then they're gone. But you don't see many whales in the strait anymore." He shook his full head of white hair, remembering. "Used to see *big* whales, besides the blackfish — oh gosh, lots of 'em — sei whales, finbacks, even the occasional humpback. The whaling company at Coal Harbour came through the strait 10 or 15 years ago. Fished 'em out."

As we hiked back to the boat, warmed by the coffee and conversation, I kept thinking about the whales coming right into the cove. Maybe they were out there in the misty twilight right now, resting their chins on the rocks and watching us.

> JULY 9. A noisy night at anchor. Tides constantly shifting, sounding at times like waterfalls, the boat swinging on its anchor. Then there was rain. In the morning, the wind shifts from southeast to light westerlies. I am awakened by ravens perched atop one of the tallest Douglas firs on the island shore, 50 yards from the boat. They seem to have a lot to talk about. I look out the hatch. They cackle, then are quiet. Minutes later, they take off, flying toward the boat. Directly over me, two of them fold their wings simultaneously and drop down 10 yards. I listen to the breathy "whuh-whuh" of their great black wings. As they continue on their way, I notice patches of blue sky through the dense cloud cover. Then, across the strait, some sunlight catches my eye, pouring yellow-green through patches of trees on the mountain. A new colour scheme makes the world seem fresh.

We spent the day combing Johnstone Strait for whales, tacking back and forth from Vancouver Island to the Cracroft Island side. Stately snow-capped Mount Derby, 5,400 feet high, shone above Robson Bight, a wide-open bay on the Vancouver Island side. Beautiful? Yes. But we were surfeited with beauty, and Derby was "just another mountain." I did not know then how familiar that mountain would become — that one day some of us would climb the peak and watch whales spouting down in the strait and that we would fight for the preservation of this place. The adjacent valley is formed by the basin of the Tsitika River, the last unlogged, untouched river valley on eastern Vancouver Island. In 1973, the MacMillan Bloedel logging company, which held most of the timber rights, was already starting to survey.

The opposite side of the strait is formed by a series of islands and islets. Cracroft Island, the largest, is 17 miles long and 5 miles wide at its broadest point. It is thickly wooded with second-growth timber and reaches a height of about 1,150 feet in the centre of the island. Behind Cracroft, we could see the bald hills of other islands, with trees reduced to sticks by logging and forest fires — an eyesore until a sunset turns the hills a soft pastel purple.

JULY 10, EVENING. It was a rough Johnstone Strait afternoon, decks awash, boat heeled over. Yet all is calm by sunset. The gulls cross the strait en masse from their feeding grounds in Robson Bight, beneath Mount Derby, to their roosts on Cracroft Island, above Boat Bay. We follow the gulls into the bay and drop anchor for the night.

Johnstone Strait weather alternates between two major patterns. Steady westerlies are the prevailing "fair weather" wind of the Northwest Coast. In this pattern, mornings in Johnstone Strait are foggy, overcast and calm, but by noon, the fog lifts, revealing the sun. Then the wind starts to build. Peak velocity is 15 to 25 knots, usually whipping up a white-capped sea by late afternoon. Before sunset, wind speed drops quickly, and by darkness, at 10 p.m., the sea is again flat calm, generally remaining so throughout the night.

Southeasters bring the other major weather pattern to the coast. Southeasters mean rain and unsettled weather. Both westerlies and southeasters funnel through east-west Johnstone Strait, but southeasters sometimes bring fierce winds that can arise with almost no warning.

En route to Johnstone Strait, we had already experienced one southeasterly gale. On a calm, almost no-wind day, our big genoa sail was trying to seduce even the hint of a breeze when the gale struck. It built to 45 knots in less time than it took our skipper to decide that we'd better pull down the sails. We nearly capsized. Eight hours later, tired and near mutinous, we limped into port, though by then, the storm had abated.

We had yet to see a killer whale. In the two weeks since we'd left Victoria harbour, all our whale "sightings" had been verbal accounts from luckier crews. Until we learned more about whale movements and their habits, we would have to keep asking and searching. Johnstone Strait seemed at times a vast area.

JULY 11. The break in the southeasterly weather this morning gave us a lift. The rain was beginning to wear on us, though no one wanted to admit it. Today, each of us finds more pleasure in daily tasks. There is none of the petty squabbling of last week. Vatcher and O'Neill work on a few bugs that have developed in the camera equipment. I work on the hydrophones. We have no choice but to share in O'Neill's obsession with salt air. That archenemy of electrical and mechanical gear is becoming a stern teacher and will make electronic technicians of us all.

Late afternoon. Bott takes the rowboat and his telescope to scout for whales and to catch dinner. On the way back, he stops to talk to a young couple whose trimaran is anchored at the other end of the bay. The couple saw several orcas in eastern Johnstone Strait yesterday, headed this way. How do they know they were orcas? "By the dorsal fins." The orca's tall dorsal is the creature's most unusual and striking feature. It has no muscle but may serve the whale as a keel does a boat. The couple described one whale as having a dorsal that towered above all the others. A bull's dorsal fin is more than twice as high as a female's or an immature male's.

As an anchorage, Boat Bay left something to be desired, since it was open to the strait. But that meant we could listen for the whales. That night, we were alerted by a faint, yet distinct, high-pitched, reedy sound on the hydrophone. It was a machinelike "bleep" that recurred at eight-second intervals, growing steadily louder. O'Neill could see nothing from on deck. A minute later, a fast-moving Canadian Navy destroyer came into view across the strait. We had been tuning in to its depth sounder, set at about 8 to 10 kHz, within the whales' frequency range. No whales — yet I was encouraged by the fact that the hydrophone was picking up sounds some three miles away.

JULY 12. The sun and the wind come up together. The westerly breeze blows ocean cold in our faces while the sun makes a brave show of strength. We pull anchor at Boat Bay and sail into the strait, the wind catching our sails, the boat and the mast creaking in submission.

"Killer whales!" Bott yelled, pointing toward them and throwing the tiller hard over at the same time.

I craned my head through the open hatchway for a glimpse. A hundred feet off to starboard, five killer whales blew simultaneously, billowy steam shooting out of huge, glistening, black bodies. Their dorsal fins wavered in the wind. The whales stayed no more than three seconds at the surface — long enough to blow, take a deep breath and dive.

I cranked up the sound equipment below decks, threw a hydrophone into the water, put on headphones and started recording. Vatcher and O'Neill grabbed movie cameras and braced themselves on deck for action. Bott handled the boat, reefing the sails to try to stay with the whales until we could gauge their direction and speed of travel.

Twenty seconds passed before they surfaced again. The small orca family included one calf, whose tiny curved fin and less-than-10-foot-long body made it look like a porpoise. The calf's mother and two other whales surrounded the youngster in a protective circle. They hung at the surface for a few seconds, and I was struck by their wild beauty — a quality that I had never observed in the docile aquarium captives. The bull, who had been leading them, angled toward our boat. All the whales sounded.

"Can you hear them on the hydrophone?" Vatcher shouted.

I shook my head. I was straining through the ocean roar for some sign of vocalization, but I heard nothing.

They seemed to stay down for a long time. We kept looking around, wondering where they might surface.

"That's five minutes now," Vatcher said, looking at his watch.

"Behind us!" shouted Bott.

The bull's tall, black dorsal fin, seeming to wobble from its own weight, knifed the water 20 feet from our stern. O'Neill swung his camera around and filmed the bull's fin slicing the water. When the fin had nearly disappeared, the bull rotated a quarter-turn onto his side. His head emerged, revealing a blunt profile, with only a hint of the dolphin snout. Just behind and below his white eye patch was a black, almost invisible, slightly protruding eyeball. For an instant, he looked at us. Then he was gone, his wide flukes pushing off, driving him deep, leaving three rings of water on the surface.

Two seconds later, I heard the bull's cry, so loud he must have been underneath the boat. "YEEEEEEEEEEEE-oooo-ee!" he sang in his finest boy soprano. It was a three-note two-second-long cry. The sound was almost too loud for the headphones. I watched the tape recorder's needles dancing in the red before I could turn down the volume. Then he repeated himself, and from farther off, with five-second intervals between each vocalization, he intoned two different phrases: first a quick upward glissando, then a long, warbly call. The clean power of his voice filled me with awe. I wanted to communicate with him, to tell him that we meant no harm but were interested in him and wanted to be close. I had no sense that the bull was afraid of us — unlike other animals I'd encountered in the wild — yet I wanted to reassure him of our intentions.

A minute later, the bull rejoined his pod, and the group surfaced and blew some 50 yards off our bow. They milled together, seeming indecisive, for about 20 seconds. Then they headed east, down the strait.

As we learned later, this was typical killer whale behaviour toward man. Often, the first thing that the whales did whenever they encountered us was to approach the boat. Sometimes, they would poke their heads out of the water and look at us. Other times, they would not surface near the boat but would use echolocation to find it. I could hear the clicks on the hydrophone. Then, looking over the side, we would often see a whale swim underneath the boat, like a dark shadow, but with the white patches surprisingly visible through the water. Perhaps this whale would then broadcast information about us to the others so they wouldn't need to investigate, since often, as soon as one had made the initial close pass, the pod's curiosity seemed satisfied, and they went about their business. This behaviour was probably normal predator curiosity, for an opportunistic predator like the killer whale needs to be aware of new additions to its environment. Sometimes, it was a bull who conducted the investigation, but more often, we found, it was one or two youngsters, juveniles or cows. The whales' lack of fear undoubtedly stemmed from their position as top predator in the sea, with no natural enemies.

The whales were moving, and we followed them for almost an hour, staying about 50 yards behind. With the bull leading, they headed due east, parallel to and about 100 yards from the Cracroft Island shore. They came up for air almost simultaneously — three or four times over the space of a minute and a half. Then they submerged for four to five minutes. They travelled about two miles in this pattern. We were getting good at judging where they would come up when they suddenly changed pattern.

First, the bull turned south and started to cross the strait, then the pod followed. For a while, we kept pace, the wind on our beam, but then the whales started swimming faster and pinching the wind until they were heading directly into it. During the next two hours, the whales steadily moved away from us — from 100 yards to 300 yards to one mile, then several — until, in the binoculars, their dorsal fins became little black dots on the horizon and their blows occasional white geysers against the distant shore of Vancouver Island. Then the black dots disappeared, and the geysers were indistinguishable from whitecaps crashing and spraying against the rocky coastline. They seemed to have entered Robson Bight, a large open bay, so we spent the afternoon tacking across the strait, hoping that they would slow down or perhaps turn around.

It was early evening when we sighted whales again. At a few hundred yards, we weren't certain they were the same ones. But as we neared, I saw the bull with the tall, wobbly fin and his four cohorts. The whales were crossing the strait from Robson Bight to the Cracroft Island side. We headed toward them. For 20 minutes, the distance between us was less than 100 yards as the whales turned and moved east, but we were unable to get close enough to film them or to make more recordings. The sun was setting in our sails as we approached Boat Bay on Cracroft Island, where we had met the whales seven hours earlier. Conveniently, the whales had brought us to our safe anchorage just as night fell and the wind died. They were still visible on the horizon, heading east, when we dropped anchor and made provisions for the night.

JULY 13. Foggy morning. Set sail about 1 p.m. We decide to move slowly west, staying in the middle of the strait, so that we might see or perhaps hear the whales on either side. One thing we've noticed is how far sounds carry over water, especially when wind and sea are calm. We can hear whales several miles away, even before we see them. If we aren't moving fast, I can also monitor them on the hydrophone.

At about 2 p.m., we heard a buzzing sound on the horizon and saw a grey speck coming toward us. It was the Zodiac inflatable boat with our friends from Victoria, James Hunter and Graeme Ellis. They'd said that they would meet us "somewhere in Johnstone Strait," and here they were. We planned to work together, coordinating whale sightings. They would approach the whales in the Zodiac, mainly to obtain still photographs. We had the sailboat, better suited for filming and recording. Ellis had received money for food and supplies as part of our expedition. Hunter, teaming up with Ellis, had brought his own Zodiac and photographic gear and hoped to pay his way by selling his photographs.

"Ahoy! Permission to come aboard?" Hunter called, straining to be heard over the sea slop and the putt-putt of the Zodiac's engine. Ellis bounced the rubber inflatable off our port stern, threw us a line and cut the throttle, and they climbed aboard.

"What are you doing down here?" asked Hunter, cleaning his wet, steamy glasses as we talked. "We found about 16 orcas at the end of Cracroft Island. We've been with 'em all morning." He pointed north, the direction from which they'd come.

Ellis studied his watch: "The whales were moving at about three to four knots, heading directly this way; at that rate, they should be here in exactly 25 minutes."

Hunter and Ellis, both blonde-haired, were decked out in shiny yellow rain gear. Hunter had a "felt-tipped-pen" moustache and wore a red baseball cap turned backward. Ellis's muttonchop sideburns made a furry frame for his wide grin.

At 22, Ellis had more experience with killer whales than almost anyone. As a kid growing up near Campbell River, he saw orcas pass by the shore and threw rocks at them. "That's what you did," he said. "And when you got older, you shot at them with BB guns, then .22s."

When Ellis was fresh out of high school in 1968, he got a job training the Vancouver Aquarium's captive orcas at Pender Harbour. Having to walk along a slippery log several times a day to feed the orcas, Ellis developed a tremendous sense of balance.

"I thought, 'If I fall in, I'm done for,'" said Ellis. "I'd been assigned to a young bull named Irving who wouldn't eat. I spent about a month calling 'Here boy, here boy, come on herring, herring' to this huge whale that just ignored me; it was really embarrassing. Then one day, I was sitting on the board splashing water at Irving. Suddenly, he lifted his pectoral fin and splashed back. So I splashed him. And he splashed me again. I thought he was responding at last. But he disappeared. And then, all at once, four tons of whale breached out of the water right in front of me. I was just about washed off the log. Within a few hours, he was coming up to get scratched and rubbed, and the next day, he was eating — though at first, only freshly killed ling cod. It was really an eye-opener for me. Until we happened upon our splashing relationship, he hadn't trusted me. Later, I worked with other whales, but Irving will always be my favourite." While studying marine biology at the University of Victoria, Ellis trained Haida and the albino orca Chimo for Sealand of the Pacific.

His 24-year-old partner, James Hunter, was a photographer and film script writer who had wandered up and down the coast from Hollywood to the Alaska panhandle and called most of it home. He was a born comedian, but he was also a keen observer, if sometimes given to hyperbole. His almost inexhaustible energy and enthusiasm made him a good expedition man.

Hunter and Ellis had arrived in Johnstone Strait a week before us, driving the logging road to northern Vancouver Island in a beat-up vintage Pontiac Strato Chief that Hunter had dubbed "the Pontasaurus" because of its size and its rattling state of near extinction. They had inflated the Zodiac at Beaver Cove and begun the search for whales in Johnstone Strait. Pitching camp on the Plumper Islands, two granite rocks a few miles north of the strait, they settled in, as Ellis put it, "for the old watching-and-waiting routine." A few days later came an encounter with eight whales: two bulls, an assortment of cows and young males, and one very young calf. They had seen the pod twice since. They were able to identify it by one bull whose dorsal fin hooked forward and had a notch midway down the trailing edge — they called him Hooker.

I wondered about the bull with the wobbly fin in the five-whale group we had followed. Neither Ellis nor Hunter had seen a whale fitting that description, but they told us about a larger pod they had seen a few times.

"Maybe the five are part of the bigger group," suggested Ellis. They had watched Hooker's pod split into subgroupings for a few hours, but it always re-formed into an eight-whale pod. "But the other group," said Ellis, ". . . or maybe it's several groups . . . sometimes there are 8 or less, sometimes 12 or 16 or even 20. Hard to say whether we're seeing several groups that periodically join together or one large group that sometimes splits." Indeed, it would take many encounters that first summer before we established the integrity of certain pods; however, it was obvious from the start that some of the pods were cohesive units.

While we were chatting on the deck of the *Four Winds*, the whales came into view. This was the indefinite group we had been discussing. Spread out in every direction, the whales gave no hint of cohesive formation. We counted and recounted them, coming up with different figures each time. They surfaced at different times and at irregular intervals and were not moving in a straight path.

Then we saw the wobbly-fin whale, travelling in a spread-out subgroup with two other bulls. I had a good look at him through the binoculars. A mature male, he arched his back, showing his tall dorsal fin to full advantage before it tottered and sank beneath the sea. The killer whale dorsal fin is mainly cartilage, containing no bones or muscle. On mature males, it tends to wobble due to sheer height and weight. But this bull's fin seemed to have a unique wavy contour on its trailing edge, and Wavy became his name.

None of the other bulls seemed to have distinguishing characteristics or marks on their fins. But we did see one whale with a mangled fin lying motionless on the water, some 200 yards behind the group. The odd-looking animal's dorsal fin was chopped off, a stub, the edges mangled.

"Stubbs!" Ellis announced.

I had heard the name before. Paul Spong, a former killer whale researcher at the Vancouver Aquarium who had visited Johnstone Strait for several summers, had told me about the whale with the stubby fin. Some fishermen claimed to have seen Stubbs as far back as 1967.

At first, Stubbs's sex was in question. It is impossible to distinguish between mature females and young males; both have small curved fins. The fact that this whale had been seen in the area for some years indicated a mature animal. If so, Stubbs was female.

We wondered about the injury. A birth defect? A fight? Or, more likely, the result of an encounter with a boat propeller?

JULY 13, EVENING. I made more recordings today despite equipment failures from saltwater shorts. Most of the whale sounds are faint, barely decipherable through the ocean noise. Several times, I heard that first sound — the one I recorded from Wavy when he was in the group of five — but from a distance. No way to tell whether it is the same whale or not. The three-note phrase seems to be a characteristic whale phrase, at least of that pod. Mostly, however, the whales were keeping their distance today. After observing them for a short while, we ran into a big westerly blow. We could see it approaching: a dark line on the water and frothy whitecaps following behind. It ended our visit with whales and people prematurely. Ellis and Hunter bumped off in the Zodiac, back to their protected camp in Blackfish Sound, while we nipped into Boat Bay.

We were pleased to have found an area of killer whale concentration. The stories of local boaters and fishermen and the reports by Ellis and Hunter (who had had an opportunity to scout the area the week before we arrived) further confirmed our observations. It also seemed that we would be able to identify certain individuals and, from them, establish pod groupings. Individual identification of animals is essential to any study of their social behaviour.

Next day, we planned to sail to the small island community of Alert Bay to get food and supplies and to make some repairs. Every time it rained, our bunks collected water from the leaky deck, and problems had developed with the boat's rudder. Alert Bay — a colourful salmon-fishing centre, an important supply depot, a rest stop for boats plying the Inside Passage between Seattle and Alaska — was the best place for ship repairs. It was also "Home of the Killer Whale," according to its tourist brochures. The lives and legends of its large native population — the seagoing Kwakiutls — have been intertwined with the killer whale for centuries.

©Peter Thomas

A young killer whale puts on an impressive display of lobtailing, a popular orca pastime. Since the smack of an orca's tail on the water can be heard for miles, it is a useful guide for locating pods.

The whales are capable of quick bursts of speed during which they "porpoise" along the surface.

Using their good vision, orcas sometimes "spy hop" to orient themselves above water.

The rear view of a bull orca may provide a clue as to the whale's age, since an older bull's dorsal fin sometimes becomes "wavy."

A breathtaking exhibit of wild-orca showmanship off Vancouver Island. The outstretched flippers measure seven feet in length.

Cause of death: unknown. In August 1973, the expedition found this dead young killer whale near Bauza Cove in Johnstone Strait, but despite a hole in the carcass, which could have been caused by a bullet, careful examination did not reveal any more clues.

Hooker and the boys. Hooker, third from the left, is easily distinguished, as his dorsal fin arches forward, giving the impression that he is swimming backwards. His pod consists largely of males, which generally live up to 60 years — 10 to 20 years less than females.

Evening sets on Blackfish Sound. Top Notch's pod, foreground, and Stubbs's pod, background, come together for the night in a superpod. The big bull in the foreground is Top Notch, while Nicola can be seen at the far left of the rear pod.

THE
SONIC CREATURE

It was sunny the afternoon we sailed into Alert Bay's harbour. The light filtered through the tall trees of the island and bounced off the 1 1/2-' storey wood-frame houses and stores that line the single main street. We fought our way through stiff tides and traffic to approach the dock. As we drew closer, I saw the famous Kwakiutl totem poles, which have brought visitors to the island since before the turn of the century. Ethnographer Franz Boas, who arrived in 1886, made the Kwakiutls well known through his many papers and books. In 1893, he took a group of Kwakiutls to the Chicago World's Fair. Then, beginning in 1910, photographer Edward S. Curtis spent four seasons with the Kwakiutls, devoting the largest volume in his 20-volume series on the American Indian to them and making the world's first feature-length ethnographic film.

Alert Bay of the 1970s bore little resemblance to the village shown in the turn-of-the-century photographs and films of Boas and Curtis. The best totems were taken long ago by museums. The few dozen that remain are rotting and faded or overpainted in gaudy greens and yellows on a glossy white base — bright colours not used by the early natives. Some stand in the front yards of houses along Fir Street. Two matching beakless eagles perched atop grizzly bears flank the old Indian Industrial School, a massive brick fortress covered in peeling white paint. Most of the remaining poles stand guard over the Nimpkish Cemetery, the tallest now dwarfed by the Shell Oil towers on the hill behind them. But there are a few new poles in the cemetery. Alone among all the Northwest Coast Indians, the Kwakiutls have kept alive the carving tradition. Today, there is a full-scale revival in progress.

We were met at the dock by Paul Spong, a psychologist who had worked with killer whales at the Vancouver Aquarium. He offered us a grand tour of the village while we shopped. "Then we'll go for a beer," he said, "and I'll show you the social life."

We walked along a narrow street that had no sidewalk, sidestepping cars, people and the occasional mud puddle. First, we checked out "the bay," the Kwakiutl reserve built around the heart of the harbour in the oldest part of town. Here were typical Canadian wood-frame houses dating from 1920 to 1950; the imposing Indian Industrial School erected in 1929 to house more than 200 school-age children; and Christ Church, built in 1881, where services are still conducted in the Kwakiutl language.

Climbing the hill to a grassy field behind the homes, we saw the massive Big House, which was built in 1967 in the old native style with fitted cedar beams. It is the place for winter native dances and for native social gatherings, called potlatches.

As we toured, Spong pointed to Kwakiutl killer whale designs carved on totems and painted on cars, trucks, house fronts and business signs. Seaplanes of the Alert Bay Air Services are decorated with bold black orcas on a yellow background. Most are primitive two-dimensional representations of orca, some with two dorsal fins or a man riding on the back, others showing a salmon or a seal in the stomach. Many designs are almost abstract. "You can tell the Kwakiutl killer whale by the interlocking teeth and the obvious dorsal fin," said Spong. The Chamber of Commerce has mounted a large placard of a Kwakiutl killer whale on a prominent dockside building to attract visitors aboard Alaska-bound cruise ships. When I asked about it, Spong laughed. "Actually, the whales avoid Alert Bay because the harbour is polluted and too busy most of the time." Nonetheless, Alert Bay is one of the few places in the world where, in the summer months, a visitor can charter a boat for a day and count on seeing killer whales.

Spong waved to a young Kwakiutl man carving cedar bowls on a beach log near the road; the carver was wearing an Alert Bay "Home of the Killer Whale" t-shirt that barely covered his paunch. Beyond him, three near naked children waded into the cold harbour, their dark forms silhouetted against the sparkling highlights off the water. The natives appear unfriendly at first meeting; some resent whites. But more, I found, were only shy and sometimes self-effacing. Some became my friends, although it took time. "It's not always this quiet," said Spong, as we continued on our way. "When the fishermen return, Alert Bay becomes a real party town. Everyone hits the beer parlours — the Harbour Inn or the Nimpkish — for a three-day binge."

In the Nimpkish Hotel beer parlour, we sat next to picture windows overlooking the harbour. "This place is like a Wild West saloon sometimes," said Spong, "but she's like a ghost town in here today. We'll be able to talk, mate." Spong calls everyone mate. His New Zealand accent is still evident, although the 34-year-old physiological psychologist left the country of his birth more than a decade ago. In 1967, Spong was hired by the University of British Columbia to study the sensory system of killer whales at the Vancouver Aquarium.

"I approached the whales as a clinical experimental psychologist," said Spong, "getting them to do things as if they were no more than laboratory rats." He and co-researcher Don White first measured orca's visual acuity. They found that a young male named Hyak could see about as well underwater as a cat could in air. They tested a young Pacific white-sided dolphin and obtained similar results. "Cetacea's use of vision is probably very specialized," Spong theorized, referring to his 1969 report written together with White. "In the wild, orca probably uses his eyes only to orient himself above water and when auditory information is not enough underwater. Living in the ocean, these social mammals use sound to navigate, find their food and stay in touch with each other. It's a very complex and varied world of sound. And we put them in concrete pools where the isolation and reverberations from their own voices tend to silence them."

At the Vancouver Aquarium, Spong began to play sounds to individual whales. From the beginning of his studies, he had discovered that food as motivation was not always enough. A hungry whale might withhold a response as determinedly as a satiated animal. "So we decided to reward Hyak with three minutes of music every time he swam or vocalized," said Spong. "We used one tone at a frequency of 5 kHz to signal 'trial onset' for the swimming and another tone, 500 Hz, for the vocalizing."

Hyak began to swim more every day, but Spong and White still had problems getting him to vocalize. After nine months of isolation, his vocalizations had become rare. "We tried playing a tape recording of his own sounds. No response. Then we tried recordings from another whale. Immediately, Hyak began to vocalize. After that, we had no problems shaping vocal responses to the 500 Hz signal. Yet Hyak got bored very quickly — and we found this held true for Skana and other captive orcas." Spong drained the last of his beer. "It was far out, mate. We had to keep changing the tunes to keep him swimming and vocalizing."

Spong's attitude toward the whales began changing in early 1969. "For more than a year, I'd been working with Skana at the Vancouver Aquarium, but we were just getting to know each other and share physical contact. Skana enjoyed having me rub her head and body with my hands and my bare feet."

Spong ordered another round of beer. "Early one morning, I was sitting at the edge of Skana's pool, my bare feet in the water. She approached slowly, until she was only a few inches away. Then, suddenly, she opened her mouth and dragged her teeth quickly across both the tops and the soles of my feet. I jerked my feet out of the water!

"I thought about it for a minute and, recovering from the shock, put my feet back in. Again, Skana approached, baring her teeth. Again, I jerked my feet out.

"We did this routine 10 or 11 times until, finally, I sat with my feet in the water and controlled the urge to flinch when she flashed her teeth. I no longer felt afraid. She had deconditioned my fear of her. And when I stopped reacting, she ended the exercise."

It was about then that Spong began to think the whales were conducting experiments on him at the same time as he was on them. "Eventually, my respect [for orca] verged on awe," Spong wrote later. "I concluded that *Orcinus orca* is an incredibly powerful and capable creature, exquisitely self-controlled and aware of the world around it, a being possessed of a zest for life and a healthy sense of humour and, moreover, a remarkable fondness for and interest in humans."

In 1970, Spong decided to investigate the creatures in their natural habitat. He brought his family to Alert Bay, went out by boat to look for the whales and found them. He started coming up every summer. In contrast to the free orcas, he said, Skana seemed lonely and bored, and her pool looked small. Every time Spong returned to Vancouver, he visited Skana and talked with Vancouver Aquarium director Murray Newman about obtaining the whale's release. The aquarium's position was that releasing Skana after so many years in captivity (since 1967) would be irresponsible because the whale might die without her pod. *If* she could find her pod, went the argument, would she even be accepted? Asked whether Skana could survive, Ellis said that he believed an ex-captive would have no trouble catching ling cod, at minimum. "It might take her a week or two to adjust, but she could go for a long time on the fat she's got on her." Spong suggested a gradual release programme, staying with Skana until she readjusted to the wild. But both Ellis and Spong admit that it is unlikely that any aquarium will consent to free its relatively rare and costly killer whales. More than any other exhibit, the orcas attract the paying customers.

By the time I met Spong in Alert Bay in 1973, he had become an outspoken advocate for the rights of all whales and was dropping his scientific pursuits to campaign full-time to save them.

Ten years before Spong began working with killer whales, John C. Lilly had begun to study captive dolphins. By 1968, his personal involvement was similar to Spong's, and he could no longer, in his words, "run a concentration camp for my friends." It was Lilly who started people thinking that whales and dolphins might be conscious, intelligent creatures. Through the 1960s and 1970s — the era in which aquariums went from old fish-tank museums to sprawling marine mammal oceanariums and entertainment complexes — everyone working with captive dolphins and orcas read John Lilly religiously and talked about "the possibilities." On the *Four Winds* that summer of 1973, Lilly's *The Mind of the Dolphin* was easily the most-thumbed volume aboard. Scientists read him and so did the public. He was controversial, yes, but exciting.

Trained as a neurophysiologist, Lilly had begun, in the late 1950s, by mapping dolphins' brains and attaching electrodes to the various brain centres. Many of the first animals died, but one, a certain No. 6, managed to "get through" to Lilly. No. 6 was quick to comprehend the experiments that stimulated his brain's pleasure centres. One day, he began mimicking laughter and other human sounds. Lilly expanded his research to investigate dolphin intelligence. The earlier numbered dolphins gave way to Lizzie, Elvar and Peter. They had gone, literally, from being numbers to becoming friends, individual beings with whom Lilly shared his excitement of learning about another species.

In 1961, Lilly published *Man and Dolphin*, his first book on dolphins, about which there is still much debate. The first chapter began boldly: "Eventually, it may be possible for humans to speak with another species." He went on to theorize about how it might be done. The ideal subject would be a species with an intelligence comparable to man's. But how to define intelligence? Scientists have yet to come up with a satisfactory definition. Perhaps the most that can be said is that the development of *human* intelligence has been critically dependent on three factors: brain volume, brain convolutions and social interactions among individuals. Toothed whales — orcas, sperm whales and dolphins — compare with or sometimes surpass humans in all three areas. *Homo sapiens'* intelligence is associated with his hands and, specifically, the opposable thumb. Speculating on the nature of whale intelligence, Lilly wrote that "without benefit of hands or outside constructions of any sort, [whales and dolphins] may have taken the path of legends and verbal traditions, rather than that of written records." Whales and dolphins are sonic creatures. Perhaps their brains function as giant sound computers.

Zoologist Roger Payne of the New York Zoological Society and his wife, Katy, began recording humpback whale songs in 1967. After more than a decade of research, Payne wrote in *National Geographic*: "So far, the study of humpback whale songs has provided our best insight into the mental capabilities of whales. Humpbacks are clearly intelligent enough to memorize the order of those sounds, as well as the new modifications they hear going on around them. Moreover, they can store this information for at least six months as a basis for further improvisations. To me, this suggests an impressive mental ability and a possible route in the future to assess the intelligence of whales."

Analyzing tapes made each year, the Paynes discovered that the whales constantly change their songs, "which sets these whales apart from all other animals," according to Roger Payne. "All the whales are singing the same song one year, but the next year, they will all be singing a new song." The Paynes found that the whales change their songs gradually, from year to year, incorporating some of the previous year's song into the new one. Over several years, the song evolves into something completely different.

Lilly's dolphin research provides other evidence of Cetacea's sound abilities — although critics challenge his interpretation of the data. Lilly found that the bottlenose dolphin could match numbers and durations of human vocal outbursts and could even mimic human words and simple sentences. But their responses were often speeded up and sometimes beyond the limit of man's hearing. It seemed logical to Lilly that since sound travels 4 1/2 times faster in water than in air, dolphins would process and send sound at about 4 1/2 times the speed that man could and would also use a frequency band about 4 1/2 times that of man's. Lilly, therefore, simply slowed down the tape to decode the dolphins' responses. Eventually, he came to believe that they were trying to communicate with him. They would vocalize out of water — a concession to man, according to Lilly, something rarely done in the wild or among themselves. Lilly also cited the persistent efforts of individual dolphins to imitate various human sounds — laughter, whistles, Bronx cheers and even certain simple human words.

Captive killer whales also seem able to reproduce a wide range of sounds, some of them humanlike. A talent for mimicry is probably important for their survival in the wild. Like the young of many birds and primates who mimic their parents, shaping their "accents" to fit the group's norm, orca calves probably mimic their pod-mates to perpetuate a set of signals unique to their social group, by which they could recognize one another at a distance.

Orcas at the Vancouver Aquarium, according to Spong, seemed as eager as Lilly's dolphins to interact with man. Spong said that they would vocalize at him out of water, and when music was played to one of them, the serenaded whale would come over to the side of the pool, lift its head out of the water and then turn it slowly from side to side as it oriented to the sound. But when Spong visited Johnstone Strait, he did not find free orcas quite so eager to interact. He had taped whales with a hydrophone from a moving boat in Blackfish Sound in 1970, but the sounds were sparse and the recording quality poor. The whales seemed to have avoided his boat.

I told Spong about recording the bull's loud vocalizations underneath the *Four Winds* the week before and that by using an electronic synthesizer, I planned to play imitation whale sounds the next time we saw the whales. I hoped that the electronic synthesizer — the only instrument capable of duplicating the frequency range and harmonic complexity of whale sounds — might arouse their curiosity. "If we can attract the whales' physical presence, if they decide to investigate the new sounds occurring in their environment," I explained, "then we'll have the cameras going, and we'll be able to film them. And if we can elicit some kind of sound response, we could record it for the film's sound track."

The notion intrigued Spong, even though he shook his head a little dubiously. When Spong first visited the Johnstone Strait area, he had played music to orcas as they passed an underwater speaker that he had mounted off nearby Hanson Island. He had played recorded music to them and then taped whale sounds, trying to get the whales to stop and react or, maybe, to respond vocally. But nothing happened. Then, in August 1970, Spong brought a Vancouver rock band, *Fireweed*, to Alert Bay and staged a live concert for the whales on the concrete-hulled sailboat *D'Sonoqua*, as both whales and men moved down Johnstone Strait. Spong did not have his underwater speaker to amplify the sounds into the water, but he thinks the whales heard the noise on the surface. They stayed in the vicinity of the boat. "Maybe the presence of musicians and the wider frequency range of the live sounds attracted their interest," said Spong, looking out the window of the Nimpkish Hotel. "But if you can actually synthesize whale sounds on your machine and spontaneously vocalize with them underwater *and* record the whole interchange, that should be very interesting."

I asked Spong about his plans for the summer. He had arrived from Vancouver a few days before, flying up with his quiet, dark-haired wife, Linda, and his elflike 5-year-old son, Yasha, "to spend the summer with the family watching for whales." He was building a shack on Hanson Island that looked out over Blackfish Sound, a mile north of Johnstone Strait. "Later in the summer, I'll be taking people whale-watching on the *D'Sonoqua* for Project Jonah. I'd also like to make some better underwater recordings of the whales." Spong generously offered to lend me his recording equipment, until he needed it, in case mine broke down. We talked about underwater recording techniques. It was essential to record from a stationary position. Best of all, we agreed, would be to find a place where the whales moved slowly or perhaps congregated on some regular basis, even if only for a short time.

Spong planned to motor to nearby Hanson Island that afternoon. We agreed to coordinate whale sightings whenever possible. With Spong on Hanson Island, Ellis and Hunter across Blackfish Sound on Parson Island and the *Four Winds* concentrating in Johnstone Strait, we had a good network to keep track of any orcas moving through the area.

That afternoon, I began synthesizing whale sounds, a slow and methodical process. I would play the tape-recorded whale sound at slow speed, analyzing it by ear. I would then try to play it on the synthesizer, adjusting the settings until the phrase seemed whalelike. The pitch and the rhythm of the phrases were fairly easy to approximate. The complex tone took longer. I made notations in my journal for each whale phrase in my electronic shorthand scrawl. Then I memorized the settings and practised moving the knobs and keys in the patterns I'd devised. By the next afternoon, I knew three killer whale phrases, each about two seconds long.

It didn't take long to patch the boat leaks, but the rudder problem brought several days of waiting in Alert Bay. Meanwhile, we held a party on the boat, playing music through the night; following that, we had a continuous stream of visitors. After four days in town, we were more than ready to set sail. Casting off, we looked up to see Ellis and Hunter motoring into the harbour in the Zodiac. They had come for supplies.

"Seen any whales?" I asked.

"Nothing the last few days, since you've been gone — until last night," Ellis replied.

"Shoulda' been there, man," said Hunter. "We spent an hour drifting with 'em — their fins silhouetted in the moonlight. We turned off the engine. The currents carried us . . . just the sound of the tides and their blowing . . . and then they began vocalizing, these long, eerie shrieks. Not very loud, but we could hear 'em."

"Without a hydrophone!" said Ellis.

It was exciting to imagine Ellis and Hunter huddled in the Zodiac in the middle of the night, whales singing beneath them. (In calm seas, loud underwater whale vocalizations sometimes penetrate the hull, producing audible sounds. Centuries before hydrophones began eavesdropping on ocean creatures, whalers and mariners heard the sounds of singing whales from their anchored sailboats.)

As we pushed off from the dock, Hunter said that they might see us in the strait the following afternoon. We coasted out on the tide. A fresh westerly came up from behind, sending us down Johnstone Strait. In three hours, we were back off Boat Bay, in prime whale country. At noon, we dropped sail in the middle of the strait. It was a high overcast day, with thick clouds racing, stacking up against the mountain peaks of Vancouver Island. It was an ideal place to wait for whales.

After lunch, the westerly wind came up strong, so we ducked into Robson Bight for shelter. The horseshoe-shaped bight is deep, a sheer wall along the rim, except at the extreme heel, where a sandy shoal extends almost half a mile out from the Tsitika River mouth. The *British Columbia Pilot* says nothing about anchoring in the bight, but we had seen fishing boats do it, so we decided to try. Seventy fathoms of anchor line had not yet hit bottom when Bott spied whale blows through the whitecaps, about two miles away, halfway across the strait. We pulled anchor, literally — we had no winch (a winch was strictly an extravagance as far as the skipper was concerned and definitely out of place on a 1906 sailboat). It took 20 minutes to haul the hook aboard. By then, the whales had disappeared. I could hear them on the hydrophone, but we couldn't see them. We sailed into the open strait. The tide was against us. The wind also fought us, but it quickly dropped to a light breeze, and then we had no power. For half an hour more, we bobbed around in the sea slop, still looking for whales. The ocean began to calm, and when the swells had almost died, we were surprised to find ourselves surrounded by whales, in a near perfect 200-yard radius.

> JULY 20. Black bodies sliding in and out of a blue sea, fins all around, like periscopes from cruising black submarines. Three groups: about seven whales in one, five and four in the others. It's hard to count them. They mill about, circling and crossing each other's paths, apparently going nowhere. Three calves, each staying close to a cow, surface a few seconds after their mothers. There are three, maybe four, bulls.

We drifted toward a group of seven whales that contained two bulls. They moved as we did, keeping a 200-yard distance. But at one point, we got within 100 feet of a bull that had wandered from the others. He hyperventilated on the surface, taking five or six breaths (three or four are usual when travelling); then he arched his back and showed his tail flukes, preparing to dive. We had rarely seen the whales' flukes in earlier encounters. They appear only occasionally before a long dive, indicating that the whale is preparing to dive deep, often to feed.

> The bull lifts his flukes gracefully; the water runs along the rims and drips off. He flips the giant eight-foot-wide triangle, as if to show us his flukes' ivory-white underside, the black etched carefully around the edges. Then, as he slips beneath the surface, the thrust begins, that up-and-down movement of flukes powerful enough to propel a several-ton mammal as fast as a speedboat.

Deep-diving orcas in search of bottom-feeding fish in Johnstone Strait probably go no deeper than 100 fathoms (200 yards). Most of the time, they seem to feed and travel in the top 10 to 15 fathoms. However, a few years ago, the corpse of a killer whale was found off the west coast of Vancouver Island entangled in submarine cable more than 3,375 feet below the surface.

Sailing over to the spot where the bull had disappeared, we saw the three rings of calm water left from his thrust. Then, beside the three rings, I saw silvery fish scales floating on the surface. Minutes before his dive, the bull had caught and eaten a salmon.

While the whales continued feeding, we attempted to approach closer, but without success. For most of the afternoon, they remained in those three loose groups. Individuals within each group were sometimes separated by more than 100 yards, and from what we could observe at the surface, each whale appeared to be feeding independently. While we watched, I monitored them on the hydrophone. From 200 yards, the whale sounds were loud, steady and repetitive. Only one whale would vocalize at a time, mostly one- or two-second-long screams consisting of two notes rising or falling in pitch. And sometimes, but only faintly in the background, I heard a clicking sound of varying pitch — an arrhythmic tap-tap-taaaaap-tap-TAP-tp-TP-tp-tap-tap-tp-TP — that permeated the silence between the screams.

Two thousand years ago, Aristotle and Pliny the Elder wrote about the squeaks, moans and clicks of captured dolphins, but only recently has science tried to learn why dolphins and other whales make these sounds. In 1947, Arthur McBride, the first curator of Marine Studios in Florida, was trying to catch bottlenose dolphins. When part of the net, which was supported by cork floats, was pulled beneath the surface, the dolphins immediately escaped through the opening. In McBride's private notes, he suggested that the dolphins' behaviour "calls to mind the sonic sending and receiving apparatus which enables the bat to avoid obstacles in the dark." In the late 1950s, the research of William E. Schevill and Barbara Lawrence of Harvard University and, independently, of Winthrop Kellogg, an experimental psychologist at Florida State University, confirmed McBride's echolocation theory. The studies proceeded along these lines:

First, the researchers recorded and analyzed the steady stream of clicks that dolphins make. Each click was short, on the order of milliseconds, and was composed of many frequencies — from 200 Hz to 150 kHz — some sounds several octaves above man's hearing range. They determined that these brief clicks — with their varying intensities and wide frequency range — which were focused into highly directional beams, produced echoes of a subtle and complex nature suitable for underwater echo-ranging. The researchers could even "hear" the echoes by greatly slowing down the tape or by watching the sounds on the screen of an oscilloscope.

Second, the researchers studied the "receiving apparatus" of the dolphin. They determined that the design for the dolphin's acoustic sense was ideal for decoding and analyzing the reflected echoes.

Finally, they tested the animals themselves, to see what a dolphin could do without using its eyes. They found that a dolphin could navigate at night and that a blindfolded animal would avoid submerged obstructions. The dolphins seemed to locate their food by sending out streams of clicks that would intercept a fish as it swam by. The echoes from the clicks would come back at varying speeds and frequencies, depending on the distance and the size, shape and particular variety of fish. Apparently, by "reading" the echoes, a dolphin could distinguish a favourite fish from a less satisfactory one or from an object of the same size and shape. Using the echoes, the dolphin seemed to assemble a kind of sound picture in its brain — a picture different from (though as sharply focused as) man's retinal picture.

Through the 1960s and 1970s, the sounds of other dolphins and whales were recorded and are now being deciphered. No species has been studied to the extent of the bottlenose dolphin, but each species produces unique sounds, and it appears that at least some others use clicks for echolocation. Other cetacean sounds range from the complex singing of the humpback whale and the low 20 Hz blasts of fin whales (which may be audible for hundreds or even thousands of miles) to the high-pitched pure-tone whistles of some dolphin species — all of which are probably used to keep in touch and to communicate with each other.

In 1964, Schevill and William A. Watkins from the Woods Hole Oceanographic Institution in Massachusetts came to Vancouver to record and to study Moby Doll. Killer whales had been recorded in 1956 by the Royal Canadian Navy off British Columbia's Queen Charlotte Islands, but no study was made of their sounds until the first orca, Moby Doll, was taken captive. Schevill and Watkins found that killer whales produced click trains similar to those made by bottlenose dolphins but within a narrow low-frequency band. Based on their observations of Moby Doll's orienting behaviour, they suggested that these click trains were used for echolocation. They also noticed that Moby Doll often made long, strident screams when boats would pass. They termed these "calling," or communication, signals. They were quite loud, about the level of someone blowing a trumpet in one's ear from three feet away, and had an unusually complex harmonic structure that enabled them to be recognized against almost any background noise from a distance of up to seven miles. These screams were actually speeded-up clicks; Schevill and Watkins were surprised to find none of the familiar delphinid "pure tone" whistles. Furthermore, Moby Doll's sounds were all much lower in pitch than the dolphins'; they were almost entirely within the range of human hearing.

While the whales continued feeding that afternoon of July 20, their vocalizations remained constant and repetitive. But then their behaviour and sounds changed. Cows and young males started jumping clear of the water, seeming to show exuberance. The bulls seemed lazy; two of them idly smacked their tails on the surface. Other whales rolled on their backs and splashed like novice swimmers, waving their flippers. As before, the whales surfaced and blew as individuals, rather than as a group. There was no organized formation, no obvious pattern to their movements. Many languished at the surface, some perhaps resting after their deep dives and food chases. One of the languishers

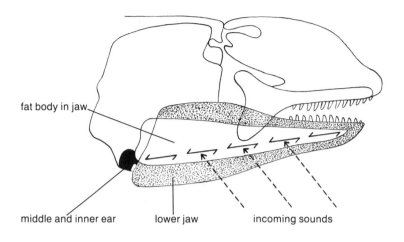

How a killer whale hears: The whale receives sounds through the lower jaw, where they are picked up by the fat body in the hollow jawbone and carried to the middle and inner ears.

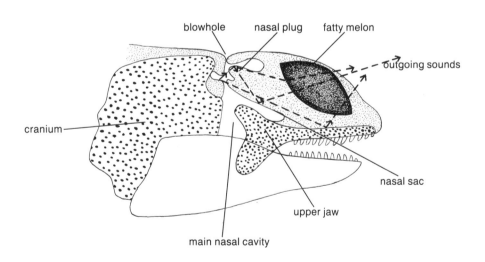

How a killer whale vocalizes: The killer whale produces its large repertoire of sounds by forcing air through various nasal sacs and cavities that can be rapidly opened and closed. The sounds are then apparently reflected toward a fatty melon in the forehead, which seems to function as an acoustic lens, focusing the sounds into a directional beam as they leave the head.

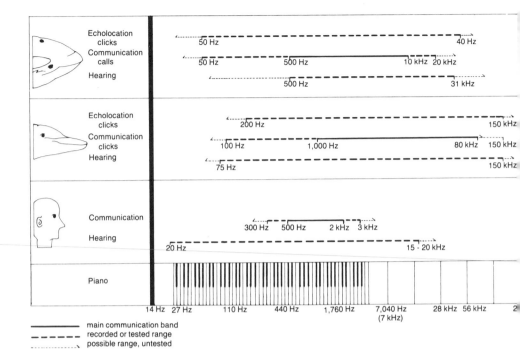

	Echolocation clicks	50 Hz		40 Hz	
	Communication calls	50 Hz	500 Hz	10 kHz	20 kHz
	Hearing	500 Hz		31 kHz	
	Echolocation clicks	200 Hz			150 kHz
	Communication clicks	100 Hz	1,000 Hz	80 kHz	150 kHz
	Hearing	75 Hz			150 kHz
	Communication	300 Hz 500 Hz	2 kHz 3 kHz		
	Hearing	20 Hz		15 - 20 kHz	
	Piano	14 Hz 27 Hz	110 Hz 440 Hz 1,760 Hz	7,040 Hz (7 kHz) 28 kHz 56 kHz	2

——————— main communication band
– – – – – recorded or tested range
················> possible range, untested

Comparison of sound production and hearing in killer whales, bottlenose dolphins and humans.

was old Stubbs. In the binoculars, I observed that she was not alone but was lying on the surface next to another mature cow. This was Nicola, so called because of a large nick on the top trailing edge of her fin. Other than this minor deformity, she was a perfectly formed mature female. We also recognized the bull Wavy, this time with a different subgroup, not the five we had first seen him with.

We never did get close to the whales that afternoon, but as we left them in the evening, we saw the three disparate groups of seven, five and four, which had surrounded us from a distance all day, finally join together. Here was further evidence that Stubbs's pod contained about 16 members and also that the five we had seen the first day were part of this bigger pod. Still, it would take many more encounters before we would know for sure. Orcas sometimes travel alone or split into small units to feed or to search for food. Sometimes, they remain within visual range of each other; other times, they spread out to the limits of long-range sound communication and beyond. Stubbs's group seemed a loose aggregation that sometimes remained apart for hours, even days, at a time. But eventually, they always came together.

After the whales had stopped feeding, the ocean grew thick with their cries. The full orchestra of killer whale sounds inspired me, and I was anxious to try the synthesizer. I described that first whale concert in my journal:

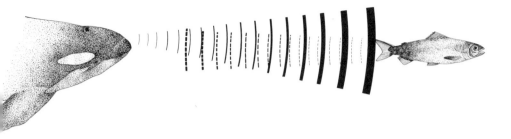

Echolocation: The whale sends out a series of clicks focused into a narrow beam. By sweeping these beams from side to side and by precisely reading the reflected echoes, the whale obtains a sound picture of everything that crosses its path.

JULY 20. I've just walked into the opera house. I have no programme. Strange new players are premiering a piece by a flamboyant new composer.

Front and centre, three, maybe four, whales begin — a swelling string section — discordant, irresolute harmonies fill the concert hall. Then two more whales, stage right, come in, playing eight-octave clarinets, counterpointing the string section. And then they, too, are counterpointed by occasional glissando slurs and passages played pizzicato by whales at the rear of the stage.

But suddenly, a programme change: The orchestra members switch clothes and pull new instruments from their cases. The French horn players begin wailing on shiny, sleazy saxophones. The trumpeters spit rapid-fire bursts into an underwater echo chamber — the deep, rocky corridor of Johnstone Strait.

I sat at the electronic synthesizer's console, awaiting an opening. I wanted to play one of the imitation whale sounds I had learned, but I was at a loss to begin. Then I heard a familiar sound — Wavy's first phrase that I had recorded when he had surfaced near our stern on July 12. It was the phrase I knew best on the synthesizer. Again and again, the whales intoned this phrase, and other whales answered with variations on the theme. The whale sounds were rising in pitch, the harmonic structure shifting. Then the rhythm changed. They had been accenting the first note with a hard attack and slurring the second and third notes, but now they switched the accent to the third note. Soon, the original phrase was unrecognizable. I peeked out of the porthole above my head, the headphones still clamped in place. The distance surprised me. From the volume of the underwater sounds, I *felt* close. A few heads bobbed above the surface. Orcas were gathering together.

Then a voice came from on deck, cameraman Vatcher yelling: "What are they saying? Have you played anything to them yet?"

The synthesizer was switched on, my imitation whale phrase programmed and ready. Yet I still had no sense of how to begin. I wondered: Would it be rude to interrupt?

"Lots of action out here," Vatcher called again. "They're jumping and splashing together."

I wanted to look, my attention distracted, but I held off. Then several whales, louder than before, directed a series of terse vocalizations toward the hydrophone suspended under the boat. With no notion of what to expect, I flipped on the tape recorder and turned up the volume pots on the synthesizer. I pressed the keys in the pattern I had devised, monitoring the imitation whale phrase as it passed out the underwater speaker. I held my breath. Two seconds went by. And then it came: A chorus of whales — three, maybe four — sang out a clear, perfect imitation of what I had just played to them — in harmony! They did not repeat their own sound; rather, they duplicated my human accent.

But wait — after the mimicry, they added something — a new phrase at the end. An invitation to continue? For a few seconds, I was speechless. I tried the other whale phrases I had learned. No response. Then that first phrase again. Still silence. Only once more, five minutes later, after I had replayed that first phrase four times, did the whales again mimic the synthesizer. It was not as loud and clear as the first choral response. (Two whales answered; one was half a second late coming in.) But again, they were mimicking my mimic of their phrase — which was a slow, stilted version of their original — rather than repeating the original. It reaffirmed the first response.

That evening, after the whales had departed, crew members gathered around as I replayed the tape — first the synthesizer, then the whales' response. There was a hushed silence of disbelief.

The whales' spontaneous mimicry showed a quick computation of my three-note phrase, probably easy work for their giant sound computers. Of course, mimicry is not a sign of intelligence or of language. Yet the possibility of a "consciousness" *behind* the mimicry intrigued me. The whales' critical perception of sound would likely have eliminated the possibility that my sounds were whale sounds. Furthermore, their passive sonar would have informed them that the sounds had come from our boat, thereby establishing that the sounds were man-made. But did they realize that these were meant to be imitation whale sounds?

The mimicry had occurred in the wild and had come voluntarily, not being bought with food or other reward. For us, the mimicry suggested that at times, the animals were willing to interact with man — as researchers had found with captive orcas and dolphins.

Hearing the tape a few days later, Spong reacted, like Bott, Vatcher and O'Neill, with stunned silence. Ellis and Hunter, however, were excited and vocal. Hunter was convinced that I had found the basic killer whale greeting signal. Earlier, Ellis had said that he often felt like a pesky mosquito (a "mozzie") buzzing around the whales in the Zodiac and that he wanted to "give them something." He said: "We have nothing to offer them in the wild, except, perhaps, sound. That's why the synthesizer is so full of promise." He told us about a whistle that he blows whenever he is close to whales. "It's the whistle

I used to train old Irving before he escaped from Pender Harbour. We had a good relationship. I know he's out there somewhere, and, who knows, maybe the whistle will bring him over to the boat.''

My original hope had been that the synthesizer might attract whales. Yet unlike Ellis's whistle — which at least in captivity had called whales — the synthesizer so far functioned in no such way. Much to the chagrin of our cameramen, the whales had maintained a 150- to 200-yard distance from us all afternoon. The synthesizer seemed to have aroused the whales' interest without bringing them close. Yet perhaps in the whales' sound world, 150 yards away from another species *was* close. Within the pod, the whales did not have to maintain physical or visual contact to be close socially to each other, since they could communicate in the open ocean at distances up to at least seven miles. But visually oriented man must be close physically to be close socially and to communicate. Only technological man with his 20th-century tools, especially the telephone, approaches the kind of "close" long-distance communication that is probably routine for whales.

The July 20 encounter was our third meeting with the whales and the first time that I had used the synthesizer. It led us to believe that we would soon be able to observe many aspects of their daily life, but it would be some time before we received another response to the synthesizer. And no single response could ever have the impact of that first chorus.

THE PREDATOR AND MAN

AUGUST 5, AFTERNOON. Some 300 fishing boats wait for 6 p.m., the official opening of the fishing season. We watch them, all lined up, clinging to the rocky shore on both sides of Johnstone Strait as far as the eye can see: west to Alert Bay, east almost to Kelsey Bay, north into Blackfish Sound. There are compact one- and two-man gill-netters, their wood hulls 30 to 40 feet long, painted white with green, blue or black trim or yellow with brown trim. There are huge seiners twice the length of gill-netters, most with the old wood hulls, a few newer ones in fibreglass or aluminum or steel painted gunmetal grey.

The seiners and gill-netters had arrived during the previous week, motoring in on long open-ocean swells from the north. They had come from Rivers Inlet and Fitz Hugh Sound — many stopping overnight in Alert Bay or Port Hardy or Sointula, an old Finnish settlement on Malcolm Island — to fish the summer salmon run in Johnstone Strait. Each boat was parked in its favourite opening spot along the shore, ready to make the first set. We saw men on deck leaning against the man-sized metal drums that held the seine or gill nets; others stood at the bow. There were dark Kwakiutls in black wool pants and plaid coats and pasty-faced Finns from Sointula fitted out in yellow rain suits. There were the deck-pacers and the water-watchers — always with hands in pockets. But most of the men were cardplayers and coffee drinkers who stayed below deck, waiting until it was time.

Passing the boats as we moved down the strait, we could hear radios over-riding the sound of the ocean. The radios squawked with salmon talk that competed with and often lost to the skip and static. The fishermen's CB radios blasted away night and day. Fishermen talked to each other, listened for weather reports and traded fishing conditions and, with friends or partners, secret tips in comic codes ("Donald Duck's got the Lone Ranger up against the wall at Hakai Pass") while they waited for the 6 p.m. signal.

And they're off! Engines revved. Gears engaged. The metal drums began turning, clanking as they spun out the nets. We watched two young natives in a red skiff push off from the *Chief Takush* and row wildly for the Vancouver Island shore. Taking one end of the net, they scurried up the rocks and tied it to a sturdy Douglas fir. Then the *Chief Takush* pulled out, dropping a perfect 600-foot arc of cork-supported net. Twenty minutes later, the ends were joined, and the purse line was pulled up underwater, entrapping the salmon. The seine net bulged with salmon; the big drum began hauling it in. Fishing with purse seines is like scooping out a block of ocean with a giant colander. The treasure could turn out to be pure silver (sockeye salmon) or seaweed or, worse than seaweed, dogfish.

Successful seining depends on making a fast set on a moving school. A seine fisherman must take into account tide, wind and currents; the drift of the vessel; and the speed and direction in which the fish are travelling. Gillnetting, on the other hand, is a matter of finding a good place to set the net and then waiting. The gill net is a rectangular net that the fish cannot see. They push their heads through the diamond-shaped mesh, discover they cannot pass, try to back up and find their gills are ensnared. They drown and hang limply in the net by the time they are pulled in.

From the flying bridge of the *Chief Takush*, the captain was yelling orders at his six-man crew. The boat heeled over as hundreds of salmon churned in the ocean cauldron. "All right, bring her aboard!" the captain shouted. We dollied in to watch them hoist the flapping mass of salmon onto their boat. For a few minutes, all hell broke loose in the stern of the seiner as the salmon fought for their lives.

Hunter and I — standing in his Zodiac inflatable clicking our cameras — watched the replay of an age-old drama of men and the sea. Hunter had come for me that afternoon while I was fixing hydrophones on the anchored *Four Winds* in Boat Bay. Ellis had returned to Victoria for a few days, and Hunter was hungry for company. "Want to go find some orcas?" he asked. I had been stuck on the sailboat for several days, awaiting the return of Bott and O'Neill from Alert Bay, where they had taken the movie cameras for repair, and I jumped at his offer.

Hunter suggested that we explore new waters and catch some salmon for dinner. It was to be an afternoon excursion; it became a three-day nonstop whale chase.

AUGUST 5, 7 P.M. And now the killer whales have arrived. We didn't hear them, with all the commotion of the fishing. Neither, it seems, did the fishermen. First, one big bull surfaces and explodes a few feet on the far side of the *Chief Takush*, busy making its second set. The bull hangs at the surface a moment, makes a deep dive underneath the net and comes up on the other side. Minutes later, we see the other whales — a procession of fins. Only eight actually, but it seems like more. They are spaced 30 to 40 yards apart, and they come up alternately, weaving back and forth through the traffic congestion of Johnstone Strait. They are coming down from the north, as the fishermen did a few days earlier.

These whales were new to me. I studied the fins through the binoculars, looking for distinguishing marks. Then Hunter cried, "It's Hooker!" A well-marked bull in an eight-whale group that Hunter and Ellis had followed several times, Hooker had a big dorsal fin, hooked forward, with a distinguishing notch halfway down the trailing edge. Hunter had been telling me about Hooker's pod, and I had been anxious to see them. There were two bulls and a cow with a young calf that Hunter called Rusty, because he still had the characteristic orangish tan colouring of a newborn whale on his white areas. Hunter said that Hooker's pod moved faster than the other whales he'd seen. Stubbs's pod was often slow-moving, scattered, an extended family. But Hooker's pod, as Hunter described "the boys," was like a rambunctious gang of bikers. Even Rusty seemed especially frisky and boisterous for his age.

Hunter and Ellis knew about Hooker's pod from their northerly travels in the Zodiac. More manoeuvrable and flexible than the sailboat, the Zodiac could manage the narrow, tide-swept passages between the islands as easily as the open ocean swells of Queen Charlotte Strait. And it did not depend on wind.

The killer whales and fishermen had come to Johnstone Strait for the same reason: salmon. Each year, both whales and men follow the migrating schools from the open ocean to the narrow straits and inlets, where the salmon gather in great numbers near the river mouths before spawning upstream. Whales and men have been following the salmon for centuries. The early Northwest Coast natives considered the salmon's movements to be part of a mystical cycle and celebrated their arrival with a great ceremony. This welcoming party was the most important group religious activity of the native year, for the natives believed that the salmon had to be treated well, or they would not return the following year. For the Kwakiutls, the killer whale — the animal that used its cunning and intelligence to catch the salmon — was the model fisherman; the salmon, the symbol of a fisherman's wealth and prosperity.

Months later, Hunter and I would walk up the Tsitika River in Robson Bight to watch the salmon flinging themselves against gravity and impossible odds to get upstream — back home — to spawn and die. Beside the pools in the river were the corpses, those that hadn't made it. Hunter saw one that had been recently grounded on the bank. It looked healthy. When he replaced it in the stream, off it shot. A few scales came off on his fingers. The scales tell a lot, he explained, not just about the species. They tell the exact streambed where each salmon is born. For scientists, learning to read the scales has been crucial to unlocking the mysteries of migrating salmon.

The salmon cycle begins in streams where the fry are born — sometimes 700 miles from the sea. Each streambed has its unique race of salmon, perpetuated for thousands of years by spawners returning to their birthplaces to lay their eggs. The young grow for a year or more in the freshwater lakes and creeks before swimming down to the open ocean. From then on, as Hunter put it, life becomes a hard-luck story for the salmon. Constantly searching for plankton, insects and, in the case of coho and spring salmon, small fish, the fry must compete with other ocean creatures to satisfy their voracious appetites. In a few years, they grow from inch-long fingerlings to mature fish, some weighing more than 85 pounds. And the larger they grow, the more they are exposed to predators — seals, porpoises, killer whales and fishermen.

Once mature, the salmon begin the biggest struggle of their lives. Driven by the instinct to propagate, they leave the ocean and swim upstream in great numbers. They no longer feed but summon all energy for the uphill fight. The male sockeye turns bright red as his body cavity swells with the milt that will fertilize the eggs. The body of the female — now pregnant with roe — changes to a paler red, and her head turns green. But nothing happens until the males and females arrive at their home stream. They stay on course unless captured or blocked. If their progress is impeded, only a very few will turn around and spawn in unfamiliar streambeds. Most who fail to reach their destination will die and, with them, sometimes their entire race.

When the salmon arrive home, each male chooses a mate, defending his interests from unlucky bachelors while the female digs the redd, or nest, with her tail. The female will wear her tail to a stump scooping out three to five redds, about 15 inches deep. She then deposits her bright orange eggs in each redd, and the male releases a cloud of sperm. Their life's work done, the salmon look like thin spectres compared with the healthy specimens that began the fight to find their way home weeks before. One-third of their weight has been lost during the upstream migration. Within three days, the spawners die. The fertilized eggs will not hatch until the following spring. The parents never see the children. They leave a yolk sac to nourish the young until the tiny fry emerge from the gravel bed to begin again the ancient cycle.

Five species of salmon live in Northwest Coast waters: sockeye, spring, humpback, coho and chum. Each has its favourite rivers and streams and special times for spawning. Spring salmon come first — "smileys" the fishermen call them — from spring through early July, mainly to the Nass, Skeena and Campbell Rivers in northern British Columbia. Then come the sockeye, which spawn up the Fraser River, the largest sockeye river in the world; the Fraser has also been colonized by springs. Coho, humpbacks and chum, found in most coastal rivers, are the latecomers, spawning throughout fall and, in the case of chum, sometimes in winter.

Salmon have always been the most important fish in the northwest, and today, they represent about 70 percent of the annual B.C. catch. The sockeye are the smallest but the most numerous and the most valuable, because of their red flesh. Humpbacks, chum and coho, however, make up most of the catch. The spring, by far the largest, average 25 pounds and sometimes top 85 pounds.

The fishing industry in British Columbia is second in economic importance only to logging, which was started by the first white settlers, expanded quickly and, before long, came into conflict with fishing interests. The building of roads and railroads destroyed some salmon-producing watersheds. Fallen trees, crisscrossing a riverbed, block the salmon's path; erosion creates heavy silting, which smothers salmon eggs in the gravel, raises temperatures and reduces oxygen levels in the water. Much of the damage occurred during the late 19th and early 20th centuries, reducing the salmon runs by half, according to some estimates. Then came the dams, blocking salmon runs and ruining many streambeds. In recent decades, many methods have been tried to help the salmon navigate upstream through damaged watersheds; finally, elaborate concrete fish ladders were constructed in crucial areas to replace the rivers that had handled things all right for millennia.

The modern fisherman is faced with smaller schools of salmon, stricter regulations for catching them and increasing costs to outfit and maintain his boat. A fully equipped wooden seiner might go for a quarter of a million dollars; an aluminum- or steel-hulled seiner could cost up to a million. The seine net itself costs about $25,000 and must be repaired constantly and replaced every five to seven years. Add to this the cost of radar and depth sounders (about $5,000). Gill-netters are within a one-man or a one-family price range, from $50,000 to $100,000 and up — if you can find a boat with a valid licence. Since the early 1970s, Canada's federal government has issued no new salmon licences and has revoked existing licences of part-time or unsuccessful fishermen.

At the turn of the century, as the salmon industry grew on this coast, the canneries owned most of the boats; by 1926, more than half were owner-operated; now the pendulum is moving again toward company ownership. It seems that one-man and one-family native fishermen are on the way out. But it will not happen without a fight. Many Kwakiutls still own and operate their own boats. A few families own several. And some native boats, like the *Twin Sisters* — a seiner owned by Alert Bay native Jimmy Sewid — are among the top fish producers year after year. Sewid's father and his uncles were fishermen, as were his grandfather and great-grandfather. The native skipper stands on the flying bridge surveying the same waters as his ancestors. He may have one eye on the sonar and depth sounders to confirm the location of the salmon schools, but he still watches for the old signs: the seagulls aloft, the brown spot on the water, "finners" breaking the surface or jumping and flashing their silver mirror scales. And he always has an eye peeled for blackfish, the killer whales that might be driving a school of salmon ahead of them.

Hunter and I watched, staying off at some distance, as the fishermen and the killer whales pursued the salmon. We wondered about the interaction of man and whale. We had heard stories of fishermen shooting at orcas in Northwest Coast waters. In one study sample, about 25 percent of the killer whales captured for the aquarium trade and subsequently examined had bullet holes in their bodies. We watched the whales swimming along the seine floats, blowing only a few feet away from some of the big seiners. Though the whales surfaced mostly away from the floats, they could have been raking the nets clean underwater. We couldn't tell. The fishermen didn't seem to mind the whales. At least, there was no open hostility. We heard no gunshots, only the continual clanking of the boats hauling in their catches. It was the height of the summer salmon run, and the fishermen had their hands full. There seemed to be plenty of salmon for both whales and men.

Near nightfall, we stopped to talk to fishermen who had ducked into Growler Cove to unload on company packer boats. The lights from several boats, tied up together, illuminated the cove. A few men stood around drinking coffee as the packer unloaded their haul. They had seen us out in the little Zodiac and had wondered what we were doing. They seemed skeptical but interested in our film of the killer whales. One fisherman handed us two steaming coffee mugs as he emerged from the galley. We asked about the fishing.

"The catch was big, but spotty," said Bob Dick, a native who commanded a large seiner, part of a fleet owned by B.C. Packers. "It was mostly chum, a few spring yet — but we were hoping for sockeye by now. Some sets were 50, 60 ton. Others, barely 50 fish."

We asked about the blackfish. Had they seen them? Did they figure the blackfish had caused the erratic fishing?

"Oh yeah, we seen 'em," said a white fisherman. "But what're you gonna do?"

We talked to many fishermen that night and over the next two days. Opinions on the killer whales differed. In general, native fishermen were more accepting of blackfish, feeling that there were enough fish for all. Most of the others felt that way, too, or didn't care, but a few of the white fishermen who got "skunked" claimed that wherever the blackfish went, the salmon disappeared. "The blackfish are either wolfing 'em or scaring 'em or both!" said one frustrated gill-netter.

An old seine fisherman on the *Wa-yas* ("sweetheart" in Kwakwala) told us he had sometimes seen blackfish diving deep, pulling salmon out of his net just before he drew it closed. "It's a miracle they don't get caught," he said. "Now, that would be some set — one $50,000 fish!"

He smacked his lips, quoting the live-capture aquarium price at the time for killer whales. Then his mood changed: "But they don't allow it no more. Got t'have a permit. And no fisherman gonna get no permit t'catch no $50,000 fish, or we'd all be tryin' t'catch 'em."

The fishermen still talk about Namu, the bull orca that was accidentally captured in a gill net in 1965 near Namu, British Columbia, about 125 miles north of Johnstone Strait. Gill-netter Bill Lechkobit had set his net in Fitz Hugh Sound late one night when the wind came up strong. The net was entangled in a reef, and he began drifting toward the rocks. To save his boat, he cut the net loose and motored in to nearby Namu for the night. In the morning, when the sea had calmed, another gill-netter, Bob McGarvey, cruised over to investigate his friend's net and found two killer whales — a bull and a calf.

At that time, Moby Doll had been the only whale kept in an aquarium, and although he had died after 87 days, several West Coast aquarium directors believed the creatures could be groomed into performing stars. The two fishermen offered their prize catch for sale and encouraged prospective buyers to move fast, as there were problems with keeping the two whales in the nets. The first day, McGarvey had watched as the bull slipped out through a place between the net and the rocks, as if showing the calf the route to freedom. The baby stayed put, so the bull returned. Two days later, the calf was gone, but for some reason, the bull remained. McGarvey and Lechkobit offered the bull to the first $8,000 cash bid. Ted Griffin, owner of the Seattle Public Aquarium, flew up the next day, paid the two fishermen for the big bull and towed his prize to Seattle in a floating cage.

Most fishermen agreed that it was a fluke that Namu got caught in the net, as most blackfish seem to know how the nets work. The nets that catch whales for the aquarium trade have been used in special shallow bays in Washington's Puget Sound and at Pender Harbour and Pedder Bay in British Columbia, with the captors waiting sometimes for months, then ambushing the whales. As unsuspecting orcas enter a narrow inlet or bay, the captors seal it off with a series of nets. Once captured, most whales do not attempt to escape, although they easily could; no one knows why they don't try. Still, when cruising near a salmon net, "they're fearless," say fishermen. Some fishermen told us about blackfish "working the nets." A gill-netter described them going along his net, eating the trapped fish. "All but the head, which they leave for me to clean out!" This obvious mooching does not seem to be common in Johnstone Strait; it could be the work of seals and sea lions. Many fishermen blame them more than the blackfish.

B.C. fishing regulations allow commercial fishermen to shoot harbour seals or sea lions caught in the vicinity of the nets or other fishing gear "for the purpose of protecting [such] gear and fish caught" — a law sometimes "interpreted pretty liberally up here," according to Dick. The killer whales are protected, "but that doesn't stop some guys. And the whales may be only passing through the strait. It all depends how busy some of these fellows are or how bored they get."

Dick respects the blackfish and sometimes uses them to catch *more* fish. "When the blackfish are coming," said Dick, "more 'n likely they're driving schools of scared salmon in front of 'em. So what you do is, you make your set directly in their path. This takes fast action, precise timing and some luck. But if you manage to close your net right before the blackfish arrive, you got yourself a bonus catch. I seen it happen with gill-netters too, setting the net right across the whales' path. Time and again, they get big catches. But you got to be quick . . . and smart. Pretty hard to be quicker 'n' smarter than a blackfish out there."

Dick said that he had to get back to work. "We'll be fishing most of the night, I guess, if the fishing holds . . . you fellows like salmon?"

Hunter and I grinned as he tossed us a couple of eight-pounders. The friendly skipper would take no money. Eager to partake in that ancient ritual of barbecuing a salmon, we headed to Hunter's camp on Parson Island. We passed fishermen and whales, both silhouetted against an orange and pink horizon still aglow at 10:30 p.m. Both were still fishing; both were still chasing the salmon.

Man and killer whale forage for the same food side by side in many oceans of the world. In the North Atlantic, Icelandic fishermen and orcas follow the herring schools. In the Indian Ocean, Japanese fishermen and orcas chase the tuna. In the Antarctic and in the southern ocean, whalers hunt baleen whales beside orcas.

Sometimes, there is peaceful tolerance between man and orca. Sometimes, there are gunshots. But in one remarkable case, man and orca actually helped each other in herding and catching large baleen whales.

It happened in Australia over a period of about a hundred years, beginning in 1828 where whalers put to sea from remote Twofold Bay, near the south-eastern tip of Australia. It was whaling in the old style, as described by Herman Melville in *Moby-Dick*. Men rowed out from shore in long whaling dories, harpooned and lanced the whales by hand, then towed their catches to the brick tryworks on the beach. The blubber was rendered into oil, and the bones were cleaned to be sold for fertilizer to the Sydney market. In 1846, Alexander Davidson began whaling at Eden near Twofold Bay's Kiah River. Thereafter, whaling was carried on by four generations of Davidsons. Even into the 1920s, the Davidsons maintained their primitive whaling style. They obtained as many as 100 whales a season, year after year; and they attributed their success to the assistance of a pack of 20 to 30 killer whales.

Every Down Under winter, from June to November, the killer whales came to Twofold Bay, making their home near Boyd's Tower on Red Point. Each day, they cruised about the bay or a few miles north or south, returning most evenings. The orcas fed on seals and on the Eden grampus (the local name for the minke whale), but they were really waiting for the same thing as the whalers — the humpback whales, soon to arrive on their migration routes from Antarctica. En route to warmer waters, male humpbacks and females heavy with calves passed and sometimes stopped in Twofold Bay, beginning about a week after the orcas arrived. The average humpback is about twice the length and four or five times the weight of a mature orca.

As a humpback approached the bay, orcas would slowly surround it, attacking like pack dogs. Two killers would grasp its flippers on each side. Others attempted to latch on to its lips. Still others would swim in a line on the outside, splashing their tails and making noise, to confuse and thus discourage its escape to deep water.

Orca pack-hunting of large baleen whales has been witnessed in every ocean. Killer whales — with their superior speed, agility and pack strength — can hassle a baleen whale several times the size of an individual orca, though they cannot always subdue it. Russian studies conducted in the southern oceans during the early 1970s compared stomach contents of captured orcas with orca bite marks on the fins of large whales. From the number of bite marks, it was obvious that killer whales often attacked the larger whales. But since there were few remains of the baleens in orca stomachs, they apparently did not often succeed.

But the Twofold Bay killer whales had a special arrangement with man. Whaler lookouts stationed at Boyd's Tower were quick to notice any commotion from the orcas and to give the "rush oh" alarm call, sending the whalers to the beach like volunteer firemen. It took time to row out to the scene of battle, but the killers would hold the big whale at bay. Leading the way through the flanks of killers, approaching the monster, the harpooner drove his harpoon into its back. Then came the wild ride, the dangerous moments. The killer whales continued to harry the whale — some even jumped on the blowhole to hamper its breathing — until the steersman lanced the dying creature. Finally, there was the long tow to the shallows of the bay; the orcas followed eagerly, while the whalers cheered them on, calling them by name (Hooky, Humpy, et cetera, after their dorsal fins) and sometimes cursing them, as when mischievous Old Tom would grab hold of the harpoon line, hanging on for a free ride.

Nearing the beach, the Twofold whalers would attach an anchor to the harpoon line, drop it and go home, leaving the carcass for the killers "to take their reward," as the whalers put it. The killers would pull apart the mouth, tear off chunks of the lips and then dive in for that delicacy, the huge tongue, each orca in turn having its feast. The killers left the rest of the carcass for the whalers. Distended by the gases of putrefaction, the corpse would rise to the surface in 20 to 28 hours. The whalers believed that the killers were sharing the spoils of victory with them because they had assisted in the hunt. But, in fact, killer whales that subdue large whales in other seas often take only the lips and tongue, these obviously being not only the delicacies but also the most accessible parts of the whale. They ignore the rest of the carcass whether there are whalers around to take it or not.

In accounts from other oceans, orcas sometimes trail whaling ships, looking for an easy meal. U.S. biologist Victor B. Scheffer writes that when Norwegian whalers harpooned but did not kill a bottlenose whale, three killers swam in to finish it off. Canadian zoologist David E. Gaskin photographed orcas following the factory ships in the southern ocean, feeding off the carcasses. Whalers say that they shoot at the marauding orcas, but sometimes even bullets do not disperse them for long. Certainly, killer whales have no fear of men and boats when their stomachs are rumbling and food is on the table.

To a remarkable degree, orcas are opportunistic predators. In the Indian Ocean, they follow tuna boats and pull the tuna off the fishermen's lines. By the mid-1960s, the situation had become so demoralizing for tuna fishermen that whenever orcas came anywhere near their boats, the fishermen packed up and went home. The difference between the tuna fishermen's situation in the Indian Ocean and that of the Australian whalers, of course, is that the Twofold Bay orcas' predatory instincts happened to benefit man. Had the killers taken the entire humpback carcass, for example, the symbiotic association would never have developed. Also, had the whalers converted to newer methods of whaling, with fast catcher boats and exploding harpoons, the orcas would have been a nuisance.

THE WHALE CENSUS

AUGUST 5, LATE EVENING. Salmon smoking on the fire. Sitting on the high lookout rocks of Parson Island, watching the dancing lights of the fishermen working the strait. Boats clanking, whales puffing. "Like Friday night in the city," says Hunter.

AUGUST 6, DAWN. Everything quiet, the strait empty. The sober stillness of "the morning after" — after a wild night of revelry. Hunter and I slide down the rocks and flop into the Zodiac, anxious to find the whales and the fishermen. It's sunny, a rare morning treat. The sea has a mirror finish. No trace of fog. We shut off the engine in the middle of Johnstone Strait and commence to watch, wait and listen.

In an hour, the tide turns; then the wind blows, and the strait starts to come alive. Gill-netters emerge from sleepy burrows along the shore to begin the day's work. A few seiners start their engines. The fishing boats fall into position like pieces on a chessboard, each with its own space in which to make a set before moving on. Then come the whales, out of the east, moving slowly but steadily through the strait, following the contour of the shoreline. Most pass between the fishing boats and shore; young ones and cows swim only a few feet from the rocky coast. Bulls stay to the outside.

Hunter yelled, "Little Stubby!" Then I saw Nicola and Wavy, and soon we counted Stubbs's full pod of about 16. I recognized another bull that we'd been seeing; we elected to christen him Sturdy, because of the erect way in which he carried his big dorsal fin (it had two tiny nicks on the trailing edge, the tinier one near the base, the other near the top). Sturdy was travelling beside a calf, the first time that we had seen a bull and calf subgroup. The day before, Hooker's pod had combed the fishing-boat-packed strait, staying around most of the day. Today, Stubbs's pod was passing through.

"Maybe they're not hungry," said Hunter, "or they're tired of the boats." "Or maybe there are no fish down here," I said. And, when we checked with the fishermen, that turned out to be the case.

As the whales moved through Robson Bight, Hunter and I chugged behind, pleased to have found Stubbs's pod again and to have gotten an early start trailing them. For a mile, the pod hugged the Vancouver Island shore. We passed waterfalls, in the mad gush of summer runoff. We passed Kaikash Creek and the place where an abandoned cabin stood on the beach. Still the whales kept moving, and our engine droned on. The calm morning sea had given way to ripples; then a fresh westerly met our advances, advising us to turn back. At noon, we approached Izumy Rock, where the tides pull in contradictory ways — a tricky spot in a storm. The whales broke pattern. First the bulls blew out in the channel, challenging both wind and tide. Then the whole pod turned and headed for open water. We motored along well behind them, fighting the long swells that built as we crossed the open waters of the strait.

Halfway across, we glimpsed a sailboat in the narrow passage at the mouth of Blackfish Sound, racing on the tide. Many boats travelling the coast took this passage, despite the currents, because it was the quickest route. Sometimes, we saw tugs and freighters come screaming through the passage almost sideways — like canoes fighting white water. The motorized sailboat did little better. Why, we wondered, were they going through when the tide was at its strongest? Then we saw tiny spouts on the horizon, around the sailboat. They looked like whitecaps, but Hunter's eagle eye and the high-powered binoculars soon confirmed that they were more killer whales. "That sailboat," said Hunter, "must be another group of crazy whale watchers."

We were headed in their direction, they in ours. Their whales were a 10-member pod led by a single adult male we called Top Notch. This was the third orca pod that we had met in Johnstone Strait. I had seen them a week ago, and for two days, they had travelled with Stubbs's group. The pods seemed like friendly neighbourhood families. Unlike Stubbs's pod, Top Notch's pod usually travelled as a tight family. They had few, if any, adolescent animals. With perhaps one exception, they were either mature animals or new calves. Recognizable individuals were Scar, who had deep gouges across her saddle and back; Saddle, who had had a V-shaped saddle on her port side; a cow with three nicks on the trailing edge of her dorsal fin; and another cow with a wide nick near the top. Top Notch, the lone bull, had a quarter-round chip, or notch, out of the tip of his giant dorsal. A mature bull in his prime, like Wavy from Stubbs's pod, he had no fear of man's approach.

Top Notch's 10-whale pod looked like a flotilla of tugs leading the sailboat safely through the passage into Johnstone Strait. The sailboat turned out to be the 52-foot-long *Amethyst II*, chartered by Canada's Pacific Biological Station for a killer whale census of B.C. waters. We had seen the boat every day for a week, had heard much about the study and wanted to talk with

Michael A. Bigg, the marine mammalogist directing the study. This "first orca census anywhere in the world" had come about in response to the growing public controversy over capturing killer whales for aquariums. Almost all the aquarium orcas were being taken from Puget Sound and B.C. coastal waters; the Canadian Ministry of the Environment needed a reliable scientific count for management.

In 1971, Bigg's research team sent out 16,500 questionnaires to boaters, fishermen, lighthouse keepers and coastal residents asking them to keep track of orca sightings for one day, July 26. They were to note the time of the sighting, the number of orcas (including the number of mature bulls and calves, if possible) and the direction of travel. Almost 500 questionnaires were completed and returned, deemed a successful response, and the census was held again in August 1972 and 1973 — an annual tally, based on a collection of individual estimates by untrained observers. It gave Bigg what he felt was "a reasonably accurate figure" of 200 to 250 killer whales for the entire B.C. coast. But he still didn't know whether these were year-round residents or transients that had wandered in from the open ocean from points as far away as Alaska or California. And he knew little about the pod unit itself. He needed to establish the reproduction, or "recruitment," rates for orcas to see if they were high enough to sustain the pods and the aquarium captures.

Bigg had arrived in Johnstone Strait a week earlier, on August 1, to begin an intensive photographic census with fellow biologist Ian B. MacAskie, concentrating first on the Johnstone Strait/Blackfish Sound region of British Columbia. (Over the next several years, they would carry the study into every area of the B.C. coast.) They had followed the whales, and after a few encounters in which they had photographed each animal with telephoto lenses, Bigg realized that individual whales could be identified. The whales we knew, some of which Spong had seen in earlier years, could be identified on sight — Stubbs, Nicola, Wavy, Top Notch and Hooker. Bigg was discovering that almost every whale could be distinguished by dorsal fin shape, saddle markings or by nicks and scratches usually found on the dorsal's trailing edge, even though some marks were so subtle that they showed up only in the darkroom. Bigg was using a system of fine-detail fin photography, effectively fingerprinting every whale on black-and-white Tri-X film pushed to 1200 ASA and shot at a shutter speed of 1/1000 of a second. It was like placing each fin under a magnifying glass, revealing every cut, scratch and abrasion.

As part of the orca study, Bigg's research team in Nanaimo was analyzing thousands of photographs taken during orca captures in the 1960s and early 1970s, looking for telltale nicks and scratches on the dorsal fins of animals that had been captured and released. It was real detective work. Bigg discovered that some B.C. orca pods had been captured more than once; pod members, usually young, were removed, or cropped, each time. He was concerned about repeated cropping of the same pods, curious whether it had affected family units, aware that it might take years of observation. Yet, through his research, Bigg was starting to piece together fascinating pod histories, dating from the early captures in the 1960s. The pod history of Top

Notch's group, for example, showed that it was once a much different pod.

On a stormy December night in 1969, Top Notch's pod — at that time 12 whales — wandered into Pender Harbour, a tiny fishing community 50 miles northwest of Vancouver. They were about 125 miles from their home range in Johnstone Strait. Seven fishermen on four boats, nets ready, were waiting — men who had been there off and on for 19 months after catching and selling another pod in April 1968. No whales had since entered the harbour.

The fishermen corralled 4 of the 12 whales after an all-night battle in gale-force winds and driving rain, a storm that they believed had driven the whales close to shore. When daylight came the next morning, they saw that the rest of the pod had remained with their captured mates, just outside the nets. So the fishermen bagged them, too, herding the whales into a separate fishnet corral 100 yards away. The harbour was crisscrossed with herring nets strung inside salmon nets; everywhere, there were nets, and all of them were full of whales.

Not long after the capture, a massive senior bull (not Top Notch) escaped. This big bull apparently "knew" nets. In any case, he had no respect for them. Though free, the big bull tried to liberate his pod-mates by repeatedly crashing back through the nets and then — as if to show the others the escape route — punching out again. The fishermen were frantically sewing up the nets. For a time, the bull made new holes faster than the fishermen could sew, but eventually, he gave up. He waited around for a few days, then disappeared.

The captured whales, disoriented by the nets and perhaps suffering from shock, would not budge — all except one cow that kept swimming up to the nets, as if searching for the escape route. She couldn't find it. Graeme Ellis was there representing Sealand (Victoria, British Columbia), and that's when he first saw the distinctive V-shaped saddle and, when the whale came close, two softball-like tumours at the corner of her mouth. "Saddle," Ellis told me later, "was probably saved from captivity by her oddness." Of the 11 whales in the nets, 7 were considered saleable. Offers poured in from U.S. and European aquariums. The remaining four, all mature animals, were released. (Mature killer whales, besides being large and heavy for transport, do not fare well in the tank, and they are more difficult to train.) These four were the whales that we knew, the elders of Top Notch's pod: Top Notch himself; the cow Scar; the wide-nicked cow; and Saddle. Staying in the harbour, one of the three cows — probably Saddle, according to Ellis and the fishermen who had watched her swimming up to the nets — delivered a calf. Had Saddle been trying to escape to have the calf? Was the bull that had crashed through the nets trying to help? Top Notch and the other two cows waited outside the harbour for a day or so and then, with the new mother and calf, swam free, leaving the others to their fate.

One subadult female, Corky II, one subadult male (no name) and a female calf, Patches, were shipped to Marineland of the Pacific, south of Los Angeles. Patches died the following year of salmonellosis and "no name" a year later of pneumonia. The remaining female, Corky II, has survived to date, mating with Marineland's resident bull, Orky II.

A mature female, 16 feet long and weighing more than two tons, was flown 6,000 miles to England's Cleethorpes Zoo. Calypso, as she came to be known, was transferred soon after to France's Marineland Côte d'Azur, where she died within the year. A male and a female subadult, Nepo and Yaka, were flown to Marine World Africa U.S.A. near San Francisco.

The seventh whale, a cow also destined for Marine World, slipped through the nets in a successful freedom dash while her captors were guiding her into a sling designed to hoist her from her native waters. The whale left the harbour in a hurry, and it is not known whether she ever rejoined Top Notch and the others released the previous week.

In 1973, could we discern any aftereffects of the 1969 capture that had cut Top Notch's pod in half? Was the fact of its survival evidence of the resilience of the killer whale pod?

The unnamed massive bull that knew the nets and tried to save his pod has not, to date, been seen by Bigg or his researchers. He may be dead, or he may have joined another pod; there is no way to tell because the photographs taken of him at the capture were too distant and out of focus. Top Notch is the only bull left in the pod, but there are three calves, born between 1970 and 1973. Top Notch's pod seems to have bounced back — although it is still two members short of its precropped size of 12.* It is noteworthy that these whales, despite man's disruption of their family life by capture, remain as approachable as Stubbs's group (and Bigg is fairly certain that there have been no captures from Stubbs's group). It may be that Top Notch's pod associates its unfortunate experience only with man in Pender Harbour. No whales have been seen there since the 1969 incident.

Hunter and I were no longer alone with Stubbs's pod. The Biological Station's sailboat hovered nearby. Top Notch's pod had joined Stubbs's pod, and now, out of Baronet Passage to the east, yet a third group of whales steamed into view. It was Hooker's pod, all eight of them. The bulls formed the first flank, then came several young males or females. A cow and the young calf we called Rusty brought up the rear. They surfaced all at once, blowing and snorting, holding their ground as if preparing to charge the other two pods. It was a momentary face-off. Then they swam into the larger group, forming the Johnstone Strait superpod.

Three whale pods together: some 34 killer whales! To Hunter, it was "orca soup." It was the largest number of killer whales that we had seen at one time, and it did seem an entire seaful. We were only beginning to learn about the periodic formation of superpods. At Penn Cove in Puget Sound in August 1970, the Seattle Public Aquarium netted about 80 orcas that had been travelling together. These whales were identified from photographs as belonging to several pods, perhaps four, which Bigg would later track off southern Vancouver Island. Superpods have been observed in other areas of the world, notably the southern ocean. Zoologist Gaskin tells of groups of 200 to 300 near Cape

*An April 1968 capture in Pender Harbour may have also involved Top Notch's pod, according to recent evidence. If so, the precropped size might have been as high as 18.

Horn, South America. Antarctic scientists and whalers talk about groups of perhaps 1,000.

Yet even with only 34, it seemed that everywhere we looked, the sea boiled with blackfish. They started diving deep, combing the tide rips of Blackney Passage, probably feeding. Hunter winced, saying that they had found his favourite fishing spot, a legendary sure-fire cod hole where fish lie in wait for the Hunter hook. "Now I know how the fishermen must feel when they see orcas," he said, only half kiddingly.

Then we noticed two small black fins, similar to the tiny dorsals of young killer whales, but with bodies larger than bulls. They broke the surface, arching their long, broad backs gently, unlike the orcas. They were minke (pronounced MINK-ee) whales, those lesser rorquals, which, at 30 feet, are the smallest of the baleen whales. Unlike the killers, the minkes have no teeth; they feed on plankton and occasionally on small fish and crustaceans, taking their food in great gulps and straining out the water through slatlike baleen plates that grow from the roofs of their mouths. Minutes later, a school of tiny porpoises puffed into view, joining the other whales. They were speedy Dall's porpoises, about a dozen of them. With their black-and-white colouring, up-to-seven-foot body lengths and tiny curved dorsal fins, these porpoises look a little like orca calves, when they can be clearly seen. However, they move so fast, they're usually just a blur.

Hunter and I trained our cameras on the scene before us, waiting for a bloody battle. The Russian studies of orcas' stomach contents in the early 1970s had revealed that minke whales were the main and sometimes exclusive food item for orcas at certain seasons and in certain sectors of the Antarctic. Porpoises and dolphins were third after fish and squid, according to Japanese whaling captains who conducted studies of 364 orca stomachs from animals killed off Japan's coast between 1948 and 1957. In 1968, U.S. biologist Dale W. Rice examined the stomachs of 10 orcas from the North Pacific — Alaska to California — and reported mostly marine mammals, including three Dall's porpoises and one minke whale. Off the west coast of Vancouver Island in May 1964, biologist David Hancock saw an orca pod slaughter a minke whale, and the next day, he found the carcass, minus the lips and tongue, neatly stripped of its skin, " the appearance being that of a freshly peeled orange." Two months later, he discovered another minke in the area that had apparently met a similar fate. In the open Pacific, off Vancouver Island, in May 1962 and 1963, the crew of the *St. Catherines* witnessed several killer whales attacking a group of Dall's porpoises; their logbook reported "much blood in the water."

We watched the orcas, minkes and Dall's porpoises — but, as it turned out, nothing happened. In fact, we would see the Johnstone Strait killers cross paths with the minkes and porpoises many times that first summer. The minkes and porpoises never altered course because of the orcas nor did they show a reluctance to share feeding areas with them. "The killer whales obviously have plenty of fish," said Hunter. In the Johnstone Strait area during the summer, there are only two to four minke whales and perhaps two to three groups of Dall's porpoises, with about a dozen individuals in each. Yet we were surprised to learn that the killer whales here would ignore what was obviously a food source in other areas off the B.C. coast.

The three cetacean species — the orcas, minkes and porpoises — worked the tide rips, foraging peacefully, almost side by side. Above the scene, eagles and herring gulls hovered, waiting to dive for leftovers. It was a convention of predators: gulls screaming and eagles laughing in their high-pitched cackle against a background of the rushing cacophony of wind and tide, all of it punctuated by the whales' shotgun-blast blows and by quick puffs from the porpoises. They milled all about us. We watched, waited and tried to photograph the scene. Meanwhile, the waves were slopping into the Zodiac. The surf sprayed our eyeglasses and chilled our waterproof suits. Our cameras were plastic-bagged, with holes for lenses and to allow our hands to reach in and focus and shoot. The cameras escaped the saltwater assault, but it was almost impossible to use them because the Zodiac had become a roller coaster. We were busy just hanging on.

Then, oblivious to wind and surf, the killer whales started to move — the three pods together — pushing north and west into Blackfish Sound, fanning out as the sound stretched wider into what soon became Queen Charlotte Strait and would eventually become the Pacific. They moved slowly at first, then at a steady six to eight knots. This was the third time we had seen more than one pod travelling together, and each time, we had observed that these super-pods travelled almost twice as fast as individual pods.

The westerly swept across the sound — just an afternoon blow, not a storm — but we were taking a beating in our open boat. We motored over to the Biological Station's *Amethyst II* and were welcomed aboard and fed hot coffee and tea as we talked whales, while skipper Danny Welch kept them in sight.

We told Bigg we had met Stubbs's pod in Robson Bight that morning and had followed them through Johnstone Strait. He had met Top Notch's pod in Blackfish Sound, just before noon.

Together, we surveyed the three whale pods stretched across the 2 1/2-mile-wide gateway to Queen Charlotte Strait, from Bold Head to Donegal Head. Bigg recalled the story of an old-timer, Billy Procter from nearby Echo Bay, who claimed to have seen more than 1,000 blackfish in this spot several times during the 1950s: "So thick you could walk on their backs."

"But killer whale numbers can be deceptive," said Bigg. "It's very difficult to make an accurate count of more than 20 or 25 animals who are widely dispersed and constantly moving — but at individual speeds and sometimes in odd directions — and who spend only about 5 percent of their time on the surface."

The most accurate method of counting whales, Bigg theorized, was to get to know the individual group sizes, then, when they join up, add the numbers of all the pods present. That was how we came up with the figure of 34 whales that day.

Why do they join up in these large groups? To hunt? To play? To socialize?

Bigg didn't know. I told Bigg that I had watched pods joining up and, at the same time, had monitored them on the hydrophone. The whale talk at such times was thick and various, different from the sparse routine sounds that a single pod makes on its daily travels. The large gatherings seemed to be social occasions of some sort.

Are the individual pods permanent groups or loose aggregations of individuals who join together for the summer hunt?

Bigg, who planned to monitor them for several years, thought that he would eventually find an answer.

Are they migratory? Do they return to Johnstone Strait in the summer like the Twofold Bay whales did every winter?

"They're probably not migratory," Bigg said. "The reports of sightings in B.C. waters are nearly year-round. There are fewer sightings in the winter and early spring months, but I suspect that reflects the fact there are fewer boats on the water and the weather is often stormy, which makes sighting them more difficult."

Are there specific pod territories?

Again, Bigg didn't know.

Do pod movements follow regular daily patterns?

Bigg said that adverse tides and weather conditions do not seem to affect travel routes. Perhaps it is as the fishermen say: The whales follow the spawning salmon schools from the open ocean to the river mouths.

Where do they go at night? Are their nights the same as their days? When do they sleep or rest?

More I-don't-knows.

"Being able to identify them as individuals is the first step," said Bigg. "Now, we'll see what they do."

As we watched, the large group dispersed, the whales assembling into individual pods. Stubbs's pod headed west, away from the others. Hunter and I decided to try to follow them; Bigg and MacAskie would stay with Top Notch. Warmed by the coffee and the conversation, we set out in our rubber boat, but suddenly, the engine quit on us. Hunter pulled and pulled on the outboard cord. Each time, the engine sputtered then died. Finally, as he cursed away, it started, but by then, the whales were almost out of sight.

It was getting late, and the sea was still windy and cold. I mentioned dinner. Hunter suggested that we grab a quick snack at his cod "hole of plenty" on the way back to camp. He had boasted about the spot, claiming that he could pull up dinner in two minutes flat. "Sometimes I put the pan in the fire before dropping my line!" That was before the whales had found the spot. Now Hunter wondered if they had left any for us.

Down went the jigging line. No bait, just a long, banana-shaped, shiny metal lure with a large, naked treble hook on the end of it. I held the boat at the head of the tide rip, watching with amusement but expectation. Hunter jigged the line half a dozen times, barely giving it time to drop. Thirty seconds passed. He cursed and jigged harder. We moved a few feet to the top of the tide rip. "Try a little deeper," I suggested. As he let the hook down to about 90 feet, Hunter was intent. Then came the tug, a big one. It took the two of us to pull the monster into the boat. Forty-five pounds of fish lay flopping at our feet — a big ling cod. Hunter was all smiles, frankly relieved that his local fish market was still giving handouts.

"What are we going to do with all this?"

"Maybe," said Hunter, "we should invite the whales back for dinner, tell them they forgot one. I guess there's enough for everyone."

In the evening, reclining on the rocks beside the fire, we heard the wind ease and the sea calm to nothing. The fog rolled in, thick and wet like a heavy blanket left out in the rain. Early fog warnings had sent the fishermen home. The strait was strangely still. We slept well, only the occasional foghorns through the night reminding us that we were near the sea.

By midmorning, we were back on the water, and our good fortune continued: We met up with the whales almost immediately. There were 10 to 15 of them. Although we couldn't see them, we could hear them through the fog patches that hung over the water. We had trouble following them and had to keep shutting off the engine to listen for their blows before proceeding. Around the islands at the head of Knight Inlet, I said: "If we lose them, we'll have nothing to follow them by; they leave no trail." (One cannot "track" a sea mammal.) But Hunter replied: "Be glad they don't leave a trail." Earlier, we had talked about scientists who study the movements and habits of land mammals: half their working lives are spent sifting through animal droppings. "Can you imagine if we had to be going around picking up whale dung? The size of it, for one thing!"

We followed the whale sounds through the fog till the sun burned off the haze. It was Stubbs's pod. Again that afternoon, Stubbs's pod joined up with Top Notch's. We followed the two groups through Knight Inlet and back down Blackfish Sound to Johnstone Strait; by then, it was almost dark. The two pods parted company.

For three days, Hunter and I had followed the whales into new areas north of Johnstone Strait, through the island passages and across Queen Charlotte Strait. We had watched three different pods for long periods and had become fairly confident about their individual numbers and integrity as pod units. Though individuals might spread out and even seem to stray at times, each pod would re-form into the same number of individuals. The whales kept returning to Johnstone Strait. Stubbs's pod and Top Notch's pod seemed centred here. (Hooker's range was farther north, but that group also spent many hours in the strait.) I was keeping daily maps of the whales' travels, and when I looked at them all together, the central whale area (among the places we had followed them) appeared to be Robson Bight on the Vancouver Island side of Johnstone Strait. As soon as the whales arrived in Robson Bight, they would slow down, seeming in no hurry to go anywhere. If any place could be called home, it was here: a place they seemed to pass during the morning and almost always returned to in the afternoon or evening.

When Hunter brought me back to the *Four Winds* that night, I suggested to Vatcher and Bott that we build a shore camp and stay anchored in Robson Bight to conduct our film and sound operations. It would give us something to do while we waited for O'Neill to return with the repaired movie cameras.

Vatcher liked the idea because the bight had little traffic: For decades, it had been closed to commercial salmon fishing to protect the Tsitika River salmon run. Also, there were no logging operations or booming grounds here, as there were inside many Vancouver Island bays. The Tsitika River watershed was the last unlogged, untouched river valley on eastern Vancouver Island. In February 1973, a moratorium on logging and road building in the valley had been declared by the B.C. provincial government. There seemed a good chance that the valley, including the river mouth at Robson Bight, would be set aside as a wilderness ecological reserve. In the quiet of the bight, we felt sure that we had found the ideal spot to film and record the whales.

SWIMMING
WITH WHALES

AUGUST 7. Night on the sea. Clear, cool, no wind. Lying on my back, alone in the dinghy, counting stars. Aquarius, Orion, Pisces and Scorpio — the known constellations. Those bright ones are surrounded by a thousand tiny pinpricks — more stars than I've ever seen. And, as if to mark the half hour, shooting stars stream across the northern sky, falling into the horizon's ocean.

I had the all-night whale watch on August 7. From our anchorage in Robson Bight, tight against steep-treed Vancouver Island, I had rowed a mile to the centre of the bight, where I was picked up by the main Johnstone Strait current. At midnight, the tide had been high, almost 18 feet, near peak of the month, but then it began ebbing fast. I was letting it carry me. At some three to four knots, the outgoing tide gave the strait the appearance of a river — wide, deep and slow-moving for a river, but a river. Change the trees from conifers to broad leaves, remove the mountains, and I could have been on a raft floating down the Mississippi to the Gulf of Mexico. The early Kwakiutls, in fact, thought that Johnstone Strait was a river. Now I understood why. I could row the six-foot-long wooden dinghy "upriver" against the current, but my headway would be cut almost to nothing. Instead, I planned to go with the tide and return a few hours later on the slack.

From time to time, I checked the kerosene mast light on the *Four Winds* and the steady blinking light across the strait at Boat Bay, lining them up to establish my position. "Don't want to lose sight of the sailboat," I thought to myself. It was a passing concern. Storms rarely came up at night. If the wind started to blow, I could turn and row hard, cross current, to shore. The danger, if any, was being swamped by the freighters and barges that passed every hour or so, leaving large wakes that, 10 minutes later, lifted and sometimes curled over the dinghy's bow to jolt me from my midnight reveries. I began rowing again — to keep alert, to ease the tightness in my limbs. It felt good, moving through the water. My eyesight sharpened. The ocean was alive, knowing no night. Phosphorescent plankton — thickest at this time of year — lit up every movement through the water. As I rowed, the water around me was churned into a froth of glitter. The oars dipped, stirred the glittery brew and then, as they lifted, dripped luminescent drops. I was painting pictures with the patterns of my rowing, my serious brushwork distracted only by schools of lantern fish that alternately fluttered and streamed through the water beside the boat. I imagined whales shooting the phosphorescence sky-high like a coloured fountain; but in order for me to see such blows, the whales would have to come very close. Then I heard something: splashing water, breathing, something swimming toward me. I stopped rowing. A bald head emerged through a glowing ring of sea. A mottled white harbour seal, who looked like an old man out for a midnight swim, was as curious about me as I was about him. Old-man harbour seal ducked in and out of the water, splashing all around the dinghy. Suddenly, he took off after a fish. I watched as his shimmering trail faded to black.

Then came the sounds I'd been searching for, the whale blows. Off and on for the rest of the night, they blew — phantoms camouflaged by darkness. Mostly, the sounds came from the far-off distance, but twice, the whales passed within 100 yards of the rowboat, and for 30 seconds at one point, I was surrounded. The blows were like distant or muted guns firing against the night quiet. The gunshots bounced off the mountain faces of the bight and echoed down the Tsitika River Valley — and I never saw a whale. I could count them by listening to their blows and mentally arranging them in patterns. The whales were in a number of subgroups, two to four individuals each. At first, it was confusing, deciphering whether three successive blows meant three whales or one whale blowing three times; but each blow varied in length. The big slow blows were from bulls; quick short ones, usually from calves or juveniles. Cows and young males were somewhere in between. From their blows, I could classify each subgroup according to its unique composition of bulls, calves and cows or young males. Then I added the subgroups together to obtain the pod size. The system was not foolproof, but it gave me some indication of the size and subgroup composition of my nocturnal visitors. I counted and recounted them as they moved past the dinghy, heading west. They were travelling steadily, in the usual pattern of three to four breaths within a 1 1/2-minute period, then down for about 4 minutes. I determined that there were at least 12, perhaps 18, whales passing by.

For several nights running in that first week of August, the whales had skirted our anchorage at Robson Bight, moving back and forth along roughly a one-mile periphery, sometimes for hours. They were not coming in daylight, except Stubbs. Her pod had come twice at sunset, both times heading east. We had instituted the all-night whale watches on August 1 to keep track of the nocturnal movements of Stubbs's pod and the other whale groups.

We were ourselves becoming creatures of the night, sleeping at odd hours.

Since our movie cameras were still in the shop being repaired and since we could not film at night in any case, we were happy to attend to the whales' nightly visits, rowing out in the dinghy to wait for them or staying on the sailboat, listening for them on deck and monitoring their underwater sounds on the hydrophone. By listening, we thought we'd always know when they were coming, usually from three or four miles away.

One night, after a late supper, we were relaxing, playing music in the boat. Bott sucked on his harmonica; I played the guitar — slow blues. We were bending the blue notes soulfully, the chords resonating through the cave chamber of the old wooden boat, warming us. Bott went up to check the anchor and thought he heard something. We were quiet for a few minutes. Then whale sounds started coming through the hull — loud and growing louder. Once our ears became attuned to them, we heard three-note whistles intoned over and over again — the same three-note whistle that a human uses to call another person or a dog or sometimes a taxi. It can mean "Come here" or simply "Hey!" Was this phrase part of a whale's vocabulary, or had our whale friends heard fishermen and other boaters whistling it? Perhaps a boater had called to the whales. We started whistling the phrase back to them, projecting our calls through the hull. At the same time, I turned on the hydrophone to find out whether our whistles were being heard in the water. They were there, faintly, interspersed with whale whistles that were coming in very loud through the hydrophone. We had been exchanging "Come here" whistles for two minutes when I cranked up the synthesizer and played a synthesized version of it through the underwater speaker. The whales responded by dragging out the phrase and pitching it higher and higher, as if in play. We played, too, continuing to use both synthesizer and our whistles, although we were a bit incredulous at the whole business.

Once, on a miserable rainy winter day at Pender Harbour, Ellis had heard a young captive whale whistle a perfect rendition of the first two bars of "It's raining, it's pouring, the old man is snoring." "I still don't believe it," said Ellis. "Was it a fluke that he'd got a combination of sounds that came out that way, or had he heard someone whistle it?" Ellis, a professional whale skeptic, was not given to telling far-out whale stories. ("You'll probably send for the men in white, but it really did happen.") Almost everyone who has worked with whales or dolphins has his "It's raining, it's pouring" story. The whales whistling "Come here" that night beside the *Four Winds* is one of mine.

For 15 minutes, whales and men called to each other from a distance, back and forth across the blackness of night. Then I heard a sharp thump on the hydrophone. Something was hitting the instrument that hung alongside the boat, 15 feet below the surface. From the time we had first heard the whales, Bott had opened the hatch. He had kept a constant check on the surface but had seen nothing, and we had heard no blows. Now it seemed that they were right beside the boat. Bott jumped on deck to investigate.

"They're splashing in the kelp bed," he said.

Several whales were frolicking in the shallows between the boat and the shore, near where the rocks dried at low tide. I poked my head out the hatchway and saw a phosphorescent blow exploding like a tiny Roman candle against the blackness. It was our first visual evidence of the whales at night. And in two seconds, they departed, leaving us speechless, unable even to whistle good-bye.

In the first-light hours of August 8, a seaplane circled twice above Robson Bight, landing near the river mouth and taxiing slowly to the boat. By sound, it was a single-engine Beaver with a de Havilland engine; by colour and design, an Alert Bay Air Services seaplane. The bold black orca on the yellow cockpit door could be seen hundreds of feet away. Reaching out as they approached, Bott caught one wing of the plane before it sliced into the rigging. The pilot waved. Michael Bigg stepped out on the pontoon and said, "Where the heck is Stubbs?" In little more than a week of following them around, he had developed an intense personal interest in the lives of the killer whales of Johnstone Strait. He said he had left Stubbs's pod yesterday afternoon in western Johnstone Strait, but the pod seemed to have disappeared from the area overnight. He had searched for them by sea the previous night, and today, he was searching by air from a chartered seaplane.

I told Bigg that we'd seen Stubbs's pod yesterday at sunset, heading east through the bight. This was two hours after the pod had left him in western Johnstone Strait. Then, after midnight, we had heard a group — by rough count, the size of Stubbs's pod (about 16 whales) — moving west again. "If this group was Stubbs's," I said, "then they're probably west or north of the strait." Bigg said that he would continue his search, flying north and west across Queen Charlotte Strait, past Malcolm Island, then backtracking across Blackfish Sound and into Knight Inlet and Kingcome Inlet where, according to Billy Procter, some 60 killer whales lived in the summer. Days later, Bigg informed us that he had not seen a single whale on his northern flight. Yet within 24 hours of disappearing, Stubbs's pod was back in the strait. Where had they gone?

This sudden disappearing act happened from time to time with all the resident whale pods of Johnstone Strait. For days, Stubbs's pod, Top Notch's pod and Hooker's pod would travel through the Johnstone Strait/Blackfish Sound area day and night, passing Robson Bight (and our anchorage there) at least once, and sometimes four or five times, in a 24-hour period. Then they'd be gone, apparently having moved out of the area for a day or two, maybe a week. Later, we discovered that Top Notch's pod made occasional trips south to the Strait of Georgia, some 125 miles away from Robson Bight, perhaps a two-day trip. Hooker's and Stubbs's pods sometimes moved north to Rivers Inlet and Bella Bella, also about 125 miles away. It was no use searching for the whales when they took to ranging over these wider areas. On the occasions when we did find them after considerable searching, they were always already back in the strait and usually en route to the bight. (In August 1975, six orcas were captured in Pedder Bay, off southern Vancouver Island. Only six days before the capture, Ellis had photographed the same pod near Bella Bella, more than 300 miles away. Following a direct route by the sea, the whales would have averaged about 60 miles a day.

Bigg hopped back into the waiting seaplane. From the window, he told us about a small group of whales that he'd seen at dawn as he flew along the Vancouver Island shore, about 10 miles southeast of the bight. He said that they might be heading for the bight. "I counted three or four animals. If you see them, watch the fins for unusual marks." (It is impossible to identify whales from the air. In fact, Bigg found the seaplane of limited use. One could survey a large area and make approximate counts from the air only on clear, calm days. In the normal summer pattern of Johnstone Strait, mornings tend to be foggy; afternoons are windy with whitecaps that, from the air, look like thousands of whales spouting everywhere.)

Some time after Bigg took off, I found myself in the rowboat, taking my turn at the watch. It was about noon. I had brought the Nagra to record the whales' surface blows in case any should come close. A few strokes out from the sailboat, bright sun greeted me, bouncing off a mirror sea. Thick fog still hung like a steamy shower curtain from the 5,000-foot-high peaks along the shore, but in the strait, I could see and hear for several miles in all directions. I eased into rowing, long smooth strokes — swish, drip, splash. My arms grew tired, but I kept on, slipping into the floating exertion-euphoria of the long-distance runner. I rowed maybe a mile, then stopped, lay back and drank in hours of waiting and listening and solitude. It was midafternoon when I heard airborne sounds, similar to underwater whale vocalizations but too loud to be whales. Birds, then. I looked around. Nothing. I studied the high treetops along the eastern wall of the bight. Perhaps ravens. Ravens are crafty and versatile mimics. I was drunk with the day and momentarily forgot what Bigg had said about whales coming.

Then, from behind me, "Kawoof!" — a whale breathing. "Kawoof! Kawoof!" Two more. Coming out of nowhere, they were headed straight for me. I sat motionless, watching them surface and blow, their black crescents slicing the water as they went up and down. My heart started pounding. A cow and calf were hugging the shore; they would pass me. But the largest whale, a young male or mature cow about three times the size of the dinghy, was zeroing in. My rational mind fought gut fear and, for a few seconds, lost out. I was far from land, deep into whale territory, a sitting duck if the whale chose to see me that way. The dinghy suddenly seemed as tiny and frail as a toy boat in a bathtub. Furthermore, the bathwater was only 10 Fahrenheit degrees on the liquid side of freezing. If the boat overturned, death from exposure could come in 20 minutes or less. Even a strong swimmer racing for shore might lose to the mind-numbing cold. There was nothing to do but sit tight and hold on. In seconds, the whale and I would be eyeball to eyeball.

I peered down over the side of the boat, searching the dark green waters. Thirty feet below, the whale appeared, an ethereal form suspended in a liquid universe. He was just hanging there. Strange as it seems, seeing him close calmed me. He did not have his mouth open. He was obviously aware of me. Then he snapped his powerful tail flukes, driving upward for air. A cloud of bubbles surged to the surface. The water broke; the underwater etching smashed. Leviathan's surfacing erupted in a wave that nearly swamped the boat. He was so close, I could almost touch him. Then he blew with a great "Kawoof!" The spray seemed to drop in slow motion as it covered me, a cool shower on a hot day. I tried to steady the boat. The whale sucked air into his sleek, shiny black mass — a hollow, cavernous sucking sound (I did not have the presence of mind to turn on the recorder) — and rolled on his side. His tawny white belly and matching eye patch flashed in the sun. The light caught his up-to-now invisible eye. He seemed to be looking, staring, at me with the dark, penetrating eye of the killer whale.

Fuelled by adrenaline, I rowed back to the sailboat in record time. As I rowed, I thought about the encounter. The intimacy of our meeting had touched me. But the gut fear I had felt as the whale approached nagged at me like a bad dream. Even then I did not believe that orcas were dangerous to humans — but for a few days, whenever I closed my eyes, I relived the incident and wondered, "What might have happened if . . ."

For the first time, I understood the fear of orca. It had been an instinctive fear that moved in my blood as the predator approached, a fear as old as man himself, a fear of the large predator — and the killer whale is the largest predator on the planet. Might orca's famous carnivorous appetite sometimes extend to humans? Was there any substance to the reported attacks on boats and humans in the water?

Back on the *Four Winds*, Vatcher and Bott had watched my encounter with detached amusement. "When the whale came up beside you, I thought he was *in* the boat," said Bott in a teasing tone. When we had discussed accounts of orca attacks on man, we had tended to be skeptical.

The first story we heard of an orca attack came from Paul Spong. He told it one afternoon when he came by the boat to see how we were doing. Later, he included the story in a chapter of *Mind in the Waters* (Joan McIntyre, ed., 1974):

"In 1956, two loggers working on a hillside in British Columbia were skidding logs down the slope into the water. Noticing a pod . . . of orcas passing below, one logger deliberately let go a log, which skidded down and hit one of the whales in the back, apparently injuring but not killing it. The whales went away. That night, as the loggers were rowing back to camp, the whales reappeared and tipped the boat over. One man vanished, the one who had let the log go. The other man was not touched and survived to tell the tale."

It sounds more like a moral fable than an account of orca behaviour. There is no documentation of the incident. We have only the word of the surviving logger, whose story has come down to us in various versions told along the B.C. coast.

Stories of orca attacks sparked a lively debate when Ellis and Hunter visited us the day of my dinghy encounter. The fear and possible danger were matters of some concern to them — they were planning to swim with the whales. Yet when I brought up the story of the two loggers, Ellis and Hunter cracked up.

Hunter: "The logger no doubt died of fright."

Ellis: "He probably couldn't swim."

Hunter: "Probably drunk . . . and nothing sinks faster than a drunken logger. Well, one thing's for certain — a killer whale would never eat a logger. Bad for digestion!"

Hunter was equally lighthearted about his own plan for an underwater rendezvous with orca. Vatcher and I listened with a certain amount of awe. Quite frankly, we would not have exchanged places with the two divers. It was one thing to be out in a small boat — a dinghy or even a canoe — with killer whales blowing beside you; it was quite another to get into the water with them. By swimming with the whales, willingly entering their watery world, the divers would be putting themselves on display, subject to inspection. Furthermore, the inspecting would be done on the whales' terms for, once in the water, the divers relinquished all control of the situation. They planned to assume a nonaggressive posture, one of helplessness: lying face down on the surface of the water.

Even Bott sobered at the thought of entering the water with the whales; total vulnerability did not seem to him an ideal situation in which to place one-self. He did plan to dive with the whales — to obtain underwater film footage. Some of his diving experience had come with killer whales at Sealand of the Pacific in Victoria. He had worked with captured whales in the nets at Pedder Bay and had once helped rescue Chimo, a rare white orca that had become entangled in the nets and had nearly drowned. Bott was tall and wiry, an ex-boxer and an ex-competition swimmer. He was an intrepid if sometimes reck-less sailor. He was also a big talker. Yet when it came to swimming with orcas in the wild, he spoke of taking elaborate precautions. Bott was searching for the perfect underwater cave where he could lie in wait for the whales and where he could retreat, seal-like, if necessary. Hunter, on the other hand, was not worried about confronting the "myth of the killer." He told us just that, almost too loudly. In Hunter, I saw the first manifestation of killer whale macho. Perhaps since predator orcas seem so macho, they inspire a certain macho in the people who work with them, in captivity and in the wild. We all had it to some degree, but especially Hunter.

Hunter delighted in quoting the available literature:

In the early 1960s, the U.S. Navy *Diving Manual* awarded orca its highest plus-four danger rating. "The killer whale has a reputation of being a ruthless and ferocious beast . . . if a killer whale is seen in the area, the diver should get out of the water immediately."

The U.S. Navy *Antarctic Sailing Direction* reported that killer whales "will attack human beings at every opportunity."

James Clarke, in his 1969 book *Man Is the Prey*, called orca "the biggest confirmed man-eater on earth" (though he neglected to confirm a single story).

But Hunter's best quote, delivered deadpan, came from Owen Lee's 450-page treatise on diving published in 1963: "There is no treatment for being eaten by the orca, except reincarnation."

After a few good laughs, we got down to a serious discussion of alleged orca attacks on boats and on men in the water. Later, from the safety of the public library, I filled in the details of these stories. Here are the major accounts, each followed by a few comments.

June 15, 1972. Dougal Robertson's 43-foot schooner *Lucette* was hit by "sledgehammer blows of incredible force" about 150 miles west of the Galápagos Islands in the Pacific. Robertson's two sons (aged 13 and 18) saw "killer whales . . . all sizes . . . about 20 of them." Robertson himself saw only the gaping holes in the floorboard caused by what he believed were three killer whales simultaneously ramming the *Lucette*'s wooden hull. The ship sank in less than 10 minutes. The Robertson family spent 37 days adrift in a small lifeboat before being rescued. Robertson then wrote the best-seller *Survive the Savage Sea.*

Ellis didn't believe that killer whales had rammed the *Lucette.* Hunter suggested, "If they'd said they hit a deadhead, it wouldn't have had as much impact as a story." Added Vatcher: "Calling it a killer whale attack makes for a best-seller." To be fair, the book is a family's dramatic account of survival at sea. That in itself was an adventure. Perhaps, however, they were a little quick in naming orca as the probable perpetrator.

March 9, 1976. The Italian yacht *Guia III* was sailing for the Cape Verde Islands off Dakar, leading on the final leg of the Atlantic Triangle Race between Rio de Janeiro and Portsmouth, England. Radioman George Marshall, sleeping below decks, felt a "bloody great bang" against the hull. He jumped out of bed and into ankle-deep water. The first thing he saw was a gaping hole below the waterline on the port side of *Guia III*'s wooden hull. The hole would have been almost big enough to dive through headfirst had the water not been pouring in with the force of a dam break. The ship sank in a few minutes. As the six sailors transferred to the lifeboat, they noticed four or five killer whales in the area, and the whales, apparently curious, came close. The crew believed that one of the killer whales must have struck the yacht.

The similarity of the *Guia III* account to that of the *Lucette* — and some half-dozen others I found — is striking. All the supposed attacks occurred in the warm temperate or tropical zones where orcas are rare, because of food scarcity. Most were midocean attacks, which encourages further suspicion of these reports, since orcas generally stay close to the continental coastline. In each case, the orcas entered and left the area quickly. The attack itself came unexpectedly and, without exception, was not witnessed. (Since the impact occurred underwater, it would have been difficult to see anyway.) Unfortunately, in almost every incident, the evidence sank. In one story of an attack that occurred off California in March 1952, a light skiff believed to have been punctured by killer whale teeth was brought back for examination. Teeth marks on the boat's hull seemed to confirm the two mariners' account of orcas attacking the boat. Later, however, scientists reexamined the tooth marks and found that they belonged to a large shark, probably the great white shark.

No killer whale attack on a boat has been proved. If any *have* happened, the most likely explanation would seem to be mistaken identity. Some scientists have suggested that there could be instances in which orca's excellent sonar system breaks down. In the accounts in question, it is possible that these killer whales, ravenously hungry in the "desert" of a tropical sea, had attacked what they *imagined* was a large whale swimming at the surface. Following this scenario, we could say that orca strategy — in order to subdue large prey — might well have been the surprise attack. The orcas would have raced in and rammed their intended victim full force. (It must have been a rude shock for the orcas when they hit wood.) But the most important point to keep in mind is that in each instance, after depositing the boat's occupants into the water, the orcas left. They obviously had no intention of preying on man. This line of reasoning — that they are not interested in man as food — is consistent with the circumstances of several alleged orca bitings of men in the wild. One of these bitings, however, represents an almost unimpeachable case against orca.

September 9, 1972. Wet-suited Hans Kretschmer was lying on his surfboard about 100 feet from shore off Point Sur, near Monterey, California, when he felt something nudge him from behind. He looked over his shoulder.

" I saw a glossy black," the 18-year-old surfer later told James Hughes, a dentist who was head of the Pacific Grove Marine Rescue Patrol. "First, I thought it was a huge shark. Then the beast grabbed me. I hit it on the head with my fist. I thought for sure it would come after me again, but I was able to bodysurf in to the beach."

One hundred stitches were needed to close three deep gashes on Kretschmer's left thigh. Immediately after surgery, Kretschmer was quizzed. He never went into shock. Two surfing buddies were questioned as well. Neither had seen the animal until after the attack, and even then, they did not see it spouting. According to Hughes, the three men "consistently described an animal that had a huge dorsal fin and white undermarkings and was black." Hughes — a diver himself and familiar with marine mammals — was convinced from the surfers' descriptions that the attacker had been a killer whale.

Conclusive evidence of the attacker's identity came from Charles R. Snorf, the surgeon who stitched up Kretschmer's thigh. The distance between the gashes, Snorf explained, corresponded to the distance between an orca's teeth. Furthermore, the type of wounds — "clean, like three deep axe cuts" — are "just the sort that would occur in the laceration of killer-whale-type teeth." Comparing the injury to one made by a shark, sea lion or seal, Snorf said that both seal and sea lion have "a canine-type mouth, which gives a ripping type of single wound. A shark gives a devastating wound that is ragged . . . tearing out large chunks of tissue. I've treated shark attacks from the same area, and the wounds are as different as night and day." Also, the surgeon added, "Kretschmer said he hit the attacking animal and that it felt smooth. If it had been a shark, his hand would have suffered abrasions from the rough hide." Snorf, Hughes and radiologist Takashi Hattori (also a member of the local rescue patrol) reported their findings in 1975 in the semiannual proceedings of *The Journal of Bone and Joint Surgery:* "Killer Whale Attack on Surfer: A Case Report."

That seems to be the only authenticated orca attack in the wild. But the attack was not fatal. The whale, probably realizing its mistake, left the area immediately. Man was not the intended prey. Seals, which form a substantial part of the orca diet off the California coast, had been observed playing in the vicinity before the attack. Did the orca mistake the surfer for a seal in the same way that other orcas may have mistaken wooden boats for large whales — if indeed any of the boat sinkings *were* caused by orcas?

The possibility of mistaken identity is the most commonly expressed fear that divers have of being in the water with killer whales. Divers dressed in black rubber wet suits feel conspicuously like seals. They contend that even if killer whales do not consider man part of their normal prey, a case of mistaken identity could prove fatal.

I believe that orcas may indeed make mistakes, but I think it is important to point out that man — in a wet suit or not — does not really resemble a seal. Orcas are probably first attracted to potential prey by hearing them move through the water. This ability to identify and pinpoint the prey's location by listening to its sounds as it vocalizes and moves through the water is called passive sonar. Neither a snorkeler nor a diver — with tanks that hiss and tinkle — sounds like typical killer whale prey. Yet what if an orca decided to investigate the strange sound of a human swimming through the water? Here, he would probably use his active sonar — echolocation. The whale directs a stream of clicks toward the human and, seconds later, reading the returning echoes, tunes in the sound picture: one human swimming or one human dressed in a rubber wet suit. If a blindfolded orca in captivity can distinguish a salmon from a cod — both the same size — then orca in the wild can certainly tell a seal from a man. And, within a 60-foot range, orca could also confirm man's presence in the water with his eyes.

But then there is the case of Herbert Ponting. He may have been mistaken for a seal — at least initially. Ponting was the British photographer who accompanied Robert Scott on his last Antarctic expedition in 1911. He was momentarily cast adrift one morning when orcas crashed through the ice all around him. From underneath the ice, Ponting's dark shadow would have had the shape of a seal, but no doubt as soon as the orcas lifted their heads through the ice, their "sickening pig eyes" (as Ponting described them) would have immediately determined that this was neither seal nor meal. Ponting was terrified, and his oft-repeated story has inspired much fear of orca over the years. But to me, Ponting's account illustrates not "near attack" but orca curiosity. That predator trait could explain many of the close calls that men have had with orcas over the years. Jacques Cousteau interviewed divers approached by killer whales off Morocco in the early 1960s. The whales circled the divers for several minutes at close range, then departed, their interest satisfied. In another instance, 24-year-old Terry Anderson became stranded off Baja, California, in March 1972. He spent a cold, yet sweaty, night lashed to his storm-wrecked trimaran while three orcas hovered nearby. Anderson said that although the whales brushed the boat and were close enough to touch, they did not harm him.

Killer whales do investigate man. It is the business of a predator to be curious. In Ponting's 1911 incident, Antarctic killer whales had probably never glimpsed a human, certainly nowhere near the Last Continent. Similarly, our first close encounters — the bull Wavy swimming over to the *Four Winds'* stern and the orca surfacing beside me in the dinghy — may have been those killer whales' first close experiences with humans. Their curiosity had attracted them to us. And it was this curiosity that Hunter and Ellis were counting on to draw the whales to them on their planned dive.

Cases of orcas attacking men and boats are obviously rare, despite the stories and so-called eyewitness reports, despite the number of opportunities orcas have had and despite the fact that man *would* be easy prey in many cases. The killer whale remains perhaps the only large predator that, in terms of documented evidence, has a clean record when it comes to man. The same cannot be said for the sperm whales that occasionally broke up the old whaling boats (of course, they were fighting for their lives) or for the various man-grabbing varieties of sharks, grizzly bears, elephants, hyenas or even, for that matter, many domestic animals, including man's best friend, the dog. Man has been mauled to death by his best friend but never by the killer whale.

During most of our discussion, Ellis was quiet. He was a man who did not talk about things too much before he did them. But one afternoon a few days before he and Hunter were to dive, he told us about the first time he swam with captive orcas. That encounter was with Irving, the whale that had been caught in the nets at Pender Harbour in the spring of 1968. Ellis was just out of high school, and Irving, a "cool" young bull, was fresh out of the wild. Ellis had been feeding Irving every day, biding his time, trying to second-guess the big bull's receptivity to the "soon-to-be-introduced foreign object — me. At that time, not too many people had swum with captive orcas, and I was damn nervous.

"I had just a wet suit and a mask. And I thought, 'Okay, here goes!' So I popped into the pool. And I'm down there looking around. It's kind of murky. Couldn't see too much. Suddenly, this form comes looming toward me. He had his mouth open, teeth bared and ready . . ."

Hunter interrupted: "Forty-six conical teeth and a large pink tongue!"

"Exactly," said Ellis. "I thought, 'Oh jeez, here goes,' and Irv just went SNAP right in front of me. Yikes! I leapt out of that water like a shock, hopped out on the wharf right bloody now.

"Irv took off. I just sat there thinking, 'Maybe it's a bluff; I've got to call him on it.' I don't know why I thought that. But I hopped in again and, sure enough, round he came with more of the same. SNAP! Inches from my face mask. This time, I just hung there, trembling like a leaf. Then Irving came up and rubbed against me. That was it. I could scratch him and go over and sit on his stomach. Oh, sometimes he was a little rough when he bumped me, throwing me against the log. But he was learning, experimenting with me. It was just a test. I passed. And Irving never did it again."

Ellis's story brought to mind Spong's account of Skana snapping at his feet until she had deconditioned his fear. These stories were not about the possibility of violence in an in-the-water encounter. They were about orcas and humans — two intensely curious creatures — discovering each other, testing the other's reactions, sometimes psyching each other out. Of course, in captivity, the whale must depend on man for his survival — to obtain food and companionship. No such relationship has ever existed in the wild. The question remained: Would orca's kindly disposition in captivity hold true in the wild? Robert Stenuit, a Belgian oceanographer and an experienced diver, devoted a book, *The Dolphin, Cousin to Man,* to proclaiming his love for dolphins but admitted his mixed feelings about orca. Writing in 1968, Stenuit was aware that there were no documented accounts of orcas killing humans, yet he shared man's gut fear of them in the wild. He marvelled at the killer whales' routine docility in captivity as they played with dolphins; but even that did not diminish his fear.

"Aquarium killers are isolated, hand-fed, tamed," he wrote, "but in the sea, free-swimming killer whales swallow dolphins by the dozen. Would I be prepared to dive into the sea and stroke a family of free-swimming killers if I were to meet one? To that question, I have been postponing the answer for a long time."

On the lookout rocks at Parson Island camp, Hunter cooked an especially large breakfast the foggy morning of D Day (variously called Diving Day, Doomsday or Deadly Dentures Day, depending on Hunter's whim of a moment). The main entrée was part omelette, part pancake — with a distinctly fishy smell to it. "Fine cuisine," said Hunter cheerfully as he shovelled it in. Ellis, unable to boil a potato unless starvation threatened, didn't argue. When they could eat no more, Hunter tossed handouts to his bird friends — numerous ravens and Parson Island's resident eagle family. "It *smells* like fish," the birds seemed to be thinking as they flew down to look over the scraps. There were no takers. The two men loaded the Zodiac with scuba gear and broke camp. Ten minutes later, the sun cleared at the entrance to Blackfish Sound, and Hooker's pod — all eight of them — steamed into view.

The evening before D Day, as Hunter and Ellis took leave of Hooker's pod to catch dinner, a juvenile had strayed from the pod, swimming toward the Zodiac. "We'd been travelling with them so much the last couple of weeks," said Hunter later, "that the youngster figured we were one of them." Clearly, the time had come to dive with killer whales. Hunter and Ellis followed Hooker's pod at a respectful distance, heading south in Johnstone Strait. For two hours, the whales combed the Hanson Island shore, then shot across the strait to Vancouver Island. Just before noon, the whales slowed to a crawl, grouping together outside Robson Bight, about a mile from shore. They did not appear to be feeding, just loping along. Hunter shut off the engine. The whales were 200 yards away, all abreast, coming closer. The divers powdered their wet suits and squirmed into them.

"It was a mad panic," Hunter recalled. "Each of us wanted to be the first to get in the water with killer whales, but Ellis was manic about it. So I said, 'Go ahead.'" Hunter would tend the Zodiac, photographing from a distance; he would be ready to rescue Ellis in case of emergency and, if all went well, to dive after him.

Quickly and without ceremony, Ellis splashed into the chilly water and snorkeled 150 feet toward the whales. Through binoculars, Hunter's eyes stayed glued to Ellis as he swam into the arena of snorting bulls.

Hunter later wrote: "At first, the whales stayed some distance away, paying little attention to the submarine intruder."

Perhaps they hadn't noticed him. Ellis splashed in the water to attract their attention. (To a killer whale, ever alert to the sounds of potential prey, splashing might be equivalent to a matador waving his red cape at a bull.)

"Finally, one orca, a young male, broke pace and circled cautiously," wrote Hunter. "Approaching to within 75 feet, he then sounded. Ellis lay on the surface, unaware of the approaching orca. Suddenly, Ellis emitted a noise that sounded as if he had swallowed his snorkel; this was followed by a laugh and a series of unrecognizable expletives." Said Ellis later: "One whale was swimming back and forth below me, his belly up. He was so close that I positively identified his penile slit." Then, as the orca returned to his pod, Hunter motored over and plucked "the almost incoherent aquanaut" from the water.

Now it was Hunter's turn. "I cleared my snorkel and went down a few feet to see if I could hear anything. Way off in the distance, shrieks and squeals filtered eerily through the dark green abyss. I couldn't tell whether they were in front of me, behind me, under me or what. It was decidedly alien. I surfaced and gulped some air. Looking around, I noticed Ellis standing off in the Zodiac — at what seemed an inordinately great distance. I had about 600 feet of water below me and, in front of me, approaching in formation, a pod of killer whales. No place to hide! I took a deep breath and sank just below the surface. The voices stopped. It was like the moment in a Tarzan movie when all the birds stop singing. I knew something was going to happen. Then, silently, as if in a dream, a young whale glided into view, slowed almost to a halt less than 15 feet away and looked right at me. I stared back at him — and I couldn't stop smiling. Then he swam off, leaving me vibrating as the adrenaline raced through my system."

Later that day, the two exultant divers motored over to the *Four Winds*. Both were quiet, obviously moved, and we had to coax the story out of them. Ellis told me about the sound he had made through his snorkel on the whale's first pass: "I wanted to give the whales something — the way you did on the synthesizer." Ellis expressed what we'd all been feeling that summer — that we had little to offer this self-sufficient creature, except *sound*.

"And perhaps ourselves, as objects of curiosity," I added. "You two in your wet suits with Hooker's pod, and us with the synthesizer to Stubbs's.'"

Said Vatcher: "The whales are probably wondering, 'Who *are* these guys pretending to be whales, following us around, making weird whalelike sounds and jumping out of their boats in black rubber seal suits equipped with spouting devices?'"

August 9. Quiet day. Whales passing the Robson Bight anchorage but only in the distance. A gill-netter from Alert Bay stopped to give us news. He was excited. He'd found a young killer whale swimming alone in Bauza Cove (near Telegraph Cove), some 12 miles up the Vancouver Island coast. He had observed the whale the day before and early that morning. "It looked sick or maybe injured. I felt sorry for the damned thing, being abandoned by its kind." He told us that the whale had approached his boat while he was anchored in Bauza Cove and that he'd thrown it a few salmon. We listened to the fisher-

man's story with interest and also with a measure of skepticism. Most terrestrial social mammals will abandon the sick and the wounded or even kill
them in certain circumstances. African elephants stay with their wounded,
but they are an exception. Among cetaceans, and especially the dolphin family
(including orca), care-giving behaviour to sick or wounded family members
seems exemplary. Moby Doll was supported by members of his pod after he
was harpooned in 1964. On another occasion off the B.C. coast, a young killer
whale was hit by a government ferry boat, the propeller accidentally slashing
its back. The ferry captain stopped the boat and watched a male and a female
supporting the bleeding calf. Fifteen days later, two whales supporting a third
— presumably the same group — were observed at the same place. So the
gill-netter's account of an abandoned young killer whale up the coast seemed
very strange. "Perhaps it was a minke whale," said Vatcher. We'd seen
minkes swimming alone in Johnstone Strait, and the small curved minke fin
could have been mistaken, at a distance, for a young orca's dorsal fin.

August 10. Another quiet day. No whales until late in the afternoon and then
on the other side of the strait. Toward evening, a friendly couple we knew
anchored their trimaran in the bight and paddled their dinghy over to the *Four
Winds*. They brought news of the reported lone whale in Bauza Cove. The
middle-aged couple, whom we knew to be reliable observers, confirmed that
the animal was a killer whale. They had seen it "lying listlessly on the surface. It was having difficulty keeping itself upright. We tried to help it, but
whenever we approached, the whale would dive and reappear on the other
side of the cove." Bott decided to take a motorboat to investigate. Friends
from Victoria had arrived that week to help set up the Robson Bight shore
camp and had brought a 13-foot-long aluminum boat for just such emergencies.
Bott got ready to leave, but the strait remained under the influence of howling
westerlies all evening. The plan was abandoned until the next day.

August 11. Bott set out alone at dawn with diving gear in search of the young
whale. He was back by noon. "I searched the area. Nothing. I asked fishermen.
They knew nothing about it. I stopped in Telegraph Cove to talk to Bud Law
at the mill. I thought someone there might have seen or heard something about
it, but no."

August 12. No shortage of whales, but they're not coming in close. At 1 p.m.,
Johnny Bligh, a warden with the federal Department of Fisheries and Oceans,
motored into Robson Bight in his patrol boat with the news: A killer whale
had been found floating dead with a bullet hole in its back in western Johnstone
Strait. The dead whale matched the description of the one reported injured
in Bauza Cove three days earlier. It had been discovered about a mile from
where the earlier reports specified. The carcass was being towed to Alert Bay
to be cut up on the beach.

I had two questions for Michael Bigg when he came by that evening after
attending to the autopsy.

Why was the whale abandoned?

"Who knows! Maybe it somehow got separated from the pod or took a wrong
turn somewhere." Bauza Cove lay a few miles off the usual daily circuit of

the Johnstone Strait pods. Whales might not pass the cove for days, even weeks, at a time. A young whale on its own would probably not survive long.

Was the whale killed by a gun?

"We're not sure," said Bigg. "Our histologist [from the Fisheries Research Board in Nanaimo] found a hole in the animal but said the organs were healthy." The animal was not completely dissected to find a bullet or to determine the cause of death. Of course, there were no homicide detectives on the case, just a few scientists coming in to measure and sex the dead adolescent (an immature male) and a local museum to pick up the bones.

A few years later, I encountered a dead orca on a lonely stretch of Vancouver Island beach. Three days into decomposition, the whale stank beyond belief. It was the smell that had alerted people passing up the coast in a small boat. There were a number of marks, tiny indentations, on the back of this big old male. Were they bullet holes? According to Bigg, there are "all kinds of pock marks on the backs of orcas, some of which are skin blemishes; others may well be injuries suffered from bullet wounds." Cause of death was unknown or, possibly, old age. Lying there, so big and still, the animal was almost beautiful, the patches of black and white glistening in the rain, only beginning to bulge with the gases of putrefaction. But the smell of death that had come upon this immovable hulk was like an angry reproach directed against the world, as if the smell itself might somehow shake us into some sensibility of what our species had done to him.

Killer whales have been commonly shot at in every ocean of the world. In the North Atlantic, fishermen and mariners have had an unspoken "shoot on sight" policy for decades. The United States Air Force practised strafing runs against killer whales in the Atlantic in 1964. In Antarctic seas, Norwegian fishing fleets keep their guns handy for the orca superpods that sometimes enter fishing areas. In the Pacific, whalers shoot at orcas that follow their ships to feed on the unflensed carcasses of large whales in tow. In the Indian Ocean, Japanese tuna fishermen try to break up the orca pods that gather to strip the tuna off the lines.

Off Iceland's south coast in the early 1950s, orcas began following and feeding on the herring schools, damaging fishermen's nets in the process. By the summer of 1956, an annual $250,000 loss was attributed to orcas, and fishermen pleaded for immediate control measures to save the herring industry. The Icelandic government called on the United States Navy for help. According to *Naval Aviation News*, October 1956, VP-7, the airborne division of the U.S. naval forces in the North Atlantic, "completed another successful mission against killer whales. . . . Hundreds were destroyed with machine guns, rockets and depth charges. Before the Navy lent a hand . . . killer whales threatened to cut the Icelandic fish catch in half."

In British Columbia in the 1950s, a machine gun was mounted on an island near the eastern entrance to Johnstone Strait. Canada's federal fisheries department was answering the cries of sport fishermen who claimed that orcas were taking too much of their salmon. That machine gun was never fired. Yet the history of mariners shooting killer whales off the B.C. coast goes back almost to the white man's arrival. The shootings have tapered off in the last decade, mostly because of new public awareness brought on by seeing orcas in captivity. But twice, in 1973 and in 1977, I heard the sounds of gunfire mingled with killer whale blows and watched the whales scatter and leave Robson Bight. At that time, I was unable to determine who had fired the guns or whether any whale had been hit. There were fishermen cruising in the area, but none were fishing. On another occasion, in the summer of 1975, I talked to a young fisherman from Sointula. He admitted to having shot orcas "for no real reason . . . maybe boredom." He said he didn't carry a gun anymore, but he knew lots of fishermen and boaters in the area who did. "It starts when you're a kid growing up out here," he explained. "You get your first .22, and you want to go out and kill something." It reminded me of the city kid who aims his slingshot or his BB gun at robins. "But some guys never grow up," he said. "They say they hate them, that the blackfish eat all their fish. I don't know. When I was a kid, we were more afraid of 'em. That was reason enough to keep a gun handy."

The fear and hatred directed toward killer whales stem from man's age-old prejudice against all predators. Among sea creatures, orca and the great white shark have long been considered the chief villains. The killer whale is the marine counterpart of large pack-hunting land predators, like the wolf. Indeed, orca has often been called the wolf of the sea. Wolf and whale share many attributes as predators, and both are innocent of many of the charges made against them: man killing, routine surplus killing of prey, brutal violence and viciousness in their attacks on helpless prey, and unfair competition with man. I've heard some hunters and fishermen talk as if wolves and orcas needed to be controlled because, as they put it, the animals have no predators themselves. The truth is that both wolf and whale eat because they are hungry and rarely kill more than they need to survive. Moreover, they are an indispensable part of the predator-prey system through which life has evolved on this planet. In this natural order of things, there is an interdependence between predator and prey. As the numbers and quality of prey are controlled by predators, so the numbers and quality of predators are determined by their prey. Neither can exist without the other. It is a cooperative, not a competitive, relationship, one that has existed for millennia; yet its delicate balance is easily upset by man with his efficient weapons.

How common are the random shootings in the Northwest? There are no figures for the number of orcas killed by gunfire. But a 1970 statistic, already cited, indicates that in some samples, about 25 percent of the orcas caught for aquariums in Puget Sound had bullet holes in their bodies. These were all live-captured animals, not orcas killed by the bullet wounds. How many more sank at sea or washed up to rot on a remote stretch of beach? We can only guess.

Among native and aboriginal peoples of the world, there is a widespread taboo against killing orcas because it is believed that the whales will avenge bullet wounds and the deaths of pod members. I first heard about the taboo from Alert Bay native fisherman Jimmy Sewid, who told me a story from his youth. A Kwakiutl man had shot an orca, and he towed the carcass to the beach to show everyone. "No one wanted anything to do with him," said Sewid. "The elders said, 'The blackfish will get you.'" Later, the man went out fishing and never returned. "Everyone knew what had happened."

The taboo against killing orcas and the belief in orca revenge is held by other Northwest Coast native peoples, notably the Tlingit of the Alaska panhandle, who take care to avoid orcas. Yet nowhere is the idea of revenge stronger than with the Inuit. One story still told around Barrow, Alaska, is of a northern Alaska Inuit who harpooned an orca, then found orcas waiting for him every time he launched his kayak. He was forced to abandon the sea altogether. In another instance, in August 1952, two young Inuit drowned off the north coast of Alaska. Their outboard had struck a log or some other object. Many Inuit in the area said that one of the boys had once fired his rifle at an orca, and this was the result.

The revenge concept makes little sense if one considers the percentage of orcas with bullet wounds found in aquariums or in the waters off the Northwest Coast. Those animals may be a little wary, but their behaviour around humans and boats is unthreatening. In fact, the *absence* of revenge is worth discussing: In other mammalian species — elephants, tigers, grizzlies — bullet-wounded individuals sometimes become "rogues," man-killers seemingly sworn to avenge their sufferings. But not killer whales, as far as we know.

AUGUST 12. For 12 hours after hearing about the dead whale at Alert Bay, the strait is quiet. No whales. It seems a long afternoon and a longer evening. We talk about the shootings, about whales and men, and wonder, as we go to bed, whether they have left us. We are drowsing, snug in our sleeping bags, when Vatcher gives the old call: "Killer whales!"

It's midnight. A dozen, maybe more, are filing into the bight. We listen on deck to the rhythm of their blows, while we tune into their underwater sounds through the speaker connected to the hydrophone. Louder grows the cadence of the blows, the honking of their squeals and whistles. It reminds me of the sound of an approaching train. I share the notion with Bott and Vatcher. Bott nods, staring into the blackness. Vatcher smiles: "Here they come all right — regular as the midnight express."

SLEEPING WHALES

AUGUST 25. The two men in the canoe slip along the mirror surface
of the water, threading their way through the tight cluster of whale
fins. Stubbs's pod has gathered in the centre of the bight: Sixteen
orcas lie on the surface, as close together as we've ever seen them.
I'm watching the peaceful assemblage from the anchored *Four
Winds*, my headphones clamped in place, tuned in to the hydrophone; the tape recorder is running, but there's nothing happening the sound department. Sixteen whales and not a click, whistle
or groan. Were it possible to hear a pin drop on the ocean floor, you
could hear it today. It's an eerie quiet, and Vatcher and O'Neill,
paddling in the canoe, do not disturb it. Observed from the sailboat,
the canoe seems a member of the pod, moving slowly like a whale
among whales. As they advance across my binoculars' field of
vision, the silhouette of the two men sitting in the canoe appears
to be some great two-finned orca — a very strange whale. Yet
Stubbs's pod seems to accept the freak as one of its own. In Northwest Coast legend, men were always changing back and forth into
orcas (as well as other animals). Paddling out from shore, Kwakiutl
fishermen looked like men in canoes, until they moved out of range
and the focus went soft — then they would turn into orcas. The
Alert Bay totem carvings of orcas come to mind, some of them
human figures with huge dorsal fins. In my mind, the two men and
the canoe are becoming that two-finned killer whale described in
Northwest Coast legend and carved in the cedar. I understand now,
as the myth comes alive before my eyes, how the belief in that trans-
formation probably originated.

Stubbs's pod had stolen into Robson Bight at 8:30 in the morning. They seemed to have come out of nowhere and to be going nowhere. But we were taking no chances: O'Neill grabbed the movie camera and the film bag, while Vatcher and I lowered the canoe into the water. "This is it!" I yelled, as they shot off from the sailboat. Neither heard me. O'Neill, kneeling in the bow, was taking light readings with the big Gossen Lunasix and setting his apertures. Vatcher was driving hard toward the whales.

For the first time in more than a month, we had both whales and working movie cameras. O'Neill had arrived the week before, bringing one repaired movie camera minus a crucial lens mount. So back to Vancouver via ferry and bus went Vatcher to fetch one lens mount, returning days later by car and canoe. On the return trip, he had driven over almost half a day's worth of logging roads and twice that over blacktop, parking the car and camping at Telegraph Cove overnight. The next morning, he had paddled the 13 miles to the bight on the incoming tide. Bringing the canoe was Vatcher's brainstorm. Our close experiences in the dinghy suggested that using small boats without engines might be one way to approach a pod of whales and film them. Like the dinghy, the canoe was low, almost eye level to a whale swimming at the surface; but the canoe was also swift and manoeuvrable. And it moved with quietude, even grace. Spong had sometimes used a kayak to paddle near the whales. We needed something a little steadier, a lot drier and with some carrying capacity. Vatcher's canoe was not designed for ocean work, but in a flat sea with no wind and in the semiprotection of Robson Bight, it served us well.

The 16-foot-long Canadian-made Chestnut Fort canoe is the second largest in Chestnut's prospector series, with heavy ribbing and a cedar-and-spruce frame covered with heavy-duty No. 10 duck canvas. "Stronger and more stable than your average pleasure canoe," according to Vatcher, it had high sides and even higher prows that counteracted the tendency to plough under waves. Additional stability came from an oak strip under the hull, which functioned as a kind of keel. "In very calm situations," said Vatcher, "I sometimes stand up in the canoe just for a lark. As long as my weight is in the centre, I'm okay." It was calm enough that day in Robson Bight, but Vatcher was too busy paddling to do stand-up stunts. If Vatcher's canoe was the perfect candidate for initiation into an orca pod, Vatcher was the perfect helmsman to get it there. He was a strong and accurate canoeist who had learned his skills on lakes and had later tackled ocean inlets around Vancouver. Top speed in the canoe, one man paddling, one man filming, was about 2 1/2 knots on a windless, tideless sea. "The whales would have to be either very slow or very curious," Vatcher had said, "but it's worth a try."

Vatcher and O'Neill were hungry for whale footage. After a good beginning in mid-July, the problems that developed with the camera gear became a constant annoyance. We would airmail equipment to the repair shop, but first the mail was too slow, then there was a mail strike. O'Neill, Vatcher and Bott had each made at least one trip back to the city to hurry things up, and there were long-distance telephone calls every other day — and lots of waiting. Yet

Vatcher and O'Neill had somehow maintained their resolve to capture Stubbs's pod on film.

The elusive orca seems to defy film capture. Among the many tales about "the one that got away" are these:

Once, when Hunter had forgotten to rewind the film in his Nikon, he opened and thus exposed his prize photograph of a leaping orca; angry, he ripped the film from the camera and flung it to the waves.

A Toronto cameraman came up for a few days to shoot whales off Bigg's chartered boat but was always changing film when the whales were leaping or coming close. An underwater cameraman with him sat in the water for two days but got no underwater footage.

A cameraman from CBC-TV Vancouver dropped his news camera on the deck of a boat, knocking out an element and ending his shoot shortly after he had arrived.

Spong had done some great movie shooting at Pender Harbour — with the lens cap on.

Also at Pender Harbour, the bull Irving had ruined most of Spong's camera and sound equipment by leaping repeatedly out of the water during Spong's lunch break, when the door to the waterside equipment shack had been left slightly ajar. (Irving was a docile orca, not one to leap except on rare occasions, according to Ellis. Did the whale hold a grudge against Spong, who had once jumped on his back and tried to ride him? "Irving was a noble beast," said Ellis. "He didn't go for that kind of thing. He was mad.")

Our camera problems were small, but they seemed never ending. On August 14, O'Neill was bringing the repaired camera back to the bight with friends Nick and Kathy Orton and their 6-year-old son, Jorma, in their motorboat (a 13-foot-long aluminum cartop boat with leaking rivets and a 1957 15-horsepower Johnson Seahorse). They'd left Telegraph Cove late, stopping at Blinkhorn Peninsula to camp for the night. O'Neill told the story:

"We tied the motorboat to some logs, then walked up the beach to scout a campsite. It was late. There was little light left. Coming back two hours later, we found the boat filled with water. It had bumped against the logs in the rising tide. The equipment, the fishing gear, the groceries, the water jugs . . . everything was floating out to sea. Most of it was lost in the dark." O'Neill managed to grab his $4,000 Bolex movie camera just in time. "I'd mounted it in the underwater housing — for protection from the salt air while travelling — but I'd neglected to tighten the wing nuts, which keep it watertight." On its way out to sea, the camera had taken on enough ocean to become thoroughly soaked in salt water. Even in O'Neill's fearful dreams of saltwater corrosion, he could not have pictured a worse scenario. His first thought to save the camera was to bathe it in fresh water immediately. With the aid of a flashlight, they searched for a stream. Nothing! They were about five miles from Telegraph Cove. The engine had been rescued but, like everything else, wouldn't run on salt water. It was too risky to row in search of fresh water — the strait was windy and unpredictable that night, and they had only one oar. O'Neill considered the narrowing alternatives. "We spread the sleeping bags on the beach.

Kathy held the flashlight, and with the tiny screwdriver I always carry, I began disassembling the camera. When I opened it, salt water streamed out. I had no choice: I stripped the camera and, piece by tiny piece, *licked* it clean!" O'Neill's act of love and desperation on behalf of his camera took most of the night, but it saved the delicate machinery from what seemed certain corrosion. Still, the camera had to be overhauled and relubricated, and some electronic connections had to be replaced. Next morning, they limped into Telegraph Cove and rushed the camera back to Vancouver. Ten more days of waiting.

So there was an air of grim determination as O'Neill and Vatcher rode out in the canoe on August 25 to meet the whales. Within minutes, Vatcher had the canoe close in, and O'Neill was filming. He panned across even rows of black-finned bodies, taking it all in, hardly pausing, yet gasping as a bull came up 20 feet away, shot a big "Kawoof!" and pushed his tall dorsal fin into the picture and across the whole viewfinder, darkening the screen. O'Neill yelled: "All I see is fin." For a few seconds, it was a total eclipse.

"We were both tense," Vatcher explained later. "We knew it was a gift, and our job was to make the most of that gift, to capture it on film." From the start, it had been difficult to maintain a steady image. O'Neill would zoom in on the whales, but each time, the movement was magnified in telephoto, and he would retreat to avoid seasickness. O'Neill wasn't seasick, but he knew that would be the effect on any audience viewing the unedited film.

O'Neill wanted close-ups. Vatcher wanted him to hold back, keep the picture wide and wait for the whales to come close. Vatcher was cautious; he had to keep things steady. If he paddled too fast, the canoe would rock, and even if O'Neill were "wide," it could bring on the seasickness. As "dolly operator," Vatcher had to point the canoe toward the whales so that O'Neill could shoot over the bow. Then, while O'Neill filmed, Vatcher used his paddle as a stabilizer, holding it in the water to break the motion of the canoe. It was teamwork. Sometimes Vatcher kept paddling closer as O'Neill filmed, rolling up nice and easy beside a three-ton whale as if the canoe were tracking on soft rubber wheels. For Vatcher, the job was a matter of control and superb technique. O'Neill had to harness the instincts of a shoot-from-the-hip documentary cameraman with the polish of a studio photographer. Each man had to understand the whales' behaviour in order to photograph them well.

"It was timed like a ballet — the most predictable behaviour yet with killer whales," said Vatcher. "The whales would be down for 4 1/2 minutes, give or take 15 seconds, so we knew when they would reappear and that they'd be coming up together. But we didn't know exactly where. Fortunately, the range of area was not too large." As the whales surfaced, Vatcher would begin paddling, O'Neill framing the next shot. There would be three or four breaths over about 1 1/2 minutes, the whales coming up and going down, holding almost the same position. By the second blow, the filming began in earnest. The whales popped into view all around the canoe for about a minute before going down for the long breath, repeating the cycle.

As the morning wore on, Vatcher and O'Neill began to detect an overall pattern. The whales were oscillating back and forth along a line. They would come up three or four times in one area, then move about 50 yards west and do the same. Each time they zigzagged, they were a little farther from the *Four Winds* and the shore. Usually, the way they were pointing on their fourth dive — before the long-held breath — indicated where they would reappear. Yet somewhere along the line, they would turn around and come back the other way. Sometimes it was possible to tell when they were going to alter course: They would go down at an angle, turning, like an aircraft banking. Later, looking at the tide book, it became evident that the whales had let the incoming tide pull them gradually east all morning. In fact, the tide flow accounted for much of their apparent movement.

In the first half hour, more whales passed through O'Neill's viewfinder than he had seen all summer. Two hours later, he was still filming. Vatcher and O'Neill were ecstatic. They ran out of film and raced back to the boat. I had been observing the scene and trying to record the whales — but there hadn't been a sound. I leaned down from the deck, passing O'Neill a bag of fresh film as he handed over the large can of exposed film to be stowed safely. "Here's our little whale movie," he said, with a smile of satisfaction. He was right. Ninety percent of the finished film came from that can.

The whales had been there for 2 1/2 hours, and they would stay for another hour and a half.

"What do you think they're doing?" O'Neill asked. The whales were making no sounds. They were tightly grouped, cows and calves only a foot apart, the rest of the pod three or four feet at most. They were coming up and going down at the same time. Their blows were almost synchronized. Were we to have somehow asked the whales later about this day — a day that would become memorable for us and be preserved on film — they probably would not recall it. The whales were sleeping.

We were observing, for the first time, the typical behaviour of a pod of resting killer whales. We have learned much about their sleeping behaviour since then, but that morning, August 25, from 8:30 to 12:30, remains the longest sleep period yet witnessed. Orca's sleep pattern seems to be irregular; over the years, we have seen that it can occur once or even several times a day, especially in the late afternoon. (We know less about their night behaviour. We have observed them hunting and travelling at night, but they probably sleep at times too. Living primarily in a world of sound, whales function fine in total darkness, so their nights may not be much different from their days.) Only one other time — a rainy afternoon in September 1974, also with Stubbs's pod in Robson Bight — would we witness whales sleeping for more than an hour. Most whale naps probably last 10 to 20 minutes. Technically, a whale can sleep only for the length of time it can hold its breath — normally about five minutes maximum. It must awaken to come to the surface to breathe. Like dolphins and other whales — but unlike land mammals, including man — orcas are voluntary breathers. They cannot afford unconsciousness. Dolphin researcher John C. Lilly discovered this in 1955 when he anaesthetized several captive dolphins for experiments and ended up killing them.

In captivity, killer whales often "float motionlessly at the surface or move passively with the current, the blowhole usually exposed," according to researchers Susan Gabe and Robyn Woodward, who observed the Vancouver Aquarium orcas, Skana and Hyak, in the summer of 1972. Adapting to man's diurnal pattern, the two whales remained inactive mainly at night — Skana for as much as 58 minutes per hour, and Hyak up to 40 minutes. Without the freedom to travel and hunt for food, captive orcas become lethargic, undoubtedly sleeping much more than wild ones.

Rejoining Stubbs's pod, Vatcher and O'Neill worked to fill out the whale footage. In the first two hours, O'Neill had focused on the bulls. The big fins are impressive, towering over a man in a canoe. O'Neill had good shots of Wavy, some in slow motion, showing the big wobbling fin as it came up out of the water. The bull Sturdy allowed them even closer. He was slow and steady, even without the slow-motion filming, and sometimes when he went down between blows, the tip of his dorsal fin remained above the surface. For a few seconds, the tide running, the fin would appear to be cutting the water like a shark's. Then Sturdy would surface, blowing.

In the second period, O'Neill turned his camera to the cows, juveniles and calves of Stubbs's pod. There were three cows with calves close by their sides. Nicola and Stubbs were travelling alone. In the film there is a long shot of Stubbs, who had drifted away from the rest of the pod at one point. Lying there, she resembles a piece of deadwood, her dorsal fin a broken branch or a tree trunk protruding from a log. As O'Neill zooms in, she blows, tilting her body back slightly and lifting her snout, a reflex action common to all cetaceans. It prevents them from inhaling water.

The canoe approached closest to Stubbs that day, and it was the only time that Vatcher and O'Neill had a moment of apprehension around the whales. As Stubbs went down for her long breath, Vatcher drove the canoe a few feet ahead, to where he thought the old whale might surface. They waited. Other whales started coming up all around them. They were temporarily surrounded by clouds of mist. Sturdy was blowing off the bow: Where was Stubbs? Vatcher looked down into the water. Stubbs was coming up underneath them. This is it, thought Vatcher. About six feet from the canoe, the old whale jerked out of the way. Vatcher was more cautious after that, but half an hour later, O'Neill was urging him to push closer to Stubbs. This time, Stubbs, coming up six feet away, was heading straight for them.

"I was certain she didn't know the canoe was there," said Vatcher. "But as soon as she reached the surface, she made an abrupt 90-degree turn, aborting her blow and diving again. Had she followed through with her normal cycle, she would have washed us." Both Vatcher and O'Neill felt that Stubbs was making an effort to be careful around the canoe.

On many occasions since, we've observed similar whale caution around small boats. It is almost as if they know their own strength and understand the fragility of small craft. It doesn't even seem to matter if they're sleeping, which brings up questions about the nature of orca sleep: How was Stubbs aware of us if she was sleeping? How do orcas navigate and stay together without sound? I had heard nothing during the four-hour hush in Robson Bight, although several years later, I would learn from Canadian biologist John Ford, who was studying killer whale sounds, that whales do make sporadic low-level sounds during sleep periods — high-pitched whistles in the 8-to-12-kHz range, which may be used for orientation. (These high-pitched low-volume sounds carry only over short distances; thus, at my distance away, I had found nothing to record during the four-hour sleep.) While sleeping, the whales might keep attuned through passive sonar — listening and orienting to the breathing and moving of their pod-mates. This, too, would function only at very close range. Stubbs would have to be six feet away to recognize the sounds of a paddle moving through the water or the shouts of excitement coming from Vatcher and O'Neill. Whales could orient partly through touch, but though they are close during sleep times, they don't touch as a rule, at least not on the surface. They *are* close enough to use their eyes for navigation, and their eyelids apparently stay open. At the Vancouver Aquarium, sleeping whales are very quick to react to unexpected lights or sounds. If visibility is 35 feet underwater, they could easily stay in touch with each other and avoid the canoe through vision. There is much speculation, but scientists really know very little about the sleep lives of cetaceans. In fact, the sleeping of most whales and dolphins might be more accurately termed resting.

Sleeping killer whales fascinated the early Kwakiutls, according to Jimmy Sewid. In the old days, he said with a twinkle in his eye, a young man proved his manhood by paddling up to a resting blackfish, hopping out and running on its back, then jumping back into the canoe. After some prodding, Sewid admitted that the story likely came from "the vivid dreams of our ancestors." After the morning O'Neill and Vatcher spent paddling next to resting orcas, we could see how the idea might have evolved from experience. Kwakiutls in their canoes, fishing side by side with the orcas, would have seen them sleeping at the surface from time to time and would have found that they could come right up beside them, as we had. It would have seemed a terrific challenge to paddle up quietly, so as not to disturb the sleeping monster, and then run along its back and return to the canoe before the whale knew what had happened. Orcas are very sensitive to touch and, in captivity, do not take easily to being ridden by their trainers, but perhaps one very agile and light-footed Kwakiutl had tried it, once. Yet the story probably tells more about the Kwakiutls than the whales. The Kwakiutls saw themselves as crafty, able to pull a fast one — even on the cunning orca. On the day Stubbs's pod slept in the bight, Vatcher said he thought the Kwakiutl test of courage might have worked with an animal like Stubbs.

While the whales were quiet and resting that morning, at their lowest energy level, Vatcher and O'Neill were at their highest. After a summer of solving camera problems, they were racing through the film — some 1,100 feet that day. There were several thousand 16mm images of whales: coming up and going down, moving slowly, lying on the surface. It was not great action footage — no bulls leaping out of the water, no juveniles curiously poking up their heads beside us, no whales slapping their flippers or flukes, no hunting or feeding. The images were gentle ones: Stubbs's pod at rest, a portrait of family togetherness. We had photographed killer whales in a pose that contradicted the image conjured up by their name.

In the finished film, there is a sequence that suggests, more than any other, the gentleness we felt paddling among these killer whales. If the French Impressionists had painted whales and animated their canvases, it would have looked like this: a backdrop formed by tiers of mountain ridges carpeted in evergreen and carved in bas-relief, some tiers floodlit by the sun, others in shadows or etched in fog. Several killer whales are coming up, their black fins and white fountain blows backlit by the sun. They are gliding on water that is green and as still as a lily pond. (On the sound track, electronic Debussy-like phrases suggest the mood of *Reflets dans l'eau*.) As three whales blow together, seagulls caught in their path take off, cutting the air a few feet above them; other gulls, lost in private reverie, are in the water around the whales, some almost on the whales' backs, others bathing and preening. The gulls are in chorus, crying whalelike sounds, as if giving voice to the mute, dozing orcas. Usually, when we saw gulls and orcas together, it was a convention of predators — a dubious alliance between hunter and moocher. Yet on resting day, it became a ballet of white wings and black fins.

Watching the film, I am always reminded of the gentleness that the whales sometimes show toward seagulls. The fishermen call the gulls "shit hawks"; orca's opinion, based on the same one-sided relationship, ought to be no higher. Yet at Pender Harbour in 1968, according to Ellis, the young male Hyak would sometimes play with seagulls, although he periodically got "very annoyed at them." The seagulls "were stealing a lot of his fish, and he was hungry," said Ellis. " The gulls obviously hadn't heard that orcas sometimes eat birds [such as white-winged scoters off the northern B.C. coast].

"To get Hyak moving on something if he was slow, I used to make him jealous by feeding his food to the seagulls. One day, I was throwing his fish into the pool, and he got the fish at the same time a gull did. He grabbed the gull by the legs and towed it down to the bottom. I thought for sure he'd killed it, but suddenly, he let it go and up bobbed this seagull, shaking its head, paddling around, and then getting up and taking off out the mouth of the harbour. Hyak was so mad . . . but he didn't even harm it. This happened about five different times at Pender Harbour. He even grabbed one by the head, but Hyak never got upset enough to kill. It was tremendous: This 'huge ferocious animal' wouldn't even harm a bird stealing his fish."

At half past noon on the day the whales slept, the tide, which had been coming in all morning, began to turn and ebb. As it did, the whales began to stir. There was some bobbing of heads, and two quick belly-flop leaps. They were stretching their muscles, slapping warm air on their faces, yawning. They headed east down the strait against the tide. Within an hour, they were back in the bight, bringing Top Notch's group with them. As the two pods moved across Robson Bight, we moved with them — in the canoe and in the dinghy — adding to our footage. In late afternoon, I got my chance to try the canoe, to record whale blows for the film's sound track. I knelt in the bow with the Nagra tape recorder propped on the seat. Nick Orton was paddling. In the last weeks of the expedition, Orton had built a land camp in the bight as a whale-watching station for us and as a place for his family to stay. Sitting amidships was Orton's son, Jorma, who had been promised a canoe trip to see the whales. The afternoon had become a feast of blue sky and sun. Billowy cumulus clouds assumed whale shapes for us as they lazed across the sky. Soon enough, the real whales rounded the corner, entering the bight. Stubbs's pod had split into several subgroups. One started moving toward us, slowly.

First, we saw Stubbs, flanked by two youngsters. They were close to the old whale, but neither was in the typical cow-calf position. Sixty feet behind was Nicola. At 100 yards, the whale platoon halted and hung at the surface, blowing. My Nagra recorder was running; I was getting it on tape, but I wanted to be closer. As the whales slipped beneath the surface, Orton began paddling, trying to anticipate where they might come up. I held the shotgun microphone over the water, waiting for the next blow.

Then one, two, three whales — Stubbs and the two youngsters — exploded some 75 yards past us. We had misjudged their speed. Seconds later, a great "Kawoof!" sounded right in front of us. I watched the record meter jump into the red. Jorma yelled: "Daddy, look!" Despite the need for quiet, I couldn't help a muffled gasp myself. It was Nicola, less than 60 feet away. I set the microphone down and grabbed an oar, motioning Orton to paddle over. We moved stealthily, skating on the water, while Nicola waited. At 40 feet, we could hear her echolocation clicks on the hull. Penetrating the canoe, they sounded like muted machine-gun fire. Then her cries started coming through loud and clear. The canoe's canvas covering — stretched tightly over the cedar frame — had become a drum skin, and Nicola's sounds were striking the membrane.

With Nicola so near at hand, I wanted to see whether she would respond to whistled-in-air whalelike sounds. We were almost close enough for her to hear us. We had cut the distance to 30 feet but were afraid to approach closer lest we disturb her. She blew three more times. I recorded the blows. Looking up, I glimpsed a seaplane high overhead, beginning to circle. Through the binoculars, it looked like a red-and-white Beaver, but no name and no identification numbers were visible. As it approached, I tried to wave it off, but it kept coming. The plane, buzzing around us like a bothersome fly, went into a dive-bombing run. We had aroused the pilot's curiosity; flying across Johnstone Strait, he had not expected to see two men and a child in a canoe, with a whale — longer and broader than the canoe — lying alongside. The plane banked, dipped and headed for Stubbs and the two youngsters, still lying on the surface 50 yards ahead of us. It looked like a collision course, as though the plane were going to land on them. Would the whales recognize the danger in time to duck below?

At the last instant, the pilot lifted the plane, clearing the water by less than 15 feet, almost brushing the whales' dorsal fins. The whales had held their positions. Had they neither seen nor heard the plane? The plane was flying to the other side of Robson Bight, where more whales had gathered on the surface. We could still hear the buzzing aircraft. Louder, however, were

Nicola's cries coming up through the hull: She seemed absorbed in conversation with Stubbs or perhaps with the whales across the bight. (I had left the tape recorder running and was later able to recreate the entire drama by replaying it.)

Leaning forward in the canoe, I put my mouth almost to the ribbing and whistled as loud as I could into the canoe's resonant wood "chamber." I was trying to whistle the synthesized three-note phrase that I had exchanged with the whales earlier that summer. I whistled three times. No response. Could Nicola hear me? She was raising her head, the tip of her rostrum, slightly out of the water and, at the same time, turning toward the canoe. As I continued to whistle, she began moving her head slowly, just perceptibly, from side to side. I realized that she was orienting to the sound of my whistling. Orienting — cetaceans moving their heads back and forth to hear a sound in the air — had been described to me by Spong from his studies with captive whales; it is common behaviour in captivity.

In the distance, the seaplane had turned around and was again flying toward us. I looked at Nicola lying there peacefully. I felt the urgency of the moment. I put my head down and whistled to her, louder, stronger than before. In two seconds, a response came. It seemed almost an echo. It was a much stronger voice than mine, twice the power of my shrill call. *Nicola had answered!* A shiver started at the base of my spine. I felt a new closeness toward this killer whale. I motioned to Orton, and we paddled up to her. She spouted again. A faintly fishy smell drifted over us as she sucked in a deep breath. I watched the flap tighten over her blowhole. I studied the breathing black mass stretched out beside me, turning my head from side to side to take in the whole whale (human orienting behaviour). Her back was crisscrossed with scratches, like secondary highways on a road map. She was immense, almost fat, though not as large as Stubbs or the mature bulls in her pod. Her dorsal fin was elegantly curved and perfectly formed, except for the mark that gave Nicola her name. I looked back at Jorma. He was excited, but like a seasoned whale watcher, he was contained, certainly unafraid. After television and movies like *Jaws* and *King Kong*, it is not easy to impress a 6-year-old.

The plane was getting closer, too loud to ignore. Again it zeroed in on Stubbs and the two youngsters. This time, it came in virtually on top of them. With seconds to spare, the whales dived. We watched, stunned and angry. The instant before the plane touched down, the youngest whale poked his pointy head out of the water — likely the closest look he'll ever have of an airplane. I imagined Stubbs underwater, pulling the little guy's flukes to get him out of there. It was close. Nicola had gone down too. Perhaps the others had called to her. All the whales were suddenly gone.

Angry, Orton and I paddled toward the taxiing seaplane, shouting at the pilot as he took off. He waved from the plane as he flew over us one final time. We never learned who he was.

In spite of the pilot's insensitive behaviour, it had been a great day for whales and humans in Robson Bight, and by evening, we were in a mood to celebrate. It was also O'Neill's birthday. "Definitely the best!" he said, elated by his successful filming. The whales were still playing in the bight when Spong and a boat full of people sailed in unexpectedly on the 60-foot-long concrete-hulled square-rigger *D'Sonoqua*, owned, built and skippered by Jim Bates of Vancouver. It looked more like a barge or a floating fortress than a sailboat. The brown-and-white square sails didn't match; the stays and stanchions were rusting; the hull needed paint. With cast and crew, it looked like a second-class Mexican bus, complete with dogs, chickens and back-bumper and roof-rack riders. Yet when it came to whales, the *D'Sonoqua* had charisma. Spong had spent part of the summer taking city people on whale-watching day trips on the big sailboat, and no one went home without having seen orcas. At $15 a person, which included a salmon barbecue lunch, it was an educational venture that Spong had organized as the Pacific representative for Project Jonah, a nonprofit international organization to save the whales. Leaving Alert Bay in the mornings, Spong lectured on deck as the boat searched Blackfish Sound and Johnstone Strait for orcas. Usually, they would see whales in Robson Bight, right after seeing us. Often, we would sail with them on the *D'Sonoqua* so long as the whales stayed near the bight.

Paddling out in the canoe to greet the mob, we saw some 30 people on deck and another 8 or 10 hanging from the spreaders, all waving, cheering, whistling. Some were playing flutes; one honked on a saxophone. Dogs on the boat were barking, the children screaming. Approaching the massive concrete boat, we felt like Kwakiutls paddling out to meet Captain Vancouver in 1792 — a bit overwhelmed after weeks of quiet. Vatcher, O'Neill and I climbed aboard. The Ortons followed in the dinghy. Bott had been to Alert Bay and was coming back on the *D'Sonoqua*. We were glowing from our day, and everyone wanted to hear about it.

Except for Ellis, who was in Victoria, and Bigg and MacAskie, who were somewhere trailing Hooker's pod, all the summer 1973 whale people were on the *D'Sonoqua*. It was pure orca energy as we talked and partied and drifted with Stubbs's and Top Notch's group in the evening light. The whales seemed to have sensed the mood. They were leaping and lobtailing, cavorting together along the eastern rock face of the bight. Somebody on the boat made the remark that "either they crashed our party or we're crashing theirs."

AUGUST 25. The music, the commotion, seems to attract the whales. Five orcas, mostly juveniles, stick their heads out of water, all in a line. They show us their chins, reflecting orange in the sunset light. Beside these five, a bull is flopping in the kelp bed. At one point, he comes up with long strands of yellow kelp wrapped around his dorsal fin, looking like a kelp-covered rock at low tide or a Mardi Gras reveller, until he spouts. Spong's hydrophone picks up the whales' sounds while we watch them. The sounds seem as free form and various as their playing behaviour.

Whales and whale watchers celebrated throughout the early-morning hours. The *D'Sonoqua* had anchored at dusk beside the *Four Winds*, and during the night, canoe and dinghy ferries ran regularly between the two boats and our land-based camp. There was salmon aplenty, smoked Kwakiutl style on fires fed by beach wood. Someone had brought a cask of rum; there was plenty of good dry white wine. The music came from hydrophones tuned in to whale sounds. Speakers mounted on various trees around the camp broadcast the sounds so all could hear. It was a fitting near end to our summer with the whales.

We were scheduled to leave in a week, but we still needed underwater footage. That was Bott's task. It did not come easy.

During that last week in Johnstone Strait, westerly winds blew at 30 knots every day. The waves invaded the bight, smashing against the eastern wall, where wet-suit-clad Bott waited, ready to descend into an underwater grotto at a moment's notice to film the whales as they passed. The whitecaps obscured the whale blows; the noise of the surf masked their sounds; the surf hampered entry into the water. For four days, the whales went by — but not close enough. Bott waited. O'Neill kept the watch. At midweek, Jim O'Donnell, a Toronto diver-cameraman, joined them. Locked into their wet suits, encased in rubber day after day, Bott and O'Donnell were hot and sweaty, their skin pinched and red. After four days, Stubbs came in close, alone, nosing up against the eastern wall. The weather that day was the roughest. The rest of Stubbs's pod may have been with her, but they couldn't see them. They were lucky to have seen Stubbs, even though the old whale was only 30 or 40 feet away. By the time Bott and O'Donnell slipped into the water, she was gone.

The next day, August 31, was still rough but sunny and absolutely clear. Underwater visibility increased from 25 to maybe 35 feet. At 1 p.m., Bigg approached on the *Amethyst II* to ask if we'd seen any whales. It was his last day for whale tracking in 1973; tomorrow, it was "back to the lab in Nanaimo to see what we've learned from all this . . . may take months." He was yelling, and I was yelling back, and it was only 50 feet from ship to shore. Still, we had to repeat everything. We were competing with the wind and the roaring surf. "There could be whales around," he shouted, "but how do you hear them or see them when it's rough like this?"

Later that afternoon, Bott saw part of Stubbs's pod moving into the bight and heading toward the eastern wall. O'Donnell handed him the underwater movie camera, and following the plan, Bott slipped into the water. Ten feet down, he said later, everything was calm, though a bit turbid from the wave action. The bubbles from his aqualung were almost invisible in the turbidity. Within three minutes, a cow and calf swam into the viewfinder, scattering the bubbles as they approached the camera. Bott squeezed the trigger and froze. The whales did the rest. Not 10 feet away, the cow's winglike flipper turned slightly, banking, and the big whale pivoted, revealing her entire length. In the shadow of the cow's broad tail and pressing close to her white underside — like a harbour tug to a mother barge — was the tiny calf. It was nursing. The two swept past the camera and were gone. The underwater encounter had lasted eight seconds. It was a brief glimpse, but Bott had gotten the first in-the-wild underwater footage of killer whales.

SEPTEMBER 2. The wind changes to southeast in the night and by morning begins to howl. If strong westerlies make whale-watching difficult, these stormy southeasters that characterize winter in Johnstone Strait make it impossible. We have what we came for, though, and more. We're on schedule. Sailing out of Robson Bight, leaving our summer home, I know I will miss the whales. The adventure of one summer in whale country has gotten to me. I have resolved this past week to return. Hunter and I may team up next summer to make a longer film. Meanwhile, the radio is abuzz with orca news from southern Vancouver Island: Four killer whales have been captured and are being held in nets inside Pedder Bay near Victoria. We're eager to investigate, though there is little time. The whales are to be shipped out to various aquariums over the next several weeks.

Part Two
FALL/WINTER

CAPTIVES

SEPTEMBER 10. Pedder Bay. Four black blobs on the water, as inanimate as logs adrift. Only the aperiodic explosions of mist assure us that they're living, breathing whales. They are docile, seeming to accept their fate. They face out to sea. Baffled by the polypropylene nets that they could smash through or, even easier, jump over, they adopt a wait-and-see attitude — all but the big bull, who can only "sit still" for so long: He begins circling the tight enclosure, round and round in the same counterclockwise motion, like a caged lion pacing his cell.

A few days after returning from Johnstone Strait, Hunter, Vatcher and I drove 20 miles west from Victoria to visit the captured whales. It was a high-overcast no-wind day. We launched the canoe at the head of long, narrow Pedder Bay and paddled out. Ten minutes later, we glimpsed the white cork floats, a line of them extending in a wide half-circle out from shore, and the four whales just visible inside. A young blonde-haired boy dressed in plaid shirt and blue jeans stood in an aluminum skiff and yelled to the whales as he tossed buckets of herring toward them. They seemed uninterested. There was a white V-hulled speedboat tied to the logs, and anchored just outside the net was a large seine boat, the one that had been used in the capture.

We pulled the canoe up a tiny clamshell beach, 60 feet along the shore from the nets. I had brought a hydrophone and a pair of headphones to listen to the sounds. Hunter wanted a high vantage point for taking photographs. We climbed the embankment and made our way to a grassy slope overlooking the capture site. It was like being in an outdoor amphitheatre; the whales were centre stage. The nets came right up to the shore and beyond them was open

Juan de Fuca Strait and, in the distance, Washington's Olympic Mountains. We had brought a picnic lunch of cheese, bread and beer, but as it turned out, we did not feel much like eating. We watched the whales. Although they could have approached the shore, almost to our feet, they stayed on the far side of the enclosure. Hunter squinted through the long barrel of his 300mm Nikkor lens and started firing. Vatcher lowered the hydrophone into the water. I put on the headphones. At first, there was nothing happening in the sound department. Hunter grew anxious, wanting the whales to do something — to leap or bob or flip their tails. When we'd seen the Johnstone Strait whales quiet like this, they had been sleeping. Then, through the headphones, came a piercing cry — one isolated vocalization. Thirty seconds later, another cry, a little longer, pitched higher. Once before, on my farm in B.C.'s mountainous interior, I'd heard a similar shrill scream. It came from the barn. Investigating, I found a female rabbit cornered by a neighbour's dog that had climbed into her pen. The scream was a sound I had never expected a rabbit to make. It was at least as strange to me as the kinds of whale screams I heard for the first time this day.

For half an hour, the sounds continued, single whale screams repeated at 30-to-60-second intervals. There seemed to be little dialogue going on, little sign of exchange between the four captives. In Johnstone Strait, the whale sounds that I had recorded seemed more like conversations — everyday exchanges among families of whales — or, at minimum, stereotyped calls used to preserve group cohesion. But these four captives were vocalizing in sudden outbursts of urgent yet seemingly despondent tones. Later, I would learn that such vocal activity, while not common, had happened before in similar situations. These were distress calls. They were loud. Underwater, they would carry about seven miles; on the surface, under ideal conditions, perhaps a few hundred yards. They were the same as, or very similar to, sounds described in a number of accounts of just-captured killer whales:

When Moby Doll was caught and while the pod waited on the surface some distance away, the harpooned whale uttered "shrill whistles so intense that they could easily be heard above the surface of the water 100 yards away."

According to Marineland of the Pacific collector Frank Brocato, the Puget Sound female he hoop-netted in 1962 was "vocalizing badly." A few minutes later, a bull orca suddenly appeared, and together, they rushed the boat.

Shamu was making "the usual whale distress sounds" through the first day of her captivity at San Diego's Sea World in 1965.

The bull Namu had issued "loud, strident screams" regularly from his Rich Cove pen during his internment in 1965-66. At times, his cries were picked up by passing Puget Sound whales, who apparently returned the sounds.

After half an hour, the screams in Pedder Bay became more persistent, more urgent. Then I heard faint calls or whistles among the distress signals. On the surface, the four captives had swum to the edge of the net. Hunter, sensing that something was about to happen, poised his camera. The bull leapt first, and as Hunter squeezed off several frames, the others bobbed to look around.

"I see more whales out there," said Hunter. Several miles away, about a dozen killer whales were surfacing, blowing together on the horizon. The captive bull began leaping repeatedly, smashing his body on the water, while Hunter snapped photographs.

In the headphones, the distress calls grew even louder. There was no way to determine whether the calls were stimulating the other whale sounds that I was hearing in the distance. The free orcas must have heard the cries of the captives. They probably saw the leaping bull. But they did not come close. Soon, they passed out of sight, and as the afternoon wore on, the captives became calm. Their distress calls, indeed all vocalizing, became sparser and sparser. All the while, the drone of engines became more constant. Men were coming and going in small boats. While we kept our vigil, the captors were preparing to move one of the young females. Within the week, she would be put into a separate log corral, then guided into a padded sling, hoisted on the deck of a seiner and taken some 17 miles by sea to Sealand of the Pacific, outside of Victoria. Sealand had been built in the harbour, and its floating whale pool, with a net stretched across one end, was open to the sea. Living at Sealand was a male orca — Haida — the one that Ellis had trained in the late 1960s. The search for a mate for Haida had led Sealand to undertake the Pedder Bay capture in the summer of 1973. It was the second time that they had searched for a mate for Haida. The first time, in March 1970, was also in Pedder Bay, when five whales were corralled in a spot directly across from where we were observing the 1973 captives. As I sat on the hillside pondering the fate of these whales, I remembered Ellis's story of that earlier capture.

On a rough and windy March Sunday, off southern Vancouver Island, Ellis was scouting for whales. With him, aboard the 20-foot-long Bertram, were two whale researchers, Don White and Norm Cameron, visiting Sealand from the Vancouver Aquarium. Skippering the boat was Sealand's owner, Bob Wright, an audacious, fast-talking entrepreneur who had come west from the prairies and had parlayed a few dollars into a marine empire. It was Wright who first saw the whales blowing in the waves that day. Nobody believed him. Then one whale began leaping, and everyone on the boat got "just a little bit hysterical," according to Ellis. With good reason: It was a rare all-white killer whale.

"Ever since I'd started working for Wright," said Ellis, "he'd ranted about catching an albino orca. At least two had been sighted around Vancouver Island off and on for several decades, and he wanted one of them to display at Sealand. Needless to say, the chance we'd see one, much less capture one, was remote."

Escorting the white one were four normal killer whales, including a young bull. It was easy to keep them in sight. The white whale kept leaping, and the late-afternoon sun glinted off its body like a neon sign. Less than a mile from shore, the whales were heading slowly toward Pedder Bay.

Wright was "just absolutely stunned," as he put it. On a Sunday afternoon cruise, he was not prepared to capture whales. His main nets were locked up in Vancouver, 75 miles away. He tried to call his crew on the radio but could raise no one.

"We roared into Pedder Bay," Wright said. "I had a crew that I'd trained, sort of like a bunch of firemen who'd never been to a fire. We'd had a couple of dry runs and both times had ripped the nets all to hell, putting our capture boat, the *Lakewood*, up on a reef and sinking another boat. I'd built a net out of gill-net material that was more than a mile long. The first time we tried to set it on a pod of whales off Victoria, they went through it like it was a spider web."

Wright's crack crew was ready that day, but all he had was a single gill net. Even if he could catch the whales, could he hold them? It seemed a long shot. Yet Wright told the skipper of the *Lakewood* to get ready. One end of the *Lakewood*'s gill net was tied to the shore just inside the bay, while the big seiner stood by, waiting. The mouth of the bay was wide open. The whales were milling around, going nowhere. The sun was starting to go down.

"We didn't know whether we'd have to stay out there or follow them all night or what," White recalled. "We didn't want to get too close, maybe spook them. We waited. And then, just after sunset, the whales went past the *Lakewood* into the bay. The *Lakewood* ran the net across, blocking the entrance, and we captured them!"

White and Ellis were caught up in the excitement of netting the rare white whale and its pod. "We were playing the macho whale hunters," said White, "and Bob Wright was our Captain Ahab." But after the whales were captured, Ellis turned to White and said, "Jeez, let's let them go."

Ellis explained later: "It had been a challenge to catch them, like catching a big fish. But afterward, we felt bad."

The whales were in the bag, but the bag was hardly whaleproof. And as it became dark, no one could see them. No one knew whether the single gill net was holding. Sometimes, the intermittent whale blows clearly came from inside the net; other times, they seemed to come from outside. Divers sent down to check the net found it 35 feet off the bottom in some places and discovered holes in other places. One hole, according to Wright, was about 240 feet deep.

"Wright was frantic," said Ellis. "He got 10 or 11 aluminum boats and stationed them all along the net." Each boat operator was issued clubs and paddles to pound on the metal hulls — noisemakers to keep the whales away from the net — and seal bombs to be dropped over the side. (Seal bombs are used to scare seals and sea lions away from fishing areas. Equal to about a quarter stick of dynamite, they have also been used by whale captors to herd orcas into nets.)

White was on the *Lakewood*, moored alongside the net in the centre of the bay. Listening for approaching whales, he would radio Wright on the Bertram and direct him to the spot. "Wright would go roaring back and forth," said White, "warning the guys in the boats to set off the bombs and start the banging again. The racket went on all night." At one point, someone dropped a bomb on a diver who apparently had never done a night dive before. "He came up yelling, scared to death, but he was okay. Also, it was cold down there. It was March 1. They were bringing in frozen divers, thawing them out and sending them back for more. There was all this bloody macho stuff happening, and it's a miracle somebody didn't get killed."

At a bleary-eyed 7 a.m., the curtain finally "lifted to reveal five whales still in the nets, the albino among them," said White. "An hour later, two seiners arrived from Vancouver with the backup nets. The whales were securely confined. It was all over."

Twenty-four days passed before anyone tried to move the whales. Two were to go to Sealand. A cow, later named Nootka, went first. There were no problems. Then it was the white whale's turn. Everyone was nervous about handling her. Wright had hired fisherman Bill Cameron to fly down from Pender Harbour to supervise the transfer. Cameron, together with two other fishermen, had captured several whale pods in Pender Harbour. He was generally considered the best whale handler around. "As far as I know, he never lost an animal," said Ellis. "He's basically a herring fisherman, and herring are spooky fish to deal with. You have to keep calm. He treats the whales the same way. It works like a charm."

During the first 24 days in the nets at Pedder Bay, the white whale had been spooked on a number of occasions. "Once, when a couple of guys fired up an outboard boat," Wright said, "she broke through three seine nets, roared up Pedder Bay, turned around, then broke right back through the nets. She went through six seine nets the way you and I would go through a Ritz cracker." Another time, Ellis saw her "go screaming across the surface like a rocket . . . never saw a whale go that fast. She just punched into the net, slipped up under the cork line and rolled up in a ball. Everybody panicked, especially Wright." Bott, working for Sealand then, was in his wet suit. Wright sent him down with John McGuire. "John ran out of air," said Ellis, "and got hooked in the net, and they were pulling on it, and he was getting more tangled, and he bloody near drowned . . . and so did the white whale." They got McGuire out; then they finally managed to cut the young whale free and get her to the surface.

The transfer of the white whale to Sealand was accomplished without further incident, giving Sealand's veterinarian, Alan Hoey, and visiting scientists a close-up look — for the first time — at the white killer whale. Eleven and a half feet long, weighing about 2,000 pounds, the whale was, from blood samples, definitely a female. Wright had succeeded in finding a mate for Haida — if Haida would accept the freak and could wait a few years until she was mature. Moreover, the white whale was a prize, probably the rarest marine mammal ever to be captured alive and put on display.

Shortly after the news broke, Jacques Cousteau telephoned from France to say that he was coming over. A California aquarium offered $1 million to buy her, but Wright said, "No, she's a Canadian whale. She stays." However, Wright's prize whale was a prize with problems. As a genetic freak, she had special medical needs. She was susceptible to infection. She would squint in bright sunshine because it hurt her eyes. She was obviously high-strung. She had hit the nets at Pedder Bay, and later, she hit the sides of the aquarium. She seemed to have an impaired echolocation system.

In the 24 days that the two cows were at Pedder Bay, they had not eaten.

There was some concern, although Moby Doll had fasted for 54 days in 1964. The two cows seemed healthy. Nootka was the first to eat, but not without a little help. "The day before she arrived at Sealand, we divided Haida's pool in half with a big net," said Ellis. "We wanted to keep them separated for a few days until they got to know one another. First, we put Nootka in at one end of the enclosure. She was vocalizing loudly. Haida paid no attention. He was at the other end of the pool getting scratched and fed by one of the girls. After four or five minutes, he dived down close to the net to have a look and came right back to the platform to get scratched again. He behaved as if nothing was going on. He wasn't upset; he just didn't appear to be interested — at first. Then he took one of his herring down to the net and pushed it through the mesh to the new whale. Nootka came and looked but didn't take it. Then the white whale arrived. Haida responded as he had with Nootka — nonchalant initially, then pressing the fish against the white one's mouth. Haida repeated this manoeuvre several times with both cows. They began eating almost immediately."

Ellis said that the three whales got along well at first. Haida enjoyed the company of the two cows, copulating with Nootka and playfully nudging the white one, who came to be called Chimo, an Inuit word meaning welcome. The name seemed to suit her friendly disposition.

Nootka soon began to take advantage of Chimo. "Nootka was overly aggressive," Hoey explained. "She kept raking her teeth across the little whale's back. In time, Chimo developed skin problems that may have come from stress. It was obvious that one whale had to go."

Nootka was sold to Japanese Deer Park, a California aquarium, but was soon transferred to Seven Seas in Texas and, from there, to Marineland and Game Farm in Niagara Falls, Ontario. Wright always regretted selling Nootka and, years later, tried to buy her back. Of all the whales that Wright captured for various aquariums, including his Sealand, Nootka outlived every one of them.

What about the other three members of the Pedder Bay Five? None of them was eating. Hired to be a 24-hour nursemaid, Don White, who had just finished his studies with Paul Spong at the Vancouver Aquarium, moved into a houseboat alongside the nets at Pedder Bay. His chief task was to get the three whales to feed. The two cows had been sold to Seven Seas; the third, to be set free, was the big bull Charlie Chin — so called because of his protruding lower jaw. Each of the whales in Chimo's pod suffered from some malformation. Besides the white Chimo, a mutation, the other animals shared unusual jaw and head formations — perhaps genetically. There was Charlie Chin's peculiarity. Nootka had a bulbous lower jaw, an extremely large gape. Another cow had a pointed head — the entire melon was long and narrow — and her upper jaw protruded. The fourth cow had a bashed-in lower jaw with extensive scar tissue, probably from some kind of accident. "It looked as if she'd hit the bottom at about 30 knots," said Ellis. In the months that he baby-sat the Pedder Bay whales, White had only one close-up look at the scarred-jaw cow: "She was a deformed animal; her teeth were yellow-brown with cracks and were worn flat."

One theory about the pod, White explained, was that it was a reject pod, a group of outcast orcas. Hoey called them "a leper colony of killer whales." There were a lot of jokes at the time, White said, because on the day that the pod was captured, it had been seen near Bentinck Island — a leper colony at one time. But if these whales were outcasts, they had become, over time, a family unit, as close as a pod sharing blood ties.

The three remaining whales of the Pedder Bay Five staged the longest hunger strike ever recorded for captive killer whales. "First, I threw herring at them," recalled White. "Later, I tried live ling cod. I used to go down swimming with them every day and count the ling cod in the nets to see if they'd eaten any. They hadn't."

At 54 days, they had matched Moby Doll's fast. They were still not eating. At about 60 days, the whales were "so emaciated, you could see the contours of the rib cage," according to White, "and a distinct indentation below the rib cage — which is incredible on a killer whale." White suspected that the whales were suffering from malnutrition and severe dehydration. "I suggested feeding them live salmon and injecting them with glucose and vitamin B_{12}, which other aquariums had used to stimulate captive whales' appetites. But no one wanted to risk anything. No one knew for sure. So we did nothing."

"Back then," Wright said, "I didn't know how to catch killer whales, let alone how to keep them. So I got hold of the people at Marineland and Sea World, who were the only experts in the world at the time, and they said, 'Oh, don't worry, this is not unusual' — but by god, it *was* unusual."

On day 75, White watched the scarred-jaw cow "start slowly swimming around the enclosure, crashing into the logs. I would walk around on the logs with it, yelling at it, hitting the side of its head, trying to steer it around. It seemed to gulping seawater. Its mouth was open, and because the tongue was flat and had no seal, seawater was probably going in. I figured the whale was suffering dehydration from the salt water and the lack of food. That would also explain why it had become disoriented.

"I radioed to town to send a vet right away. I was yelling on the radio. No one seemed to believe me. Finally, they sent Graeme Ellis, and of course, he realized something was very wrong. At the marina, Graeme spent a long time on the phone with Bob Wright, and then he came back out alone. No vet was going to come. We were standing out there in our wet-suit bottoms. It was about five in the afternoon, and we were watching this whale go crazy and wondering what to do with it. Then, at full steam, the whale made a run at the net. It went through the heavy polyprop up to its dorsal fin. Stuck halfway, it didn't have the power to push through any farther. We tried to cut the net around it, but all I had was a diver's knife with me. So we tried to back it into the pool. I pushed on its head. And it just went backwards, opening its mouth and allowing air bubbles to escape as it sank to the bottom. That was the end of it.

"All this time, the pointed-nose cow had been floating in the centre of the enclosure, motionless. The bull Charlie Chin kept circling round and round, but before the scarred-jaw cow died, he stopped on the surface and looked over at us. There was some vocalizing between the animals. When the cow died, Charlie Chin started grabbing the net in his teeth and yanking on it. We were smacking him on the head, but he hung on. After a while, he let go and returned to his circling pattern.''

Again, Ellis went in to the Pedder Bay marina to telephone Wright. "I was really choked up," Ellis recalled. "I told Wright the cow had died, and he said, 'You better go down there and haul it out.' I was mad. I said, 'Don't ask me.' He said, 'Well, we'll try to get another diver.' I knew damn well he didn't want anyone else to know about it. So he got back to me, said he couldn't get more divers, and I was going to have to go in and help pull it out. So we went down, tied a line to the flukes, dropped a corner of the pen and towed it out.''

"The consideration was," explained White, "do you weight it or slit its belly? This was at the time when killer whales were washing up in Puget Sound [from a Seattle Public Aquarium capture]. Some had anchors attached to their tails; some were cut up. The decision was to do neither. Just take it out far enough, and let it go, and if a whale washes up . . . well, dead whales wash up all the time. But if you actually slit its belly or attach weights to it, then that's evidence that it's one of yours.''

"We waited until it was late, well after dusk," said Ellis, "pulled it out past Race Rocks — and let it go. It sank like a rock. No vet got a chance to look at it. 'Don't tell anyone it died,' we were told. Of course, there were a few people around who thought there was one animal missing and said, 'Wasn't there another animal in there?' 'No, only two.'''

The carcass was never discovered.

"I left Sealand soon after," said Ellis. "I told Wright, 'I don't want to have any part of capturing killer whales again.'" But White stayed on — upset, yet feeling some responsibility toward Charlie Chin and the pointed-nose cow, who were still fasting in the net.

"It became obvious that doing nothing was not an adequate solution," White said, "that they weren't going to start eating and that they would, in fact, die before eating." That night, White threw them some live salmon. The whales ignored the fish. He wanted to inject the whales immediately. No one would listen; Wright was out of town for a couple of days, and no one would authorize it. After Wright returned, Sealand's veterinarian Hoey came out and, without any trouble from the bull and cow, injected them with a mixture of liquid glucose and vitamin B_{12} to stimulate their appetites. It was day 77. When the whales still hadn't eaten by the next day, Hoey gave them another injection.

White reflected on the incident: "The evening after the second injection, a Pedder Bay salmon guide brought in some fresh salmon for the whales. Charlie Chin was doing his slow circling, and the cow was still just sitting at the centre of the enclosure. She had become severely sunburned, and we had been applying zinc ointment to her skin, which was cracked around the blowhole. We were squatting at the side of the water. Jerry, the salmon guide, was holding the fish out. It was maybe 20 inches long. And Charlie just came up and grabbed it. Then he swam out to the cow and started vocalizing. There were these exchanges going back and forth as they lay there on the surface.

It really seemed like a fairy tale, especially after all this time of not eating. Charlie dropped the salmon right in front of the cow's nose. She grabbed it by the tail, and with the fish hanging out the side of her mouth, she started swimming around the pool, vocalizing. Then Charlie came up beside her and grabbed hold of the head, and with the fish stretched between them, they made a circuit of the pool. All this time, they were talking back and forth. Finally, they ripped the fish apart, and each ate half. A few minutes later, the bull returned for more. He took another salmon out to the cow. This time, she ate the whole thing. Then he came back in and got one for himself.

"I think this shows a very high level of social interaction among killer whales. What I saw happen between those two whales implies an incredible degree of sophisticated socialization — the ability to form concepts and thoughts and to execute them. It's the kind of altruistic behaviour that you would like to think people are capable of, but few are."

After Charlie Chin helped the cow start eating, each of them consumed up to 450 pounds of fish a day. White fed them salmon, gradually adding ling cod, which had to be skinned and filleted, or they wouldn't touch it. Then he switched to herring, the cheapest and easiest way to keep a captive orca's belly full. The two whales slowly regained their health. Charlie Chin, the big bull that was to have been let go, was sold at a cut rate to Seven Seas in Texas to replace the dead cow.

"I was upset that Charlie, along with the cow, was going to be moved to Texas," said White. "Because of his size, he probably wouldn't survive long. I had spent some eight months living out there alone with those whales. It was depressing. I didn't want to be there, and they sure didn't want to be there. At first, there had been some interplay. The bull was curious. As I swam along the bottom, he'd come over and have a good look, and occasionally, I'd follow him around, which he didn't seem to mind. But after a few months, when I went swimming, the whales would avoid me. They'd gone through a lot. I began to feel it was wrong to keep them captive, to put them in a situation not of their own choosing, where, sooner or later, they are doomed."

Ellis was vacationing in Mexico when he heard that Charlie Chin and the pointed-nose cow had been "released." It happened on October 27, 1970. Sometime during the night, someone let a corner of the net down and threw weights over the floats until they sank. White was playing cards in the house-boat with several friends, including the McGuire brothers (who had worked for Wright during the Chimo capture and had later quit in protest). At the time, Wright apparently accused White of setting them free, but when I asked him, White denied that he'd had any part in it. Ellis believed White: "Why wouldn't he admit it to me? After all we'd gone through, I'd be proud of it. There were quite a few people who wanted to let those whales go. There was even specu-lation that Wright might have done it because he didn't have much to lose. I believe the deal was 50 percent down and 50 percent on arrival, so Texas had already paid about 20 grand for the two animals. Both were large whales, and it was something of a gamble as to whether they'd survive the flight to Texas. Wright might not collect the other 20 grand, and he stood to have his reputation smeared if they died. At the time, he was calling himself the world's best whale catcher. I still think it's a possibility he did it."

A few years later, the distinctive Charlie Chin and the pointed-nose cow were photographed by Ellis and Bigg off eastern Vancouver Island. They were travelling with a new calf.

Of the Pedder Bay Five, the white youngster Chimo was easily the most famous — but her life, if not her fame, was short-lived. Some time after arrival at Sealand, Chimo was discovered to be suffering from a rare disease. It was the little-understood genetic syndrome Chediak-Higashi, a condition inherited as a recessive trait in five known species: mice, mink, Hereford cattle, humans and killer whales. According to Washington State University geneticist and veterinary pathologist George Padgett, who diagnosed the syndrome in mink and in killer whales, Chediak-Higashi victims are *partial* albinos subject to recurrent infections and fevers. Such individuals have enlarged granules in the blood, particularly in the white cells. In all species, the condition is fatal — at an average age of one year in mink and ten years in humans. Chimo received probably the most expensive medical attention any animal has ever had. An international team of scientists studied her to learn more about this rare condition. "A mutation, which Chimo was, tells you something about the species itself," said Padgett. "Since we know that the C-H syndrome is inherited as a recessive trait, there must be considerable inbreeding in order to bring it out. This may be a bit of evidence to support the idea that killer whales live in the same pods through long-going family relationships, instead of changing pods frequently."

In late October 1972, Chimo developed interstitial pneumonia from streptococcal septicemia, an infection that she was unable to combat. At the time, Wright was in England with his veterinarian, head pathologist and curator, conferring with experts about designing a sterile environment for Chimo. "I'd left my nephew Robbie Waters in charge of the aquarium," Wright explained. "He phoned and said she'd quit eating. And I said, 'Did you get blood?' He said, 'No, I think it's sexual.' I said, 'Robbie, always get blood right away.'"

On November 2, as Wright and his medical people were boarding an airplane bound for Canada, Chimo died. The infection had raced through her body. Last-minute antibiotics were powerless. Wright said that even an earlier diagnosis probably would not have saved her.

After Chimo's death, Haida refused to eat. For a week, he lay motionless in the centre of the pool. He had picked up the streptococcal infection from Chimo, said Sealand officials, but reporters were calling his condition "more a case of heartbreak." The heartbreak notion may have been partly accurate. If so, perhaps there was a lack of sensitivity on the part of Sealand and the visiting scientists, who dissected Chimo beside Haida's pool. Haida had no choice but to attend the autopsy of his young companion.

Haida was injected with massive doses of antibiotics. At the same time, jazz flutist Paul Horn came to play beside Haida's pool for a few days. Approaching the musician, Haida seemed to perk up and began vocalizing again. Shortly thereafter, Haida returned to health. The Sealand shows went back to normal.

Sealand veterinarian Hoey, who was in England when Chimo died, said later that "after knowing the big guy for 10 years, I don't think he was the slightest bit affected. As for not eating, speaking as a veterinarian, I'd have to place emphasis on the infection — despite those people who anthropomorphize, suggesting that he was mourning the loss of Chimo."

Had Paul Horn helped Haida recover?

"Playing music has exactly the same benefit as putting a television set in a kids' ward," Hoey explained. "It keeps them involved. But I'd never trade 10 million units of penicillin for a television set or a flute."

Soon after Haida recovered, Wright declared that Haida needed another mate: "Sealand's philosophy is that all animals should be paired." The summer after Chimo's death, Wright and his team began patrolling the waters off southern Vancouver Island. The four orcas that Sealand eventually corralled in Pedder Bay in August 1973 were the ones I visited after my first summer with the Johnstone Strait whales.

What were the fates of the Pedder Bay Four?

Taku, a 23-foot-long bull, was turned over to Michael Bigg who, on October 27, 1973, had the whale fitted with a small tracking device to transmit signals to a monitoring vessel. The device was bolted on through a hole drilled in the animal's dorsal fin by Hoey. Following Bigg's orders, Hoey made two large cuts on the dorsal's trailing edge to ensure later identification in the wild. Bigg hoped to track Taku for a month, at which time the radio device was designed to fall off. Yet after only half a day, diving deep and ducking behind a group of islands, the bull evaded Bigg. Some nine months later, Bigg found Taku (minus the device) travelling off southern Vancouver Island with a cow and calf. Taku had rejoined K pod, an approximately 12-whale pod residing in southern Vancouver Island waters.

Kandy, a cow almost 18 feet long, was flown to Niagara Falls' Marineland and Game Farm on October 30. Marineland owner John Holer hoped that Kandy would mate with their resident young male, Kandu. In three weeks, Kandy was dead from acute pneumonia.

Frankie, the third whale, a 19 1/2-foot-long male, was sold to Sea World in San Diego. Four months later, on January 29, 1974, Frankie also died of pneumonia.

Nootka II, the fourth whale, a cow, seemed the most likely mate for Haida and, on October 7, was admitted to Sealand of the Pacific. Nootka II, like Taku, belonged to K pod. According to Bigg, she had been captured before with the entire pod at Yukon Harbor, Washington, in Feburary 1967, but she had been released. In that capture, three family members died, and five others were brought to the Seattle Public Aquarium. Most eventually went to Sea World, where they died, but Nootka II's "brother," old Ramu at Sea World in Florida, and her "sister," Skana at the Vancouver Aquarium, survived captivity longer than any other orcas. K pod was probably also captured at Penn Cove, Washington, in August 1970, as part of an 80-whale group corralled by the Seattle Public Aquarium. (Groups of 80 whales travelling together in Puget Sound, according to Bigg, typically consisted of pods J, K and L — although L was the only pod positively identified at the capture.) At least once, therefore, and maybe twice, Nootka II avoided captivity, only to be taken in August 1973. On May 1, 1974, she died at Sealand of a ruptured aorta. She was an old whale — Bigg estimated that she was in her thirties — one of the oldest killer whales to be aged by the tree-ring method of counting the tooth layers. She may have been a barren cow.

For the second time in two years, Haida had lost a mate. In the summer of 1975, Wright reassembled his crew and sat offshore at Pedder Bay, waiting, boats and nets at the ready.

At twilight on August 16, six killer whales (Q pod) visiting southern Vancouver Island from northern B.C. waters poked their heads into Pedder Bay. Wright quickly sealed off the entrance, and in an hour, the whales were securely confined. I was in Toronto when I heard; I flew to Victoria immediately and again made my way to the hillside overlooking the spot where the earlier pods had made their final stands. The security at Pedder Bay was tight; there had been telephoned threats and talk in the local pubs about cutting the nets, and when I arrived, the Royal Canadian Mounted Police had apparently just thwarted one attempt to free the whales. For almost a week, no one had been allowed to visit the site where the Pedder Bay Six were waiting in the nets. Through his marina at Pedder Bay, Wright controls access by land to some extent. He wanted as little publicity as possible. Regulations about capturing orcas had become more stringent since 1973. Size limits would be strictly enforced, and all whales outside acceptable limits (calves and mature animals) had to be released immediately. Then, on September 12, the B.C. provincial government declared a moratorium on future captures. Although the catching of killer whales is regulated by a federal government permit system, the provincial declaration was a sign of changing times. The abuses of previous captures and the mortality rates of collected specimens were finally catching up with the captors.

Four of the Pedder Bay Six were released immediately. One 14-foot-long male was purchased by Marineland and Game Farm. Formal protest to the sale was registered by the B.C. provincial government, which refused to allow the whale to be conveyed to Vancouver International Airport on the B.C. ferries (used to transport earlier captives). The airlift was thus delayed almost to the date that Wright, according to his permit, would have had to let the whale go. Marineland's lawyer said that it would sue the B.C. government for additional transportation costs. A federal Department of Fisheries and Oceans official, perhaps irked that the provincial government was interfering in the management of a federal resource, said that the delay could endanger the whale's life. Greenpeace, the international save-the-whales group, threatened Air Canada, the scheduled carrier, with a campaign to distribute bumper stickers proclaiming: "Air Canada Kills Whales!" No decision was reached for 72 hours. Then, at the last minute, Marineland enlisted International Jet Air, a Calgary-based charter airline, to fly the young male from Victoria International Airport to Ontario. A protest parade of honking cars was organized to follow the whale from Pedder Bay to the airport the day this orca left British

Columbia forever. Among hundreds of others in the parade was Don White, who some years before had helped capture Chimo.

The young 12 1/2-foot-long female of the Pedder Bay Six was sent to Sealand to be Haida's new companion. Flutist Paul Horn played the wedding march as the cow, Nootka III, was lowered into the pool.

Soon after the cow's arrival, Ellis visited Sealand on one of his periodic trips to Victoria. I was in Victoria too, and we saw each other on the street and stopped to talk about Haida and the new cow. Ellis, who had trained Haida when the young male came to Sealand in 1968, felt discouraged by the visit. "It's depressing to see him," he said. "And Haida probably has the best possible conditions of any captive whale." Ellis explained that Sealand's whale pool is the largest — at 1.5 million gallons, it is about twice the size of the one at the Vancouver Aquarium. It is open to the sea, thus somewhat free of the concrete reverberations that Paul Spong suggests tend to silence whales at some aquariums. Ellis said that Haida's mental health has received as much, if not more, attention as has been paid to other captive orcas.

On my visits to Sealand, I'd often seen trainers and visitors playing with Haida. That was how my first contact with him had come about one December day in 1972. As the first orca I ever met, captive or wild, Haida will always have a special place in my affections. After watching his acrobatic show that rainy winter morning, I was standing by the side of the pool when he came up with a piece of seaweed in his mouth and deposited it at my feet. No one was around except for a few seagulls, and they weren't interested. Amused, I picked up the seaweed and threw it into the water. Immediately, Haida came and got it, circled the pool and brought it to me again. It was the pass-the-seaweed-back-and-forth game. Though I didn't know it at the time, it was a game that he delighted in playing. It had probably all started with Ellis, who occasionally rewarded Haida when he voluntarily retrieved objects of value that had fallen into the pool. When he brought objects of no value — like seaweed or Styrofoam chips from the side of the tank — Ellis did not reward him, but Haida still persisted. Haida's love of simple games seemed independent of his training and even of his need for food. There was the time when the Cousteau team had come to film Haida performing and taking food from a diver underwater. Haida had hardly eaten that morning, but when the cameras started rolling, he was more interested in passing the fish back and forth with Ellis than in eating or being rewarded. When I met Haida in 1972, he was just returning to health after Chimo's death. He seemed playful, but according to Ellis, Haida had started deteriorating long before Chimo's death.

Ellis met Haida in 1968 when the young male was "enthusiastic, the most responsive and eager orca of the captives I'd seen." But after visiting Haida in 1975, Ellis said: "A captive whale has only a year, maybe two, before his mental health starts going downhill. Some get bored, lethargic. Others turn neurotic and perhaps dangerous. There was the girl at Sea World in San Diego bitten by Shamu, who started playing a tug-of-war with her leg. Other whales have held their trainers underwater, almost drowning them. Some of these accidents have happened when the trainers were riding the whales around the pool. In my experience, whales don't like to be ridden; they may tolerate it when they're young or new to captivity, but later, no. They still ride the whales at Sea World, but the whales in Canadian aquariums are not ridden anymore. When I visited the California aquariums a few years ago, I saw a big old bull at one of them that they kept in a back pool, away from the public. They said he'd killed five dolphins and taken a grab at a lady. There was a standing offer of $500 for anyone who would swim across his tank.

"How long a whale lasts in captivity depends on the animal's age at capture and his personality — also on the trainer. You have to be able to challenge them, to know how their minds work. The mark of a good trainer — to too many aquarium owners — is how many tricks can you train them to do in two months. That's not the point. It's how long you can maintain a whale's sanity. A lot of people wouldn't agree that a whale even has sanity or insanity. Do animals have it? That's a hard one. People won't accept the fact that they could be boring to a whale. I mean, whales aren't supposed to get bored." Ellis was suddenly sarcastic. "They're just dumb animals — that's the attitude, anyway. But you take juvenile orcas: They're really pretty eager for at least a year; after that, if you can keep them interested . . . but it's difficult, because the novelty wears off. Now, mind you, given the chance, they'll go the other way [escape] — but they're curious enough and interested enough that they won't be driven neurotic in a year. Based on the whales I've worked with at Sealand and at the Vancouver Aquarium and the ones I've observed in the California aquariums, they all start to get a little bit nutty in two years."

In the fall of 1975, Haida and Nootka III were "getting along fine," according to Sealand officials. Ellis's report, after seeing them, was that Haida seemed better, fooling around with the cow all day, but that it was at best a temporary diversion. In fact, they never did successfully mate. Nine months after the 1975 capture, Haida's third bride died of a perforated ulcer. According to Sealand, Haida showed no signs of distress during Nootka III's 13-day illness and death. Too far gone to be distressed? Stoic? Brave? Numbed or immunized by earlier deaths? Or "just a dumb animal"?

We spent the fall of 1973 editing and laying the sound for our 17-minute whale film. Once back in the city, we all had to return to other jobs to pay the bills, so it took evenings and weekends to complete the short documentary. The premiere on December 22, at the 3,000-seat Queen Elizabeth Theatre in Vancouver, was part of a benefit called "The Christmas Whale Show." The sold-out show was organized and hosted by Paul Spong, and it later became an annual affair in Vancouver and a travelling event that, during the following two years, toured California, Japan and several international whale conferences. Our little film was well received. It was the first glimpse that most people had had of wild killer whales. After Stubbs, Nicola, Wavy and Sturdy paraded past on the big screen, the Johnstone Strait killers received a standing ovation.

In the new year, Hunter and I began fund raising for a full-length documentary on the whales to be made in the summer of 1974. Our money finally came from the Todd family, a famous name in salmon fishing in British Columbia.

In conservative Victoria, Derek Todd was a rather adventurous financier. It seemed appropriate that Todd family money be spent to make a film that might help conserve the killer whales which fed on the salmon and which had, historically, been abused by salmon fishermen.

In July 1974, we headed north to Johnstone Strait. We were anxious to see whether the same whales would still be there, and we wanted to learn more about them. Our new film expedition provided us with a vehicle to do so.

Part Three
SECOND SUMMER

A KILLER WHALE DAY

JULY 11. Once again, I'm heading up Johnstone Strait to killer whale country. The journey that took weeks by sail in 1973 will be completed in a few hours. This year, we've chartered an old nine-passenger amphibious Grumman Goose. Seven of us — plus cameras, sound gear, supplies — are crammed into the belly of a flying tank. Travelling separately, by sailboat, is Hunter, with the underwater gear and divers, notably Stanton A. Waterman, "the dean of underwater cameramen," as Hunter describes him. Forty-nine-year-old Waterman has made a career of jumping into the water with sharks, filming the great white in the 1970 documentary *Blue Water, White Death*. Hunter figures that after sharks, "orcas'll be a cinch for Watermonster." Hunter and the divers will meet us in Alert Bay. Flying north, following the eastern Vancouver Island coastline, we look for the distinctive brown sails of their ketch, the 57-foot *Nausikaa III*. We never do see them; the rain and heavy mist blanket Vancouver Island like a patchwork quilt, obscuring the strait and softening the harsh view of the bald mountain patches left by logging companies. Heading inland to the lush Tsitika River Basin, zigzagging across the green virgin wilderness, we slowly turn up the river valley. At the mouth of the Tsitika, the sky opens, and for a few minutes, the sun shines on paradise. We come in low over Robson Bight, close enough to see killer whales — perhaps 10 of them, hanging around at the river's mouth, no doubt enjoying this year's record salmon runs. It's like coming home.

The enthusiasm of coming home quickly dissipated as we became involved in day-to-day conflicts with the filmmakers. To say that Hunter and I had creative differences with the Hollywood director would be a considerable understatement. This director appeared to be uninterested in observing the whales or even, for that matter, filming them. After spending two hours one afternoon following a few straggling whales that we were unable to identify, he informed us that we had all the surface footage we needed. In fact, the whales would not come close to the 13-foot green speedboat, for our director was at the wheel, driving the boat much as he had driven his late-model Fleetwood Cadillac only weeks before, showing us how to negotiate Los Angeles traffic. He had charged along the freeway aggressively, even dangerously, and had climbed the sidewalk to park. To him, Johnstone Strait was just another freeway, and the whales were fat black sedans to be chased and passed. After he nearly hit one youngster broadside, the whales disappeared. "Never mind," he said, "we'll get the close-up coverage in the tank." Hunter and I looked at each other. Hunter was not laughing. What had been amusing in Los Angeles got no laughs in Johnstone Strait.

Creative control — or how to shoot a whale movie — was the least of our differences with this director/producer. Twice in the first week, Hunter lost his temper, accusing the director of taking the production for a ride. Money was owed to certain crew members; contracts were not being honoured. Morale on the expedition had started low, gone lower. We were holed up in secluded Growler Cove, filming endless arrival and departure sequences, while Hunter and I watched longingly as whales sometimes passed by out in the strait. Our minds were on whales, and finally, one sunny afternoon, Hunter and I grabbed cameraman James Glennon and stole a few hours to go find some orcas. Leaving Growler Cove, we headed for Robson Bight, some four miles across the strait.

The whales seemed to be waiting for us. Entering Robson Bight, we saw their fountain blows against the dark green shore. They were crossing the mouth of the Tsitika River, heading east, almost single file — about eight or nine of them, cows and calves mostly, no bulls. We angled across the bight to its eastern point, waiting near shore, directly in their path. We shut off the engine. The bight's eastern rock face is a half mile long and irregular, and as the whales approached, some no more than a few feet from the steep-walled shore, our view of them was sometimes blocked by rocky outcrops. Then the whales seemed to disappear entirely. For 15 minutes, we did not see a spout, and we began to get edgy. Had they passed underneath us? Hunter fired up the Johnson 25, and we put-putted out from shore. Nothing. A hundred yards into the strait, we were still searching the coastline. Nothing. How could we have lost them?

We doubled back to the spot where we had last seen the whales. Moving slowly, we traced their probable path along the shore. Fifty feet from where we had sat and waited, we rounded a rocky outcrop and found ourselves staring into a tiny bay filled with whales. The air was thick with their spouts. Some whales lay on the surface; others came up, alternately. At first, it did not appear that they were going anywhere. Then Hunter yelled: "They're underneath us!" I looked over the side of the Zodiac and watched two young whales swimming piggyback, almost touching, their tails undulating in perfect synchrony. Hunter eased up on the throttle, and Glennon hoisted the big Eclair NPR to his shoulder. It was difficult for Glennon to follow them in the viewfinder. The two adolescents were moving fast, showing off, executing breathless pas de deux underneath us. Like dancers, they leapt and pirouetted, then stood poised, facing us for an instant as if waiting for applause. They swam over to the rock wall and joined several other whales. We moved a little closer. Two cows were slapping their tails on the surface. The water was glossy black in the shadows, but when they flipped their tails, the sun caught the arc of water droplets, creating a momentary curtain of brilliance. Beside one of the cows, a calf began lifting and smacking *its* tail. The porpoise-sized flukes only just cleared the water.

"He's not very good at it," said Glennon, laughing.

The calf was trying hard, though, while beside him, the two adolescents began smacking their tails too. They were a bit better. In a few minutes, all of them — the two cows, the juveniles and the calf — were lined up facing the rocky shore, smacking their tails.

"Killer whale nursery school," said Hunter. "The little guys are learning how to use their flukes in tail-lobbing class."

That was exactly what it looked like. For some 15 minutes, the exercises continued. By the end, the two juveniles were getting quite good. And the little calf was improving.

Then one cow turned and floated off to the side, another tiny calf emerging from the shadows and swimming up beside her. For the first time, we saw the cow's dorsal fin. It was perfectly silhouetted in the light of the calf's blow.

"Nicola!" I called. Nicola nudged the baby maternally. They just lay there on the surface. It was a tender moment. Since last summer, Nicola had become a mother.

"Let's move in closer," said Hunter impatiently, starting the engine. It was in gear. We bolted forward, almost losing Glennon and the Eclair over the side. The whales dove down, out of sight.

"The old *Orcinus orca* disappearing act," said Hunter after 10 minutes. Nicola was playing hard to get, and we were left to wonder where she had gone.

Then we heard a blow against the rock wall. A whale had surfaced in the kelp bed, looking like a seaweed-covered rock. Where had this whale come from? We started moving closer. The whale went down and surfaced again, minus the seaweed.

"Stubbs!" yelled Hunter. He killed the engine.

Stubbs blew and sucked a deep breath. She stayed at the surface. She blew, breathed again. Still she stayed. Stubbs had been following the other whales, but now that she had entered the little bay, the others had left. We could hear them blowing in the distance. They were moving away fast, heading north now, crossing the open windy waters of the strait.

We coasted closer to Stubbs. She wasn't moving. We studied her fin and her scratched black torso. We had tried to describe old Stubbs to Glennon, but now that Hunter and I saw her again, she seemed much odder than we had remembered. Her back was deeply pockmarked, and close up, her fin seemed even more twisted and misshapen than the year before. She blew again. She did not seem concerned about us coming close. Hunter began slapping the side of the Zodiac and splashing water with his hand. The old whale faced us, turning her head slightly from side to side, orienting. Hunter became more persistent, cupping his hand and smacking his arm from the elbow. The smacking sounds were decidedly whalelike. Hunter, too, had learned something in tail-lobbing class.

After seven blows, Stubbs pushed off with her flukes and dropped beneath the surface, her fin cutting a slight chop as it disappeared. She was following the other whales. For a few minutes, we paced her as she chugged out of the bight. Moving at a speed of only about a knot and a half, she was coming up seven, eight times for air, then going down for only two minutes. (Whales usually take three or four blows over five minutes when travelling.) Stubbs was not gaining on the pod. She seemed like an old animal. We wondered if she was sick. Still she pushed on — old, perhaps, but very determined.

The three of us felt renewed, quietly exhilarated, as we rejoined the film crew for dinner. It had been a refreshing afternoon after weeks of Hollywood insanity. It seemed so simple just to be with Stubbs and Nicola, to move with them, to share part of their day. The film we were making with the Hollywood director, which was supposed to tell the story of killer whales and men, seemed ridiculous in the light of our day's experience.

Hunter and Waterman went diving twice a day. Waterman's 20-year-old son, Gar, was light man, and Hunter's friend Mark Driscoll from Victoria was number-four diver and camera assistant. Left to their own devices, the divers were getting good underwater footage. To Waterman, who had plumbed the world's oceans, B.C. waters might be cold and murky, but they possessed some of the most prosperous flora and fauna anywhere. He photographed the huge purple anemones, the giant nudibranchs and the Pacific octopus, with its up-to-25-foot arm span, the world's largest. He also photographed a young Steller sea lion charging Hunter, stopping inches from his face mask and snarling.

The divers encountered everything *but* killer whales. They were trying every method they could think of to get close to whales: motoring ahead and dropping off in the whales' path; waiting in prime orca spots, jumping out and hoping the whales would come over; motoring as close as possible to them and trying to swim over. But the whales avoided them. And that was the story of the entire production. The logistics of 14 people, five boats and a low-budget operation with no contingency had us in deep water from the beginning. The three variables — wind, water and whales — made survival uncertain, but the lead weight that finally sank the production was the Hollywood producer/director. Every chance we could, Hunter and I, with Glennon and sometimes Driscoll, would take off to spend time with whales. On our own, we were getting some good footage. When the director lost his temper and fired Glennon, Hunter and I quit. As coproducers of the film, it was tough to turn our backs on a year's work — a big investment of time and money. Yet it was tougher to stay involved with a project which had no integrity and which, despite our best efforts, had grown into a monster. (After we sold out our interest, this film was partly reshot with captive orcas, dubbed and repackaged as a television movie entitled *Jaws of Death*.)

We were not giving up on filming the whales, however. We still had August, perhaps September. We had a loyal crew who offered to work for nothing. We had lots of whales, and the good weather showed no sign of changing. We decided to spend the rest of the summer in Johnstone Strait.

August 4 was the day that Hunter and I walked off the set. That same morning, Peter Vatcher was paddling his canoe down Johnstone Strait, headed for Robson Bight. It was a six-hour trip, and Vatcher was tired but elated when we helped him ashore. The whales had staged a bit of a homecoming for him. After our summer 1973 expedition, I had missed Vatcher. Expeditions make for lifelong friendships or feuds, no room for much in between. We hugged on the beach. "Your timing is perfect," I said. "Do you want to film orcas again?"

Strong bonds of friendship had already formed among Hunter, Glennon, Driscoll, Waterman and me in only three weeks of working together, even on a bad production. Glennon and Driscoll would stay with Hunter, Vatcher and me. Waterman wanted to, but the following week, he was due to shoot a documentary on the first exploration of the rift in the Mid-Atlantic Ridge. He did give us his blessings and the loan of his backup underwater movie camera. Other equipment we would have to rent. We needed film and supplies. We left Vatcher by himself to care for the Robson Bight camp (which, when we departed, was only three tents clustered on a lookout point near the Tsitika River) and flew to Vancouver and Victoria. When we returned five days later, Vatcher had remodelled the place. Left without a boat or much in the way of supplies, he had become an instant Robinson Crusoe, throwing up a crude shack, hewing tables and benches from beach logs, collecting berries from the forest and clams and crabs from the beach and sprouting a beard so that he even looked the part. His beard was the approximate colour·and consistency of the lichen-covered rocks that the camp was built on. After six days, he was glad to see us. I had invited a musician friend from Toronto, Jacqui Krofchak, to join us. Now we were seven. Vatcher and Glennon would man the topside cameras; Driscoll would perform as diver and camera assistant; Hunter and his girlfriend, Shirley Thompson, would help with the underwater chores; and I would record sound. But everyone helped with everything — loading film magazines, holding microphones, driving boats, cutting wood and cooking. We all rallied around Hunter's manic energy. At some point, it occurred to me that we got along as well as did (it seemed) the whales who passed the campsite daily. Our yellow, orange and blue tents were freely scattered on the point surrounding the shack, and we built a lean-to in the trees. It was cozy, but we had room to breathe under giant hemlock and balsam.

When we arrived, carting box after box up slippery rocks to Camp Robson, it seemed that we had packed enough gear to live out our days in whale country.

We had generators, banks of 12-volt batteries, an air compressor that required four men to lift, diving tanks, sacks of diving gear and enough camera and sound equipment to stock a small motion-picture studio. We brought foam mattresses, kerosene lamps and a portable kerosene heater. We had 12 large boxes of food — sacks of granola made with honey and nuts, canned milk, crunchy peanut butter, stoned wheat crackers, potatoes, carrots and a lot of lemons. Those were some of the staples, second in importance only to salmon, which we could either catch by hook or get by bargaining with the local fishermen. The fishermen — whites more than natives — considered us more than a little crazy, running around in our rubber boats and canoes all day with blackfish. But we were handy friends to have when the fishermen's nets ran afoul of their propellers, and they needed a diver — fast. We were well paid in cash and salmon, and later, one boat that we had helped, an old wooden seiner called the *W-10*, would bail us out when we were really in need.

Cameraman Glennon was the lone American, and the gadgets that he had brought with him were as American as his absolute delight in them. Our first day on the new production, he issued each of us a tiny pocket can opener (courtesy U.S. Army surplus), which would have rendered a vast storehouse of C rations readily edible had he remembered to bring them. The can openers worked on canned milk, all right, but they were even better for cleaning one's fingernails. Glennon loved any gadget that worked well — the simpler and handier, the better. His favourite was the Lightningpak, a beanbag full of crystals — one had only to add 2 1/2 tablespoons of cold water, shake and wait 15 minutes. Presto! A very hot hot-water bottle that burned for eight hours with no relief. Every night, the Lightningpak was passed from bed to bed like a hot potato. Glennon had also brought a portable Army surplus shower, which was hung from a fir branch above a back eddy near the Tsitika River mouth. The shower was a three-quart canvas bag attached to an open can with a number of holes punched in the bottom. A metal disc, similarly punched with holes, fit inside the bottom of the can; when the disc was turned, aligning the holes, the water passed through. Theoretically, the water in the bag — as well as the water in the back eddy — would be sufficiently warmed by the sun so that by late afternoon, one could enjoy a leisurely dunking, but the water was always just shy of freezing. When standing in the back eddy up to one's waist, first the goose bumps came, followed by the tiny trout fingerlings that nibbled the hairs on one's legs. We should have rigged the Lightningpak to heat the water. But it was bathing in paradise — and peaceful, too, except for the brown bear that occasionally strolled down to the river to poach spawners and the eagles that followed the bear, determined to mooch from the poacher.

Once we were set up, I moved into the shack, pounding out daily reports on the typewriter — a journal of the whales' movements and their activities. We watched them from the rocks. We had the hydrophone suspended from a mooring offshore to alert us when the whales passed. By day and by night, the whales played along the shores of the bight and sometimes rested briefly, but we didn't go out with them. With up-to-30-knot westerlies, the strait was too rough for filming. It was sunny, blue skies, but rough, cold and wet. That first week, the afternoon tides were high, and the salt spray drenched the camp. On these cloudless days, we wore rain gear and sat and talked or did our buzz-bombing off the rocks. A buzz bomb is a tapered, diamond-shaped lead fishing lure, about three inches long, attached to a treble hook. The name comes from the sound the lure makes as it is alternately lifted and allowed to fall through the water. Fishermen believe that the buzzing sound attacts the fish; the buzz bomb is one of the most successful lures ever devised for catching salmon, especially coho and spring.

Casting from the camp with our buzz bombs, we caught brown bombers — the local name for a prolific spiny brown rockfish. Hunter would curse when he got one, but Glennon could catch them all day. Most were too small, but he wanted to keep them all. We argued with him. With big sockeye and smileys around, it was hard to get excited about the spiny rockfish. So Glennon began feeding the local animal community. He would leave most of his catch on the rocks just above the high-tide mark for the ravens and eagles. Usually, the seagulls snapped the fish up first. But one day, three dark brown shiny heads peeked up from the kelp bed offshore. Glennon and Driscoll, talking around the fire, called the rest of us. We stared at the three bright faces. Their gaze was direct, unflinching and very curious. River otters. We didn't move. The bravest — or the most curious — slid up the rock to inspect the freshly killed fish. He didn't take any, but the trio returned later that afternoon and dove for the herring that we threw them. After that, they became sometime visitors, and by summer's end, they were almost as curious as the killer whales. We never saw the whales and otters at the same time, though. Sea otters are food for orcas in some areas of the North Pacific, but our otters never gave the whales a chance to test their appetites. Another occasional visitor, partial to early mornings, was a great blue heron. He would strut like a stork through the high estuary grass until disturbed — whereupon, he would take flight and, like a pterodactyl, cut a wide swath across the river mouth. Hunter's favourites were the eagles; he made certain that some of Glennon's catch got to the one family which lived in the trees above our shower installation. Hunter, who could mimic the voice of almost any creature that walked, flew or swam, was an excellent eagle mimic. The eagles, perhaps baffled or mildly annoyed, rarely answered him, but when he did get them going, they wouldn't shut up for an hour.

Glennon's principal welfare case was a young mink that visited only by night. The "little minkster," as Hunter dubbed him, was about 18 inches long, including his bushy tail. A relative of the otter, the mink is considerably smaller, with a shorter tail and short legs with unwebbed toes. Sporting a glossy dark brown pelage, our mink looked at the world through tiny yet prominent eyes set into a flat, triangular head. At Camp Robson, he had his own dish, which Glennon filled with fish scraps and fat and always left between the main tent and the shack. Every night, after we were tucked in our sleeping bags, the mink would creep along the side of the tent, stopping at the dish. Usually, we would just lie there listening. But sometimes, with a bright moon, we'd peek out the tent flap. It took awhile, but eventually, the mink permitted us to watch him from outside the tent. His head would dart from side to side. Then, like a cat, he'd begin lapping at the fat. We would slide back into our sleeping bags, and if we looked again, he was always gone.

One night, we had talked until after midnight, and the mink arrived about 2 a.m. Glennon, Vatcher and I were in the main tent, and as the mink began his little ritual, we stirred. Suddenly, a killer whale blew in the kelp bed just below the camp. If the loud blow surprised us, it put the fear of orca into the little mink. Only halfway through dinner, he rose from the table and, at a dead sprint, scrambled along the tent and disappeared into the forest forever.

"The little guy probably heard that killer whales eat his relatives," said Vatcher. It is not difficult to imagine that otter-eating killer whales would also eat mink, given a good appetite and the opportunity to exercise it.

For a month, we lived at the Robson Bight camp — happy, self-sufficient, our total focus on the whales. Like neighbours, we gossiped about them:

"Nicola certainly is protective of her calf this year."

"Standoffish."

"Did you see big Sturdy travelling with the two youngsters?"

"Hooker's boys sure like to mingle with the cows in Top Notch's pod."

"And Top Notch doesn't seem to mind."

I even dreamt about the whales:

> AUGUST 15. Paddling the canoe up to the eastern rock face in Robson Bight, I find Stubbs. At first, she seems therianthropic — part whale, part human. Then she appears as an old but handsome woman. She looks like a wrinkled Russian grandmother in a black babushka. In broken English, she tells me how her dorsal fin was damaged by a ship's propeller. She speaks matter-of-factly. The accident happened more than 10 years ago. She feels no ill will about it. Realizing that she is only temporarily in this human form, I want to seize the opportunity to talk with her. "May we photograph you underwater?" She hesitates a beat: "Yes, we could probably arrange that sometime." Then, becoming Stubbs the whale, she dives beneath the ocean.

Between August 9 and September 10, we observed killer whales for a total of 112 hours from the camp and from various boats as we travelled through the strait. There was Top Notch's pod of 10 animals. They often swam with the 16 whales in Stubbs's group. There was another group, The Six, led by a big bull with two nicks on his dorsal. We suspected that it was a splinter group of Stubbs's. The Six had a very young calf. We met them almost every day during the last weeks in August but could not get close. Although Stubbs's and the other whale pods became more and more approachable, The Six stayed wary. When we motored ahead of them and parked the Zodiac in their path, they would stop and wait for us to leave. When we drew near, they would huddle on the surface, the larger animals surrounding the calf — like a group of porpoises exhibiting protective behaviour. So we left them alone and just watched from shore as they passed the camp. Then there was Hooker's pod. They showed up only twice during the summer of 1974, although they had been frequent visitors to the bight the previous summer. We also encountered three new pods — C, D and G. (Michael Bigg had been assigning letter names to all the groups — Stubbs's pod was A, Top Notch's A5 and Hooker's B.)

C pod had three big bulls in a 10-whale group. One bull (C1) resembled Top Notch, with a similar notch near the top trailing edge of his fin. But unlike Top Notch, he also had a small nick near the base. When we first saw this pod, we thought that Top Notch had split off, leaving his cows and calves to fend for themselves. But Top Notch was approachable, whereas C1 preferred to keep some distance from our boats. There was only one calf in C pod. The pod usually travelled alone, but Ellis had seen them once near Bella Bella, British Columbia, with the two A groups and D pod.

Composed of about 12 members, D pod included three bulls. The largest was Warp Fin, whose dorsal's entire trailing edge was ragged. Hunter had photographed him alone in Johnstone Strait in 1973, then again in 1974 with his entire group. Bigg thought that Warp Fin was one of the oldest bulls on the coast. There were three calves. D pod was rarely observed in Johnstone Strait and, according to Bigg, probably frequented west coast Vancouver Island and northern B.C. waters.

G pod had 18 to 20 members. We saw them only twice. There were three big bulls and at least four youngsters. The bull G1 had a tall dorsal that curled over and slightly back at the top edge. The cow G6 had an S-shaped saddle. The bull G7 had a perfect tall dorsal but could be distinguished by three slashes across the left side of his saddle patch. This pod often swam spread apart, sometimes with Top Notch's (A5) or Warp Fin's (D) pods. They travelled the coast in the Strait of Georgia, as far south as Nanaimo, all the way to Bella Bella and perhaps farther north, a range of at least 300 miles.

Of our 112 hours with the various Johnstone Strait pods, about 85 hours were spent with Stubbs's group (often in association with Top Notch's pod). They stayed in the bight, while other pods usually passed through. They were the most approachable. During the long hours of watching and moving with them, we were becoming familiar with their daily patterns. Theirs seemed a simple life — eating, resting, playing, eating again. And always travelling. It was a rhythm unbroken even by darkness, as far as we could tell. They seemed content, living in the present, taking life as it came. They had all they needed — food, family companions, mates. There seemed no competition for these items. The scratches and fin deformities that we noticed on some animals could be signs of some infighting; occasional squabbles would be certain to develop even among the most congenial companions, but we observed none.

Animal psychologist Heini Hediger has suggested that man differs from other animals in not being chronically frightened, but killer whales would have to be an exception. Having no predators, they seem placid and carefree for the most part. This is not true of other cetaceans. Dall's porpoises, for instance, which we saw in the strait almost every day, appear to be nervous, jumpy animals by nature. (Incidentally, they do not take well to capture and captivity.)

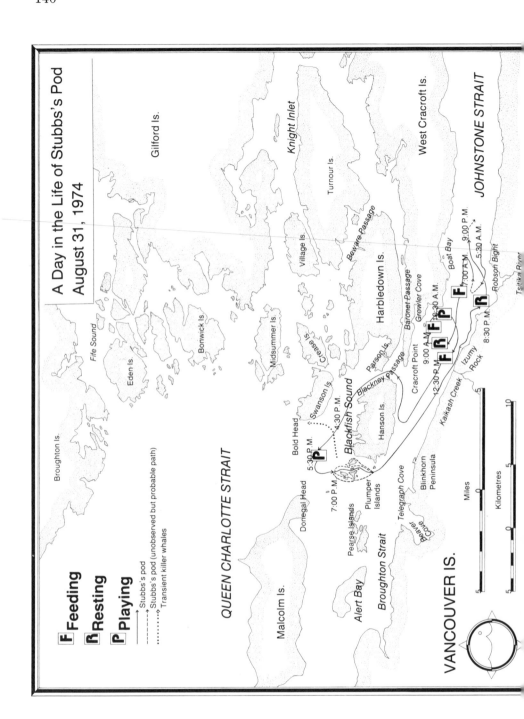

A Day in the Life of Stubbs's Pod
August 31, 1974

F Feeding
R Resting
P Playing

Stubbs's pod
Stubbs's pod (unobserved but probable path)
Transient killer whales

QUEEN CHARLOTTE STRAIT

Fife Sound

Broughton Is.

Gilford Is.

Knight Inlet

Eden Is.

Bonwick Is.

Midsummer Is.

Village Is.

Turnour Is.

Creasey Is.

Bold Head

Swanson Is.

Blackfish Sound

Blackney Passage

Hanson Is.

Parson Is.

Harbledown Is.

Beware Passage

Baronet Passage

Growler Cove

Cracroft Point

West Cracroft Is.

Boat Bay

Robson Bight

Tsitika River

JOHNSTONE STRAIT

9:00 A.M.

11:30 A.M.

7:00 A.M.

5:30 A.M.

9:00 P.M.

8:30 P.M.

12:30 P.M.

Izumy Rock

Kaikash Creek

Blinkhorn Peninsula

Telegraph Cove

Beaver Cove

Pearse Islands

Alert Bay

Broughton Strait

Donegal Head

Malcolm Is.

Plumper Islands

7:00 P.M.

5:30 P.M.

4:30 P.M.

VANCOUVER IS.

Miles

Kilometres

10

5

They normally swim at more than twice a killer whale's cruising speed. I once saw two Dall's porpoises swiftly navigate a narrow channel between two islands, then enter the strait — only to find themselves in the midst of Stubbs's pod. The two porpoises went crazy, darting back and forth across a self-imposed perimeter defined by killer whales that happened to be passing by. The whales were hardly moving, surfacing slowly, apparently unconcerned about the flurry of activity. Finally, the porpoises found a "hole" in the imagined perimeter and made good their escape. I doubt that the whales paid the porpoises more than passing attention. Seeing the two species together graphically illustrated the difference in temperament. The killer has nothing to fear, except possibly man. And even with man, only The Six seemed obviously wary. Any nervousness that Stubbs's pod may have had was allayed by our day-to-day contact with them.

The daily life of Stubbs's pod was typical of the various groups that regularly passed through Johnstone Strait. Summer 1974, during which we followed Stubbs's pod steadily throughout August and early September, must have included many of the incidents that a killer whale encounters again and again in his lifetime. Many days typically began like that of August 31. Through the night, at one-to-two-hour intervals, we had heard the blows as groups of orcas passed the camp. They came at 1 a.m., 2:30 a.m. and 3:45 a.m.

5:30 A.M. Whales wake us again. Heading west, they pass the rocks in front of the camp. I slip on my boots and step naked outside the tent into the dew-laden twilight. Vatcher comes out, half-dressed, then Driscoll. We see Wavy and Nicola — definitely Stubbs's pod. The fins are barely visible at the edge of the pink-grey mist, but the sound of their blowing carries for miles, alerting a few ravens and seagulls to the predawn patrol. A husky harbour seal pokes its bald head out of the water, looks around, sees the killers and darts off. Sleeping fishermen are oblivious, snug in their one-boat coves along the Vancouver Island shore. We crawl back to bed.

6:30 A.M. Sunrise. Vatcher fires up the Coleman stove. Driscoll and Krofchak prepare a logger's breakfast for seven. As usual, we are just sitting down to eat when the whales enter the bight, passing the camp. Again, Stubbs's pod.

We had vowed to get an early start that morning — "but this is ridiculous," said Hunter. For the last week of August, we had hired the 80-foot *Betty L*, an ex-halibut and packer boat. The *Betty L* enabled us to travel with the whales through any sea and in comfort. It had a roomy, stable platform for filming. On six successive days, as we accompanied Stubbs's pod from morning until night, the whales seemed to have accepted the big packer. Today, August 31, the last day that we could afford our charter, the plan was to get moving as soon as anyone saw or heard a whale. We would have to hurry, for the whales were leaving the bight. The *Betty L* was waiting. We gulped our coffee or tea and left our pancakes browning in a greasy fry pan.

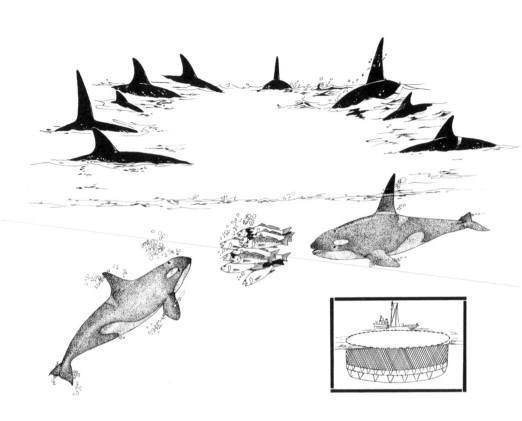

Killer whales herding salmon like seine fishermen

7 A.M. On the whales' trail. As we stand on deck, the cold dew-laden air — stronger than any coffee — slaps our faces awake. Today, as every day the past week, the whales' early morning seems reserved for active feeding. Hunter was mildly annoyed: "We skip *our* breakfast to come out here and watch *them* eat." Travelling steadily in ones and twos, the whales are spread across the strait. They take three or four breaths, then deep-dive for up to seven minutes. We are moving with about half of Stubbs's pod. The others? They are out of visual, perhaps audio, range. But this is typical. We have learned that even though the pod or family group is a tight unit, it is constantly expanding and contracting, depending, at least partly, on pod activities. As a unit, pods tend to rest and play together and feed together on marine mammals and large schools of fish. Superpods probably group feed, too, and socialize while they travel from one area to another. The small subgroups seem more limited in their range of activities, spending most of their time chasing and diving for fish individually.

8:30 A.M. The whales stop at the surface. Six of them are lying there, waiting. Two bulls bob their heads and look around. A youngster leaps. Across the strait, out of Blackfish Sound, more whales are approaching.

8:45 A.M. It's the remainder of Stubbs's pod. About 16 whales are now grouped together in a tight cluster — to rest. As with previous sleep behaviour that we have observed, the whales' breathing and surfacing is almost perfectly synchronized.

9 A.M. Nap time over, the pod assumes the hunting formation. Like marching soldiers, they present a formidable line, stretching about a mile out from Vancouver Island's shore into Johnstone Strait. The tallest dorsal fins, those of the bulls, are near one end, out in the strait. From there, fin heights step downward to the porpoiselike fins of the juveniles and calves. An exception is a young calf that travels beside its mother. The whales, including the calves, are stationed 60 to 100 feet apart.

Meanwhile, on the *Betty L*, we moved ahead of Stubbs's pod, planning to await their approach. I signalled skipper David Stanhope to cut the engines.

9:15 A.M. The whales are advancing at only three to four knots, yet they seem threatening as they shoot out of the water like thick blunt rockets. As they sound, they smash their fat heads almost defiantly against the water, making choppy waves. Some whack their tails on the surface before diving. Several juveniles and calves are hitting their tails too — almost as skilfully as their elders.

Two large seine boats, roused from their berths by the sun and by the sights and sounds of the dorsal-fin parade, steamed toward the centre of the strait, spinning out their heavy black net in front of the approaching whales.

9:30 A.M. Ignoring the fishermen, the whales form a wide circle. The bulls at one end of the line speed ahead, gradually turning in and slowing down, leading the pod into a netlike formation.

The two seiners, less than 50 yards from the whales, pursed their circular sets, and the big clanking steel drums hauled in the cork line. The fishermen smashed their plungers on the water, as is the custom when the net is being pulled in, to keep the salmon from escaping under the boat.

9:35 A.M. The whale circle closes, the odd whale still smacking its tail. Several long, silvery salmon, suddenly trapped, begin leaping, boiling in the cauldron. We watch as each whale, in turn, enters the arena.

It was the first time that I had seen killer whales apparently herding the salmon. It seemed that the whales had set their own net and then, by slapping their tails — much as the fishermen did with their plungers — had kept the salmon together. The whales and fishermen worked side by side, demonstrating the similarity of their fishing methods. The fishermen had indeed used the whales, grabbing part of what was perhaps a large salmon school for themselves. The fishermen's catch that morning was big. We couldn't know how the whales had done, but their exhilaration a moment later may have indicated success.

10:30 A.M. The whales break the circle, fall out of formation and scatter. Three-ton bulls leap clear of the water, one after another, falling forward in a belly-flop smash or, twisting as they fall, flopping down on their sides. Two youngsters thrust their tails high, as if standing on their heads underwater. Other whales bob their heads, stand poised and seem to be dog-paddling with their flippers.

On the deck of the *Betty L*, we watched the spectacle, while Glennon and Vatcher filmed it. To Hunter, it was all a "stage show . . . a regular song-and-dance routine," one that he was certain Busby Berkeley had choreographed for these "little fat men in their black-and-white suits." In some crazy way, it accurately described the whales' demeanour.

10:45 A.M. Fifty yards from the boat, a bull surfaces, belly up, squirming his nearly 25-foot-long frame while the water washes over his sun-reflecting white belly. We study him through binoculars. Propelling himself with his broad tail, he backstrokes toward us, and the water churns and swirls in wild confusion. He bats his six-foot-long disc-shaped flippers — those giant ping-pong paddles — against the water and creates an awesome disturbance. The bull's reckless play and the four-knot current are carrying him ever closer to the stern of the *Betty L*. A moment later, the bull seems surprised when he realizes that we're peering at him. Quickly, he rights himself, regains his composure and shoots off a thick vapour cloud. When the fog clears, we see his big dorsal fin, tottering in the breeze. It's Wavy, the first whale we met in the summer of 1973.

A senior bull in Stubbs's pod, Wavy was not accustomed to being caught off guard. He was somewhat curious, snooping on us from time to time, but he had never stayed long. After we surprised him, he sounded for a full five minutes, and all the bulls suddenly left the playing field. It was noon. During the morning, the pod had fed individually, slept, fed together, then played. Now they were restless. When they appeared again, they were all together out in the strait, about a mile away. A conference was being called to order. The probable topics for discussion: Where to eat today? Where to go? What to do?

The tall, dominant black fins of the bulls, surrounded by all the others, looked a bit like a cluster of high rises in the centre of a city. Standing on the deck of the *Betty L*, we awaited the decision from on high. The whales milled around, churned the water, snorted and then, without warning, took off.

> 12:30 P.M. Nomads on the move again. The pod falls into several subgroups of one to six individuals. Eighty yards ahead of the group, Wavy leaps three times in a row, his big dorsal flopping back and forth almost like the swinging door of an old-time saloon. Sturdy bobs his head. Often, when the pod begins moving or turns around abruptly, older pod members will leap and bob. Perhaps they are checking to see if the entire pod is present, taking a head count. In any case, this has become a signal to us that they are re-grouping, changing their direction and, sometimes, their activities.

Stubbs's pod had commenced its typical travelling pattern — loping along in a more or less straight path, surfacing every four to five minutes to take three or four breaths over the space of a minute and a half. Scattered in odd clusters over an area about a half-mile square, the pod moved at a speed of three to four knots, following the coastline. The younger ones sometimes nudged the shore. The bulls stayed almost a mile from shore.

Following them in the *Betty L* that afternoon, we examined the various subgroups of Stubbs's pod one by one. We were hoping to gain some insight into the social organization of the killer whale pod. From studies of other intelligent social mammals, we know that a premium is placed on individual experience and learning, and thus great respect and deference is given old animals. If killer whales have a ranking order, age probably figures prominently in determining it.

Yet during several seasons of observation, I have seen little evidence of the dominance of older pod members over junior ones. I have never witnessed dominance displays or, for that matter, any sign of intraspecies aggression — as fearsome and well equipped for carnage as orcas may be in their predatory habits. The spirit of the killer whale pod is cooperation, rather than competition. Fostering this spirit of cooperation would be a strict ranking system, with every animal knowing its place in the hierarchy.

Among orcas, there must exist strong killing inhibitions to protect weaker pod members from intraspecies aggression. Even in play, a calf could be endangered by a rambunctious senior bull. And no pod member could defend itself against an angry bull. We can compare orca's strong killing inhibitions to those of the wolf and other large social predatory mammals, of which ethologist Konrad Lorenz writes: "Large predators . . . which live permanently in a society, as wolves or lions do, must possess reliable . . . inhibition mechanisms [against intraspecies aggression, mechanisms] independent of the changing moods of the individual. And so we find the strangely moving paradox that the most bloodthirsty predators, particularly the wolf . . . are among the animals with the most reliable killing inhibitions in the world. When my grandchildren play with other children of the same age, supervision by an adult is advisable, but I do not hesitate to leave them unsupervised in the company of our big Chow-Alsatian dogs, whose hunting instincts are of the bloodthirstiest. The social inhibitions on which I rely . . . are the heritage of the wolf."

Most pod subgroups seem to be built around cows. Some contained only a cow and a calf; others also had an older juvenile and a bull. We followed a killer whale nuclear family — a bull, cow and calf. We watched the trio blowing together and compared their sizes.

Sturdy's towering 10-foot-high blow turned to mist and hung suspended in midair as his 5-foot-high dorsal fin sliced through the thick of it. He pushed up effortlessly, and his broad back seemed to go on forever before he finally sounded. At the other extreme, the tiny calf had to poke its whole head out of the water to manage a safe breath. The calf blew perhaps two feet high, about twice as high as its foot-high fin. The cow blew nearly as high as the big male; her dorsal was only about two feet tall.

The size of a killer whale is misleading when viewed in the normal breathing posture. One sees only the tip of the iceberg — from the "forehead" to the saddle patch. Another third of the body length and seven-eighths of the total bulk are underwater.

One also obtains a false impression of the relative size of bulls and mature cows because of the bulls' tall dorsal fins. Bull dorsals stand more than twice as high as those of mature cows, yet a bull grows only about 20 percent longer than a cow. Among 16 adults in a 20-member pod stranded at Estevan Point on Vancouver Island in June 1945, the males' average length was just under 23 feet, while the females averaged less than 20 feet. Record lengths for the species have been reported by Japanese whalers in the northwestern Pacific — bulls at 31 1/2 feet, with an estimated weight of nine tons, and females at 27 feet, estimated at five or six tons.

Compared to the two adults, the calf looked like a porpoise: barely eight feet long, weighing less than half a ton, having a tiny fin and a pointy head and lacking a saddle patch. Yet the eye patch and the striking contrast between back and belly marked it as a young orca. This particular calf was very young: Those areas that are white in an older animal were tan-yellow, with a slight pinkish orange hue. Soon the deep colours would fade to ivory, becoming as bleached white as an adult before the calf is one year old.

The nuclear family seemed devoted to the care and feeding of the calf. Swimming in the elders' shadows, the calf was nestled in a kind of travelling playpen formed by the two adults. Sturdy seemed to be guarding the perimeter. His position relative to the calf varied, but he was never more than 30 feet away. The cow stayed even closer and kept rigidly positioned in relation to her calf. She led the way. The calf, at her side and a little behind, tagged along almost awkwardly.

This common cow-calf positioning is most conducive to nursing. Imagine the calf nosing along underwater and sighting the mother's dramatic markings on the underside of her streamlined body to find her two mammary teats, hidden in slits far back of her navel. The hungry calf presses its mouth against the teats, and the mother squirts a jet of concentrated milk down its throat. About 50 percent fat, whale milk also contains nearly six times as much protein as human milk.

The calf – born that spring after about a 17-month gestation period – would nurse another year, maybe two. While it had most of its teeth, the calf would continue cutting new ones at the front as it was being weaned on fish. After the nursing period, the calf would spend several years with its mother, while occasionally engaging in the activities of adolescent and adult pod members. The youngster, playful and intensely curious, would have much to learn en route to maturity, at approximately age 14. The cow-calf bond is the strongest pairing in the orca pod and, according to Bigg, may be a permanent arrangement.

A number of killer whales have given birth in captivity. Two pregnant cows captured at Pender Harbour in April 1968 were sent to Marine World Africa U.S.A., where they delivered stillborn calves. According to Ellis, who was working at Pender Harbour at the time: "The two cows were big animals, and when they hoisted them into the sling to move them, both were suspected of being pregnant. After a month at Pender Harbour, the two animals were not eating. It was a gamble, but the arrangements to fly them to California had already been made." Less than two months after arrival, the cow called Bonnie gave birth to a perfectly formed dead calf, then died herself. "They did tests on the other animal, Kianu," said Ellis, "and found she was not as far along in her pregnancy. But they kept working her, training her, jumping her . . . and she finally had her stillborn calf." Kianu survived.

In the early afternoon of Feburary 28, 1977, Marineland of the Pacific's performing female Corky II delivered the first orca to be conceived and born alive in captivity. No one knew that she was pregnant, except perhaps the father, fellow performer Orky II. Corky was a large animal, and the approximately 450-pound calf did not show. At lunch on the day she gave birth, a Marineland trainer had joked, "She's probably pregnant, she's so bitchy." Returning from lunch, someone noticed a tiny tail protruding from Corky's underside and went screaming through the halls. The male calf, 7 1/2 feet long, was delivered in about 2 1/2 hours. He was assisted to the surface by Orky – who initially functioned like the auntie in captive dolphin births. Overall, the parents seemed curious, even cooperative, but in a passive, uncommitted way. Corky never offered her teats, and the calf never tried to nurse. On the eighth day, he was force-fed. He was already losing weight. By the end of the second week, he had lost about 100 pounds, or a quarter of his birth weight. On the sixteenth day, he died. The autopsy showed acute vocal pneumonia and bowel stasis as the immediate cause of death, while United States Navy research veterinarian Sam H. Ridgway, examining the brain, found "haemorrhagic areas on the surface of cerebral cortex and areas of cerebral edema." Ridgway said that in his view, "though we can't know for certain, brain damage was due to a difficult birth." Marineland curator Tom Otten described the birth as "somewhat protracted. After the tail had emerged, several times the calf fought Corky's labour, pushing back partway into the womb. After birth, the calf's behaviour seemed erratic."

Nineteen months later, on October 31, 1978, the stork again visited Marineland's Orky and Corky. This time, the baby was born headfirst. Again, Orky helped the calf to the surface. "The birth seemed normal, and the baby healthy," said Otten. "We had big hopes."

Then things began to go wrong. Brad Andrews, who succeeded Otten as Marineland curator in 1979, explained: "The calf was trying to feed all around Corky's eye patch and at the side of her mouth, but not around the nipple. He couldn't figure it out, and Corky wasn't helping. Again, Corky didn't seem committed to keeping the youngster alive."

This time, the parents were separated from the male calf on the sixth day. The calf was force-fed. "Taking the parents away was a long shot, but what could we do?" said Andrews. The baby soon developed gastric problems from the formula, and then infections invaded the lungs and liver, and colitis set in. He began losing weight — again about 100 pounds. The baby was attended by trainers and staff 24 hours a day until his death at 11 days of age.

Both calves died because Corky had probably never learned how to nurse and to care for a calf. Like other social mammals, killer whales seem to need a long period of learning, and Corky had had no one to teach her. Yet Ellis and other researchers I have talked to wonder: What was Corky doing all those years in the wild? She was an adolescent when she was caught in Pender Harbour in December 1969. At 12 feet long, she was about three or four years old. Thus for three or four years, she had travelled with her pod — Top Notch's pod — which at the time included mature cows and young calves. She had probably observed several family births. Was it Corky's lack of experience and knowledge that prevented her from nursing her calves, or was it her lack of interest and commitment brought on by almost a decade of captivity? An auntie may in fact be crucial for a successful birth — if only to provide companionship to a mother exhausted by labour and a calf new to the world. But would an auntie guarantee a successful birth in captivity? Or would the prenatal and postnatal need for privacy and space then become even more acute?

Another subgroup we followed that afternoon contained Nicola and a pair of youngsters. They were active, even playful, and quite approachable — especially the two youngsters. By early August 1974, Nicola's calf had disappeared. He was too young to have taken off on his own. The little calf with white spots on its back was never seen again. It was the first apparent fatality in Stubbs's pod during the time we'd known them. Raising killer whales may not be easy, even in the wild.

Approaching closer, we recognized the two youngsters as The Twins — a pair of whales that had already achieved some notoriety for their playfulness around our boats. They earned their name because we always saw them together, but they were likely not twins. Multiple birth for killer whales is probably rare. A twin orca birth was apparently witnessed by loggers at Von Donnop Lagoon, Cortes Island, British Columbia, in March 1949. Unfortunately, the mother, her twin calves and two males in the pod were stranded in the lagoon by a low tide. All of them died.

We had met The Twins in 1973 when they were late in their first or early in their second year. They were still under the care and tutelage of their mother, only occasionally travelling with other pod members. This was the case today, Nicola having assumed responsibility as their auntie.

Scientists have studied the auntie relationship among captive bottlenose dolphins. The dolphin auntie initially acts as a midwife, pushing the newborn to the surface to take its first breath. From then on, the auntie becomes a kind of godmother. The role of killer whale aunties may be similar; the two species belong to the same family, Delphinidae, and live in similar social groups. Yet behavioural observations of orca aunties are limited. For one thing, they may not always be females. During the twin birth at Von Donnop Lagoon, the smaller male orca played auntie, bringing the newborn calves to the surface on his back, one at a time, and supporting them until they managed the first breath. At Marineland, it was the father, Orky, who brought Corky's calves to the surface. In Stubbs's pod, we sometimes observed senior bulls travelling with calves for several hours at a time. With killer whales, though the cow-calf bond is the strongest, all pod members occasionally accompany the young.

Today, it looked as though Nicola had her flippers full. The two youngsters were all over the place. Twice, The Twins turned around and headed right for us. The first time, they stopped 60 feet short of the *Betty L.* The second time, they were steaming for the bow. Nicola raced after them, surfacing beneath them. We saw splashing water, tails flying up and flashing — a sudden scuffle. Then, as if nothing had happened, the three whales continued on together. After that, The Twins stayed in line.

Besides the various subgroups, we found one cow that stayed off to the side, lagging behind the rest of the pod. We might have overlooked her were it not for her long surface rest stops and frequent spouting. It was, of course, Stubbs, the loner, the old female — "Stumbellina, the ugly duckling," as Hunter persisted in calling her.

Was she an outcast? Stubbs had mostly kept to herself as long as we had known her. Though all the whales except newborn calves travelled alone at times, by summer 1974 this was Stubbs's characteristic pose. Still, she sometimes participated in pod activities. She slept with them. Occasionally, she played auntie to The Twins or to the other youngsters in the pod, sharing the responsibility with Nicola.

Stubbs's manner seemed to be that of a sick or ageing whale. She moved slowly, never indulged in speed swimming, leaping or tail lobbing. She was breathing up to 10 times during the routine four-to-five-minute breathing cycle, when most whales found three or four breaths sufficient. More than any other orca, she spent long periods lying on the surface. The rest of the pod often went on without her. Following the group, we sometimes wouldn't see Stubbs again until late afternoon; the pod would slow down, and she would catch up. Other times, we discovered Stubbs first, apparently alone; by staying with her, we eventually met up with the others.

She impressed us because she seemed a gentle, almost unperturbable whale. If her scars were man-made, she bore no grudge. She showed no objection to our presence — though perhaps it was a moot point whether she was friendly or simply didn't have the energy to avoid us. In late 1973 and early 1974, we had been able to approach her in both the canoe and the Zodiac while she lay on the surface for those long stretches. But from the *Betty L*, it seemed impossible. The big packer boat was difficult to manoeuvre, and Stubbs sounded every time we moved to within 50 feet. Almost every day, Glennon talked about wanting to take close-up film of the old whale from the stable shooting platform of the *Betty L*.

It was late afternoon on our daylong journey with Stubbs's pod. Beginning that morning in Robson Bight, we had followed the pod, heading west along the Vancouver Island shore to Kaikash Creek, then crossing the strait to Hanson Island. They had swum east, then north around Hanson Island and were now heading northwest into Blackfish Sound. In eight hours, they had covered about 12 1/2 miles, an average of 1 1/2 miles per hour. There had been two 15-minute rest periods. Another half hour had been spent playing. Most of the time, they had travelled steadily, probably foraging, moving at an average speed of two miles per hour. Only occasionally had there been a speed burst — perhaps up to 10 miles per hour. Probably the fastest swimming came during play periods. To jump clear of the water, an orca must reach an exit speed of at least 32 feet per second, or about 22 miles per hour. (Top speed for the orca is estimated at 30 miles per hour.) The pod was moving slowly. In a 24-hour day, the pod might travel some 35 to 50 miles. The whales usually followed the coastline, since the strait and island passages were narrow. Here, it was easy for us to keep track of them. In the open waters of Queen Charlotte Strait, where we had occasionally followed them, it was not so easy. Still, they tended to travel as a group in one direction for several hours before turning or reversing direction.

After almost two summers observing the movements of Stubbs's pod, we were beginning to see certain overall travel patterns. The pod seemed to work over a given area for a period of several days or weeks, then move to a different range. The main area was the western Johnstone Strait/Blackfish Sound region, with Robson Bight the centre. This seemed home range for Stubbs and Top Notch, at least during the summer months. But periodically, they visited other regions off northeastern Vancouver Island.

In August 1975, in the northerly Rivers Inlet/Bella Bella region, Ellis was tracking killer whales for the Canadian Pacific Biological Station, under Michael Bigg. Besides occasional visits by Stubbs and Top Notch, Ellis found Hooker's pod more often than we found it in Johnstone Strait — also C, D and G pods. Later, I pod would be found regularly in the Port Hardy region. According to Bigg, 12 pods shared the various regions off northeastern Vancouver Island. He found that while there were no individual pod territories, the concept of territoriality could be applied to larger populations of orcas. This became evident in 1974 and 1975 when Bigg extended the photographic census of whales into southern B.C. waters. He found new groups of whales that appeared to share a territory in much the same way as the northern Vancouver Island whales. There seemed to be two distinct multipod, or community, territories in British Columbia — one off northern Vancouver Island, the other off southern Vancouver Island and in Puget Sound. The boundary was Campbell River/Seymour Narrows, near the eastern entrance to Johnstone Strait. Besides the 12 pods resident to the northern territory, three more pods stayed to the south. Sharing community territories, resident pods would often travel and socialize together. Some resident pods would occasionally stray north or south of the border, but they would never form superpods with whales from the other territory. In addition to the northern and southern residents, Bigg found certain transient pods that would periodically enter the coastal areas from the open sea and pass through the two community territories. The transients never stayed long and usually wouldn't appear again for months, maybe a year.

4:30 P.M. Hanging from the spreaders of the *Betty L*, Hunter is the first to sight the transients moving toward us. We are heading due west in Blackfish Sound, and the transients are coming fast out of the northwest. There are only three animals. The big bull has a deep V-shaped notch about one-third of the way down the trailing edge of his dorsal fin. We have never seen them before. In a matter of minutes, they will cross the path of Stubbs's pod. "It's as if they're another species of whale," says Vatcher, as we stand on deck watching. The pods totally ignore each other. They cross paths. In a few minutes, the transients are gone.

On several occasions, I made underwater recordings of transient pods swimming through Johnstone Strait. Their vocalizations differed from the residents' and were certainly much sparser. When we saw transients crossing the residents' path, it was difficult to determine if there was any interchange between the two pods. The sounds collided. To us, observing them on the surface, the transients and Stubbs's pod seemed strangers, two bands of nomads passing in the desert. According to Bigg, the transients are weird pods. They look different. Transient dorsal fins are more pointed and have a bulge on the leading edge. Transients never socialize with residents. Unlike residents, they have a very broad range, and there is no way to predict their movements or their behaviour. But transients have never been observed fighting with resident pods. The territoriality of killer whales, as we know it, cannot be compared to that of land mammals. With orcas, community territories are apparently not exclusive domains with defended borders but, rather, home ranges, areas through which certain pods habitually roam.

Killer whales obviously have strong attachments to members of their own pod. Like other social mammals, they feel most secure and content among intimate friends and family, rather than among casual acquaintances or pods that they have never met. Even when resident pods sharing the same community territory meet and mingle, each animal tends to remain with its respective group. When pods mix, it is usually only for a few hours. And always, the individual pods re-form, eventually going off by themselves. Bigg's research covers more than 500 encounters along the B.C. coast, and he has rarely witnessed pod switching — long-term or permanent immigration from one pod to another.

> 5:30 P.M. Playtime again. The whole pod has gathered on the surface to relish the late-afternoon sun. Sturdy floats belly up. Sixty feet from him, a couple of youngsters flop onto their backs, bumping into each other. Excited, they begin rolling over and over. They charge over to a third whale, a female lying on her back. They nudge her and then race away, returning to Sturdy's side to lie motionless for a while on the surface.

Do whales bask in the sun? Perhaps for the sensual feel of it, but probably not for warmth. At 43 degrees F, Johnstone Strait is cold, but killer whales thrive in much colder water. Large numbers of orcas live near the polar ice caps, some right to the limits of the fast ice. Orca's three-to-four-inch-thick coat of blubber keeps him warm.

> 5:40 P.M. One calf keeps jumping on Wavy's blowhole as he basks on the surface. The big bull is patient with the youngster, but on the fourth attempt, he abruptly rotates his body to one side and whacks his dorsal across the youngster's backside. After that, the calf leaves him alone.

The youngest members of an orca pod are the most playful. Even outside of obvious playtimes, youngsters often get frisky. Our sudden appearance in a fast boat was like an invitation for them to come and romp through the waves — or so it seemed. They showed their excitement by circling us, jumping around the boat, bobbing to look at us. But bulls and older cows rarely approached close to play. When bulls played, they usually stayed alone — sometimes even away from the pod. As with many other social mammals, the older the individual, the less time was devoted to play. Stubbs, probably the oldest in her pod, was rarely observed playing.

Some play activities undoubtedly form part of sexual routines, although the week we followed Stubbs's pod, we saw no mating. In fact, orca mating in the wild has rarely been observed. Russian biologist A.V. Yablokov says that he has seen mating preceded by lengthy love play, with copulation itself lasting but a few seconds. Like dolphins and other whales (but unlike most mammals), orcas mate belly to belly — sometimes leaping out of the water in the final moments. A chance aerial photograph taken off the coast of Japan in the late 1950s showed one orca lying belly up at the surface with another on its side — joined.

> 6:30 P.M. Sitting in the large deck-level galley of the *Betty L*, the seven of us eat supper while, through open windows and doors, we watch the whales travelling on both sides of us. I suddenly under-

stand Vatcher's suggested title for our film: *Living With Killer Whales*. The feeling of togetherness has been growing in me for a week, as we moved with Stubbs's pod. Glennon is filming us relaxing and eating, and the whales are right there in the same frame. Life among a pod of orcas. I take my tea and lean against the cabin doorjamb. The smell of the sea mingles with the aroma of baked cod. Glennon is shooting from inside — Wavy and Nicola blowing beside the boat, beside me, my relaxed silhouette in the foreground. It had seemed a significant step when the whales accepted the canoe in August 1973, as Vatcher and O'Neill filmed them sleeping. For the whales to accept this massive 80-foot packer boat surprises me. Credit must go to skipper David Stanhope, who pilots the boat slowly, steadily, and is never aggressive toward the whales. Soft-spoken, bald, yet bearded, Stanhope is obviously pleased when I mention that the whales seem to love his boat, but he brushes aside compliments on his steering with his theory about the engines: "The Gardiner diesel has a very low hum and doesn't interfere with orca's sound range." What he says about the engine is, in fact, true. But whether that is what enables us to stay close to Stubbs's group for hours at a time is another matter.

7 P.M. Stubbs's pod funnels through the maze of island passages on the west side of Hanson Island. The pod is splitting up, taking different routes through the maze. Some take the high road, others the low road. We take the centre passage, following Stubbs herself, quickly losing track of the other whales. Circumnavigating some of the Plumper Islands, she seems to be taking us on a roundabout tour through a series of narrow channels. Trees, dark green and forbidding, come up close on both sides and hang over us. Even more disconcerting is the rocky bottom that we can see perhaps too clearly — purple anemones and giant orange starfish shining through strips of yellow and green-to-brown kelp. The charts say that if we keep to centre channel, we will have plenty of water to pass, but we're all standing on the bow watching the bottom come up fast. The old whale knows the way. She is smart. She lets the tide carry her. We need engines to maintain control through the swift passage. We follow her. Stubbs blows six, seven, eight times in a row, then coasts on the surface. She looks like a stray log riding the current, her broken fin a splintered piece of trunk.

Moving through the passage, I feel a camaraderie with the old whale. I wonder whether the feeling could be mutual. It is impossible to know, and perhaps there is no substance to it, no reason for me to feel the way I do. Gradually, Stubbs angles toward the *Betty L*. Five of us are lined up along the railing of the forward deck. Cradling the Eclair in his arms, Glennon is perched on the bowsprit — hanging over the water. Vatcher stands on the cabin roof filming whales and people from above. I climb the spreaders to record the action on the boat with the shotgun microphone as we all watch the big old female lumbering closer toward us.

She is truly an ugly whale. It's not just her stubby fin. She is ungainly. Silently, with morbid curiosity, we stare at the freak. It's my first close-up view of her in the harsh light of day. She is exceedingly fat around the middle and has a bulbous head and a sharply defined neck, unlike any other orca that I've seen. Hunter finally breaks the silence: "Look at the snout on her!"

Moving parallel to us, Stubbs dips just beneath the surface. She is swimming through the kelp. A yellow-brown streamer catches on the mangled edge of her fin. She turns sharply toward the *Betty L.* Glennon is filming. We are all excited. I begin whistling the simple three-note phrase that I had used with Nicola in August 1973. Everyone on the boat starts whistling it with me. At 10-second intervals, in unison, we call to Stubbs: YEEEEEEEEEEEEEE-oooo-ee!

I yell to Stanhope to cut the engines. Idling now, I am fairly certain that we can be heard. Then Stubbs comes up underneath the bow. Glennon is excited: Stubbs fills the viewfinder, and the Eclair is purring. He is filming her swimming through the water just below the surface, then coming up again and again.

It was good that we'd cut the engines. Stubbs seemed out of breath. I counted 9 breaths in a row, then down for a minute, then 12 more breaths. Every time she surfaced, we were whistling.

7:30 P.M. "Kawoof!" Stubbs blows into the camera, Glennon shooting right down her blowhole. All of us are hanging over the bow. In the split second after she breathes, we whistle to her.

At last, it comes — a cry from Stubbs — strong, piercing flute-like tones. The 2,000-Hz range is clearly audible over the low drone of the engine. She seems to be answering. For the next three blows, we repeat our whistle calls. Stubbs gives a different response each time. It's a near repeat of last year's whistling with Nicola in the canoe, but Stubbs's response is not a mimic. With all of us whistling together, there's enormous shared energy. It's one of our best moments with the whales.

8 P.M. Open water at last. Still trailing Stubbs, we spill into Johnstone Strait. Stubbs heads east, picking up speed. We fire up our engine and follow her. We are headed back toward the camp. Up ahead, blowing on the horizon a couple of miles away, we see the rest of the pod.

The wind and the sea had dropped considerably as the day and our shadows had grown long on the water. Preparing for its final descent, the sun danced down the jagged mountain edges of northern Vancouver Island. Stubbs was taking us home to Robson Bight. She cut close to shore as we neared the calm waters of the bight's western opening, opposite the campsite. The other whales had already turned. We couldn't see them. Stubbs rounded the rocky outcrop of a corner, and we followed quickly. A bit too quickly, for we suddenly burst upon a quiet, pastoral assemblage. We pulled on the reins of the *Betty L*; the engine coughed and died.

8:30 P.M. Again, the whales have stopped to rest. The pod that eats together, travels together, plays together, now sleeps. The sun is sinking. The sky and the sea have turned a molten orange and red, the colours bathe the 16 massive black bodies lying in peaceful repose. Hunter says that he is in the mood for some "heavy logging" (sawing logs, or sleeping) himself. Everyone agrees. It has been a long nonstop day in a long nonstop week with Stubbs's pod. It is growing dark, orange-red fading to purple. Soon: black.

It was a strange scene as I remember it — ethereal, dreamlike, deathly quiet. Stubbs had rejoined her pod, and the whole group lay together nose to nose, some of them almost touching. Suddenly, one of the bulls exploded: A feathery cloud of vapour shot skyward. Each drop hung there, illuminated, backlit by the sun's last rays.

Then three whales beside the bull erupted simultaneously with their giant fountains. The other bulls, Sturdy and Wavy, blew together, then Stubbs and Nicola and The Twins. In 15 seconds, they had all blown, and the whole scene was shrouded by their backlit mist. The myriad droplets drifted and spread like a cloud of feathers exploding out of a pillow. Everything seemed to be in slow motion.

9 P.M. The whales start their engines first. These night-and-day nomads, for whom family togetherness is a way of life, are on the move again. They file out of the bight like sleepy troopers on the graveyard shift. We are quiet as we watch the line of fins disappearing in the ghost shadows of twilight. Firing up the engines, we turn and chug back to camp. Tents and snug sleeping bags await us — our protection from a chill darkness unknown to the whales.

STUBBS

O n September 1 and 2, my journal entries were the same: "Empty strait; no whales." For 56 hours, Stubbs's pod had disappeared. When last seen, late on August 31, they were headed west-north-west, toward the open sea. The following day, a seine fisherman arriving from Port Hardy told us that he had seen whales, "some 40 or 50 of 'em steaming past Hardy." We wondered if Stubbs's group was among them.

Early September 3, coming out of the northwest, Stubbs's pod passed the camp. We went out to meet them. Nicola, Wavy and The Twins were in the count. Stubbs herself was not. Presuming that she was swimming off to the side or lagging behind the others, we were not concerned. Before noon, the westerlies came in rough — too rough, probably, to see a lone straggler with a chopped-off dorsal. The following day, Stubbs's pod again visited Robson Bight. The strait was sunny, with only light westerlies all day. It was the day that Hunter and his girlfriend, Shirley Thompson, dived in among the whales and filmed two youngsters streaking past them underwater. It was a high moment, culminating weeks of work, but not without the usual Hunter clowning. As the whales passed, Hunter poked his head out of the water and yelled to the rest of us waiting in the boat, anxious, wondering. But what did he say? Glennon thought that he had hollered: "I'm on it!" — meaning, presumably, the whale. Just then, one whale surfaced underneath Hunter, or as near as it could be to Hunter and not be underneath him. In fact, Hunter had said, "I've got it!" — referring to the footage.

In the evening, as the whales rested in the bight, we waited patiently for Stubbs to rejoin her pod — but she didn't show.

The following morning, September 5, Glennon, Vatcher and I took the Zodiac searching. We trailed Top Notch's pod up Blackfish Sound. At the entrance to Knight Inlet, we met Hooker's pod, and following Top Notch back to Johnstone Strait, we picked up C and D pods en route. But we wanted Stubbs's pod, with Stubbs. It was the last and probably the calmest sunny summer afternoon of the year. We nervously enjoyed the calm — sensing that the summer westerlies were already cross-fading to winter southeasters. The change often occurs abruptly on the Northwest Coast. One day, one can almost smell the coolness coming, the rain, and feel the low-pressure area forming at sea. The southeasterly pattern might not mean heavy winds or even rain, but it at least means heavy cloud cover. By that evening, clouds were invading our paradise, shaping the greyness. It was a dull sunset. The summer was beginning to live in our heads. At night, lying in our sleeping bags in the tent, we made hand-shadow pictures on the canvas walls with flashlights. We made silhouette fins of all the bulls and marked cows in Stubbs's pod, but our no-contest favourite was Stubbs. She was the star of the whale shows that we acted out on the tent walls. We still hoped to find her.

On September 6, the strait was "empty . . . no whales." Same on the seventh and the eighth. When the whales had first failed to show, we slept in, lazed through breakfast. But after a few days, we longed to be robbed of our morning granola. Every day was the same: get up late; take the Zodiac; search for whales in the afternoon; give up by dinner time; go home to bed. On the ninth, it was grey and sprinkling rain, but the calmness was holding. Returning in the Zodiac from our afternoon search party, Glennon, Vatcher and I saw spouts deep in the bight. The whales had already passed the camp and were moving toward us. In the binoculars, I saw Jacqui Krofchak near the camp, paddling the kayak hard toward shore — *away* from the whales. That should have been a tip-off, but we steered into the whales' path, turned off the engine and awaited their approach.

> SEPTEMBER 9. Five large killer whales — mature and young bulls or cows with very erect, pointed dorsal fins — advance in a line, all abreast. They are blowing quickly, slashing the water with their dorsal fins, smashing big waves with their fat, blunt heads. They are coming up fast to our boat. I feel a queasiness growing in the pit of my stomach. I am excited to see whales, but the feeling is not just excitement. (Once before, when I was alone in the dinghy on my first eye-to-eye encounter with a killer whale, I felt this way.) These whales *look* violent. The rational mind says it's purely subjective until . . .

Vatcher spoke up: "Who are these guys anyway?"
"Nobody we know," said Glennon.
"Probably just some transients," I said, controlling my paranoia.
"Don't look too friendly," Glennon finally admitted.

> The whales are almost upon us. Vatcher, Glennon and I look at each other. Our rubber Zodiac suddenly seems very small and insignificant in the path of a pack of killers. A long way from shore, we are

helpless. Therefore, all decisions belong to the whales. There's nothing for us to do but sit tight. I clutch my notebook underneath my coat and brace for the cold water, the long swim to shore. It's like waiting for a bomb to go off. Then the whales pass underneath us. It's a dud! They aren't interested in us, even slightly. An audible sigh of relief goes through the boat.

Krofchak met us on the beach. She was wet from the waist down. Her face was pale. She held out her hand to take the bowline.

"You won't believe what just happened to me!" She was a little embarrassed.

"Yes, I think I would," I replied.

Excited to see the spouts, Krofchak had paddled the kayak hard into the midst of the approaching transients, only to turn as they neared and paddle for her life. She was shivering. In her eagerness to get out of the kayak, to the safety of shore, she had fallen into the water.

Since my first close experience with a whale — in the rowboat in 1973 — I had become blasé. Stubbs and her family were not the sort of orcas to inspire panic. But since the encounter with the transient pod, I no longer laugh when I hear stories of people being, in their words, "attacked by killer whales." Based on our experiences and on all the reliable accounts, I still do not believe that killer whales are dangerous. The transients had not touched us. However, their fierce, wild appearance could inspire fear. The resident whale pods that we knew off northeastern and southern Vancouver Island appeared to be fish-eaters — large families of killer whales that followed the salmon schools and came to know the fishermen, boaters and whale watchers who frequented the same waters. The transients travelled in much smaller groups — usually three to five members per pod — over vast areas. Passing through the inland water-ways only occasionally, they frequented the remote open waters of west coast Vancouver Island. Perhaps unfamiliar with humans, the transients' reaction to them could be less predictable than the residents'. Moreover, the transients were known to be opportunistic feeders. Stomach studies of orcas stranded or caught off west coast Vancouver Island and observations of open-ocean feeding activities show a diet of, among other things, seals, sea lions, porpoises and minke whales. Probably in part because of this proclivity for hard-to-catch large-mammal flesh, the transients seem to be more aggressive. Ellis and many other divers have stated that they won't swim with open-ocean transient orcas. On our 1974 film expedition, we wanted to try to film these marine mammal-eaters in action off the west coast of Vancouver Island. it was a long shot — it is a vast area, and killer whale sightings are infrequent. In any case, we'd be able to film Steller sea lions and perhaps the grey whales, both commonly found off the west coast. There, both are potential food for killer whales.

It's only 125 miles by air from Johnstone Strait to Long Beach, on the west coast of Vancouver Island. By road, the journey is long and roundabout — some 300 miles. At Telegraph Cove, we tossed the Zodiac on the roof of Hunter's ancient Pontiac Strato Chief and headed south and west down the Nimpkish Valley. By summer 1974, Hunter's noble Pontasaurus was on its last legs. "No shocks," said Hunter, as we bounced down the first stretch — some four hours and 95 miles of potholes. The Pontasaurus became, by Hunter's description, the "Ponta-sore-ass," but it carried us and our gear. As we approached Campbell River, the gravel logging road became paved highway across the 8,000-foot-high mountains and deep forests of interior Vancouver Island. We headed due west. As we wound down the mountains, the terrain turned more rugged and wild, and the trees were windswept and gnarled. At the wheel, Hunter, our guide, talked nonstop about walking through the miniature wind-stunted forests, watching grey whales from the Wickaninnish Inn and roasting salmon on the vast expanse of sandy Long Beach. Growing up in Victoria, at the southern tip of Vancouver Island, Hunter had often visited the west coast. He had been struck by its "raw, primal beauty" and had always wanted to shoot a film there. Wild it was. But after two months of camping in the Johnstone Strait wilds, we felt that we had returned at least partway to civilization — staying in a clean motel in nearby Tofino, indulging in hot showers and iced drinks.

First day out, we headed for Sea Lion Rocks. Dressed in diving gear, Hunter and Thompson were prepared for anything — except, perhaps, trying to break up a fight between sea lions and killer whales. Vatcher and I, cameraman and sound man, respectively, were ready to record whatever happened on the three-day Long Beach excursion. Like four pack animals, we portaged the Zodiac plus engine, diving tanks and film equipment across that vast expanse of Long Beach at low tide. Launching the Zodiac bow first through the oncoming surf, we were nearly turned broadside — and swamped — three times. As we poked through the breakers, the sun reflected off the high crests and floated inside the long swells that made us more than a little dizzy after the short, stiff chop of Johnstone Strait. Yet it was good to be back on the water. In an hour, we were approaching two barren rocky islets that rose like black fortresses from the sea. There were sea lions everywhere.

> SEPTEMBER 11. The stench is overpowering. The barking, snarling and howling is deafening. Three dozen Steller sea lions, those tawny-maned blubbery giants indigenous to the North Pacific, stand their ground, eyeing us. They look formidable. I can feel the hair prickle on the back of my neck. The largest bull rears his head and bellows above the others, defying us to come closer. More than 10 feet long, weighing about a ton, he is easily twice the size of the largest grizzly bear on record. Yet I know that he is more afraid of us than we are of him, that if we go closer, all the sea lions will retreat into the water.

Hunter backed the Zodiac close to the rocks as Vatcher swung the Arriflex camera to his shoulder and fired away. I held the microphone over the side of the Zodiac, recording the roar of the lions through the din of the waves smashing on the rocks.

In sea lion society, the top bull on each rock is king. Young bulls and juveniles in nonbreeding colonies, called haul-outs, might struggle for the top playfully, a game of king-of-the-castle, but mature bulls, fighting for control of their patch of rock, battle on the rookeries as a matter of life and death. Driven by the mating instinct, warring bulls sometimes crush and kill young pups, and an even larger number of pups die by drowning during storms. As a result, there are often rotting carcasses on the rocks, and their foul smell is compounded by the smell of excrement. Only the high tides or heavy rains or wind periodically clear the decks.

Steller sea lions are the largest sea lions in the world. They live only in the North Pacific and the Bering Strait, roaming sometimes thousands of miles along the coastal rim. In British Columbia and Alaska, they tend to move north in the spring and summer to inaccessible areas to breed. In the fall, they go south, ranging along the coast while they feed. Their diet is wide and various and gets them in constant trouble with fishermen. While killer whales have been fired upon from time to time for alleged offences, sea lions have been subjected to all-out war. For most of this century, fishermen have conducted Steller purges, many off the B.C. coast. Beginning in the 1920s, Canada's federal fisheries department helped organize machine-gun expeditions that eliminated thousands each year. According to Michael Bigg and University of British Columbia zoologist H. Dean Fisher, B.C.'s Stellers have failed to recover from these purges, which continued into the 1960s. Although Steller sea lions are not an endangered species, the current B.C. population of 5,000 adults and 900 pups is about half what it was in 1950.

The sea lion purges ended when the Stellers' feeding habits were finally examined. Stomach studies by U.S. biologist Victor B. Scheffer and Canadian marine scientist David J. Spalding revealed a varied diet, obviously that of an opportunistic predator: squid, octopus, sand lance, flounder, pollock, sculpin, cod, small sharks, skates, perch and other fish. They were found to eat hake and lamprey eel, which are salmon predators. Most important, Spalding's exhaustive study showed that B.C.'s three big commercial fish — herring, salmon and halibut — were found in a relatively small percentage of sea lion stomachs. Spalding concluded that all of B.C.'s Steller sea lions and harbour seals together eat only about 2 1/2 percent of man's annual salmon catch and 4 percent of his herring catch. "Predation at this level," he wrote, "is believed to be of negligible importance in the reduction of existing salmon and herring stocks."

Still, a decade after Spalding's study, many commercial fishermen along the B.C. coast complained about sea lions — much more than about killer whales — and many frankly admitted shooting them. Fisher's study sites near Long Beach have been "shot up" a number of times; researchers find the bullet-ridden carcasses rotting on the rocks. "As soon as we get the money to do a behaviour study," said Fisher ruefully, "people get the idea we're breeding them or something." The penalty for killing a sea lion in Canadian waters is a fine of up to $1,000 or up to 12 months in jail — unless a fisherman has caught a sea lion stealing fish, breaking lines or mucking about the gear.

"Sea lions are a problem for fishermen," Bigg told me on one of my periodic visits to the Pacific Biological Station in Nanaimo. "They follow the boats and take fish off the line. Usually, one or two animals learn that they don't have to fish much, they just have to follow a boat. I've got friends who fish, friends kindly disposed toward animals. They say it drives you crazy sometimes. You get a bite, and there's a big smiley on there. Next thing, you see a puff behind you, a sea lion snorting, going down, coming up, kicking, throwing the fish all over the place. If you give him a couple of fish out of the kindness of your heart, he stays with you all day. Well, it doesn't take much of that, and a guy doesn't like sea lions anymore. But for the most part, the sea lions aren't a bother. Most live in remote areas. It's just the few individuals who learn the trick of following a boat that are a nuisance."

When I talked with Fisher at the University of British Columbia a few years later, he described a device that he was developing with a private company which he thought might solve the sea lion problem. It is an underwater speaker that plays recorded killer whale sounds to bothersome sea lions.

The idea is not new. In June 1970, Alaskan biologists James F. Fish and John S. Vania experimented by playing orca sounds to white whales, or belugas. Every year, the belugas swimming up Alaska's Kvichak River preyed on large numbers of young red salmon as they migrated out to sea. Fish and Vania found that when they broadcast killer whale sounds through underwater speakers mounted in the river, the belugas would turn and head back to sea. At the same time that the beluga experiments were taking place, U.S. biologist William C. Cummings and psychologist Paul O. Thompson of the Naval Undersea Center were testing killer whale sounds on California grey whales. Like the belugas, the greys turned and swam away. In October 1974, South African ornithologist Peter G.H. Frost tried playing killer whale sounds to groups of jackass penguins swimming on the surface near Cape Town. Each time he played the sounds, the response was immediate: The penguins formed into a tight group and exhibited "synchronous high-speed 'porpoising,'" which Frost termed "obvious antipredator response." Penguins eat fish, but they are not a problem for fishermen in South African waters. South Africa's jackass penguin is, in fact, an endangered species. Frost's study was funded by the Society for the Prevention of Cruelty to Animals to see whether orca sounds would keep penguins away from oil slicks. It seems they can.

As for sea lions, they, too, run from killer whale sounds, but Dean Fisher said that there are problems in developing a device that B.C. fishermen can use because the recorded killer whale sounds seem to scare away both sea lions and smileys. "And in time," said Fisher, "some smart gill-netter will find he can use killer whale sounds to drive salmon into his net — an unfortunate effect from the viewpoint of the Department of Fisheries and Oceans. But if we can figure out exactly what frequencies the sea lions respond to, maybe we can filter out the part of the signal salmon respond to."

"It's not as simple as it might appear," biologist and orca sound researcher John Ford told me in his basement laboratory at the University of British Columbia. "Sometimes I play killer whale sounds to Stellers, and they get really excited, but instead of running, they come right over to the boat and start mobbing the underwater speaker." At other times, Ford said, the sea lions didn't respond at all, and he expressed some doubt about the effectiveness of playing orca sounds recorded in one area to sea lions living elsewhere. With different orca dialects, it's possible that the lions would not respond to unfamiliar sounds. Also, the sounds might not be associated with feeding behaviour. It is just possible that playing sounds from a pod of fish-eating killer whales would elicit no reaction from even a timid sea lion.*

Riding the swells off Sea Lion Rocks, we wondered if the killer whales would show. Hunter had heard that whales periodically patrolled the rocks. He told us about a "showdown between killers and lions, which happened on these very rocks." A few years ago, his friend Wayne Campbell, a B.C. Provincial Museum biologist, had been observing the Stellers when orcas suddenly appeared out of nowhere. Circling the rocks, they were patiently waiting while the tide slowly rose, as if knowing that this would force the sea lions into the water. "One by one," said Hunter, "the sea lions jumped to their deaths. Then one killer breached with a massive Steller in his jaws." Hunter shook his head, opening his mouth in imitation. "With a single chomp, he converted the victim into two bite-sized pieces — wolfing down one still-squirming half."

Hunter had hoped to witness just such a confrontation and, failing that, thought he might film the sea lions underwater. "But only if conditions are just right," he said. Despite having swum with killer whales on two occasions, Hunter was nervous about the lions. "Killer whales are smart, curious yet cautious around divers. But a sea lion's curiosity is like a playful puppy's — and a one-ton playful pup could be dangerous!"

In Johnstone Strait, we had heard about an abalone diver who had been thrown from the water by one such oversized puppy and had sustained a few broken ribs. Hunter himself had had a near tangle with a young sea lion only weeks earlier on a dive with Stan Waterman. Out of the blue void the sea lion had come, mouth ajar, gnashing its teeth, stopping just short of Hunter's face mask. It was a big bluff by a little sea lion, but Hunter's account of it helped me to understand his reluctance to jump into the water with the big bulls of Long Beach. These animals might be ungainly and timid of man on land, but once in the sea, they became acrobatic torpedoes, full of daring, seemingly fearless.

Hunter's dilemma was soon resolved by the rising seas. The swells were whitecapping, breaking as we rode them, smashing against the rocks, sending great geysers of spray skyward, which the wind whipped in our faces. We grabbed what surface footage we could and headed back to shore. Seeing the Stellers and hearing the stories about them, I gained a new respect for the killer whales — the only creatures that could subdue the fearsome sea lions, outwitting them with shrewd hunting tactics, speed, agility, brute strength and cooperative effort. Yet I also felt sympathy for the Stellers, which are obvious underdogs among marine mammals. Not as cute as seals or as brainy,

---

*In time, whales and sea lions seem to become habituated to the killer whale sound recordings, but a 1983 device developed by Oregon State University biologist Bruce Mate and electrical engineer Charles Greenlaw has proved effective, at least with seals and sea lions. Called the Acoustic Harassment Device, it produces a pinging in the ear that functions as a physiological repellent. The sound does not affect birds or fish, including the eggs and fry of commercial fish.

it seems, as whales, they have been slow to earn public favour and a share in the benefits of conservation.

On day two, we encountered the Vancouver Island grey whales. Following them, we watched as these 40-to-45-foot-long baleen whales grubbed along the bottom, sucking up their food — tiny marine invertebrates — from the sandy shallows of Wickaninnish Bay. Every fall, some 16,500 greys migrate from Alaskan waters down the B.C. and California coast to their winter calving lagoons on the Baja California peninsula. The following spring, they head north again to feed in polar waters. It is a 6,000-mile journey, but not all the whales make it. Some decide to stop off, summering in quiet bays like Wickaninnish. That's where we ran into a few of them.

In the mid-1970s, in Wickaninnish Bay, biologist James D. Darling was working among the summering greys, photographing their skin pigmentation patterns to identify them — in much the same way that Bigg had photographed orca dorsal fins and saddle patches. In his master of science thesis, "The Behaviour and Ecology of the Vancouver Island Grey Whales," Darling estimated the summer resident population at 26 in 1975 and 34 in 1976. About 65 percent, or 18, of 1975's summer residents returned in 1976. He saw some individuals in the area every year for five or six successive summers.

More than once, Darling was monitoring his resident greys when killer whales moved in. Once, the orcas swam right underneath two greys. His findings were similar to ours in Johnstone Strait, when we saw orcas swimming with the resident minke whales. Never did Darling observe the orcas and greys minding each other's presence. But in other areas of the Pacific Coast, killer whales *do* harass the greys. U.S. biologists Dale W. Rice and Allen A. Wolman found that 18 percent of the grey whales they examined at a California whaling station in the 1960s showed evidence of having been attacked by orcas. Accounts of successful attacks, however, are rare. In 1874, Captain Charles M. Scammon watched three orcas harry a grey cow and calf, killing and eating the calf. Russian biologist B.A. Zenkovich reported finding the tongue and baleen plates of a grey whale in the stomach of an orca taken in the western Bering Sea in 1954.

In 1967, Alan Baldridge from Hopkins Marine Station at California's Stanford University observed five or six orcas stalking a grey cow and calf. The killers charged, killing the calf. Three days later, examining the 20-foot-long carcass, Baldridge found that the grey calf had been stripped of its blubber on the ventral surface, and its tongue had been eaten. On the flukes and flippers, which were intact, there were teeth marks. "Such marks," wrote Baldridge, "might be made if a group of *Orcinus* forcibly restrained and drowned their prey."

On our three-day excursion to Long Beach, we never did see the killer whales. We asked various fishermen about whale sightings. No one had seen a killer whale for weeks. And no one had ever heard of a whale called Stubbs. Secretly, I had entertained the remote possibility of seeing Stubbs alone or with her pod. I knew Long Beach was probably out of the pod's range, but that didn't stop me from hoping.

At Long Beach, we learned more about orca the predator, especially when we compared accounts of west coast Vancouver Island orcas with Johnstone Strait orcas and other orcas from around the world. There was the fact that orcas never seemed to bother the Vancouver Island greys, but farther south, along the California coast, where food supplies differed, they did. There were the stomach studies and witnessed accounts of west coast killers feeding on minke whales and Dall's porpoises, two species that, in the Johnstone Strait area, the whales apparently never touch. There were the descriptive accounts of sea lion attacks.

We were learning about orca the opportunistic hunter with an expansive repertoire of predatory skills. At the same time, we were also realizing that in orca's day-to-day food habits, in each area of the world, he tends to be a specialist. For orcas, as for any other predator, specialization is the most efficient way to survive. The Johnstone Strait orcas were fish-eaters; the west coast Vancouver Island orcas preferred porpoises, sea lions, seals and small whales. In open sectors of the Antarctic, killer whales — according to stomach analyses — eat minke whales exclusively, while near the ice, they usually feed on seals.

The orca diet often varies by season. The birth of sea lions off Patagonia's Península Valdés in the South Atlantic attracts hungry killer whales to the sea lion rookeries. For two months, orcas feast on sea lion pups, but for the rest of the year, the two species share the same waters without incident. In the North Atlantic, orcas follow seasonal herring runs; and in Johnstone Strait and most of the Inside Passage, orcas seem to be associated with the various seasonal salmon runs.

As specialists, killer whales develop techniques adapted to particular prey and feeding conditions. In the Antarctic, orcas bump and spill ice floes, sometimes sliding to the top to grab unsuspecting seals. In the South Pacific and Indian Oceans, orcas pull tuna from fishermen's longlines, cleanly and neatly devouring all of the fish except the part containing the hook. In Johnstone Strait and in other oceans, orcas work fishermen's nets, sometimes pulling out the herded fish seconds before the net closes. Off Península Valdés, orcas grab sea lion pups by the folds of skin on their necks, tossing them about and thumping them with their flukes, perhaps to stun them. And at Twofold Bay, as described earlier, orcas associating themselves with man learned to corral big baleen whales.

Some aquarium orcas have to be taught how to eat herring. The young bull named Irving from Pender Harbour would close his mouth, squirting the herring out the sides. In B.C. waters, the bountiful supply of salmon and other fish probably made it unnecessary for Irving to bother with the tiny herring. Aquarium economics (herring is one-quarter the price of salmon) forces certain captive whales to become herring specialists.

As previously detailed, when Icelandic killer whales became herring specialists, to the detriment of the fishing industry, the United States Navy intervened. Fishing economics forced these whales to become herring avoiders.

Orca's keen ability to learn and to adapt sets it apart from many predators.

Other specialized predators have become extinct or endangered species, victims of their specialization, when the environment changed radically.

Orca learns — and learns quickly. Orcas mooching on tuna longlines in the Indian Ocean — where the whales avoided the hook but got the fish — began in the 1950s as seasonal and only incidental poaching. By the early 1960s, this practice had become a year-round phenomenon and was spreading to new fishing areas in the South Pacific and Indian Oceans. Orcas also became herring specialists in Icelandic waters almost as quickly.

It had been a week since we'd seen Stubbs's pod. The absence of whales and the change of weather eroded our resolve to stay at the camp. It was definitely fall, racing on to winter. We moved into Alert Bay and spent two days at the elementary school viewing some 10,000 feet of film that we'd shot. There we found Stubbs's pod: Nicola, Wavy, Sturdy, The Twins and, lying off to the side, Stubbs. Stubbs and Nicola taking care of the youngsters. Stubbs swimming beside the *Betty L*. Stubbs coming up underneath the bow, blowing into the camera. The film had some good moments, but still it was incomplete. Hunter and I voted to continue on a scaled-down budget, with one camera and Vatcher to operate it. Glennon had to go, and we all lamented the loss of his energy. Purchasing fresh supplies, we got ready to return to Robson Bight. Four days after the decision to go, our departure still awaited a reprieve in the weather. When the wind and the sea seemed to let up a little, the evening of September 17, we decided to set out the following morning.

> SEPTEMBER 18. All morning, southeasterly whitecaps file past Alert Bay. It's rainy and cold. No better than last night, maybe worse. Slowly and without enthusiasm, we make final preparations to leave, carrying four boxes of groceries and supplies down to the Zodiac. A tight fit. Four large boxes and five of us: Hunter, Thompson, Driscoll, Krofchak and myself. Vatcher now seems the lucky one to have been left to care for the camp. Thinking of the roller coaster ride that awaits us in the Zodiac, my stomach is uneasy, but we have sat around too long in Alert Bay.

Hunter was driving as we slowly motored out of the harbour, ready for the worst, yet not knowing quite what that meant. Maybe it would not be so bad. Rounding the point, we turned and faced the southeaster that was funnelling through Johnstone Strait. It was no less than 30 knots of driving rain and ocean spray. We would be going into it all the way to Robson Bight, some 18 miles.

Hunter buttoned his rain gear and pulled his hood on tight. "It's going to be a rough, wet ride," he said, hoping that a little dry humour would ease the tension.

The Zodiac took off, instantly becoming almost airborne. Surfing off a wave at a 45-degree angle, the bow was caught by the wind, which blew the boat nearly perpendicular to the sea. We slowed down. It happened again. Hunter told Driscoll to sit on top of the groceries in the bow to distribute the weight more evenly. Still it happened. We decided to turn and cross the strait first, then head into the southeasters close to the Vancouver Island shore. "It should be calmer over there," yelled Hunter. Approaching midchannel, we still couldn't see the far shore. It was getting rougher. The waves were six feet plus, and it was difficult to see over them. Hunter was standing up, navigating by feel. His eyeglasses were awash with every other wave, yet he was determined. Hunter's profile — the high forehead, thinning light blonde hair combed straight back and hanging down over the ears — was the picture of determination. It reminded me of the painting of General George Washington crossing the Delaware River with his men after the bitter 1774 winter at Valley Forge. To me, our enterprise seemed crazy. Coming out of Alert Bay, we had seen at least a dozen fishing boats, big seiners and gill-netters, all heading in. Too rough for them. I looked at Krofchak, Thompson and Driscoll. No one said anything.

"Should we turn back?" I asked Hunter.

"We're *in* a goddamn lifeboat!" shouted Hunter against the dual roaring of waves and engine.

Killer whale macho? I could smell it in the air.

The Zodiac was a lifeboat. It was not going to sink. But one might die of exposure just sitting in it. If there is a rougher, nastier craft in a choppy sea, I do not know of it. Even driving a Zodiac into the teeth of a moderate chop could be a real gut pounder. "Just be glad I'm driving, not Graeme Ellis," he said. "He'd take this sea flat out."

As we lurched slowly down the Vancouver Island shore toward Robson Bight, the wind shot from 30 to 35 knots, then 40. It was gusting, too, picking up our boat again and again. Once, as we were rounding Blinkhorn Peninsula, I was certain that we were going to flip over. At the last instant, Driscoll and Krofchak lunged forward, throwing the weight to the bow and averting disaster. Hunter slowed even more. The engine was alternately chugging and racing, as we rode up, then down each wave. Inebriated with salt water, the engine sputtered twice, then died. Hunter pulled on the outboard cord. There was no response. He was trying to stand in the wave-tossed boat, but he kept tripping over us as he yanked the cord. In the confusion, we got turned around. Then the waves started breaking over the transom. We were taking on a lot of water. Soggy cardboard grocery boxes were giving birth to potatoes and grapefruit, which rolled across the bottom of the boat. Picking up the occasional grapefruit and stashing it in the bow, Driscoll seemed almost lighthearted, as if trying to be cheerful in the face of doom. Krofchak was laughing giddily. Thompson was alternately cajoling and screeching at Hunter — but she did that even at the best of times. I sat, not cracking a smile, probably looking stony silent but really half frozen. With only half a set of rain gear, I was soaked to the skin and shivering. And Hunter? The picture of eternal patience. Hunter, whose fiery temper normally exploded at the first sign of frustration, pulled again and again on the outboard cord. On the eighth pull, as he turned his head to shout something to us, a wave struck him squarely in the jaw. We heard the slap — loud and clear. I didn't look up, just waited for the stream of expletives. Nothing. No sign of that legendary temper. He just kept pulling at the outboard. On the fourteenth pull, the engine coughed and started. I said no more about turning back. Clearly, this was no ordinary case of killer whale macho.

Within the hour, things grew even worse. Two hours out, we were barely a third of the way to Robson Bight — normally less than an hour's trip. The rain let up, and above the troughs, we could just see Mount Derby, the snow-capped peak above the bight, at the base of which was the camp. But the waves were getting higher and trickier as the afternoon tide came flooding out of Baronet Passage from the northeast at a steadily increasing rate. That same flood tide was also coming from the west, funnelling through Johnstone Strait. At about the spot where we were attempting to navigate in the Zodiac, along the Vancouver Island shore, the two tide streams collided. The Baronet tide piled the waves ever higher; the main Johnstone Strait tide sucked us into them, twisting our bow from side to side, subverting our control.

We were getting low on gas. A five-gallon tank was usually good for a one-way trip to town, but we were burning gas three times faster than normal. The extra gas was stashed in the bow. The problem was to transfer the gas to the fuel tank in such a sea. Running on near empty for half an hour, we angled closer to the rocky shore to search for a landing.

We had been three hours at sea and were not even halfway to Robson Bight. Then they appeared. We would never have seen them if they hadn't passed right beside us.

"Ah . . . the rescue party!" said Hunter, his iron mask breaking. "And none too soon."

> SEPTEMBER 18. It's Stubbs's pod! Sturdy, Nicola and The Twins in the front line. Then Wavy, with several cows and juveniles. The younger animals fly from wave to wave; the older ones ride up and down the swells or plough right through them. Looking down the ocean troughs, we see them blowing, their entire bodies, save for the heads and tails, revealed between the waves, straddling the trench. The sea is grey on the slopes; foamy white at the tops; black in the troughs. The killer whales, too, are grey, white and black. Yet they stand out in the moody light of the storm. Their bodies and fins are black, coal-black; their patches and bellies, a scrubbed ivory white; their saddles, a deep grey. In the fourth line, we see Top Notch and Saddle; then Scar, the cow with the cuts in her back, clearly visible from dorsal fin to tail. All our old friends except Stubbs herself. In groups of threes and fours, they slowly move by, heading in the opposite direction.

For Top Notch and Stubbs's pods, it was an afternoon social, a pleasant stroll through Johnstone Strait. If they were having any difficulties travelling, we did not notice. Although, as I was quick to point out to Hunter, "at least they have the good sense to be going with it." Perhaps they were pushing up a little higher to blow, to obtain a good breath. They seemed more to frolic through the waves than anything else. For the killer whales, this was not a "hostile, lonely sea." Twenty-five feet or more below the surface, where whales spend most of their time, there was no storm. It was a little darker than usual, but to a sonar-equipped creature, the amount of light makes little difference.

In a few minutes, they were gone, disappearing in the mountainous swells, leaving us to think about the differences between men and whales.

Heading in to land — we had just rounded Izumy Rock — we saw a seiner anchored tight against the shore, the first sign of man we'd seen since leaving Alert Bay. We were still in the worst part of the storm, but our spirits were lifted, first by whales and now by men. "We can load our gas on the lee side of the seine boat," Hunter shouted, heading for it.

As we approached, the fishermen waved us in. The seiner was the *W-10*, an Alert Bay black-and-gold wooden vessel captained by Mel Stauffer, who remembered us well. Earlier that summer, Hunter and I had helped Stauffer when another seiner's nets had fouled the *W-10*'s propeller. We had been passing by, and when they explained their predicament, Hunter had suited up immediately, gone down, cut the nets out and saved them a day's fishing. Now, pulling up on the lee side of the boat, we threw them our bowline.

"Come aboard," the captain ordered.

Inside the galley, over scalding coffee, Stauffer said: "You're crazy! Out in weather like this!" He had seen more than one boat capsize in the tricky tides around Izumy Rock. "You're lucky you made it." Even Hunter was too frozen to defend our recent enterprise, and our appearance, that of half-drowned rats, was material evidence of our folly and no defence at all.

Stauffer would not hear of our climbing back in the Zodiac. He insisted that he would get us to the bight. In 45 minutes, we arrived at the camp. Vatcher was surprised to see us on such a day. It had been raining and blowing rough inside the bight for days. He hadn't even been able to take the canoe upriver for water. He had caught plenty of rainwater inside the shack, however, in various tin cans that gave us some idea of his menu over the past week. He had recorded whales on the hydrophone but had not seen any.

Vatcher built a roaring fire on the beach, and we tied a canvas tarp between several high tree branches overhanging the fire. We hung our clothes on the low branches to dry. We huddled close and roasted soggy, salty potatoes, which we ate with canned beans. We didn't talk much. We were glad to be home, but we knew that our summer with the whales was over.

Three days after the storm, on September 21, we left. We had prearranged with Stauffer to pick us up then unless the weather had changed for the better. the night of September 20, it was raining, but we ate our last meal on the rocks in front of the camp. We were watching for whales, any whales, but especially Stubbs's pod. One by one, everyone went to bed. Vatcher was the second to last to go. We stood talking, and he echoed my feeling of irresolution about Stubbs. I didn't want to leave Johnstone Strait without knowing what had happened to the old whale.

SEPTEMBER 21. It's after midnight when I finally turn in. I lie awake for hours, listening for whales, the events of the summer turning over in my head. The light rain scatters drops; the wind blows fir needles across the roof of the nylon tent. At about 3:30, I look at my watch and, exhausted, drift off — into one of those dreams so real that when you awake, you remember every detail:

. . . We are on the beach watching the whales navigate a narrow passage — Stubbs's full pod, except for Stubbs — sliding one by one through this shallow tidal area, revealing their full bodies. Standing beside me, Glennon is filming. Beside him are Vatcher and Hunter. Driscoll, Krofchak and Thompson are on my other side. We're all quiet, our mouths hanging open. We can hardly believe what we are seeing.

Sturdy slides by. Then another cow. Then a calf. But the calf gets stuck halfway across, grounded in shallow water. Driscoll wades into the water to help the youngster. The mother turns, instinctively throwing herself between us and the calf. Frightened, Driscoll races out of the water.

The cow assists her calf and begins to swim away, then turns to us with a look that seems to say, "I meant no aggression." With her flipper and her eyes, she beckons us into the water.

Other whales begin to gather now. I remember walking into the water, blind at first, trying to catch someone's eye or smile — the way one walks into a crowd or maybe a gathering, looking for a sign of welcome. I see this cow. Our eyes meet. We touch. The experience of touching seems to make all words unnecessary.

Whales and people are standing around now, as if at a party. Hunter jokes with The Twins. Glennon and Vatcher and the others exchange pleasantries with various cows and calves. I make my way over to Sturdy. Dark, formidable, massive, Sturdy is, nevertheless, friendly. We touch, and then we forget about touching. I consciously think of a question. I want to use the opportunity to learn more about the whales.

"You know the whale we call Stubbs?" I ask, hesitantly. "What is your name for her?"

Sturdy smiles. "Oh yes, she is Smirilak."

"Where is she?" I ask. "Why isn't she with you?"

Sturdy points down and over toward the side of the narrow passage to the beach. I don't understand the gesture.

"She died?"

Sturdy nods.

I look down, feeling upset. Sturdy is puzzled at my reaction. It makes no sense to him that I should feel badly about her death. She shrugs. "She is dead, that's all."

I say nothing, but I am sad, thinking of Stubbs's death. Yet I am also relieved to know. Sturdy makes it easier to accept.

Seeing the whales, talking with them, I feel alive, completely aware at this moment. I tell myself that this is really happening; it is not a dream. Between men and whales, all things suddenly seem possible.

But the whales are already beginning to leave our focus. They are talking among themselves about things we do not understand. I turn to Sturdy: "Can we talk like this again sometime?"

He says, "Sure . . . sometime," in a casual tone that suggests he's very busy, but it would be all right if I approached him sometime when he wasn't too busy. He is friendly yet his is a feeling that I have often had with whales. To them, we are but a passing curiosity.

As the whales are leaving, I turn to a male juvenile and ask, "How old was Stubbs?"

He says, "Well over a hundred years."

I make a mental note of this — to inform Michael Bigg — remembering that the oldest killer whales aged by their teeth were in their thirties or early forties.

The whales leave now, but we are glowing. Looking at each other as we move to the beach, we realize that the killer whale and man have touched and talked. Between the two species, the door has at last been opened. . . .

A flurry of raindrops sweeps across the tent. My eyes open. I am sweating, out of breath, as the shock of "it's only a dream" sinks in.

Yet somehow, I feel resolved about Stubbs. And I can accept that our time with the whales has ended — at least for this year.

Part Four
THIRD SUMMER

THE RUBBING BEACH

AUGUST 25. It's raining. Sky and sea fuse into a uniform greyness. Searching for whales in the Zodiac, feeling at one with the greyness. We all share colds. Veteran whale man Peter Vatcher, bearded this year, crouches at the helm over our 30 horsepower Chrysler, blowing his nose. Tall, wiry photographer John Oliphant — on his first whale expedition — stands with me. Cameras and binoculars tied around our necks, both of us brace ourselves against the pontoons, hacking and sneezing. The rag each of us carries in a back pocket doubles at opposite ends for lenses and noses.

I t was the third season in Johnstone Strait for Vatcher and me. Only three of us made it this year. Unable to obtain more financing for our whale movie, Hunter and I had parted company. Finishing the whale documentary would have to wait for some other year. Hunter had gone to Los Angeles to write film scripts. At the last minute, I had organized a small photographic expedition, hoping to find Stubbs's pod. We had driven up in Hunter's Pontasaurus, which he had sold to Oliphant for $50. Leaving Telegraph Cove in a new rented 14-foot Zodiac, we had been up and down Johnstone Strait and back through Blackfish Sound several times. Yet in three days of searching, the 1975 whale crew had not seen a spout. The nonstop rain was making the search difficult and unpleasant. Top Notch, Hooker, Stubbs — their pods — we were sure, were out there somewhere in the greyness. But where?

Funny thing about waiting for whales — you start thinking about past encounters, and things begin to take on an air of unreality. The old experiences seem far away, to have happened as a matter of luck — *past* luck — and you think you'll never see them again. You begin to wonder if those old times happened only in your head. Then suddenly, out of nowhere, "Kawoof!" It always happens that way.

"Look. Underneath us!"

A dark shadow was pacing us, 10 feet beneath the surface: a young killer whale. It spiralled, its belly momentarily flashing white through the water — a sleek surface-bound projectile arching upward and . . .

"Kawoof!"

From *behind* us came the explosion — another whale on the opposite side of the boat. We swung around instantly, firing our cameras, but we missed the whale as it ducked beneath the surface.

Then: "Kawoof!" The whale we'd first focused on blew, surprising us again. And by the time we had regained our footing and faced it, it was gone.

The two playful young whales gave us no time to recover. Together, they shot out of the water off our bow, belly flopping in our path. Oliphant and I managed to photograph the splash. Niagara Falls, close up.

The two youngsters wriggled and rolled against each other. They popped up on opposite sides of the boat, gazing at us with their black eyes, then dove and popped up together behind us, then in front of us — always when we weren't expecting them. They started swimming circles around us, just below the surface, breathing every 10 to 15 seconds, faster and faster, sometimes skimming the surface, creating a near whirlpool, with the Zodiac in the middle. We tripped over each other and our equipment cases trying to follow them with our cameras, to anticipate their surfacing and to capture the image. The resulting photographs were black shadow blurs or blank pieces of ocean. Not once did we get a shot.

At one point in the midst of the chaos, Oliphant cried out that the two whales could easily tip us over if they surfaced underneath us. But the real danger was our own recklessness. Vatcher was trying to steer a straight course, but every time the whales blew beside us, he flinched. And when Vatcher flinched, the boat flinched too. To avoid hitting the whales, Vatcher kept cutting the engine from half-throttle to neutral, hurtling Oliphant and me forward with dangerous abruptness. It would have been pure slapstick to any passing fishermen: three crazies buzzing around in a rubber boat flanked by a couple of orcas doing a Sea World audition.

Our ineptness made even us laugh, and we were exhilarated that we had found the whales and had been so well received. Then Oliphant and I noticed one youngster nosing dangerously close to our propeller, its tail flukes thrashing underwater, and we shouted. Vatcher, who hadn't seen the youngster trailing behind, looked over the transom, straight down into the water, and turned pale. He stopped the boat, tilted the engine up and shouted: "That whale had his mouth up against the prop." (Young whales nosing, or "eating," the prop became a frequent occurrence that year. Vatcher's theory was that the whales enjoyed the feel of it. "It's a jet stream with air bubbles," he said. "It's probably like when you stand with your face in front of a fan.")

As soon as Vatcher stopped the boat, the whale took off, leaving bubbles in its wake as it rejoined its friend. We watched the two of them up ahead, skimming the water lightheartedly, and laughed: Who were these diabolical young whales?

The answer came almost immediately. Appearing in the grey swells were a dozen or more whales, their long, fat, black bodies coasting up and down as they approached. It was Sturdy, Wavy and Nicola — Stubbs's pod. Our frolicsome friends had to be The Twins. They rejoined their pod, no longer acting like flighty Dall's porpoises, and surfaced with the others in dignified whale fashion.

The Twins had grown since we'd seen them the year before. Straying from their parents, they had become more playful and curious and seemed eager to test their strength, speed and daring. Judging from their exuberance around our Zodiac, they may even have recognized it or us. They almost seemed to be asking: Aren't these the same guys in the rubber boat who followed us around the last two summers?

In July and early August 1973, James Hunter and Graeme Ellis had travelled in a Zodiac with Stubbs's pod. It was the same Zodiac that Hunter and I had used in late August that year for our three-day odyssey with Stubbs's pod. In 1974, Hunter and I had moved with the pod for a week, observing them from the *Betty L*, towing the Zodiac when we weren't using it for close-up action. It was then that we had seen the first signs of The Twins' playfulness. Probably born in 1971 or 1972, they were still regularly accompanied by their parents or an auntie in 1974. At two to three years of age, their curiosity, characteristic of young mammals, was budding and led them frequently to inspect the towed Zodiac, circling and nudging it. In late August 1974, we'd been travelling with Stubbs's pod for most of a week when mysterious visitors approached the Robson Bight camp one night. Three of us were sleeping snugly in the big yellow tent near shore. The entry in my journal reads:

1 A.M. Waking to the sounds of noisy splashing, I yell, "Whales!" Vatcher sits up instantly, but Glennon continues snoring. Climbing out of warm sleeping bags, we yank the tent's cold metal zipper and step out into the night. Swift black winds seem to whistle through our bones. The splashing stops. We slide down the rocks. Wait awhile. No sign of them. "Maybe just the tide," offers Vatcher. We go back to bed.

As soon as we are settled, the commotion erupts again, even louder. The sounds are coming from the area around the Zodiac, moored a few feet from the rocky shore. This time, a blow sounds amid the splashing and frolicking, and now we are certain that our mysterious visitors are whales. Again, we grab at clothes and tent zippers to investigate. Again, everything is quiet as soon as we step outside. Returning to our sleeping bags, we are suddenly alert to an emerging pattern; so we are not surprised when the splashing resumes, full force. It sounds as if a whale is slapping its flukes against the side of the Zodiac.

"I think we're the butt of a joke," I tell Vatcher.

Groggy tent mate Glennon finally stirs: "What's the joke?"

The three of us, thoroughly awake, sit outside the tent watching and waiting. It's a clear, bright, moonlit night. Our eyes are wide, but we see nothing. After 10 minutes: a barely audible whale blow. It comes from behind the 50-foot-wide rock island that sits just off the camp, perhaps 75 feet from the Zodiac. Two small whales now appear from behind the rock island. They leap twice together and are gone. The Twins — playing their version of hide-and-seek.

Vatcher, always searching for the essential truth in a situation, remarks, "It looks as if The Twins have discovered where the little rubber boat lives."

It was always a delight to be around The Twins — whether they were rousing us in the middle of the night or hassling us during the day with their wild, wet shows around the Zodiac. We only wished that they would stay interested longer. Their warm, though wet, reception at our first encounter in 1975 soon turned into mere tolerance of our presence. The Twins may have wanted to play, but the pod obviously had things to do.

After that initial meeting, Vatcher, Oliphant and I took a break to gather our wits. Watching the whales from a distance, we pulled out our portable lunch of peanut butter and stoned wheat crackers, with lemons as the only medicine we had to fight our colds. We all wished that we'd been better prepared: Oliphant and I with our cameras, Vatcher in handling the boat.

That afternoon, we followed the whales east through Johnstone Strait, past Robson Bight. They travelled in uneven formation, arranged in four or five subgroups, but close together. Sturdy moved alone. The Twins swam with a mature cow; Wavy, with a cow and calf. Poor Stubbs had indeed disappeared, and we finally had to conclude that she had died. I missed old Stubbs, although the youthful exuberance of The Twins helped make up for the loss.

As evening neared, the whales slowed to a crawl, and the sea became calm. Far to the east, blue skies peeked out over Kelsey Bay — the first sign of changing weather in a week. But daylight was already fading. The whales had steadily kept their distance from us since morning. Vatcher's instinct had been to hold off and wait for them to come to us, but he finally acknowledged that it was no use. Shifting the Zodiac into high gear, he headed for the leader bulls.

AUGUST 25. We cut the distance quickly — too quickly. At 175 feet, the pod veers to avoid us. Vatcher says it's obvious that they just want to be alone. Oliphant insists that we try again. I don't argue. Vatcher respects Oliphant but doesn't feel right about being aggressive with the whales. We motor ahead of them and wait in their path. (In 1973, Hunter and Ellis used this approach with success; but in 1974, for Hunter and me, it failed more often than it worked. Still, we try again.) Vatcher shuts off the engine. The whales' response is instant: Led by Sturdy and Wavy, they turn sharply toward shore. They want nothing to do with us.

While half the pod moved down the strait, the other half headed for a white-speckled rock face beside a tiny beach that faced west. We had dubbed this landmark the rubbing beach, because of reports that whales came here to rub themselves. Around the rubbing beach, the water was calm, though usually rippled, pushed and pulled as it was by strong tides. The entire area was dark, shadowed by spruce spires that stood along the 35-foot-high cliffs above the beach. Through boat-rocked binoculars, we watched the whales congregating, many of them lying on the surface. They appeared to be tight against the shore, going nowhere. The growing darkness lent an air of mystery to the scene.

Since 1973, our first summer with the whales, we had heard stories from local fishermen about whales rubbing themselves on various rocks along the Vancouver Island shore, close to the Robson Bight camp. As early as 1965, in Johnstone Strait, Marineland of the Pacific's collector Frank Brocato had heard about whales "playing and perhaps rubbing on a beach about half a mile east of Robson Bight." In 1973, biologist Ian MacAskie apparently observed whales rolling on this beach, and Paul Spong said that he thought whales might be rubbing on a number of rocks in the area. There are also reports of rock rubbing in the Indian Ocean. At Marion Island, between 1975 and 1976, South African biologist Peter R. Condy and his colleagues found orca pods playing in shallow sheltered coves, "lying belly up on the bottom, possibly rubbing themselves on the rocky seabed." Following Stubbs's pod on the *Betty L* in 1974, Hunter and I thought that the whales might be rubbing their chins against rocks on the eastern wall of Robson Bight and, later, on Hanson and Cracroft Islands, both on the north side of Johnstone Strait. But the area that we called the rubbing beach, located a half mile east of Robson Bight on Vancouver Island, seemed the most popular. It was not only the most likely rubbing area but also a regular hangout for the resident whales — Stubbs's and Top Notch's pods.

Yet we had never actually seen a whale rubbing. We were not certain whether the whales were rubbing on these rocks or were merely close to them. The murky and often rippled water hampered our vision. We'd never come close because we feared that the whales would disappear if we did. For about 20 minutes, Vatcher, Oliphant and I watched Stubbs's pod from a distance. As our curiosity gnawed at us, we chugged in cautiously.

Ten whales swim slowly, round and round, in a tight counterclock-wise circle. They come up alternately, sometimes blowing, sometimes just lying still, before dipping below. Occasionally, they slap their tails on the surface. The black water oozes and rolls over their bodies like oil. It looks like some strange and primitive ritual.

Tension mounts as we put-put toward the circling whales, and before we know it, we are upon them. We try to hold off, but the tide is sweeping us along too fast. In a few seconds, it's all over. One by one, the whales sink beneath the surface and are gone. One bull turns toward us and surfaces violently, like the creature sprung from the black lagoon. The wave that he pushes at us washes our boat. We feel a bit threatened. Then he, too, disappears. The next time we see the whales, they are more than half a mile from shore, heading away.

We were disappointed — mostly at our own impetuousness. We had encroached upon them. We had broken their circle. And they had left. Motoring back to the camp, we saw the whales turn around and slip back to the rubbing beach. This time, we let them be. The last thing that we noticed before turning into Robson Bight were their blows against the beach, a few heads bobbing in the fading light.

The notion that the whales rubbed themselves, that they engaged in certain furtive, perhaps "illicit," activities, seemed immensely appealing, if somewhat humorous at times. We imagined *Orcinus orca* as "the sensual whale," and the rubbing beach as a kind of massage parlour for horny orcas. Perhaps our jokes were close to the truth. Like other whales and dolphins, orcas are tactile creatures that play and express affection for each other through their sense of touch. Like dolphins, they are nudged to the surface at birth and, like other mammals, are coddled and doted on as calves. The killer whale's size and reported ferocity, however, make its sensual nature an especially engaging attribute. The Twins first showed us orca's sensual side, and fortunately for us, they were bold exhibitionists. Otherwise, we would have witnessed little of the killer whale's sensuality.

Our initial impression of The Twins was that they were like puppies in their tag-along playfulness. Oliphant wrote in his journal that they "chased boats, instead of cars." Even more puppylike was the way that they nuzzled and fought together in play. Sometimes, older animals joined in the fun, and it became a free-for-all, with several pod members rolling and sliding against each other. During one of these group body-rubbing sessions, we saw a youngster's foot-long pink penis. Group play among orcas, as among other social mammals, probably helps prepare youngsters for appropriate behaviour at maturity — in this case, mating.

Sex education for the young male orca is probably first conducted by his mother. With bottlenose dolphins, orca's close relatives, the male calf will usually attempt copulation with his mother — generally within a few weeks of birth. The infant's nursing and nosing in the mother's genital area undoubtedly stimulates her. In *Mammals of the Sea* (Sam Ridgway, ed.), dolphin experts Melba and David Caldwell of the University of Florida write: "The mother's response may range from passive acceptance to active solicitation of the infant by nosing his genital area, which elicits an erection. The young male then continues his copulatory attempts as he develops and may achieve what appears to be an effective copulatory pattern within a few months. This is significant in an animal such as the bottlenose dolphin, which has not been known to achieve sexual maturity before seven years, as it permits a long learning period for sexual patterns." (With killer whales, sexual maturity in males occurs at about 10 to 12 years of age.)

After a young orca male's sexual initiation, probably by his mother, other males and even bulls may participate in educational sex play. On one occasion in Johnstone Strait, I watched a bull engage in apparent sex play with two male juveniles. Similarly, with the Vancouver Island grey whales off Long Beach, biologist Jim Darling once thought that he was witnessing mating and perhaps a ménage à trois, until three males rolled over on their backs, their stocky pink penises slowly unfurling.

In a behaviour study conducted by Susan Gabe and Robyn Woodward in the summer of 1972, at the Vancouver Aquarium, the killer whales "often rubbed themselves against the sides and floor of the tank, sometimes swimming with genital areas touching the floor or wall as they moved."

Sharing the tank with the mature female orca Skana and the junior male Hyak were three Pacific white-sided dolphins. "The dolphins generally moved actively around Hyak," wrote Gabe and Woodward, "each rubbing its body or head against [Hyak's] body. Sexual contacts short of mating were frequent, and Hyak and Skana sometimes swam together belly to belly. When swimming side by side, the flipper of one was often inserted into the genital slit of the other. When one swam below the other, its dorsal fin touched that area. Both [female] dolphins behaved similarly with Hyak, and Diana [one of the female dolphins] often with Skana.

"Often, Hyak would sink to the floor of the tank and lie belly down, awaiting the arrival of a dolphin or, less often, Skana. The dolphins, singly or together, would dive down and rub head and body against Hyak's body and appendages — either a simple desire for touching or part of a courtship pattern. When Skana joined Hyak on the bottom, however, the rubbing became mutual, each nuzzling the other's body, appendages and genital area."

Much of the rubbing behaviour between Skana and Hyak, as with other captive orcas, undoubtedly occurs as part of solo or mutual masturbation — something that Gabe and Woodward seem loath to mention in their study. With captive bottlenose dolphins, masturbation was common among females of any age, but male juveniles were observed masturbating most often. According to the Caldwells, this was accomplished by "rubbing the genital area against the dorsal fin, the tip of the fluke or the flipper of a female, usually resulting in an erection. Even the appendages of a dead animal of either sex on the bottom of the tank have been used. Sometimes, the edge of a sea turtle's shell is utilized, with the male inserting his erected penis under the edge of the turtle's shell as they both swim slowly around the tank. At Marineland of the Pacific, a juvenile bottlenose used the frame of one of the observation windows as a source of stimulation for several days, and the management was greatly relieved when he found other sources of stimulation and discontinued the practice. (This sort of behaviour can be a great source of embarrassment to the management of a public exhibit and thus can present a husbandry problem.)

There is also some evidence that penile erection is, at least in part, under purely voluntary control in dolphins (males have been known to use the penis as a manipulatory organ). As an in-house joke, one trainer at Marineland of Florida taught a dolphin to have an erection on cue and then to carry a hoop around on his penis. The cue for the behaviour was the trainer's raising his arm, which proved to be an unfortunate choice. When this animal, along with his hoop, was transferred into a tank available to the paying public, the behaviour created quite a stir whenever an innocent, friendly tourist raised his arm to wave at the seemingly smiling creature."

Many captive cetaceans enjoy being touched by their trainers and seek out such attention, although younger animals do so more often than older ones. If two or three orcas share a tank, they sometimes vie for this attention, offering their bellies to be scrubbed. "At the Garden Bay Whale Station," wrote Paul Spong and Don White, describing their experiments with the captive Pender Harbour orcas in the late 1960s, "we found all three killer whales to have a virtually insatiable appetite for the tactile stimulation of a scrubbing brush. This type of stimulation appeared to us to be as effective as food for reinforcement." At some aquariums, touching supplements the Skinnerian food-reward system in training the whales for public shows. Except for older individuals (usually whales kept captive for more than five years), who will not tolerate much physical contact with man, touching also seems to be essential to maintaining a captive orca's mental health.

In August 1975, we were learning that orcas were sexual creatures and that they rubbed against each other and, in captivity, on various objects, but that did not mean wild whales were necessarily rubbing on rocks. Except for possible pleasure, why would they *need* to rub on rocks? Orcas do not collect skin parasites or barnacles, as do grey and humpback whales, for example. Could rubbing help remove algae or dead skin? Possibly, but a killer whale's skin is extremely sensitive to touch and susceptible to injury. Orcas are "tender," as a Vancouver Aquarium trainer put it; if Skana lightly mouthed Hyak's fins, he screamed. This vulnerability, coupled with the fact of northern Vancouver Island's sharp and often barnacled rocks, led us to reexamine our rock-rubbing suspicions. Those rocks are sharp. We've ripped holes in the Zodiac landing on the beaches in the area. We've ruined rubber boots and shoes traipsing below the camp at low tide.

During the summer of 1974, we had begun investigating suspected rubbing-rock locations in Johnstone Strait. Some areas could be viewed at low tide, but most had to be examined by divers. Typically, much of each area is barnacle-encrusted and lethal if rubbed against. To our amazement, some rocks in each area were smooth, almost like velvet to touch.

Then, early in September 1975, on a very low tide, Oliphant, Vatcher and I discovered large, smooth rocks along the rubbing beach's cliff wall. We also noticed that the stones on the beach — from the high-tide line to below the low-tide mark — were unusually smooth and round, each about the size of a thumbnail. And, for the first time, we saw several underwater sand patches. We wondered if the whales might also be using the tiny stones and sand on the beach for rubbing.

On September 3, we staked out the rubbing beach to wait for the whales. From the 20-foot-high cliff above the beach, we could watch discreetly yet photograph them in action. We brought along the canoe, our trump card: From the beach, we could launch it quickly and quietly — if the situation seemed appropriate. Paddling the canoe, Vatcher might be able to approach closer than we had in the Zodiac. If possible, Oliphant and I wanted to photograph Vatcher with the whales playing all around.

Two days later, the whales arrived. They had followed the shore closely; we had not seen them until they were almost on our doorstep. There were eight, all from Stubbs's pod, The Twins in the lead. Sturdy and a few others followed and, last, Nicola and Wavy. They filed in almost in a straight line and then about 125 feet from shore, right before our eyes, formed into that same tight circle that we'd seen before.

At first, there was an eerie silence. Then, faintly yet distinctly, whale whistles started coming up through the water. The whales were jabbering away. It was our first hint that intense vocal play is as characteristic of rubbing-beach gatherings as near silence is to resting times. Even so, without a hydrophone, we were missing most of it. Whenever I had recorded the whales playing (in 1973 and 1974), their vocalizations were thick, different, and seemed to follow no patterns. But the rubbing-beach sounds seemed stranger than strange.

Counterclockwise round and round the circle went Stubbs's pod, singing their new music. Patches of sun, leaking through the high trees, glinted off their fins. But the spell seemed to be breaking. One by one, the whales left the circle and, staying just underwater, approached the base of the cliff wall where we stood. We saw one whale's white belly turned emerald-green by the thick algal water. Another wriggled through the kelp jungle that grew out from shore. A moment later, he swam close, almost breaking the water, his dorsal fin tangled in a 10-foot strand of yellow-brown kelp. Oliphant and I, our cameras ready-focused, waited for the whale to surface. But then, like an apparition, he drifted deeper and was gone.

SEPTEMBER 5. Below us, along the rock-face wall, huge foamy air bubbles boil to the surface. At six feet across, some bubbles look like miniature craters of molten lava from a soon-to-erupt volcano. Emanating from the craters are whale sounds — an eerie musical score for what looks like the climactic scene from a science fiction movie. Dispatching those big air bubbles (perhaps to lose buoyancy) and vocalizing from 30 to 50 feet down are our favourite creatures of the deep, but we can't see them for the kelp and murky water. Trying to get their attention, Oliphant and I both whistle at the whales. At the beach, we would be able to see them clearly and photograph them in the shallows and against the sand patches. Fifteen minutes pass; the whales stay put.

Except during sleep times, we had rarely seen the whales remain in one spot.

At my prompting, Vatcher launched the canoe on the far side of the beach and paddled out alone to investigate. He had not gone far when a senior bull, probably Wavy, pushed his fat head out of the water and took a good look around. He approached Vatcher as if to examine him.

> Things begin to happen fast: Wavy explodes off the bow of Vatcher's canoe. A second later, behind the canoe, The Twins bob up, flapping their pectorals and looking at Vatcher. Bug-eyed, Vatcher stops paddling. From the cliff above, Oliphant and I are snapping pictures like a couple of manic tourists. Then six or seven whales start zigzagging underneath the canoe, popping up in sudden explosions of whale mist and splashing their flukes furiously. The sea churns with fins and foam.

For 30 seconds, the sea itself seemed to come alive. Then everything was quiet. The whales had all sounded. We looked around, waited, then realized that they'd left the rubbing beach to us. They'd moved on.

That night in the tent, Vatcher described what he'd seen from the canoe — his closest look ever at the whales. He talked about the lines and scratches on their backs — similar to the marks that I had noticed on Nicola when I had paddled up to her in the canoe at the end of summer 1973. "But the two youngsters seem to have even more lines and scratches," said Vatcher. The marks seemed to be not so much the accumulations of lifetime injuries, not marks of age, but more the result of constant playing and rolling against each other, possibly rubbing on rocks and even mouthing each other.

Later, examining the photographs, we found parallel scars on the orca bodies corresponding to the distance between their teeth — about an inch apart. The scars were most evident on our pictures of The Twins.

At the Vancouver Aquarium, "the bodies of all the [whales] show scars of past encounters," wrote researchers Gabe and Woodward, "even though very few aggressive acts have been noticed." Skana, the dominant animal, had the fewest scars. She had less physical contact with the others. And, as the oldest animal, she played the least.

Activities at the rubbing beach remained something of a mystery. Perhaps the whales wanted their privacy. When we had approached in the canoe, they had suddenly come alive, then disappeared. Again, we were forced to conclude that they had been bothered by our presence.

For two weeks, through mid-September 1975, Oliphant, Vatcher and I lived out of the Zodiac. We spent long days travelling with the whales, day by day growing closer to them. Mostly, we moved with Stubbs's pod, though there were several days when Top Notch's group joined in. We didn't see Hooker's pod that summer. Along with C pod and D pod (led by Warp Fin), Hooker's pod (B) had been classified by Michael Bigg as a more northerly group, ranging mostly from Port Hardy to Bella Bella and often passing Pine Island.

We saw a few new whales in 1975. Twice when we moved with Stubbs's and Top Notch's pods, groups of transients passed by. Both times, it was late in the day, however, too dark to get any IDs. Then one afternoon with Stubbs's pod, a large new group joined in — I pod. The lead bull had the oddest dorsal fin since Stubbs. It looked as if it had been bitten off at the top, the tip replaced with a crude, twisted hook. We called him Captain Hook, but when Bigg saw him that summer, he named him Finger Fin. Besides Finger, I pod had a bull (Tube) with a large fin notched at the base and curled over to port, a smaller bull (Accordian), whose fin flopped from side to side as he swam, and a cow with a hole in the top trailing edge of her fin. Still other dorsal fins in the pod were mangled, and several were collapsing. It was a pod full of fin oddities, which later prompted Bigg to speculate that "genetically, the pod may have a weak dorsal fin structure."

The day I pod travelled with Stubbs's pod, they both visited the rubbing beach. Resident and northern pods alike seemed to know about the rubbing beach, but only Stubbs's and Top Notch's pods visited regularly. Stubbs's pod, when it was in Johnstone Strait, made daily pilgrimages. Perhaps it had introduced the northern pods to the exotic pleasures that we imagined were found there. Even when the whales travelled together, however, they never converged on the beach all at once. There would be six or eight — at most ten — at a time, and then they took turns in the rubbing area.

The rubbing beach was frequently the eastern terminus of a pod's journey through Johnstone Strait. Many times, it seemed that the whales would come out of Blackfish Sound only to rest in the bight, usually by late afternoon, and would then proceed to the rubbing beach around dusk. We often watched them — at some distance from the beach. After previous encounters, we were going to give them plenty of room. As Vatcher said, "We must win their trust by our gentle persistence." If Vatcher would be gentle, Oliphant and I could be relied on to remain persistent. But we worked smoothly together: Oliphant and I taking photographs, Vatcher the perfect helmsman. After three summers navigating every kind of boat around whales, Vatcher was finely attuned to whale moods and travel patterns. And in 1975, he became a virtuoso at manoeuvring the Zodiac when the whales were close. After our encounters with The Twins, he could handle anything. He seemed to know just when to move in and when to hold off. He tried never to force the whales into an awkward position but left them the choice of approaching us or not. In 1973, we had thought whales wouldn't come near boats with engines, especially outboards; our experiences in 1974 and especially 1975 had put that notion to rest. More and more, the whales tolerated our presence, and we were getting to know individuals better. Of all their activities, only the rubbing beach remained off limits.

The Twins were our greatest source of joy that summer of 1975. Often playing, they seemed to escalate their assault as time went by, and they became constantly more daring. Sometimes, we could even get them going with a little playful prodding. One afternoon, we watched The Twins — together with several other whales, including a bull — surfing in the wake of the Canadian Pacific's Alaska steamer. Surfing was one of The Twins' favourite pastimes. Suddenly, Vatcher had an idea: "I'll give them a wake of my own!" It seemed to contradict his principles, but Vatcher knew what he was doing. He revved the Zodiac and screeched past the whales, boldly, blatantly.

Right away, one Twin leapt into the wake. Then its partner joined in, and both began speed swimming off our bow, falling away from the boat as the waves fell away. After surfing on our bow waves, they raced ahead, ploughing the water and surfing on each other's bow waves.

On other occasions, The Twins performed somersaults in the water beside the boat, their backs curving down, down, until we saw the white underside of their tail flukes. For an instant, they'd be gone. Then two heads would bob up, each giving us the eye. At other times, they would race right under the Zodiac, rolling over on their sides, gazing up at us without ever breaking stride. And sometimes, we actually applauded — they seemed so proud of their tricks.

On the afternoon of September 10, we observed The Twins toying with a long strand of bull kelp. One swam on his side beside the moving Zodiac, the brown ropelike kelp clenched in his teeth and trailing through the water like a streamer. Oliphant photographed him perfectly. Then the other came from behind, and both darted off, playing with the kelp, a game of tag or tug-of-war. That same afternoon, we watched The Twins catching salmon. Even this they did with sportive zeal, seeming to trap the silver fish between them. We saw one salmon dance on the water for some 35 feet — hopping like crazy to get away — until one Twin reached up and grabbed it. Blood trickled down the youngster's chin in the instant before it dove. All that was left of the fish were silver scales floating on the surface.

When they were eating, The Twins were not always so lighthearted. But a few 25-mile-an-hour bulletlike leaps would signal their success — and leave us, time and again, wet and breathless. What impressed us more than anything as we motored along was the everyday casual proximity of The Twins. They repeatedly approached close enough for us to touch them. We no longer needed to chase them. We merely travelled alongside the pod, staying out of their way, and when The Twins were in the mood, we got together. Perhaps, after all, the whole pod was beginning to trust us. We had established some kind of relationship with The Twins based on their curiosity and playfulness and on our tolerance of their mischief.

Then one evening, after we had spent a day travelling with the whales and had suffered the usual teasing and terrorizing by The Twins, the whales turned and headed toward the rubbing beach. We decided the time had again come to try to follow. The Twins escorted us most of the way — until we were less than 100 yards from the beach. The moment of truth seemed finally at hand. As we motored in, that cold, sweet air which comes down off the mountains only at dusk rushed at our faces. The last light of day illuminated the mountaintops, but already, the rubbing beach was growing dark. Oliphant and I loaded two cameras apiece, push-rating the Ektachrome two stops beyond the recommended speed, and hoped for the best.

SEPTEMBER 13. Seven whales swim around in their tight counterclockwise circle, as if lining up to rub. In the pale light, it looks like some kind of ritualized drama about to be enacted before our eyes. Oliphant and I click away. Vatcher attempts to hold us steady, but a strong tide pulls us closer. Then the Zodiac engine quits. We are headed for the shallow water below the rubbing beach, right for the whales. And we are caught in a back eddy that is sucking us ever closer. Should we start up the engine? A sudden noise might disturb them more than our encroaching presence. We decide to go with the tide. The whale sounds, already loud, grow louder.

Seconds later, looming beneath us through the surprisingly clear water is a 23-foot-long bull killer whale rolling on the sandy bottom. We can see his moving silhouette against the sand, his massive flippers fluttering the water like wings. It's Wavy!

We were only 10 feet away, watching this big bull underwater as he gyrated and squealed like a child at play. But we soon learned that there was more to this than child's play.

Wavy swims over to join several already frolicking whales in very shallow water 60 feet ahead of us. The closer the tide pulls us, the wider our eyes open. Three or four whales are rolling in the shallows of the beach, nearly half of their bodies exposed. We watch the dorsal fins bend as they turn over and over. We watch them thrashing, sliding against each other. Then two animals, Wavy and one of the cows, come together — belly to belly.

"They're mating!"

It was a smothered yell. I held my breath, afraid to disturb the scene, yet clicking away for 10 minutes, as the last rays of sunset faded, and night finally closed in.

We had won the full trust of Stubbs's pod at last. The whales had allowed us close enough to witness this very intimate moment. As it turned out, it had been too dark to capture the scene on film, but we had seen it and shared it. We were glowing inside that night, as we quietly left the whales and headed back to the camp.

Part Five
IN LATER YEARS

A FUTURE
FOR ORCAS IN
THE NORTHWEST?

After our 1975 summer with The Twins, there were still more seasons with whales. In the pods that we had photographed and identified, a number of the older members disappeared. They had probably died. Balancing the casualties were several newborn calves, youngsters every bit as curious and playful as The Twins once were. We always enjoyed the new whales. They took the sting out of the deaths of the whales we had known and The Twins' near indifference to us as they grew older. There was always change, and with it came new concerns.

I was thinking about the future of whales and men in September 1979, as I headed north to Johnstone Strait. It was my seventh annual visit to killer whale country. I was driving a comfortable new Ford Mustang on a highway that had recently been cut through the northern Vancouver Island wilderness. It was a fine road, as roads go, yet I missed the bumpy 10-mile-per-hour logging road full of potholes and lined with quicksand shoulders, as well as the old Pontasaurus that used to get us there.

The new road had been opened just that spring. It joined populous and prosperous southern Vancouver Island (and the mainland) to the near isolated logging communities of the north. The road meant different things to different people. To most north-island residents, who had been asking for it for three decades, it meant cheaper groceries and supplies, faster trips to Vancouver and Victoria and the prospect of visitors once in a while. To other residents — older settlers like sawmill owner Fred Wastell of Telegraph Cove — the road spelled some loss of peace and quiet, but it was a change that was inevitable. Certainly, it meant that large numbers of people would now have easy access to previously remote areas. About two million people (Vancouver, Victoria, Seattle) were now within 10 hours' easy car travel.

The entire north island would be affected, but the most dramatic impact would fall upon the 26-mile-long Tsitika River Valley — the last unlogged, untouched watershed on eastern Vancouver Island. Now, as we drove along, the highway was empty, but the red carpet had been rolled out. The people would find it.

The new highway cuts through the mountainous interior of northern Vancouver Island. My two companions, Françoise Roux and my sister, Victoria Hoyt, were first-time visitors from the East who had never seen whales or wilderness. They could not believe how hard it was raining, and in fact, I was having some trouble seeing the road. At 55 miles per hour, though, we were making good time, and when the sky cleared, we found ourselves deep in virgin forest. There were black-tailed deer by the road; occasionally, we saw mink running for their lives as we passed.

At dusk, we crossed the headwaters of the Tsitika River. I had seen the route marked on a map before it was constructed. Now, the big steel-and-concrete bridge spanning the Tsitika seemed a tombstone. There was no sign, no epitaph, to mark the river's passing. Before explaining my concern to my companions, I stopped talking altogether. I wanted them to be as impressed as I had been upon first seeing the virgin forest.

Some might say that a single bridge spanning a river, a road crossing a valley, were small things. I knew that it was only the beginning. A concrete sliver across a virgin valley, the road was a tiny fault line through paradise. And in September 1979, the ground was moving — the beginnings of an earthquake shaking the valley. Even as we drove north, dozens of logging roads — an intricate network of fault lines that would eventually extend over more than 750 miles — were being cut and scraped through these woods. Twentieth-century man's tools of progress, the bulldozer and the chain saw, were at work on a big job: one virgin rain forest.

The logging companies owning the largest tree farm licences in the Tsitika River Valley are MacMillan Bloedel Limited — Mac'n'Blo, or M'n'B — and Canadian Forest Products Limited — Canfor. MacMillan Bloedel's TFL (tree farm licence) gives them 109 square miles (72 percent of the Tsitika watershed); Canadian Forest Products' TFL contains 37 square miles (25 percent of the Tsitika); Rayonier Canada holds 3 percent, about 4 square miles. These companies acquired the rights to cut the valuable hemlock and balsam decades ago, and although they didn't touch it until 1979, the area had figured in their calculations for "sustained yield." Mac'n'Blo and Canfor claimed that they *needed* the Tsitika. Without it, Mac'n'Blo in particular would have exhausted all its timber in a matter of a few decades. B.C.'s economy — about 50 cents of every dollar — is based on timber. The Tsitika would provide about 146 jobs per year (until the year 2008) from direct logging activity and an additional 1,128 jobs from associated manufacturing, trades and services.

Despite economics that seemed to have doomed the Tsitika without a second thought, the regional wildlife biologist for Vancouver Island had, in the fall of 1972, proposed the establishment of an ecological reserve encompassing the 150-square-mile Tsitika watershed. An ecological reserve, under B.C.'s 1971 Ecological Reserves Act, would have afforded complete protection to the region in perpetuity. The land area proposed for the reserve, about 1/8 the size of the U.S. state of Rhode Island, represented 1/80 of Vancouver Island and 1/2400 — a drop in the bucket — the total land area of British Columbia. Yet had it been approved, it would have been the largest reserve in the province. In February 1973, the B.C. Minister of Lands, Forests and Water Resources honoured the proposal by declaring a moratorium on logging and road building in the area. For the next five years, various government and conservation groups prepared their studies and argued pro and con.

Among the first to hike through the region with cameras and notebooks were biologists Alton Harestad and Allan Edie. As detailed in their 1971 report to B.C. Fish & Wildlife, they found several thousand black-tailed deer, small groups of resident Roosevelt elk and many bear and cougar. Biologists who followed Harestad and Edie found wolves and discovered that the Tsitika River had perhaps the largest summer steelhead (rainbow) trout run on Vancouver Island. They also counted a number of cutthroat and Dolly Varden trout and roughly 10,000 spawning salmon — 6,000 pinks, 2,000 coho, 1,200 chum and a smaller number of sockeye and chinook. With additional lake and stream species, the Tsitika boasts one of the most diverse fisheries on Vancouver Island.

Still other groups came to conduct specialized ecological studies in the region. They examined mountains and meadows and the interrelationships between bogs, streams, lakes and the prolific fish-rearing habitat in the Tsitika estuary at Robson Bight. The estuary, or river mouth, was only about 200 yards from the Robson Bight base camp, and at low tide, we had observed the large crab population from the thick eelgrass beds close to shore. Following bear, deer and wolf trails, we had often hiked up the valley. We had watched some of the study groups come and go between 1973 and 1978. We had talked with them and exchanged notes, making sure to point out that the killer whales which frequented Robson Bight and the river mouth were also part of the Tsitika ecosystem and should be included in any plan for its management. What is the relationship between whales and trees? We did not know for sure why Stubbs's and Top Notch's groups, among others, spent more time around Robson Bight than anywhere else, but three reasons came to mind: (1) salmon that schooled near the river mouth before navigating upstream; (2) rubbing rocks inside and just to the east of the bight; and (3) peace and quiet. Robson Bight is one of the few eastern Vancouver Island bays that has never housed a log boom. It is completely closed to the fishing seiners and gill-netters, and boat traffic is at a minimum. To each whale watcher who stayed at the Robson Bight camp, the Tsitika was like his own backyard, and we did not like the idea that it was to be invaded. All three of the reasons why whales came to Robson Bight were threatened by the logging of the Tsitika River Valley.

On November 1, 1978, the B.C. provincial government killed the moratorium on logging the Tsitika and, with it, all hope for an ecological reserve encompassing the entire valley. Under the terms of the Tsitika Watershed Integrated Resource Plan (TWIRP), some 90 square miles — 60 percent of the Tsitika River Valley — would be open to clear-cut logging, and more land along watercourses and in proposed recreational areas would be accessible through selective cutting. Much of the remaining 40 percent consisted of non-productive alpine areas and lakes, and only 5 percent was *proposed* ecological reserves. Yet TWIRP's decision was hailed by some as a compromise between loggers and conservationists because of a number of concessions to conservation:

1. The vital deer winter range would be identified and reserved from logging for 150 years.
2. A four-mile "fishing corridor" of virgin timber would be left along the Tsitika River (to give hikers and fishermen the feeling of walking through wilderness).
3. The visual impact of logging would be minimized by using landscape logging techniques on those areas highly visible from the North Island Highway and from Johnstone Strait.
4. MacMillan Bloedel Limited would study alternatives to using the Tsitika estuary as a log dumping ground, and if alternatives were economically unfeasible, further environmental-impact studies would be undertaken.

TWIRP made no mention of the whales, except indirectly in tenuous provision number 4. The fact remained: Mac'n'Blo wanted to ship a large portion of their logs through the Tsitika River mouth, assembling massive log booms in Robson Bight to be towed south to southern Vancouver Island and mainland B.C. processing plants. This was the way that it had been done in almost every other B.C. river valley, and it was the cheapest way to do business on the Tsitika. Mac'n'Blo also planned to use the gravel beach just west of the river mouth for a dry-land sort — an area where logs are graded and selected before being shipped, usually by water, to processing plants. With booming grounds and dry-land sorts, there would be little peace and quiet for the whales. Furthermore, the gravel beach earmarked for development was part of the Robson Bight rubbing-rock area.

To assess the environmental impact of using the Tsitika estuary as a dumping ground, TWIRP's follow-up committee asked Michael Bigg about the whales. Bigg explained that Robson Bight was a unique core area, a kind of home territory for one of the largest concentrations of killer whales anywhere in the world and that in his view, "excessive risk would be involved in gambling that nothing would happen in making a booming ground [there]." Assured that the whales would be considered, Bigg told me when we talked in September 1979 that "the killer whale seems to be the strongest argument for keeping industry out of the bight." But the debate was only beginning.

TWIRP's so-called concessions to conservation, the first ever given by a B.C. government, included no guarantees for the future. If a few decades from now the demand for lumber — and the cost of harvesting it — greatly increases, anything could happen. Many have expressed dissatisfaction with TWIRP, among them the B.C. Wildlife Federation, the United Fishermen and Allied Workers Union, the Sierra Club and the Federation of B.C. Naturalists.

"It's nothing but a good public relations job on the part of the forest indus-

try," said David Orton, spokesman for B.C. Naturalists. "We're not opposed
to logging, but we are opposed to logging this valley in the traditional manner
[that is, creating large clear-cut zones on steeply sloped valleys]. The large-
scale clear-cuts of up to 600 acres, as proposed by the report, will degrade
and fundamentally change the environment to the detriment of fisheries and
wildlife."

Orton and many others felt that with the Tsitika, it was time for the forest
industry to try new methods of harvesting trees. They believed that the old
methods had proved inadequate again and again. No doubt more sensitive
styles of logging will be developed in the future. But for the Tsitika, it's too late.

More than anything, the Tsitika debate has been based on a conflict of
values. The economic values of B.C.'s biggest industry once again easily over-
shadowed the less tangible values of science, recreation and aesthetics. "It
would cost a fortune in lost jobs and industrial profits to save the last virgin
forest of Vancouver Island's east coast," wrote Mark Hume, who covered
the Tsitika story for the *Victoria Times*. "But once gone, it cannot be bought
back. Wilderness is a priceless commodity."

As I drove along, leaving the Tsitika River Valley, my two companions,
Victoria and Françoise, were very quiet, and my thoughts began to wander.
I remembered walking through the Tsitika for the first time in 1973, seeing
the giant trees standing shoulder to shoulder, denizens of an ancient forest;
giants that had been 100-year-old youngsters back in 1792 when Captain
George Vancouver, the first white man to sail up Johnstone Strait, had seen
them; giants that were soon to fall. I thought of the time that I had heard one
of the giants die a natural death. Standing at the grassy river mouth watching
whales feeding at the Tsitika estuary, I heard a scream come from behind me.
It was the squeal of dead wood splitting, followed by a clap of thunder as the
tree slammed onto the forest floor. The sound had emanated from deep in the
forest, but the echoes, bouncing off the mountain faces, carried clear to the
river mouth. One whale had lifted its head and looked around. I'd wondered
if he had heard and perhaps been curious about the crash.

Would the whales understand what was happening as the bulldozers and
chain saws edged ever closer to the Tsitika River mouth? Or would they, with
the dirtying of the water and perhaps the declining number of fish, sense the
coming of change long before? Would they then still swim up to the eelgrass
beds of the estuary, to that lush place where the fresh water meets the sea?
Driving on, I felt my concern grow into an obsession.

On my 1979 trip to Johnstone Strait, I intended to gather the last bits of
research for this book. It was to be a quick trip to make a final check on the
whales that I had known, some since 1973. I had talked with Bigg before leaving, and he had asked me, as before, to keep track of whale sightings. That
summer, Bigg had spent a few days in Johnstone Strait and twice had travelled
to Port Hardy, on northern Vancouver Island, to monitor orca pods north of
the strait. On one of these excursions to Port Hardy, he was accompanied by
biologist John Ford, who was studying killer whale sounds at the University
of British Columbia. Graeme Ellis was taking care of sightings near Nanaimo.

It had been eight years since Bigg and his colleagues first began counting killer whales and six years since he had developed his photo-identification system. The base study and most of the legwork had been done, and now, it was mostly a matter of checking up on the whales every summer to monitor births, deaths and changes in the various pods. In 1976, with Ian B. MacAskie and Ellis, Bigg had written a preliminary report on the abundance and movements of B.C. killer whales. Along the B.C./Washington coast, there were about 261 orcas in 30 pods. The recruitment, or birth, rates of these orcas, Bigg estimated, is "as low as 4 or 5 percent per year, probably the lowest of any cetacean group." Such a low rate emphasizes the importance of parental care and highly developed social habits to the survival of the species.

Our first day on the water, we found Stubbs's pod — Nicola, Wavy, Sturdy, all the regulars. With them was Top Notch's group — the lone bull Top Notch; the cows Scar, the wide-nicked cow, and Saddle; and five calves. Scar's calf, born in the early 1970s, was coming along fine. And there was a new calf, the second born in seven years to Saddle. Old A7, a cow with three nicks on her fin, was missing, and we would later conclude that she had died. Through a sunny afternoon, some 31 whales travelled together and, in the evening, split into three separate groups. There was little doubt that the pods are long-term family units. Over seven years of observation, the main recognizable individuals have never varied, although from the beginning, there was some discrepancy in the various fin counts of A pod — Stubbs's "extended" pod. In July 1973, we had isolated Top Notch's group of 10 as a distinct pod within the 25-whale aggregation. That left Stubbs's pod with about 15 animals. But usually, there were only eight or nine in the core group; it was difficult to account for the remaining whales. It was not until 1979 that Bigg "cleaned up the A's," as he put it, with the help of Ford. Within A pod, there was a distinct pod of six whales, led by a single bull that Bigg called A4 — who had two nicks in his dorsal's trailing edge, the large one near the top. Besides this bull, the pod was composed of three cows and two youngsters. We had called this group The Six in 1974, although we were not certain whether it was an integral pod or a subgroup of some larger pod.

In previous summers, it seemed that the A's had more often travelled in a group of 20 to 30 and only later had become several distinct pods. One reason for this belief was certainly the fine-tuning of our ability to recognize the cohesiveness of various groups, but there was reason to believe that the A's had once formed a single pod (perhaps as recently as decades ago) and that as the pod grew larger, it had gradually divided into three groups. Two points supported this theory:

1. According to Bigg's studies of the 30 pods along the B.C./Washington coast, the larger pods are the productive ones. These large pods, Bigg believes, spin off smaller ones periodically.

2. In killer whale sound studies begun in 1978, Ford has established the existence of dialects. What earlier researchers recording orca sounds thought to be true, Ford was able to quantify. Each pod has a set of characteristic sounds. The three A pods, however, share most of the same vocalizations,

and initially, Ford thought that they had the same dialect. Their sounds were first recorded in 1964 by University of British Columbia zoologist H. Dean Fisher in Johnstone Strait. They were then recorded by Paul Spong when Top Notch's pod was captured in Pender Harbour in 1969 and again on Spong's visits to Johnstone Strait in 1970-72. The same sounds formed the repertoire of the 25-odd A's that I had recorded in 1973 and 1974. Ford eventually found a few unique calls in each of the three pods, but sharing most of the same sounds seems evidence that all the A's are closely related and probably come from a single pod.

Learning how pods developed and will continue to develop is crucial to understanding the population biology of killer whales. Beginning in 1971, Bigg had counted whales in answer to the controversy over orca captures. But to provide "a reliable scientific basis for management," he had to know much more. The small pods, the 15 or so transient pods — like Charlie Chin's group, seen in the harbour at Nanaimo in September and October 1979 — are doomed to die out, said Bigg. They have an average of three members per pod. They don't associate with other pods. And with the low killer whale birthrate, they can't reproduce fast enough. Charlie Chin and the pointed-nose cow were the only survivors of the Pedder Bay Five, captured in 1970. Between 1972 and 1975, they had had a calf, which Bigg saw them with about once a year until 1977. By 1978, that calf had disappeared. In September 1979, Charlie Chin and the cow were seen with a new calf. "Even if this new calf survives," Bigg explained, "that would mean only one additional pod member in 10 years. In another 10 years, that youngster could be mature. But Charlie, who would then be about 30 years old, could be gone. And that's the end of the pod."

There is little doubt that it will be the large pods, the productive ones, that we must look to for the survival of B.C. whales. These large family organizations, like the A's in Johnstone Strait and J pod in the southern territory, live mainly in the inshore waters of Vancouver Island. Most of them seem to be fish-eaters, at least in the summer and early fall months. And because of their diet and inshore range, they have come into constant contact with man: salmon fishermen, boaters, whale captors and, more recently, whale watchers and researchers. So far in the history of man and orca, one can almost say that to the degree that these large pods have come into contact with man, they have been threatened. These pods have been the ones most frequently captured — some, like the large southern Vancouver Island pods, J and K, perhaps two or three times each. They have also been shot at the most. As for whale watchers and researchers like ourselves, I do not believe that we pose an immediate problem, but with many more people following the pods closely, the potential for harassment exists. The situation must be monitored, and if it becomes necessary, guidelines should be introduced.

In September 1975, John Oliphant, Peter Vatcher and I had been inspired by our closeness to Stubbs's pod, but in later years, it became a matter of some concern. In October 1977, Port McNeill diver Jim Borrowman and I were motoring along in our 10-foot inflatable Beaufort (a smaller version of a Zodiac) when The Twins suddenly "attacked." They had grown since 1975. One surfaced on our starboard side, close enough that I could have put my arms around him without getting out of the boat. Actually, I was too busy driving and trying to hold on to display any affection. Still, we did get wet. His surfacing sent a wave into the small inflatable that soaked me from the waist down. A second later, the other Twin blew on our port side. As the two whales exploded alternately in typical Twins' fashion, they were porpoising ever closer to the inflatable boat. I saw that they were going to hit us. I swerved, but one grazed the rubber, his skin squealing against it like tires braking on the highway. Turning around to look at me, Borrowman's usually red face was almost white.

The following September, Borrowman and I, along with divers Michelle Pugh and Lou Crabe, encountered G pod on one of their rare visits to Johnstone Strait. When they stayed near us, we took that as an invitation to swim with them. Like hornets, several whales buzzed the two scuba divers, Borrowman and Pugh. Pugh was a blonde, blue-eyed diver that Borrowman and I had met while doing a photographic assignment in the Virgin Islands. She had swum with whales before but never with killer whales. "They seemed to go for our legs," she said after the dive. "I didn't think they'd attack, but I feared they might playfully grab our fins and swim off with us." One cow came within 10 feet of Borrowman and invited him to a staring contest. Like Davy Crockett, who, according to legend, once outstared a bear, Borrowman held his ground, focusing his Nikonos almost leisurely. The interplay between whales and divers was clearly visible below the surface, and Crabe and I took it all in. Eventually, both divers had shot their rolls. We helped them out of the water to reload their cameras. The whales waited, bobbing their heads, looking at us, asking for more. They whistled, and we whistled back. The divers jumped back in. The whales remained, and in the next very long 20 minutes, Borrowman and Pugh stayed with them, swimming, drifting through Johnstone Strait. It was the kind of scenario that we could not have imagined in previous years.

In September 1979, when Borrowman and I returned with other divers, we encountered the resident A pods at the rubbing beach. Initially, the whales were slightly skittish, but they stayed and stayed while five scuba divers floated around them. When they began swimming up to the divers, close enough to touch, we finally had to conclude that the whales were becoming "tame." Our closeness was no longer the breakthrough that it had been in previous years. In 1979, we spent only three days with the whales, but the sum of our closeness was about equal to the three-month total for 1973. I couldn't help worrying about their tameness in light of the opening of the North Island Highway and the logging of the Tsitika.

Graeme Ellis was the first to express concern about people who might take advantage of the closeness that we had cultivated with the whales. For days, one juvenile in Hooker's pod had taken to tagging after Ellis and Hunter's Zodiac in July 1973. At first, Ellis had been delighted, then distressed. "Perhaps it's all right for us in the summer," Ellis said, "but what if in the winter, a youngster starts following some boat that doesn't particularly care for orcas?" If the surprised mariner felt fear or hatred, the youngster "might get his head blown off."

Ellis was sometimes a pessimist, but we had all shared the same feeling in August 1973 when a young orca was found floating dead near Alert Bay. We were not certain how it had died, but there was a possible bullet hole in its back. Then in August 1977, about 30 miles south of Johnstone Strait, there had been another similar incident. A baby killer whale was discovered, apparently sick and bullet-wounded — but alive.

It was low tide, August 2, 1977, when Bill Davis and his fishing buddy Gerry Kool saw the calf. All alone in the shallows of Menzies Bay, near Campbell River on Vancouver Island, it was covered with brown algae and looked to be in trouble. Approaching the whale in his motorboat, Davis "threw a herring out, and she took it. Pretty soon, I had used up all my fishing bait." The next day, Davis made three trips for herring, and by the following day, "she was eating out of my hand, and I could touch her and pat her." Davis moved his camper to the bay to be close to the whale. Soon realizing that the calf needed medical help, he telephoned the Vancouver Aquarium on Monday, August 8, and, through them, reached Michael Bigg. Bigg called Bob Wright of Sealand of the Pacific, Victoria, who was looking for another killer whale at the time. That afternoon, Bigg, Wright and New York Aquarium veterinarian Jay Hyman (visiting Wright) motored out with Davis to see the whale. I talked with Bigg on the telephone a week later.

"Davis knew exactly where the animal was," Bigg said. "He just tapped on the side of his boat, and then this whale approached, slowly puffing around in the shallow water. Davis took a bit of bait herring and threw it near the whale, and the whale slowly turned around and obviously ate it. As he kept throwing more bits, it came closer and closer, until it was right up beside the boat. Most unheard-of thing. I think it was starving."

One month earlier, Bigg had seen the lone calf "swimming vigorously" near Nanaimo. For the next few weeks, fishermen and residents reported sighting it moving steadily north along the Vancouver Island coast. "By the time Davis found it," said Bigg, "it was a mopey little animal. The edges of its flukes and its dorsal fin were abraded, and it was bleeding and covered in parasites. I'm sure it would have died had it been left as it was." Bigg recommended that an aquarium be allowed to try to save it, and after a day of haggling, the federal Department of Fisheries and Oceans issued the permit — to Sealand. Late the following day, the 10-foot-long youngster was on a flatbed truck headed for Victoria.

What had happened to the young whale? Why was it alone? Bigg was as mystified as anyone: "We've never seen a calf before that's been separated from its pod. It's probably just an accidental thing — the animal made a wrong turn somewhere along the line, and they lost it. I don't think it was abandoned deliberately, but we don't know how complicated these whale societies are."

Most disturbing was the bullet wound. Ballistics experts and several veterinarians at Sealand confirmed that it had come from a .22 rifle. Had the young whale, either before or after becoming separated from its pod, nosed up to some boat? There were also propeller cuts behind its blowhole. This youngster, never mind having been shot and probably run over by some boat, had trusted a fisherman, Davis, enough to take food out of his hand. And when Sealand came to get the whale, to take it forever from its wild waters, the youngster had swum into the tiny holding pen without a struggle. This whale had a trusting nature. For a wild animal, trusting humans rarely has survival value.

For the first few months, Miracle — as the trusting calf came to be called — fought various infections and ulcers. Several times, the whale sank to the bottom, only to be brought to the surface to breathe. Once, the whale's heart stopped, and she was clinically dead. It took round-the-clock medical attention from Sealand, but the plucky orca, who seemed to have the crucial will to live, finally pulled through. Rescuing Miracle had boosted Sealand's public image, which had sagged further each time Haida had lost one of his three mates, between 1972 and 1976. Sealand had taken a big chance by trying to save the baby. Now, it had not only good press but also a new whale. Davis said that he'd like to see her set free but could never ask for that since he felt that there was no alternative to captivity at her age. As Bigg explained: "It would be like putting a 6-year-old child out in the wilds and saying, 'Look after yourself.' It takes quite a few years for these animals to learn the ropes." Yet even if Miracle survives to adulthood, she will not be released. As an adult, Miracle will become the mate of Haida — if Haida is still alive. Miracle will spend the rest of her life performing tricks to earn her keep and to pay off her medical bills.

When I talked to Wright, he made much of the fact that the baby had been shot, pointing out that his aquarium obviously still had the job of educating the public by exhibiting whales. Some days before picking up the starving, battle-scarred calf, Sealand had already requested another permit to capture whales. Miracle's survival meant that Sealand would not be going whale hunting. Since Sealand's 1975 capture of the Pedder Bay Six, Canadian federal government policy required that capture permits be granted only to established whale catchers and only to replace performing whales that had died in Canadian aquariums. The "established whale catcher" in Canada since 1970 was Bob Wright, and although five of the last seven whales that Wright had sent to aquariums (including his Sealand) had died within a year, he would be the one doing any catching. At the time of the ruling, there were seven orcas performing in Canadian aquariums — three at Marineland and Game Farm in Niagara Falls, two at the Vancouver Aquarium and two at Sealand of the Pacific. When Sealand's Nootka III died in 1976, Wright was the first to request a new permit. Miracle became that replacement. Since Miracle, there have been no new captures — and Wright said that he didn't want to go hunting again for himself or for anyone else. Yet as Bigg says: "When another captive orca dies, there likely will be another capture."

At the current rate of exploitation — new captives only to replace ones that die — killer whale numbers in the Northwest will not be endangered. There is no biological argument that can be presented against capturing a few animals. The scientific and educational reasons for keeping killer whales, on the other hand, are questionable. Much has been learned in the new science of orca husbandry — how to keep a captive whale alive. Yet behavioural studies are of limited value, especially when there is a wild population accessible for study. "How much do you learn by watching a wolf pacing back and forth on the other side of a chain-link fence?" asks Ellis.

The scientific value of keeping animals in captivity was a source of outrage to Desmond Morris, author of *The Naked Ape* and ex-curator of animals at the Regent's Park Zoo in London, England. In 1968, he caused an uproar among his fellow zoologists when he wrote that "a zoo animal without a challenge, with all its problems neatly solved or eliminated, is a travesty of evolution. . . . There is something biologically immoral about keeping animals in enclosures where their behaviour patterns, which have taken millions of years to evolve, can find no expression. . . . [The captive becomes] a battery chicken that provides no food to eat and precious little food for thought."

With killer whales, we could, in fact, learn something by releasing an individual — such as Haida, Skana or Hyak, each of whom has lived in a tank for more than a decade. Bigg knows the pod that each animal belongs to. During the summer and fall, these pods can be seen almost daily and within easy boating distance of Vancouver and Victoria. It would be feasible to reintroduce these whales to their pods and then see what happens.

Visiting the Vancouver Aquarium a few years ago, I asked its director, zoologist Murray A. Newman, how he felt about continuing to keep orcas captive. In 1964, Newman had displayed the first live orca, Moby Doll, in a makeshift pen in Vancouver harbour.

Newman said that he believed an important function of his institution was teaching conservation — to everyone, but especially to schoolchildren. "If they never see a whale, they won't care about them." He called Skana and Hyak "ambassadors from their species" and said that the whales have a continuing mission, "as do we at the aquarium, to foster public sympathy for the whole species."

Newman made his points well, but I was left with nagging questions. Isn't there more to conservation than just displaying the animals? What about the notion of "recycling" — putting back as much as possible of what one has taken? I talked about this with Paul Spong, who had hashed it out with Newman on numerous occasions. Spong had suggested temporary sentences for killer whales, and Newman, as diplomatically as possible, had said: No. We can't do that. Yet of all the organizations exhibiting marine mammals — the various Sea Worlds and Marinelands — the Vancouver Aquarium, which is operated by a nonprofit society, is one of the few that would even seriously discuss the matter. The others, often described as marine circuses, may profess corporate commitments to conservation, but their first responsibility is to their shareholders. Orcas, wherever exhibited, become the star performers that attract the paying customers.

Spong's cohort Robert Hunter, the first president of Greenpeace, summed up many of the arguments and made some concrete suggestions in a series of columns he wrote for the *Vancouver Sun* in 1974. In one, he boldly declared that the aquarium's espoused "cause of conservation is not rightly served by a giant corpse." (We all knew that sooner or later, that would be Skana's fate.

As the longest-surviving orca in captivity, she was, statistically, living on borrowed time.) "Why wait for Skana to die," asked Hunter, "before going out and capturing another whale? Why not do it now? And let Skana herself go free to join her relatives. . . . Another whale could be brought in to replace her. And it, too, could be released after a period of time. The point is that the whales would leave the pool alive — not dead." Hunter went on to suggest that the Vancouver Aquarium was willing "to pioneer in the capture of whales. Just as easily, with its resources, it could pioneer in the releasing of whales by setting up a halfway house in the water up the coast and gradually reintroducing [whales] to the natural world. The lesson would be a tremendous one for a whole generation of young Canadians who have already gotten the message about conservation but who have not yet been given any guidance about what to do."*

Still, any discussion concerning whether aquariums should serve the animals, the public or only themselves fails to reach the heart of the matter. Beyond all the arguments is what could be called, quite simply, a growing public distaste for the idea of keeping large marine mammals like orcas as captives. Some of that public sympathy for the species, which the aquariums have indeed fostered, also extends to the captives and, paradoxically, is directed against the aquariums themselves. In the words of biologist Ian B. MacAskie of Canada's Pacific Biological Station, "Not enough consideration has been given the moral implications of confining a huge animal like the killer whale in a relatively tiny space like an aquarium tank. There'd be quite an outcry if a dog were kept in a cage of the same relative size."

The treatment of wildlife — in captivity and in the wild — is "something I've given a lot of thought to," said U.S. biologist Victor B. Scheffer, a world authority on marine mammals. Scheffer presented a case for the conservation of all whale species in the final chapter of *Marine Mammals of Eastern North Pacific and Arctic Waters*. "At the core of humaneness," he wrote, "is the idea of *kind-ness*, or the idea that we and the other animals are basically of one kind." Scheffer suggested that because we are all "part of the living animal world . . . caught up together in a sort of spiritual biomass . . . we have the right to insist not only that animals be spared distress (pain and fear) but that they be used in ways acceptable to large numbers of thoughtful men and women."

Determining the uses of wildlife is the job of wildlife managers, but Scheffer said that the managers must listen to biologists (who tell us how animals *could* be used) and to sociologists (who tell us how they *should* be used). Scheffer, whose numerous writings on marine mammals bespeak his knowledge and, more recently, his concern, nevertheless confessed his "inability to deal adequately with the problem of how one learns what the general public wants from, and for, the whales, seals and other marine mammals." But, he wrote, "I myself believe that what men and women are saying today about them is,

---

*On October 5, 1980, after 13 1/2 years of captivity, Skana died. In 1982, a few months after Miracle died in Victoria, Sealand of the Pacific proposed that the mature male Haida be returned to the wild and that it be allowed to capture two new young whales from the pods living off southern Vancouver Island. The Canadian government approved the plan, but before Haida could be replaced, he died.

'Let them be.' A useful marine mammal, they say, is one out there somewhere in the wild — free, alive, hidden, breathing, perpetuating its ancient blood-line.''

Scheffer freely admits that beyond scientific reasons for conserving marine mammals, "my real argument is emotional or, if you wish, sentimental. I believe, quite simply, that sentiment is one of the best reasons for saving not only some of these animals but all of them.''

As for the live capture of killer whales, public sentiment had become a powerful force for conservation by the mid-1970s. The 1976 capture of six orcas in Budd Inlet, Washington, amply demonstrated that. Through the late 1960s and early 1970s, Sea World's Don Goldsberry had captured more than 50 percent of the killer whales removed from the wild and sent to the world's aquariums. With Ted Griffin of the Seattle Public Aquarium, he was the first, in October 1965, to mount a successful live-capture operation, bringing back the first Shamu. Later, on a dozen occasions, he captured more than 200 orcas. Of these, about 30 were sent to various aquariums, but mostly to Sea World. At least nine others died in the nets. When it came to capturing orcas, Goldsberry had been called a cattle rancher more than once. It was his lack of subtlety plus bad timing that finally finished him at Budd Inlet.

For most of March 7, 1976, Goldsberry was busy driving a pod of whales ever deeper into Puget Sound. He herded them into Olympia Harbor, right past the capitol dome where the legislature was in session debating, among other things, a possible Puget Sound killer whale sanctuary. He herded them in full sight of Ralph Munro, an assistant to Washington State Governor Dan Evans. Munro happened to be out sailing that afternoon, and he did not like what he saw: buzzing aircraft and motorboats equipped with exploding seal bombs to move the whales. Finally, Goldsberry herded the whales into Budd Inlet, setting his nets only a few miles from Evergreen State College, where a three-day killer whale conference was in progress. The theme of the conference — if not at the beginning, then certainly by the end — was that Puget Sound orca captures must stop. Goldsberry himself was scheduled to speak. After catching the whales, he was not talking. Spong was at the conference, screening our 1973 whale film of Stubbs's pod. I was there, too, showing slides and playing sound recordings. Whale photographer Ken Balcomb, just then beginning his census and studies of Puget Sound orcas, was also there. The conference was well attended by whale researchers, students and conservationists who were members of Greenpeace and Friends of the Dolphin. The air was charged. "Free the whales" was the cry of the conferees. More than a thousand people descended on the capture site at Budd Inlet. People watched from shore or rowed and kayaked out to the nets. Flowers were dropped from a passing seaplane. Newspaper and television reporters pounced on the story, and it brought international headlines.

Goldsberry had incensed not only the conservationists and whale conferees but also Washington State public officials. Governor Evans and Attorney General Slade Gorton filed suit against Sea World, Incorporated, in federal court, charging that Goldsberry and Sea World had violated the terms of their collecting permit by using aircraft and explosives "in an inhumane manner" to net killer whales. The suit bounced from court to court while six whales waited in the nets, held by court injunction, though the injunction did not keep three of them from making good their escape. After a series of drawn-out proceedings in Seattle, a district court judge dismissed the case but stipulated several conditions: He ordered the remaining whales released but recommended that two of them be turned over to University of Washington researchers for not more than two months. Furthermore, Sea World had to give up its permit-granted right to collect orcas in Washington waters. Goldsberry and his men limped out of the state.

In October 1976, the killer whale capture scene shifted to Iceland, with Goldsberry representing Sea World's interests. After Puget Sound, Sea World did not want to be officially involved, but Goldsberry agreed to assist two newcomers to the capture business – W.H. Dudok van Heel, zoological director of Holland's Dolfinarium Harderwijk, and Jón Kr. Gunnarsson, director of Sædyrasafnid, an aquarium near Reykjavík. The group netted two young whales during the fall herring season. Both were airlifted to Holland. One stayed, while the other was forwarded to Sea World in San Diego after six months. The following October, the same consortium captured six orcas. In October 1978, Goldsberry and Gunnarsson caught another five; then Sea World, with nine new whales in less than two years, dropped out of the picture. Gunnarsson took over all the catching in Icelandic waters, with International Animal Exchange of Ferndale, Michigan, handling sales and distribution to the world market. (The going rate in November 1979 for a healthy young orca was $150,000 FOB Reykjavík, but in 1980, the price rose to between $200,000 and $300,000.) According to Gunnarsson (in a letter dated April 1980), some 21 Icelandic killer whales, mostly youngsters, were sent to aquariums from 1976 to 1979. Besides Sea World's nine, two each went to Dolfinarium Harderwijk, Marineland of France, Canada's Marineland and Kamogawa Sea World in Japan. Single animals were sent to Windsor Safari Park in England and to new aquariums in Hong Kong and Switzerland.

In November 1978, International Animal Exchange ordered five Icelandic orcas, planning to ship them to Japan, but had difficulty arranging transport. As winter came on, Gunnarsson was left holding them at Sædyrasafnid. "We had an unusually hard winter," he wrote, "very stormy and very low seawater temperature. In the middle of January, we came into pumping trouble. . . . The animals got frostbite. Two died. The [other] three got medicine against pneumonia and were doing well again, but after more cold weather and delay in arranging transportation, we removed the animals out to sea and let them free." A few weeks later, on February 26, 1979, five Japanese orcas were netted by the town of Taiji for its Taiji Whale Museum and for nearby Shirahama World Safari, which had planned to buy orcas from Iceland. Unfortunately, three of the five whales – all mature females – died within three months.

Since 1979, Iceland has been the site of most orca captures. Gunnarsson reports seeing orcas in the hundreds around the herring boats every fall, when they are "easy to catch in purse seines." The Icelandic government, limiting permits to from 4 to 10 most years, has welcomed the new "industry." But the high cost and the problems of shipping whales from Iceland — plus the denial of Sea World's request to import Icelandic orcas in 1980 — rekindled interest in capturing Northwest Coast orcas.

In 1976, Puget Sound became an unofficial sanctuary for killer whales — at least in terms of capturing them. Since then, public sentiment — the "let them be" philosophy — has effectively precluded anyone from even asking for a permit. And in Canadian waters, where permits may still be requested to replace whales that die, Sealand owner Bob Wright obtained a permit in 1982, but Greenpeace blocked all capture attempts. Sealand finally gave up, buying three orcas from Iceland and flying them in secretly.

In 1983, Sea World, Incorporated, announced that it was expanding its facilities and wanted to mount a five-year capture operation in southeast Alaska waters. The plan was to catch 100 killer whales — 90 for research and eventual release, 10 for permanent exhibition. The permit application — condemned by many biologists, environmentalists and Northwest Coast residents — was approved by the U.S. National Marine Fisheries Service. Sea World's corporate director of collection, Don Goldsberry, got his nets ready, but opposition in Alaska, from the governor down, steadily mounted. Finally, Sea World withdrew. Sea World did not want to have another Budd Inlet incident on its hands.

Since the Alaska operation fell through, Sea World has relied on buying killer whales from existing aquariums to replace dead animals and to stock a new park in San Antonio, Texas. It also developed the first successful orca breeding programme. On September 26, 1985, Baby Shamu, a female, was born at Sea World in Orlando, Florida. Since then, five more Baby Shamus have been born — three in the autumn of 1988 — and a total of five survived through October 1989.

Yet bad publicity continues to plague Sea World. In late 1986, Sea World, through its parent company, Harcourt Brace Jovanovich, purchased Marineland of the Pacific, orcas and all. Two months later, after promising to keep the park open, it moved longtime residents Orky (II) and Corky (II) from Los Angeles to San Diego in the dead of night and closed down Marineland. The following year, in an unfortunate case of crossed signals during a Sea World show, Orky landed on trainer John Sillick, breaking his ribs, pelvis and femur. After this accident and several other near tragedies, three executives were fired. Former trainers are now suing Sea World.

In August 1989, disaster struck again at the San Diego park. As several thousand spectators watched, Baby Shamu (III)'s mother Kandu (V) raced at Corky, mouth open, smashing into her. This "attack" may have been prompted by Corky's role as "auntie" to the then 11-month-old baby. Kandu, though 2,000 pounds lighter than the much older Corky, was nevertheless the dominant animal. Kandu was also known to be aggressive. She had twice taken trainers in her mouth and had once pinned one against a wall. With Corky, she had roughed up a male trainer, causing him minor injuries. But after biting Corky, Kandu herself started spouting blood. Sea World trainers tried to keep the show going, but the pool soon turned bloody. As the crowd was ushered out, she died at poolside. The necropsy showed an upper-jaw fracture that had triggered a massive haemorrhage. Sea World officials called it a "freak accident" following routine aggressive behaviour. But others saw the incident as neurotic behaviour brought on by years of captivity. Corky escaped with minor rake marks on her back. Baby Shamu, who was nearly weaned at the time, seemed disoriented by the loss of her mother. The following day, however, the baby performed in the show beside Corky. Sea World trainers were optimistic about the youngster's future.

A month after the accident, in September 1989, Harcourt Brace Jovanovich sold all the Sea World parks to Anheuser-Busch, the world's largest brewer, for $1.1 billion. The sale had been in the works for months; Harcourt Brace Jovanovich needed cash, and the profitable Sea World was the most saleable part of its empire. Meanwhile, at Anheuser-Busch, now the second largest operator of theme parks in the United States, there were jokes about "Spuds MacKenzie," the Bud Light dog, joining Shamu by the pool. Sadly, the show must go on.

But on the last day of our 1979 expedition, we were in Robson Bight and wild whales were blowing rainbows in the low sun of late September. There were five of us on the 26-foot Bell Boy. Jim Borrowman, a veteran of three whale summers, and fellow diver Bill Harrower had joined Françoise Roux, Victoria Hoyt and me for three days of whale watching. Françoise was driving Harrower's boat, while Victoria, Borrowman and Harrower were sprawled on the deck. The divers were hoping for another chance to be invited in by our orca hosts. Clutching a camera, I was waiting for all the whales to blow at once, Robson Bight in the background – one photograph to tell the whole story. We were all quiet.

As we watched and listened to the whales, they seemed to be arguing, passionately, for Robson Bight and the Tsitika estuary. The three A pods were travelling together as in the old days. Saddle's brand-new calf was rolling over its mother. Saddle's 7-year-old and Scar's 7-year-old were playing with Top Notch. Against the bight's eastern wall, the three bulls in Stubbs's pod were giving feeding lessons to another group of youngsters. Near the river mouth, several cows and young males were lying on their backs, sculling across the river waves that spilled into the bight. It seemed a day in paradise, fresh and new, and at the same time, it was like hundreds of others we had spent with the whales.

Deep in the Tsitika River Valley, some 12 miles upstream from Robson Bight, Mac'n'Blo and Canfor were already pulling down the old giant trees and building roads to pull down even more. The road had been surveyed down to the estuary, and Mac'n'Blo was determined to reach tidewater by 1984. Never mind the whales, Mac'n'Blo wanted to haul their logs out of the river mouth, dumping them in the bight, and the growing fear was that despite continuing environmental studies, it would take a major effort to stop them.

In November 1979, Borrowman, Harrower and I spoke on several occasions with the executive director of B.C.'s Ecological Reserve Committee, zoologist J. Bristol Foster. Borrowman asked if there was any hope of protecting the bight as an ecological reserve. Foster said yes, that a proposal was being made.

We looked at the map. The reserve turned out to be less than 100 acres at the river mouth; it included only a small part of the bight and none of the rubbing rocks along its shore. With Foster's help, we redrew the boundary lines for the proposed reserve. Most of the Tsitika River Valley was going to be logged. Could we not obtain full protection at least for Robson Bight? It represented less than 1 percent, a crumb of the total Tsitika watershed. While Foster encouraged us, he warned that it could be a big fight. "You'll be effectively killing the proposed logging port, asking the logging companies to find another route, undoubtedly more expensive. They're not going to like that." Foster advised us to organize public support.

After our talks, Borrowman and Harrower, joined by Telegraph Cove resident Bill Mackay, designed posters and handbills, prepared a talk and slide presentation and took their show on the road. Biologists Michael Bigg, John Ford and Dean Fisher lent their names and their expertise, writing letters and appearing before committees, to verify the whales' use of the bight. A film crew led by Michael O'Neill, who had first filmed the orcas in 1973, documented the whales in the act of rubbing. In the meantime, I wrote a series of articles for local and national magazines. We were publicizing Robson Bight, inviting the world to come and meet the whales. It was either publicize the place or let it die quietly. The challenge was to convince people and government that marine creatures which roam the open seas need habitats. We tried to give the bight an international perspective – comparing it to Scammon Lagoon in Mexico, where grey whales spend the winters calving and raising their young, and to Golfo San José in Argentina, the home of Patagonia's right whales. Both Scammon Lagoon and Golfo San José had been set aside as permanent government reserves for whales, and we wanted the same kind of protection for B.C.'s killer whales. Designation of the bight as an ecological reserve was the only way to protect it from logging booms, logging traffic, gravel pits and pollution and to keep it forever for the whales that are its rightful owners.

Late afternoon on that last day of our expedition, there was one moment when three whales suddenly lifted their heads and bobbed together, looking at us. A sigh went through the boat. I framed and shot the whales' portraits – with Robson Bight, the Tsitika River Valley and snowcapped Mount Derby in the background.

The whales slid back into the water, but the image stayed, clearer in mind than on film. It is an image that nourishes our dream that the killer whales will continue to come to Robson Bight and that we will be able to visit them there for many years to come.

EPILOGUE

Our understanding of killer whales has come a long way since I first set sail for "killer whale country" in 1973. We have learned that:
• Killer whales live about as long as humans and reproduce over roughly the same age span.
• Most females first give birth at age 14, bear four to six calves over the next 25 years, then enjoy life as doting grandmothers into their sixties and seventies, sometimes even eighties.
• The males also mature at about age 14, and they live to about 60. As with males of many mammals, they do not live as long as females.
• A killer whale pod is an extended family with as many as four generations of related whales living and travelling together.

These facts — the sifted wisdom from thousands of pod encounters — emerge from the work Michael Bigg began in the early 1970s, with important contributions along the way from Graeme Ellis, John Ford, Kenneth Balcomb and others.

Because of their work, we now know that the big male, Top Notch, was probably born in 1958 when his mother, Scar, or A9, was 26. And in 1989, Top Notch, at 31, still travelled with his mother, then 57, and his younger brother, A26, who was about 18. Scar is no longer having calves; rarely do the females reproduce beyond their late thirties. Scar has no known grandchildren. Her sons could have fathered several calves, but the calves would stay with their mothers, who may well be in another subpod of A5 pod. Scar would have to have had daughters to become a doting grandmother.

Sadly, grandmother Nicola, who did have a daughter and at least four grandchildren, died in 1988. At the time of her death at age 64, she was the second oldest killer whale living off northern Vancouver Island. The only older female, G30, was born in about 1918 and is still alive. The oldest known killer whale on the British Columbia-Washington coast is a female, identified as K7, who is in the southern resident community, ranging off southern Vancouver Island and in Washington State waters. In 1989, she was believed to be 83 years old.

Back in 1981, when the first edition of *Orca: The Whale Called Killer* was about to be published, I wrote that we hoped to revisit our orca friends "for many years to come." I had no idea then that those whales I had grown so fond of on my first orca trip in 1973 might still be around in the year 2000 and beyond.

But neither did I realize as fully the dangers to orca longevity. Today, many people are wondering:
• How well will the world ocean be cared for?
• Will the dumping of sludge and other toxic wastes at sea increase or abate?
• Will fishermen be allowed to continue stringing miles and miles of gill nets that unselectively catch and drown anything which swims into them?
• Will destructive oil spills, such as the tanker *Exxon Valdez*'s fouling of Alaska's Prince William Sound in March 1989, be tolerated by future world citizens as the fragile nature of Earth becomes more evident?

There is only one world ocean, and pesticides and contaminants, such as PCBs, DDT and others banned decades ago, are cycled throughout it. As we examine the tissues of marine animals, we find high concentrations of these poisons. We also find more and more marine animals with cancers and suppressed immune systems.

I wonder, too, whether we can control the burning of fossil fuels in cars and factories that apparently is leading to the greenhouse effect. Will the increase in world temperatures eventually make the sea a desert by warming polar waters and damaging the productivity of the plant-plankton source for much of marine life?

If we can avoid some of these ecological disasters, we will owe a special debt to the whales. They have given the environmental movement around the world some glamour and have brought into the conservation crusade many who would not otherwise have become involved. Initially, the killer whales played a key role through their performances at aquariums, and later, as they became better known in the wild, people marvelled at their power, intelligence and sleek elegance.

Whaling of certain whale species continues on a limited scale, mainly by the Japanese, but it has diminished. We have in large part saved the whales. Yet it will be a temporary reprieve if we are unable to save their watery habitat.

In their home at Robson Bight, Top Notch's pod and others now enjoy some of the protection that we fought for in the early 1980s. MacMillan Bloedel Limited agreed to drop its logging-port proposal, and in 1982, the B.C. government awarded the killer whales a marine ecological reserve at Robson Bight. In late 1987, MacMillan Bloedel sold the Tsitika River estuary to the province, Wildlife Habitat Canada and the Nature Trust of

British Columbia. Since then, additional shoreline was acquired to provide a land buffer between the whales and the logging activity, and now the reserve covers about 1,000 acres.

It has taken more than a decade for us to secure minimal habitat protection for Top Notch and Scar, plus Sharky and her newborn calf and the next generation of killer whales. But it is a start. Robson Bight is now a real sanctuary — the first for killer whales anywhere in the world.

©Peter Thomas

Captured in March 1970 at Pedder Bay, Chimo was the only white killer whale ever to be held in captivity. One aquarium offered Sealand $1 million for her. But Chimo's fame was short-lived, as she died 2½ years later of Chediak-Higashi syndrome.

Researcher James Darling comforts a mature bull orca stranded near Tofino in 1976. The whale, thought to have beached itself while pursuing harbour porpoises near shore, could not be saved.

Marineland's Corky and her second calf. Born in captivity in October 1978, the calf — weighing 450 pounds and measuring 7 feet — died 11 days later. Corky belonged to Top Notch's pod before her capture in Pender Harbour in December 1969.

Peter Thomas

Killer-turned-tourist-attraction. Orcas have lived down their past image and are now the principal attraction of many West Coast tours.

Peter Thomas

Dorsal-fin deformities, perhaps genetically linked, distinguish the members of I pod. The whales in the foreground are, from left to right: Tube, whose notched fin lists to port; Finger, whose fin is collapsing; and Accordian, whose fin wobbles from side to side.

APPENDICES

APPENDIX 1

THE DIET OF THE KILLER WHALE: A LIST OF KNOWN PREY

COMMON NAME	SCIENTIFIC NAME	LOCATION	EVIDENCE	SOURCE
CETACEANS				
Baird's beaked whale	*Berardius bairdii*	Japan coast	stomach	Nishiwaki & Handa, 1958
Beluga	*Delphinapterus leucas*	Arctic	seen feeding	Scammon, 1874
		Greenland coast	attack	Dergerböl & Neilsen, 1930
Blue whale	*Balaenoptera musculus*	Baja Calif. coast	seen feeding	Tarpy, 1979
Bowhead whale	*Balaena mysticetus*	Arctic	prey scars	Tomilin, 1957
		North Pacific	seen feeding	Bullen, 1948
Common dolphin	*Delphinus delphis*	Baja Calif. coast	seen feeding	Brown & Norris, 1956
Cuvier's beaked whale	*Ziphius cavirostris*	Japan coast	stomach	Nishiwaki & Handa, 1958
Dall's porpoise	*Phocoenoides dalli*	California coast	stomach	Rice, 1968
		N.E. Pacific	attack	Pike & MacAskie, 1969
		Alaska coast	attack	Barr & Barr, 1972
		North Japan coast	stomach	Nishiwaki & Handa, 1958
Dusky dolphin	*Lagenorhynchus obscurus*	Patagonia coast	attack	Wursig & Wursig, 1979
Fin whale	*Balaenoptera physalus*	South temperate zone	prey scars	Shevchenko, 1975
		Bering Sea	stomach	Tomilin, 1957
		British Columbia	attack	Pike & MacAskie, 1969
Finless porpoise	*Neophocaena phocaenoides*	Japan coast	stomach	Nishiwaki & Handa, 1958

COMMON NAME	SCIENTIFIC NAME	LOCATION	EVIDENCE	SOURCE
Grey whale	*Eschrichtius robustus*	Bering Sea	stomach	Zenkovich, 1954
		Baja Calif. coast	seen feeding	Scammon, 1874
		California coast	prey scars	Rice & Wolman, 1971
		California coast	seen feeding	Baldridge, 1972
		British Columbia	attack	Pike & MacAskie, 1969
Harbour porpoise	*Phocoena phocoena*	California coast	stomach	Rice, 1968
		W. Vancouver Island	stomach	Ford & Ford, 1981
Humpback whale	*Megaptera novaeangliae*	S.E. Australia	seen feeding	Wellings, 1944 Dakin, 1934
			attack	Tomilin, 1957
Killer whale*	*Orcinus orca*	South temperate zone	stomach	Shevchenko, 1975
Minke whale	*Balaenoptera acutorostrata*	California coast	stomach	Rice, 1968
		W. Vancouver Island	seen feeding	Hancock, 1965
		Near Port Hardy, B.C.	prey scars	Ford & Ford, 1981
		Antarctic	stomach	Shevchenko, 1975
		Antarctic & S. Indian Ocean	stomach	Yukhov et al., 1975
		S.E. Australia	seen feeding	Wellings, 1944 Dakin, 1934
Narwhal	*Monodon monoceros*	Greenland	attack	Freuchen & Salomonsen, 1958
			attack	Kellogg, 1940

*Possible case of cannibalism in which orca remains were found in the stomachs of two males belonging to the same group. Shevchenko (1975) notes that it may have occurred because of the insecure food supply. Eleven of 30 stomachs — a very high percentage — studied in this area (30° to 50° southern latitude) were empty.

COMMON NAME	SCIENTIFIC NAME	LOCATION	EVIDENCE	SOURCE
Northern bottlenose whale	*Hyperoodon ampullatus*	Norway coast	seen feeding	Jonsgård, 1968
Right whale	*Eubalaena glacialis*		attack	Tomilin, 1957
Sei whale	*Balaenoptera borealis*	Japan coast	stomach	Nishiwaki & Handa, 1958
		South temperate zone	prey scars	Shevchenko, 1975
Short-finned pilot whale	*Globicephala macrorhynchus*	Japan coast	stomach	Nishiwaki & Handa, 1958
Sperm whale	*Physeter macrocephalus*	South subtropics	stomach	Yukhov et al., 1975
		Southern ocean	prey scars, attack	Shevchenko, 1975
Striped dolphin	*Stenella coeruleoalba*	South Japan coast	stomach	Nishiwaki & Handa, 1958

PINNIPEDS

COMMON NAME	SCIENTIFIC NAME	LOCATION	EVIDENCE	SOURCE
Bearded seal	*Erignathus barbatus*	Bering Sea	stomach	Zenkovich, 1938
California sea lion	*Zalophus californianus*	California coast	stomach	Rice, 1968
Crabeater seal	*Lobodon carcinophagus*	Antarctic	prey scars	Yukhov et al., 1975
		Antarctic	attack	Smith et al., 1981
			attack	Tomilin, 1957
Harbour seal	*Phoca vitulina*	W. Vancouver Island	stomach	Pike & MacAskie, 1969
		Denmark coast	stomach	Eschricht, 1862
		North Japan coast	stomach	Nishiwaki & Handa, 1958
		Puget Sound, Wash.	attack	Scheffer & Slipp, 1948
Leopard seal	*Hydrurga leptonyx*	Antarctic	stomach	Yukhov et al., 1975

COMMON NAME	SCIENTIFIC NAME	LOCATION	EVIDENCE	SOURCE
		Antarctic	prey scars & attack	Siniff & Bengtson, 1977
Northern elephant seal	*Mirounga angustirostris*	California coast	stomach	Rice, 1968
		Baja Calif. coast	attack	Samaras & Leather- wood, 1974
		S.W. Indian Ocean	seen feeding	Condy et al., 1978
		W. Vancouver Island	stomach	Ford & Ford, 1981
Northern fur seal	*Callorhinus ursinus*	Bering Sea	seen feeding	Tomilin, 1957
Ringed seal	*Phoca hispida*	N.E. Japan coast	stomach	Nishiwaki & Handa, 1958
South American sea lion	*Otaria flavescens*	Patagonia coast	attack	Bartlett & Bartlett, 1976
Southern elephant seal	*Mirounga leonina*	S.W. Indian Ocean	stomach	Voisin, 1972
		S. Indian Ocean	attack	Paulian, 1953/64
Steller sea lion	*Eumetopias jubatus*	California coast	stomach	Rice, 1968
		W. Vancouver Island	stomach	Pike & MacAskie, 1969
Subantarctic fur seal	*Arctocephalus tropicalis*	S.W. Indian Ocean	attack	Paulian, 1964
Walrus	*Odobenus rosmarus*	Bering Sea	stomach	Zenkovich, 1938
		Arctic	seen feeding	Scammon, 1874
Weddell seal	*Leptonychotes weddelli*	Antarctic	stomach	Yukhov et al., 1975
		Antarctic	seen feeding	Cromie, 1962

MUSTELIDS

COMMON NAME	SCIENTIFIC NAME	LOCATION	EVIDENCE	SOURCE
Sea otter	*Enhydra lutris*	North Pacific	seen feeding	Nikolaev, 1965
		North Pacific	attack	Tomilin, 1957

COMMON NAME	SCIENTIFIC NAME	LOCATION	EVIDENCE	SOURCE
FISHES				
Basking shark	*Cetorhinus maximus*	S. California coast	seen feeding	Norris, 1958
		South subtropics	stomach	Yukhov et al., 1975
Bonito	*Sarda orientalis (?)*	Japan coast	stomach	Nishiwaki & Handa, 1958
Capelin	*Mallotus villosus*	Arctic/N.W. Pacific	stomach	Tomilin, 1957
Cod (Pacific)	*Gadus macrocephalus*	Japan coast	stomach	Nishiwaki & Handa, 1958
		Puget Sound, Wash.	stomach	Balcomb et al., 1979
Cod (Atlantic)	*Gadus morhua*	Norway coast	stomach	Tomilin, 1957
Eagle stingray	*Myliobatis*	S. Brazil coast	stomach	Castello, 1977
Electric ray	*Torpedo californica*	California coast	seen feeding	Norris & Prescott, 1961
Flat fishes	*Heterosomata*	Japan coast	stomach	Nishiwaki & Handa, 1958
Greenling	*Hexagrammidae*	Puget Sound, Wash.	stomach	Scheffer & Slipp, 1948
Halibut (Pacific)	*Hippoglossus hippoglossoides*	Kodiak Island, Alaska	stomach	Rice, 1968
		W. Vancouver Island	stomach	Pike & MacAskie, 1969
Herring (Atlantic)	*Clupea harengus*	Icelandic waters	stomach	Jonsgård & Lyshoel, 1970
		S.W. Norway coast	seen feeding	Collett, 1912
		Norway coast	stomach	Grieg, 1906
		Norway coast	stomach	Christensen, 1978
Herring (Pacific)	*Clupea pallasi (?)*	Puget Sound, Wash.	attack	Scheffer & Slipp, 1948

Common Name	Scientific Name	Location	Evidence	Source
Ling cod	*Ophiodon elongatus*	Puget Sound, Wash.	stomach	Scheffer & Slipp, 1948
Mackerel/Atka mackerel	*Scombridae*	Japan coast	stomach	Nishiwaki & Handa, 1958
Opah or moonfish	*Lampris regius*	California coast	stomach	Rice, 1968
Rockfish	*Sebastes*	Japan coast	stomach	Nishiwaki & Handa, 1958
		Puget Sound, Wash.	stomach	Balcomb et al., 1979
Salmon	*Oncorhynchus*	Japan coast	stomach	Nishiwaki & Handa, 1958
Salmon (chum)	*Oncorhynchus keta*	North Pacific	stomach	Tomilin, 1957
Salmon (coho)	*Oncorhynchus kisutch*	North Pacific	stomach	Tomilin, 1957
Salmon (spring or chinook)	*Oncorhynchus tshawytscha*	North Pacific	stomach	Tomilin, 1957
		Puget Sound, Wash.	prey scars	Scheffer & Slipp, 1948
Salmon (pink)	*Oncorhynchus gorbuscha*	Puget Sound, Wash.	seen feeding	Balcomb et al., 1979
Sardine	*Sardinops melanosticta (?)*	Japan coast	stomach	Nishiwaki & Handa, 1958
Shark (Carcharhinid: blue or white-tip)	*Prionarce glauca (?)*	N.E. Pacific coast	stomach	Rice, 1968
Skate	*Rajidae*		stomach	Tomilin, 1957
Smelt	*Osmeridae*		stomach	Tomilin, 1957
Trevalla	*Carangidae (?)*	Tasmania coast	prey scars	Tilley, 1979
Tuna (albacore)	*Thunnus alalunga*	Indian Ocean	prey scars/ seen feeding	Iwashita et al., 1963
Tuna (blue fin)	*Thunnus thynnus*	Morocco coast	seen feeding	Bourne, 1965

Common Name	Scientific Name	Location	Evidence	Source
Tuna (big-eyed)	*Thunnus obesus*	Indian Ocean	prey scars/ seen feeding	Iwashita et al., 1963; Sivasubramaniam, 1964
Tuna (albacore)	*Thunnus alalunga*	Indian Ocean	prey scars/ seen feeding	Iwashita et al., 1963
Tuna (yellowfin)	*Thunnus albacares*	Indian Ocean	prey scars/ seen feeding	Iwashita et al., 1963; Sivasubramaniam, 1964

BIRDS

Common Name	Scientific Name	Location	Evidence	Source
Black brant	*Branta bernicla nigricans*	E. Vancouver Island	attack	Scheffer & Slipp, 1948
Cormorant	Phalacrocoracidae	Boundary Bay, B.C.	stomach	Ford & Ford, 1981
Penguin	Spheniscidae	Falkland Islands	seen feeding	Strange, 1973
		Antarctic	seen feeding	Tomilin, 1957
Emperor penguin	*Aptenodytes forsteri*	Antarctic	stomach	Prevost, 1961
King penguin	*Aptenodytes patagonica*	S.W. Indian Ocean	seen feeding	Condy et al., 1978
Marconi penguin	*Eudyptes chrysolophus*	S.W. Indian Ocean	attack	Condy et al., 1978
Rockhopper penguin	*Eudyptes chrysocome*	S.W. Indian Ocean	seen feeding	Condy et al., 1978
White-headed flightless steamer-duck	*Tachyeres leucocephalus*	South Atlantic	seen feeding	Straneck et al., 1983
White-winged scoter	*Melanitta deglandi*	Near Prince Rupert, B.C.	seen feeding	Odlum, 1948

REPTILES

Common Name	Scientific Name	Location	Evidence	Source
Leatherback sea turtle	*Dermochelys coriacea*	St. Vincent Island (Lesser Antilles)	stomach	Caldwell & Caldwell, 1969

CEPHALOPODS

Common Name	Scientific Name	Location	Evidence	Source
Octopus	Octobrachia	Norway coast	stomach	Christensen, 1978

COMMON NAME	SCIENTIFIC NAME	LOCATION	EVIDENCE	SOURCE
		Japan coast	stomach	Nishiwaki & Handa, 1958
Squid	Decabrachia	California coast	stomach	Rice, 1968
		Japan coast	stomach	Nishiwaki & Handa, 1958
		Norway coast	stomach	Jonsgård & Lyshoel, 1970
		Antarctic	stomach	Shevchenko, 1975
		Kuril Islands	stomach	Tomilin, 1957
		Puget Sound, Wash.	stomach	Scheffer & Slipp, 1948

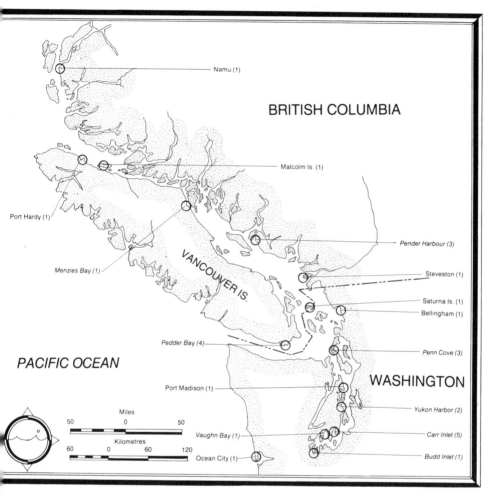

Namu (1)

BRITISH COLUMBIA

Malcolm Is. (1)

Port Hardy (1)

Pender Harbour (3)

Menzies Bay (1)

VANCOUVER IS.

Steveston (1)

Saturna Is. (1)
Bellingham (1)

PACIFIC OCEAN

Pedder Bay (4)

Penn Cove (3)

WASHINGTON

Port Madison (1)

Yukon Harbor (2)

Miles

50   0   50

Carr Inlet (5)

Kilometres

60   0   60   120

Vaughn Bay (1)

Ocean City (1)

Budd Inlet (1)

e Killer Whale Capture Locations in the Northwest (1962-77)
Appendix 5, page 234)

APPENDIX 2

POPULATION OF KILLER WHALES IN BRITISH COLUMBIA AND WASHINGTON WATERS: POD SIZE AND COMPOSITION 1981-1987[1]

Pod Name	Subpods[2]	Cows	Bulls	Young[3]	Total in Pod 1987	Total in Pod 1981
Northern Community						
A1 (Stubbs's)	3	4	6	5	15	14
A4 (The Six)	2	2	0	6	8	7
A5 (Top Notch's)	2	5	3	5	13	12
B1 (Hooker's)	1	1	3	3	7	80
C1	2	3	3	4	10	9
D1 (Warp Fin's)	2	3	1	5	9	10
G1	4	9	5	9	23	19 ± 1
G12	1	3	0	6	9	6
H1	1	2	1	4	7	?
I1	1	2	1	4	7	?
I2	1	2	3	3	8	?
I11	2	4	0	10	14	?
I18	2	4	0	9	13	?
I31	2	2	1	4	7	?
R1	3	7?	6	6	19	19 ± 1
W1	1	1	1	1	3	?
Southern Community						
J1	1	7	4	7	18	19
K1	2	9	3	4	16	10
L1	3	19	5	23	47	50 ± 1

Northern Community

Range: off northern Vancouver Island (from Campbell River north at least to southeast Alaska)

Total 1981: 12 known pods of 135 whales

Total 1987: 16 pods of 172 whales[4]

Southern Community

Range: off southern Vancouver Island (from Campbell River south to Puget Sound and Grays Harbor, Washington)

Total 1981: 3 pods of 79 whales

Total 1987: 3 pods of 81 whales[4]

Transient Community

Range: off Washington, British Columbia and southeast Alaska

Total 1981: 15 known pods of 47 whales

Total 1987: 29 pods of 74 whales[4]

Pod	1981	[2]		1987	
E1	1	1	0	1	?
F1	1	1	0	1	1
M1 (Charlie Chin's)	1	0	1	3	3
M3	1	1	0	1	1
N1	1	1	0	1	1
O2	1	0	2	2	?
O5	1	1	1	2	?
O10	1	0	2	3	?
O21	1	1	2	4	?
P1	1	1?	0	2	2±1
P27	1	0	5	7	?
Q1	1	0	2	3	?
Q3	1	0	2	3	?
Q4	1	0	1	2	?
Q9	1	0	2	3	?
S1	1	?	1	3	4
S3	1	0	0	2	?
S8	1	0	0	1	1?
S10	1	0	0	1	?
T1	1	>1	3	5	4±1
U1	1	?	0	5	4
V1	1	1	1	2	2
V10	1	>1	2	4	?
X1	1	?	0	5	5?
X10	1	1	1	3	?
Y1	1	1	1	3	3
Z1	1	1	0	2	2
Z50	1	1	0	1	?
Z60	1	1	0	1	?

Grand Total 1981: 30 known pods of 261 whales

Grand Total 1987: 48 pods of 327 whales[4]

[1] Adapted by permission from Bigg, M.A. (1982), based on 1981 census figures, and Bigg, M.A. et al (1987), with 1987 census figures.

[2] Number of subpods within the pod. Subpods often travel apart from each other and probably represent future pods.

[3] Less than 14 in 1986 (born in 1973 or earlier).

[4] The difference in the number of pods between 1981 and 1986 results from the reclassification of certain pods into distinct units and the discovery of several new pods.

APPENDIX 3

LOCAL AND NATIONAL NAMES FOR ORCINUS ORCA

NORTH AMERICA

United States and Canada	killer whale, killer, grampus, orca, orc
British Columbia	blackfish
Eastern Canada	swordfish
Quebec	épaulard, espadon (swordfish)
North Alaska (Inuit)	aaxlu
South Alaska (Inuit or Chugach)	takxukuak
Cook Inlet, Alaska (Tanaina)	axlot
Alaska (Yupik)	mesungesak
Alaska (Aleut)	agliuk
Kodiak Island, Alaska (Aleut)	polossatik (the feared one)
Northwest Coast, Alaska (Tlingit)	kit
Northwest Coast, Alaska-B.C. (Haida)	skana (killer demon; supernatural power)
Northwest Coast, B.C. (Kwakiutl)	mahk e-nuk
Northwest Coast, B.C. (Nootka)	qaqawun
St. Vincent, Lesser Antilles	whitefish
Mexico	orca (female or either), orco (male)

SOUTH AMERICA

Spanish America	orca (female or either), orco (male)
Brazil	orca
Tierra del Fuego (Yaghan)	ëpãĭăci

EUROPE

England	killer whale, killer, grampus, orca, orc
Scotland	pictwhale
France	épaulard, orque, epée de mer
Germany	Mörderwal, Schwertwal (sword-whale), Schwertfisch (swordfish)
Netherlands	zvaardwalvis (sword-whale), zvaardvis (swordfish), orca
Spain	orca (female or either), orco (male)
Portugal	orca
Italy	orca
Czechoslovakia	kosatka drava
Denmark	spækhugger (fat-chopper), hvalhund (whale-dog), sværdval (sword-whale), tandthoye
Iceland	hahyrningur, hahyrna, sverdfiscur (swordfish), huyding
Greenland (Inuit)	ardluk (female), ardlursak (male)
Sweden	spækhuggare (fat-chopper)
Norway	spækhogger, spekkhogger (fat-chopper), staurvagn (farmer's pole; swinging back and forth), staurhynning (pole-shaped horn), staurhval (pole-whale), vaghund (hunting together like dogs), vagnhogg (hunting together for fat or blubber)
Lapland	akan, fakan

AFRICA

Union of South Africa   killer whale, killer, grampus, orca, orc

ASIA

Russia   kosatka, kasatka, svinka
Siberia (Koryak)   wúli-yū´ñin (the wedge-whale)
Chukotski Peninsula, Russia   niss'onkhgyssyak
(Inuit and Chukchee)
Kuril Islands, Russia (Ainos)   nookur, dukulad
Japan   sakamata, shachi
Japan (Ainu)   repun kamui (master of the open sea)
Japan (Shachi)   sadshi
Korea   innuatu

AUSTRALIA

Australia and New Zealand   killer whale, killer, grampus, orca, orc

APPENDIX 4

WORLD CATCH STATISTICS FOR KILLER WHALES

These figures, arranged by whaling ground and month, provide some idea of local and seasonal killer whale concentrations around the world.*

WHALING GROUNDS	YEAR	Jan	Feb	Mar	Apr	May	Jun	Jul	Aug	Sep	Oct	Nov	Dec	TOTAL
NORWAY														
Coastal districts	1954				5	8								13
	1955				3	5	7		2					17
	1956				5	3	7		1	2				18
	1957				14	10	7		2					33
	1958			7	9	8	3			1				28
	1959													13
	1960													40
	1961													57
	1962													46
	1963													47
	1964													25
	1965													26
	1966													62
	1967			1	5	4								10
	1968			23	14	6	3							46
	1969			167	4	9	3		6					189
	1970	5	135	66	9	14	2	1						232
	1971	9			3		6							18
	1972				2	5								7

Catch statistics by locality and year (reported numbers).

Year											Total
1973											1
1974											6
1975											2
1977	2	5									7
1978	7	5	1						22	27	62
1979			6	102	9	45	7	3	36	3	221
1980				48	4						52
1981											13

Barents Sea, Spitzbergen and Bear Island

Year											Total
1955	1	1									2
1956	2	5	2								9
1957			2								2
1958	2	8	1								11
1959											24
1960											14
1961											11
1962											11
1963											15
1964											5
1965		3	3								6
1966	2	2	1								5
1968	1	1									2
1969	1		2								3
1970			2								2
1978			1								1

Shetland

Year											Total
1955				7							7
1956	4			3						6	13
1957				10			1	1		1	13
1959											32
1960											28
1961											43

*Catch figures are *reported* numbers only based on International Whaling Statistics 1930-82, with additional information from G.C. Pike and I.B. MacAskie (1969), A.G. Tomilin (1957), and E. Mitchell (1975).

WHALING GROUNDS	YEAR	Jan	Feb	Mar	Apr	May	Jun	Jul	Aug	Sep	Oct	Nov	Dec	TOTAL
	1962													67
	1963													28
	1964													47
Shetland, Iceland, Greenland, Jan Mayen	1965				6	2	6	24	34					72
	1966				6	14	15	13	46					94
	1967				3	6		7	10					26
	1968					16	5	2		15				38
	1969					10	1		22	6				39
	1970				3		6	2	1					12
	1971					2	1	9	26					38
	1972				16	5								21
Antarctic	1965/66													2
	1969/70		2							6	3			11
	1970/71				6	8								14
NORWAY	1954-81	All Districts												2,059
	1938-54	Additional Reported[1]												393
	1938-81	All Districts												2,452
								Grand Total						
								Avg. Catch/Year						56
DENMARK Greenland	1964													1
	1965							1						1
	1969										1			1
	1970									1	1			1
	1971									1				2
	1974													3
	1977						2							2
Faeroe Islands	1966													2

Region	Year	All Districts	Grand Total	Avg. Catch/Year
	1971		1	
	1978	31	31	
DENMARK	1964–78		45	3
Iceland	1981	3	3	
U.S.S.R.				
Kamchatka	1948		3	
	1949		4	
	1954	2, 2	4	
	1955	2	4	
	1956	15, 7, 2, 1	26	1
	1957	3	3	
	1958	4, 3	7	
	1960	8	8	
	1963	6	16	10
	1964	2, 1	3	1
Kuril Islands	1949	4, 3	24	
	1955	4, 3	11	
	1956	3, 18, 16, 2	47	8
	1957	3, 9, 7, 3	27	5
	1958	5, 5, 5	18	3
	1959	25, 8	36	3
	1960	2, 3, 15, 1, 21	45	3
	1961	4	4	
	1962	3, 1	7	3
	1963	3, 1	4	
Antarctic (including catch north of 40° south)	1953/54	8	21	13
	1954/55	1, 7	11	3
	1955/56	2, 16, 8	33	7

[1] An additional 393 orcas were taken (5 to 57 per year) in the coastal districts and in the Barents Sea by Norwegian whalers from 1938 to 1954.

WHALING GROUNDS	YEAR	MONTHS												TOTAL
		Jan	Feb	Mar	Apr	May	Jun	Jul	Aug	Sep	Oct	Nov	Dec	
	1956/57	6											48	54
	1957/58	4										16	55	75
	1958/59											36	74	110
	1959/60											25	30	55
	1960/61			8								19	37	64
	1962/63			1										1
	1963/64													10
	1964/65													1
	1965/66													7
	1966/67													4
	1969/70			5	2									7
	1970/71	1	6									2		9
	1971/72	2												2
	1972/73	5		7	1								2	15
	1973/74		13	7	7	1						4	16	48
	1974/75	13	19			1						7		40
	1975/76	10	2	4										16
	1976/77	26		2									1	29
	1977/78	37	16									7	17	77
	1978/79	6	30										13	49
	1979/80	284	252	380										916
U.S.S.R.	1948-80	All Districts (as above)												1,955
	1950-54	Additional Reported[2]												91
	1935-48	Additional Reported[3]												43
	1935-80	All Districts				Grand Total								2,089
						Avg. Catch/Year								45
REPUBLIC OF KOREA	1981								2					2

JAPAN
Coastal Districts[4]

Year												Total
1946												18
1947												25
1948												48
1949												44
1950												24
1951												66
1952												58
1953												66
1954			8	1	3	17	15	16	18	19	3	100
1955			9	21	17	7	1	1	8	18	3	85
1956		3	1	1	4	2	5	6	6	3		38
1957		2	5	4	10	21	5	9	11	8	3	78
1958		7	2	8	25	3	5	4	7	8	4	73
1959		3	4	1	3	2	3	8	6	6		36
1960	2		2	2	4	7	6	10	3	10	2	48
1961	1	2	5	9	4	4	4	4	5	5	2	54
1962		5	5	2	4	5	5	13	8			47
1963		3	5	2	2	3	2	1	1	12	12	43
1964	3	2	3	1	6	11	4	11	19	23	16	99
1965		4			10	6	17	14	29	42	40	169
1966	10	2	6	4	5	6	6	14	20	30	34	137
1967		8		3	3	3	6	3	35	15	11	101
1968		4	1	2					6	8	1	22
1969		2	1		2			5	3		3	16
1970		2						8		2		12
1971			2			2			3	3		10
1972		2					2			1		3
1974		2										2

[2] An additional 91 orcas were taken in the North Pacific from 1950 to 1954.
[3] An additional 43 orcas were taken in the North Pacific from 1935 to 1948.
[4] Most were caught off northern and eastern Japan, especially around Hokkaidō.

WHALING GROUNDS	YEAR	Jan	Feb	Mar	Apr	May	Jun	Jul	Aug	Sep	Oct	Nov	Dec	TOTAL
	1975			1		2								3
	1976	1												1
	1977							1						1
	1980			2										2
	1981													5
JAPAN	1946-81	All Districts								Grand Total				1,534
										Avg. Catch/Year				43
SOUTH AFRICA														
Natal	1971							1	1		3			5
	1972				2	10				5				17
	1973								6	2				8
	1974							2						2
	1975				2			2						4
SOUTH AFRICA	1971-75	All Districts								Grand Total				36
										Avg. Catch/Year				7
CANADA														
British Columbia	1955					1								1
Newfoundland	1955						1							1
	1971							2						2
Nova Scotia	1964					1	1							2
	1967									1				1
Eastern Arctic[5]	1977										14			14
CANADA	1955-77	All Districts								Grand Total				21
										Avg. Catch/Year				1

UNITED STATES			
California	1963	1	1
	1966		1
	1967	1	1
UNITED STATES	All Districts	Grand Total	3
1963-67		Avg. Catch/Year	1
WEST INDIES	1968		6
	1969		4
WEST INDIES	All Districts	Grand Total	10
1968-69		Avg. Catch/Year	5
PERU	1966		1
CHILE	1969		1

[5]A group of orcas stranded near Pangnirtung, Baffin Island, in September 1977, were killed by the Inuit.

APPENDIX 5
LIVE-CAPTURE STATISTICS FOR KILLER WHALES[1]

DATE	PLACE	CAPTOR	AFFILIATION	NOTES	CAPTURED	DIED[2]	KEPT	ESCAPED OR RELEASED
CALIFORNIA								
11/61	Newport Harbor	F. Brocato/F. Calandrino	Marineland (Calif.)	disoriented in harbour	1		1	0
WASHINGTON AND BRITISH COLUMBIA								
9/62	Haro Strait, Wash.	F. Brocato/F. Calandrino	Marineland (Calif.)	hoop-netted, shot	1	1	0	0
7/64	Saturna Island, B.C.	S. Burich	Vancouver Aquarium (B.C.)	harpooned	1	0	1	0
6/65	Namu, B.C.	B. Lechkobit/B. McGarvey	fishermen	accidental	2	0	1	1
10/65	Carr Inlet, Wash.	T. Griffin/D. Goldsberry	Seattle Aquarium (Wash.)	seine netted	15	1	1	13
7/66	Steveston, B.C.	fishermen	none	entangled and drowned in net	1	1	0	0
2/67	Yukon Harbor, Wash.	T. Griffin/D. Goldsberry	Seattle Aquarium (Wash.)	seine netted	15	3	5	7
7/67	Port Hardy, B.C.	fishermen	none	accidental	1	0	1	0
2/68	Vaughn Bay, Wash.	T. Griffin/D. Goldsberry	Seattle Aquarium (Wash.)	seine netted	12-15	0	2	10-13
2/68	Pender Harbour, B.C.	Cameron/Reid/Gooldrup/etc.	fishermen	seine netted	1	0	0	1
4/68	Pender Harbour, B.C.	Cameron/Reid/Gooldrup/etc.	fishermen	seine netted	7	0	6	1
7/68	Malcolm Island, B.C.	fishermen	none	accidental	11	0	1	10
10/68	Yukon Harbor, Wash.	T. Griffin/D. Goldsberry	Seattle Aquarium (Wash.)	seine netted	25-33	0	5	20-28
4/69	Carr Inlet, Wash.	T. Griffin/D. Goldsberry	Seattle Aquarium (Wash.)	seine netted	11	0	2	9
10/69	Penn Cove, Wash.	T. Griffin/D. Goldsberry	Seattle Aquarium (Wash.)	seine netted	7-9	1	0	6-8
12/69	Pender Harbour, B.C.	Cameron/Reid/Gooldrup/etc.	fishermen	seine netted	12	0	6	6
2/70	Carr Inlet, Wash.	T. Griffin/D. Goldsberry	Seattle Aquarium (Wash.)	seine netted	6-14	1	1	5-13
3/70	Pedder Bay, B.C.	B. Wright	Sealand (B.C.)	seine netted	5	0	3	2
8/70	Penn Cove, Wash.	T. Griffin/D. Goldsberry	Seattle Aquarium (Wash.)	seine netted	80	4	7	69

Date	Location	Captors	Destination	Disposition				
8/70	Port Madison, Wash.	T. Griffin/D. Goldsberry	Seattle Aquarium (Wash.)	stranded	1	0	1	0
8/71	Penn Cove, Wash.	T. Griffin/D. Goldsberry	Seattle Aquarium (Wash.)	seine netted	15-24	0	3	12-21
11/71	Carr Inlet, Wash.	T. Griffin/D. Goldsberry	Seattle Aquarium (Wash.)	seine netted	19	0	2	17
3/72	Carr Inlet, Wash.	D. Goldsberry	Seattle Aquarium (Wash.)	seine netted	9-11	0	1	8-10
3/73	Ocean City, Wash.	D. Goldsberry	Seattle Aquarium (Wash.)	stranded	1	0	1	0
8/73	Pedder Bay, B.C.	B. Wright	Sealand (B.C.)	seine netted	2	0	1	1
8/73	Pedder Bay, B.C.	B. Wright	Sealand (B.C.)	seine netted	2	0	2	0
8/75	Pedder Bay, B.C.	B. Wright	Sealand (B.C.)	seine netted	6	0	2	4
3/76	Budd Inlet, Wash.	D. Goldsberry	Sea World (Calif.)	seine netted	6	0	0	6
8/77	Menzies Bay, B.C.	B. Wright	Sealand (B.C.)	lone, sick, disoriented calf	1	0	1	0
ICELAND								
10/74	SE coast	herring fishermen	none	accidental	1	0	1	1
10/76	SE coast, Medallandsbugt	R. de la Grandiére	Marineland (France)	seine netted	1	0	0	0
10/76	SE coast, Medallandsbugt	W.H. Dudok van Heel/ J. Gunnarsson	Dolfinarium (Holland)/ Sædyrasafnið (Iceland)	(practice catch)	1	0	0	1
10/76	SE coast, Medallandsbugt	W.H. Dudok van Heel/ J. Gunnarsson	Dolfinarium (Holland)/ Sædyrasafnið (Iceland)	seine netted	2	0	0	2
10/76	SE coast, Medallandsbugt	J. Gunnarsson/D. Goldsberry unofficially associated	Sædyrasafnið (Iceland)/ Sea World (Calif.)	seine netted	2	0	2	0
10/77	SE coast, Ingolfshöfdi	W.H. Dudok van Heel/ J. Gunnarsson/D. Goldsberry unofficially associated	Dolfinarium (Holland)/ Sædyrasafnið (Iceland)/ Sea World (Calif.)	seine netted	1	0	1	0
10/77	SE coast, Ingolfshöfdi	W.H. Dudok van Heel/ J. Gunnarsson/D. Goldsberry unofficially associated	Dolfinarium (Holland)/ Sædyrasafnið (Iceland)/ Sea World (Calif.)	seine netted	3	0	3	0

[1]Washington and B.C. statistics were derived from M.A. Bigg and A.A. Wolman (1975) and E.D. Asper and L.H. Cornell (1977). Additional information came through interviews with Michael Bigg, Edward Asper, Frank Brocato, Bob Wright and Bill Cameron. Brocato also provided information on the California capture. Varied numbers in Washington captures (at Penn Cove, Carr Inlet, Yukon Harbor and Vaughn Bay) represent conflicting reports from captors, National Marine Fisheries Service and the published accounts of Bigg/Wolman and of Asper/Cornell: "In many cases, accurate records were not kept," said Bigg, "and anyway, it is difficult to count exactly a large group of whales in an enclosure unless you photograph each one." In most cases, the Bigg/Wolman figure is the low (conservative) estimate. Icelandic statistics were obtained through correspondence with W. H. Dudok van Heel, Jón Kr. Gunnarsson, Brian Hunt (International Animal Exchange), A.G. Greenwood and Martin R. Dinnes (International Zoo Veterinary Group), Jóhann Sigurjónsson and in J. Sigurjónsson and S. Leatherwood (1988). The Japanese report came from Teruo Tobayama (Kamogawa Sea World).

[2]Refers only to mortalities during capture.

DATE	PLACE	CAPTOR	AFFILIATION	NOTES	CAPTURED	DIED[2]	KEPT	ESCAPED OR RELEASED
10/77	SE coast, Ingolfshöfdi	W.H. Dudok van Heel/ J. Gunnarsson/D. Goldsberry unofficially associated	Dolfinarium (Holland)/ Sædyrasafnid (Iceland)/ Sea World (Calif.)	seine netted	2	0	2	0
10/78	SE coast		Anna h/f (Iceland)	seine netted	1	0	1	0
10/78	SE coast, Medallandsbugt	J. Gunnarsson/D. Goldsberry	Sædyrasafnid (Iceland)/ Sea World (Calif.)	seine netted	1	0	1	0
10/78	SE coast, Tvisker	J. Gunnarsson/D. Goldsberry	Sædyrasafnid (Iceland)/ Sea World (Calif.)	seine netted	1	0	1	0
10/78	SE coast, Tvisker	J. Gunnarsson/D. Goldsberry	Sædyrasafnid (Iceland)/ Sea World (Calif.)	seine netted	1	0	1	0
10/78	SE coast, Skardsfjara	J. Gunnarsson/D. Goldsberry	Sædyrasafnid (Iceland)/ Sea World (Calif.)	seine netted	3	0	3	0
11/78	SE coast, Ingolfshöfdi	J. Gunnarsson	Sædyrasafnid (Iceland)	seine netted	1	0	1	0
11/78	SE coast, Ingolfshöfdi	J. Gunnarsson	Sædyrasafnid (Iceland)	seine netted	1	0	0	1
11/78	SE coast, Ingolfshöfdi	J. Gunnarsson	Sædyrasafnid (Iceland)	seine netted	1	0	0	1
11/78	W coast, Malarrif	J. Gunnarsson	Sædyrasafnid (Iceland)	seine netted	1	0	0	1
7/79	SE coast, Ingolfshöfdi	J. Gunnarsson	Sædyrasafnid (Iceland)	seine netted	1	0	1	0
10/79	SE coast, Ingolfshöfdi	J. Gunnarsson	Sædyrasafnid (Iceland)	seine netted	2	0	2	0
11/79	SE coast, Medallandsbugt	J. Gunnarsson	Sædyrasafnid (Iceland)	seine netted	1	0	1	0
11/79	SE coast, Medallandsbugt	J. Gunnarsson	Sædyrasafnid (Iceland)	seine netted	1	0	1	0
10/80	S coast, Alvidra	J. Gunnarsson	Sædyrasafnid (Iceland)	seine netted	1	0	0	1
10/80	S coast, Alvidra	J. Gunnarsson	Sædyrasifnid (Iceland)	seine netted	1	0	1	0
11/80	E coast, Reydarfjördur	J. Gunnarsson	Sædyrasafnid (Iceland)	seine netted	1	0	1	0
11/80	E coast, Reydarfjördur	J. Gunnarsson	Sædyrasafnid (Iceland)	seine netted	1	0	1	0
11/80	E coast, Reydarfjördur	J. Gunnarsson	Sædyrasafnid (Iceland)	seine netted	2	0	2	0
10/81	SW coast, Selvogsbanki	J. Gunnarsson	Sædyrasafnid (Iceland)	seine netted	5	0	4	1
10/81	S coast, Alvidra	J. Gunnarsson	Sædyrasafnid (Iceland)	seine netted	2	0	2	0
10/82	NE coast, Héradsflói	J. Gunnarsson	Sædyrasafnid (Iceland)	seine netted	3	0	3	0
10/82	SW coast, Stokkseyri	J. Gunnarsson	Sædyrasafnid (Iceland)	seine netted	2	0	2	0
11/83	E coast, Berufjördur	H. Jónasson	Fauna Co. (Iceland)	seine netted	3	0	3	0

Date	Location	Collector	Destination	Method	Captured	Died	Kept	Escaped or Released
11/84	E coast, Berufjördur	J. Gunnarsson	Sædyrasafnid (Iceland)	seine netted	2	0	2	0
11/84	E coast, Reydarfjördur	J. Gunnarsson	Sædyrasafnid (Iceland)	seine netted	3	0	3	0
10/87	E coast, Seydisfjördur	H. Jónasson	Fauna Co. (Iceland)	seine netted	4	0	4	0
10/89	SE coast, Hornafjord	H. Jónasson	Fauna Co. (Iceland)	seine netted	1	0	1	0
10/89	SE coast, Hornafjord	H. Jónasson	Fauna Co. (Iceland)	seine netted	1	0	1	0
10/89	SE coast, Hornafjord	H. Jónasson	Fauna Co. (Iceland)	seine netted	1	0	1	0
10/89	SE coast, Hornafjord	H. Jónasson	Fauna Co. (Iceland)	seine netted	1	0	1	0

JAPAN

Date	Location	Collector	Destination	Method	Captured	Died	Kept	Escaped or Released
?/72	Abashiri, Hokkaido	fishermen	none	harpooned	1	0	1	0
?/78	Taiji, Wakayama	fishermen	none	harpooned	1	0	1	0
2/79	Taiji, Wakayama	fishermen	Town of Taiji	herded and netted	5	0	5	0
2/82	Taiji, Wakayama	fishermen	Town of Taiji	herded and netted	5	0	3	2
10/85	Taiji, Wakayama	fishermen	Town of Taiji	herded and netted	3	0	1	2
10/85	Taiji, Wakayama	fishermen	Town of Taiji	herded and netted	1	0	1	0
2/86	Taiji, Wakayama	fishermen	Town of Taiji	harpooned	1	0	1	0

TOTALS

PLACE	CAPTURED	DIED?	KEPT	ESCAPED OR RELEASED
California	1	0	1	0
Washington	223+	10	31	182+
British Columbia	52	1	25	26
Iceland	64	0	55	9
Japan	17	0	13	4
TOTALS	357+	11	125	221+

APPENDIX 6
KILLER WHALES KEPT CAPTIVE[1]

NAME	SEX	SIZE length (cm.)	SIZE weight (kg.)	CAPTURE date	CAPTURE place	POD[2/3]	AQUARIUM[4]	STATUS	FINAL SIZE length (cm.)	FINAL SIZE weight (kg.)	TIME IN CAPTIVITY
No name	F	521	1,857	11/61	Newport Harbor, Calif.	?	Marineland, Calif.	Died 11/61; gastroenteritis, pneumonia	521	1,857	1 day
Moby Doll	M	467	?	7/64	Saturna Island, B.C.	J[3] or K[3] or L[3]	Vancouver, B.C. (held at Burrard Drydocks)	Died 10/64; drowning (exhaustion?)	467	1,034	3 mos.
Namu	M	655	3,600	6/65	Namu, B.C.	C[2/3]	Seattle, Wash.	Died 7/66; drowning, clostridium perfringens	?	?	1 yr.
Shamu (51)	F	410	1,090	10/65	Carr Inlet, Wash.	J[3] or K[3] or L[3]	Sea World, Calif. (Seattle, Wash., until 12/65)	Died 8/71; pyometra, septicemia	544	?	6 yrs.
Skana (Walter)	F	439	1,360	2/67	Yukon Harbor, Wash.	K[2/3]	Vancouver, B.C. (first at Seattle, Wash.)	Died 10/80; general mycotic infection	577	2,985	13½ yrs.
Ramu (SWF-00-13)	M	406	1,000	2/67	Yukon Harbor, Wash.	K[2/3]	Sea World, Fla. (Seattle, Wash., until 3/67)	Died 1/82	623	3,272	15 yrs.
Kilroy (72)	M	277	390	2/67	Yukon Harbor, Wash.	K[2/3]	Sea World, Calif. (Seattle, Wash., until 3/67)	Died 9/78; gangrenous pneumonia	538	2,364	11½ yrs.
Katy	F	249	270	2/67	Yukon Harbor, Wash.	K[2/3]	Seattle, Wash.	Died 5/67	?	?	3 mos.
Kandu (94)	F	312	700	2/67	Yukon Harbor, Wash.	K[2/3]	Sea World, Calif. (Seattle, Wash., until 12/69)	Died 6/71; liver necrosis, pneumonia	442	?	4 yrs.

Name	Sex			Date	Capture Location	Pod[2]	Exhibition Location	Fate			Duration
Lupa	F	556	2,495	2/68	Vaughn Bay, Wash.	?	New York, N.Y.	Died 9/68; respiratory ailment	?	?	7 mos.
Hugo	M	399	900	2/68	Vaughn Bay, Wash.	?	Miami Seaquarium, Fla.	Died 3/80; aneurysm of the brain	700	4,536	12 yrs.
Hyak	M	500	1,800	2/68	Pender Harbour, B.C.	?	Vancouver, B.C. (held at Pender Harbour)	Released 2/69			1 yr.
Irving (Skookum Cecil)	M	600	3,600	4/68	Pender Harbour, B.C.	A5?[3]	Vancouver, B.C. (held at Pender Harbour)	Escaped 8/68			4 mos.
Natsidalia	F	579	?	4/68	Pender Harbour, B.C.	A5?[3]	Vancouver, B.C. (held at Pender Harbour)	Died 11/68; heart failure	?	?	7 mos.
Hyak II (Tung Jen)	M	304	450	4/68	Pender Harbour, B.C.	A5?[3]	Vancouver, B.C. (first at Pender Harbour)	Alive as of 9/89			21½ yrs. +
Corky	F	401	1,150	4/68	Pender Harbour, B.C.	A5?[3]	Marineland, Calif.	Died 12/70; mediastinal abscess	501	?	2½ yrs.
Orky II (SWC-00-8726)	M	510	?	4/68	Pender Harbour, B.C.	A5?[3]	Sea World, Calif. (Marineland, Calif., until 1/87)	Died 9/88; acute pneumonia, chronic wasting	665	3,450	20 yrs.
Kianu	F	579	2,722	4/68	Pender Harbour, B.C.	A5?[3]	World Safari, Japan (Marine World, Calif., until 4/78)	Died 6/80; gastrointestinal disease	587	?	12 yrs.
Bonnie	F	610	2,948	4/68	Pender Harbour, B.C.	A5?[3]	Marine World, Calif.	Died 8/68; stillbirth	?	?	4 mos.
Tula	M	399	?	7/68	Malcolm Island, B.C.	?	Dolfinarium, Netherlands	Died 10/68; fungus (external)	?	?	3 mos.

[1]Includes all orcas kept for exhibition or research plus those kept for more than a month with the intention of exhibition, even if they were later released or escaped; also includes orcas born alive in captivity.
[2]According to Michael Bigg's system of letter designations for B.C./Washington population of killer whales. "?" indicates that designated pod was present at the capture site in the company of orcas from unidentified pods, which may have been among those taken captive. No letter names are given for live births or for the Japanese and Icelandic orcas that have not been identified photographically.
[3]Evidence from sound recordings analyzed by John Ford to determine the dialect(s) of whales present.
[4]See Appendix 7 for full names and addresses of aquariums that have exhibited killer whales.

NAME	SEX	SIZE		CAPTURE		POD[2,3]	AQUARIUM[4]	STATUS	FINAL SIZE		TIME IN CAPTIVITY
		length (cm.)	weight (kg.)	date	place				length (cm.)	weight (kg.)	
Ishmael	M	518	2,041	10/68	Yukon Harbor, Wash.	J[2] or L[3]	U.S. Navy, Hawaii	Escaped 2/71	?	?	2 yrs.
Ahab	M	579	2,495	10/68	Yukon Harbor, Wash.	J[2] or L[3]	U.S. Navy, Hawaii	Died 1974	?	?	5½ yrs.
Haida	M	427	1,452	10/68	Yukon Harbor, Wash.	J[2] or L[3]	Sealand, B.C.	Died 10/82; lung infection (airborne staphylococcus)	700	4,500	14 yrs.
Mamuk	M	396	1,361	10/68	Yukon Harbor, Wash.	J[2] or L[3]	Sea-Arama, Tex.	Died 6/74	?	?	5½ yrs.
Cuddles	M	351	?	10/68	Yukon Harbor, Wash.	J[2] or L[3]	Dudley Zoo, Great Britain (Flamingo Park, Great Britain, until 1971)	Died 4/74; streptococcal mediastinal abscess, osteomyelitis of rib	?	?	5½ yrs.
Ramu II	M	604	4,000	4/69	Carr Inlet, Wash.	?	Marineland, Australia	Died 5/70	?	?	1 yr.
?	F	457	?	4/69	Carr Inlet, Wash.	?	Seattle, Wash. (?)	Died	?	?	?
Calypso	F	518	2,000	12/69	Pender Harbour, B.C.	A5[2,3]	Marineland, France (Cleethorpes Zoo, Great Britain)	Died 12/70; cause unknown	?	?	1 yr.
Corky II (SWC-00-8727)	F	366	?	12/69	Pender Harbour, B.C.	A5[2,3]	Sea World, Calif. (Marineland, Calif., until 1/87)	Alive as of 12/89	?	?	20 yrs. +
Patches	F	290	499	12/69	Pender Harbour, B.C.	A5[2,3]	Marineland, Calif.	Died 8/71; salmonellosis	365	?	1½ yrs.
No name	M	412	?	12/69	Pender Harbour, B.C.	A5[2,3]	Marineland, Calif.	Died 5/72; pneumonia	483	?	2½ yrs.
Nepo	M	366	1,136	12/69	Pender Harbour, B.C.	A5[2,3]	Marine World, Calif.	Died 7/80; pneumonia	686	4,082	10½ yrs.

Yaka	F	320	682	12/69	Pender Harbour, B.C.	$A5^{2/3}$	Marine World, Calif.	Alive as of 12/89			20 yrs. +
?	?	457?	?	2/70	Carr Inlet, Wash.	?	Seattle, Wash. (?)	Unknown			
Chimo	F	335	900	3/70	Pedder Bay, B.C.	M^2	Sealand, B.C.	Died 11/72; Chediak-Higashi Syndrome	427	?	2½ yrs.
Knootka (Nootka) (SWC-00-8628)	F	411	1,814	3/70	Pedder Bay, B.C.	M^2	Sea World, Calif. (first at Sealand, B.C.; Japanese Deer Park, Calif.; Seven Seas, Tex.; Marineland, Ont., until 4/86)	Alive as of 11/89			19½ yrs. +
Scarred-jaw Cow	F	579	?	3/70	Pedder Bay, B.C.	M^2	Sealand, B.C. (held at Pedder Bay)	Died 5/70; malnutrition		?	2½ mos.
Charlie Chin	M	670	?	3/70	Pedder Bay, B.C.	M^2	Sealand, B.C. (held at Pedder Bay)	Released 10/70			7 mos.
Pointed-nose Cow	F	610	?	3/70	Pedder Bay, B.C.	M^2	Sealand, B.C. (held at Pedder Bay)	Released 10/70			7 mos.
Lil Nooka	M	320	?	8/70	Penn Cove, Wash.	L^2 or J? or K?	Sea-Arama, Tex.	Died 3/71		?	7 mos.
Winston (Ramu III) (SWC-00-7601)	M	406	?	8/70	Penn Cove, Wash.	L^2 or J? or K?	Sea World, Calif. (Windsor Safari Park until 10/76)	Died 4/86; chronic cardiovascular failure		?	15½ yrs.
Lolita (Tokitae)	F	430	909?	8/70	Penn Cove, Wash.	L^2 or J? or K?	Miami Seaquarium, Fla.	Alive as of 10/89			19 yrs. +
Jumbo	M	475	1,300	8/70	Penn Cove, Wash.	L^2 or J? or K?	Kamogawa, Japan	Died 7/74; liver dysfunction	533	1,600	4 yrs.

NAME	SEX	SIZE length (cm.)	SIZE weight (kg.)	CAPTURE date	CAPTURE place	POD[2][3]	AQUARIUM[4]	STATUS	FINAL SIZE length (cm.)	FINAL SIZE weight (kg.)	TIME IN CAPTIVITY
Chappy	F	350	600	8/70	Penn Cove, Wash.	L[2] or J? or K?	Kamogawa, Japan	Died 4/74; periostitis of lumbar bone	382	655	3½ yrs.
Clovis	M	335	?	8/70	Penn Cove, Wash.	L[2] or J? or K?	Marineland, France	Died 2/73; clostridial myositis	520	?	2½ yrs.
Ramu IV	M	351	726	8/70	Penn Cove, Wash.	L[2] or J? or K?	Marineland, Australia	Died 8/71	?	?	1 yr.
Whale	F	280	?	8/70	Port Madison, Wash.	L[2] or J? or K?	Munich, West Germany (first at Seattle, Wash.)	Died 10/71; cause unknown	?	?	1 yr.
Kona (16)	F	434	?	8/71	Penn Cove, Wash.	L[2]	Sea World, Calif.(Seattle, Wash., until 9/71)	Died 9/77; septicemia	582	2,409	6 yrs.
Kandu II	M	396	818	8/71	Penn Cove, Wash.	L[2]	Marineland, Ont. (first at Seattle, Wash.; Bremen, West Germany)	Died 10/79; pneumonia	?	?	8 yrs.
Kandu III (15)	F	379	864	8/71	Penn Cove, Wash.	L[2]	Sea World, Calif.(Seattle, Wash., until 9/71)	Died 6/75; uraemia-nephritis	508	1,361	4 yrs.
?	M	401	?	11/71	Carr Inlet, Wash.	?	Seattle, Wash. (?)	Died	?	?	?
?	M	411	?	11/71	Carr Inlet, Wash.	?	Seattle, Wash. (?)	Died	?	?	?
Kanuck (27)	M	354	800	3/72	Carr Inlet, Wash.	J[2]	Sea World, Calif.	Died 11/74; candidiasis	419	?	2½ yrs.

"0" (Zero,Go)	?	?	?	?/72	Japan	?	Kamogawa, Japan	Died 1972	?	?	?
Sandy (301)	F	488	?	3/73	Ocean City, Wash.	?	Sea World, Fla. (Seattle, Wash., until 10/73; Sea World, Calif.)	Died 10/77; cerebral haemorrhage	579	3,182	4½ yrs.
Nootka II	F	579	?	8/73	Pedder Bay, B.C.	K²	Sealand, B.C.	Died 5/74; ruptured aorta	579	?	9 mos.
Taku ("K1")	M	700	?	8/73	Pedder Bay, B.C.	K²	Sealand, B.C. (held at Pedder Bay)	Released 10/73; radio-tagged			2½ mos.
Kandy	F	540	1,818	8/73	Pedder Bay, B.C.	L³	Marineland, Ont.	Died 11/73; pneumonia	540	?	3 mos.
Frankie (302)	M	594	?	8/73	Pedder Bay, B.C.	L³	Sea World, Calif.	Died 1/74; pneumonia, influenza	594	?	5 mos.
Nootka III	F	381	864	8/75	Pedder Bay, B.C.	Q²	Sealand, B.C.	Died 5/76; perforated post-pyloric ulcer	394	1,040	9 mos.
Kandu IV (SWF-00-8701)	M	427	1,364	8/75	Pedder Bay, B.C.	Q²	Sea World, Fla. (Marineland, Ont., until 1/87)	Alive as of 11/89			14 yrs.+
04	F	610	?	3/76	Budd Inlet, Wash.	O²	Seattle, Wash.	Released 4/76; radio-tagged			1½ mos.
05	M	549	?	3/76	Budd Inlet, Wash.	O²	Seattle, Wash.	Released 4/76; radio-tagged			1½ mos.
Kim	F	450	1,400	10/76	Iceland		Marineland, France	Died 7/82; lung abscess	?	?	5½ yrs.
Kenau (SWC-00-7602)	F	300	420	10/76	Iceland		Sea World, Calif. (Dolfinarium, Netherlands, until 5/77)	Alive as of 11/89			13yrs.+
Gudrun (SWF-00-8702)	F	270	300	10/76	Iceland		Sea World, Fla. (Dolfinarium, Netherlands, until 11/87)	Alive as of 11/89			13 yrs.+

NAME	SEX	SIZE length (cm.)	SIZE weight (kg.)	CAPTURE date	CAPTURE place	POD[2/3]	AQUARIUM[4]	STATUS	FINAL SIZE length (cm.)	FINAL SIZE weight (kg.)	TIME IN CAPTIVITY
No name	M	231	200	2/77	Live birth		Marineland, Calif.	Died 3/77; pneumonia, bowel stasis, cerebral edema	228	148	18 days
Miracle	F	305	364	8/77	Menzies Bay, B.C.	?	Sealand, B.C.	Died 1/82; drowning	500	1,225	4 yrs.
Kona II (SWF-00-7701)	F	351	?	10/77	Iceland		Sea World, Fla. (Dolfinarium, Netherlands, until 12/77)	Died 10/87; lung abscess	?	?	10 yrs.
Kanuck II (SWC-00-7705)	M	350	?	10/77	Iceland		Sea World, Calif. (Dolfinarium, Netherlands, until 12/77)	Died 8/81; chronic kidney disease	402	820	3½ yrs.
Kandu V (SWC-00-7706)	F	370	?	10/77	Iceland		Sea World, Calif. (Dolfinarium, Netherlands, until 12/77)	Died 8/89; upper-jaw fracture, massive haemorrhage after collision with another orca	525	2,700	12 yrs.
Hoi Wai (Susie Wong)	F	270	350	10/77	Iceland		Ocean Park, Hong Kong (first at Dolfinarium, Netherlands; Windsor Safari Park, Great Britain, until 1/79)	Alive as of 10/89			12 yrs. +
Winnie	F	275	?	10/77	Iceland		Windsor Safari Park, Great Britain (first at Dolfinarium, Netherlands)	Alive as of 11/89			12 yrs. +
Magnus	M	326	?	10/77	Iceland		Dolfinarium, Netherlands	Died 12/77; agranulocytic anaemia	326	490	2 mos.

Name	Sex				Origin	Location	Status			Age
No name	M?	?	?	?/78	Japan	Taiji Whale Museum, Japan	Died 1978; harpoon wound	?	?	5 days
No name	M	236	210	10/78	Live birth	Marineland, Calif.	Died 11/78; pneumonia, colitis	236	159	11 days
Kotar (SWC-00-7801)	M	210	?	10/78	Iceland	Sea World, Calif.	Alive as of 11/89			11 yrs. +
SWC-00-7802	F	295	?	10/78	Iceland	Sea World, Calif.	Died 9/79; pneumonia	325	500	1 yr.
Kahana (SWF-00-7803)	F	312	?	10/78	Iceland	Sea World, Fla.	Alive as of 11/89			11 yrs. +
Shamu (SWC-00-7804)	F	292	?	10/78	Iceland	Sea World, Calif. and Ohio	Alive as of 11/89			11 yrs. +
Betty	F	375?	?	10/78	Iceland	Marineland, France	Died 1987?	?	?	9 yrs.?
Kandu VI (SWC-00-7806)	F	350	?	10/78	Iceland	Sea World, Calif. and Ohio (Marineland, Ont., until 6/79)	Alive as of 11/89			11 yrs. +
No name	M	310	?	10/78	Iceland	Sædyrasafnid, Iceland	Died 2/79; heart attack	?	?	3 mos.
No name	F	320	?	11/78	Iceland	Sædyrasafnid, Iceland	Died 2/79; pneumonia	?	?	3 mos.
No name	M	330	?	11/78	Iceland	Sædyrasafnid, Iceland	Released 2/79			3 mos.
No name	?	360	?	11/78	Iceland	Sædyrasafnid, Iceland	Released 2/79			3 mos.
No name	?	320	?	11/78	Iceland	Sædyrasafnid, Iceland	Released 2/79			3 mos.
Tai-chan	M	700	4,000	2/79	Japan	Taiji Whale Museum, Japan	Died 1982	?	?	3 yrs.

NAME	SEX	SIZE length (cm.)	SIZE weight (kg.)	CAPTURE date	CAPTURE place	POD[2/3]	AQUARIUM[4]	STATUS	FINAL SIZE length (cm.)	FINAL SIZE weight (kg.)	TIME IN CAPTIVITY
No name	F	610	3,100	2/79	Japan		Taiji Whale Museum, Japan	Died 5/79	610	?	3 mos.
No name	F	635	3,100	2/79	Japan		World Safari, Japan	Died 3/79; stillbirth	635	?	1 mo.
No name	F	650	?	2/79	Japan		World Safari, Japan	Died 4/79; nutritional disorder	650	?	2 mos.
Benkei	M	535	3,000	2/79	Japan		World Safari, Japan (Taiji, Japan, until 4/79)	Died 1/89; acute pneumonia	687	5,000	10 yrs.
Dzul-ha (Shamu)	M	307	600	7/79	Iceland		Aquarama on Parade, Mexico (first at Sædyrasafnid, Iceland; Mannheim, West Germany; Connyland, Switzerland)	Died 1983	?	?	3 yrs.
Nootka V (Noni)	F	370	?	10/79	Iceland		Marineland, Ont. (first at Sædyrasafnid, Iceland)	Alive as of 10/89			10 yrs. +
Caren	F	362	915	11/79	Iceland		Kamogawa, Japan (at Sædyrasafnid, Iceland; Marineland, Ont., until 3/80)	Died 5/87; agranulocytosis	495	1,760	7½ yrs.
King	M	270	760	11/79	Iceland		Kamogawa, Japan (at Sædyrasafnid, Iceland; Lübeck, West Germany; Marineland, Ont., until 3/80)	Died 10/83; pneumonia	445	1,220	4 yrs.

Name	Sex				Origin	History / Location	Status			Age
Kago	M	366	?	11/79	Iceland	Reino Marino, Mexico (first at Sædyrasafnid, Iceland; Marineland, Ont.)	Alive as of 11/89	?	?	10 yrs. +
No name	F	370	?	11/79	Iceland	Marineland, Ont. (first at Sædyrasafnid, Iceland; died at Marineland en route to Kamogawa, Japan)	Died 1/80; acute enterotoxaemia	?	?	3 mos.
Benkei II	M	290	400	10/80	Iceland	World Safari, Japan (at Sædyrasafnid, Iceland; Vancouver, B.C., until 1/81)	Died 7/83; malignant lymphoma	315	450	2½ yrs.
Ulises	F?	395	?	11/80	Iceland	Zoo Barcelona, Spain (first at Sædyrasafnid, Iceland; Rioleon Safari, Spain, until 1983)	Alive as of 11/89			9 yrs. +
Vigga	F	320	?	11/80	Iceland	Marine World, Calif. (first at Sædyrasafnid, Iceland; Vancouver, B.C.)	Alive as of 11/89			9 yrs. +
Bjossa	F	404	820	11/80	Iceland	Vancouver, B.C. (first at Sædyrasafnid, Iceland)	Alive as of 12/89			9 yrs. +
Finna	M	394	600	11/80	Iceland	Vancouver, B.C. (first at Sædyrasafnid, Iceland)	Alive as of 12/89			9 yrs. +
Ruka (Orca)	F	350	600	10/81	Iceland	World Safari, Japan (first at Sædyrasafnid, Iceland; Hagenbeck Tierpark until 2/85)	Alive as of 10/89			8 yrs. +
Nemo	M	280	?	10/81	Iceland	Windsor Safari Park, Great Britain (first at Sædyrasafnid, Iceland; Clacton Pier, Great Britain)	Died 11/86; essential thrombocytosis	455	1,075	5 yrs.

NAME	SEX	SIZE length (cm.)	SIZE weight (kg.)	CAPTURE date	CAPTURE place	POD[2/3]	AQUARIUM[4]	STATUS	FINAL SIZE length (cm.)	FINAL SIZE weight (kg.)	TIME IN CAPTIVITY
?	M	260	?	10/81	Iceland		Clacton Pier, Great Britain (first at Sædyrasafnid, Iceland)	Died 12/81; ruptured kidney, traumatic shock	?	?	2 mos.
Neptune	M	410	?	10/81	Iceland		Clacton Pier, Great Britain (first at Sædyrasafnid, Iceland)	Died 6/83; appendicitis	?	?	1½ yrs.
Kiska	F	340	634	10/81	Iceland		Marineland, Ont. (first at Sædyrasafnid, Iceland)	Alive as of 11/89	?	?	8 yrs. +
?	F	415	?	10/81	Iceland		Marineland, Ont. (first at Sædyrasafnid, Iceland)	Died	?	?	?
No name	M	700?	?	2/82	Japan		Taiji Whale Museum, Japan (was awaiting shipment to Enoshima, Japan)	Died 6/82; pneumonia	?	?	4 mos.
Benkei III	M	275?	?	2/82	Japan		Private home, Japan (first at Taiji Whale Museum, Japan)	Alive as of 6/82			4 mos. +
No name	?	?	?	2/82	Japan		Taiji Whale Museum, Japan	Escaped			
No name	?	?	?	2/82	Japan		Taiji Whale Museum, Japan	Escaped			
Sacchi	F	655	4,500	2/82	Japan		Enoshima, Japan (Taiji, Japan, until 3/82)	Died 4/84; pneumonia	655	3,500	2 yrs.
No name	M	230?	200?	5/82	Live birth		Enoshima, Japan	Died 5/82	230	200	10 days
Kiva	F	241	205	6/82	Live birth		Marineland, Calif.	Died 8/82; colic, respiratory failure	241	239	46 days

Name	Sex			Date		Location	Status			Age
Haida II	F	290	?	10/82	Iceland	Sealand, B.C. (first at Sædyrasafnid, Iceland)	Alive as of 11/89			7 yrs. +
Nootka IV	F	380	?	10/82	Iceland	Sealand, B.C. (first at Sædyrasafnid, Iceland)	Alive as of 11/89			7 yrs. +
No name	M	310	?	10/82	Iceland	Sealand, B.C. (first at Sædyrasafnid, Iceland)	Died 6/83; haemophilia	350	900	6 mos.
Kim II	M	290	?	10/82	Iceland	Marineland, France (Sædyrasafnid, Iceland, until 3/83)	Alive as of 11/89			7 yrs. +
Freya	F	300?	?	10/82	Iceland	Marineland, France (Sædyrasafnid, Iceland, until 3/83)	Alive as of 11/89			7 yrs. +
?	M	430	?	11/83	Iceland	Acuarama, Brazil (first at Sædyrasafnid, Iceland)	Died			?
Tilikum	M	350	?	11/83	Iceland	Sealand, B.C. (Sædyrasafnid, Iceland, until 11/84)	Alive as of 11/89			6 yrs. +
SWO-00-8951	F	400	?	11/83	Iceland	Sea World, Ohio (first at Sædyrasafnid, Iceland; Acuarama, Brazil, until 5/89)	Alive as of 11/89			6 yrs. +
Junior	M	351	?	11/84	Iceland	Marineland, Ontario (Sædyrasafnid, Iceland, until 12/86)	Alive as of 11/89			5 yrs. +
Patty (Freyja)	F	350?	?	11/84	Iceland	Kamogawa, Japan (Sædyrasafnid, Iceland, until 11/85)	Died 9/87; acute enteritis	415	1,040	3 yrs.
Candu	M	490	?	11/84	Iceland	Marineland, Ont. (Sædyrasafnid, Iceland, until 12/86)	Alive as of 11/89			5 yrs. +

NAME	SEX	SIZE length (cm.)	SIZE weight (kg.)	CAPTURE date	CAPTURE place	POD[2/3]	AQUARIUM[4]	STATUS	FINAL SIZE length (cm.)	FINAL SIZE weight (kg.)	TIME IN CAPTIVITY
No name	M	410	?	11/84	Iceland		Sædyrasafnid, Iceland	Died 1/85; neck damage	410	?	2 mos.
Bingo (Thor)	M	340	?	11/84	Iceland		Kamogawa, Japan (Sædyrasafnid, Iceland, until 11/85)	Alive as of 10/89			5 yrs. +
No name	F	231	180?	7/85	Live birth		Marineland, Calif.	Died 8/85; failure to nurse	231	?	1 mo.
Baby Shamu (SWF-00-8501)	F	206	135	9/85	Live birth		Sea World, Fla.	Alive as of 11/89			4 yrs. +
Goro	M	260	345	10/85	Japan		World Safari, Japan (Taiji, Japan, until 11/85)	Alive as of 9/89			4 yrs. +
Nami-chan	F	370	?	10/85	Japan		Taiji Whale Museum, Japan	Alive as of 10/89			4 yrs. +
Baby Shamu II	?	213	135	1/86	Live birth		Sea World, Calif.	Died 1/86; heart defect	213	?	11 days
Shachi	F	490	1,600	2/86	Japan		Izu-Mito, Japan (Taiji, Japan, until 5/86)	Died 3/88; pneumonia	476	1,470	2 yrs.
Magy (Miss Piggy)	F	401	?	10/87	Iceland		Kamogawa, Japan (Sædyrasafnid, Iceland, until 3/88)	Alive as of 10/89			2 yrs. +
Bubba	M	399	?	10/87	Iceland		Ocean Park, Hong Kong (Sædyrasafnid, Iceland, until 3/88; Kamogawa, Japan, until 4/89)	Alive as of 10/89			2 yrs. +

251

Name	Sex			Date	Origin	Status	Location			Age
Stella	F	274	?	10/87	Iceland	Alive as of 10/89	Kamogawa, Japan (Sædyrasafnid, Iceland, until 3/88)			2 yrs. +
Oscar (Wolfie)	M	320	?	10/87	Iceland	Alive as of 10/89	Kamogawa, Japan (Sædyrasafnid, Iceland, until 3/88)			2 yrs. +
Baby Shamu III (SWC-00-8826)	F	200?	135?	9/88	Live birth	Alive as of 11/89	Sea World, Calif.			1 yr. +
Baby Shamu IV (SWC-00-8801)	F	200?	135?	11/88	Live birth	Alive as of 11/89	Sea World, Fla.			1 yr. +
No name	F	233	150	11/88	Live birth	Died 12/88; malnutrition	Vancouver, B.C.	233	150	22 days
Baby Shamu V (SWT-00-8876)	F	200?	135?	11/88	Live birth	Alive as of 11/89	Sea World, Tex.			1 yr. +
Baby Shamu VI (SWC-00-8901)	F	200?	135?	7/89	Live birth	Alive as of 11/89	Sea World, Fla.			4 mos. +
Katak (Baby Nootka)	M	175	70	8/89	Live birth	Alive as of 12/89	Marineland, Ont.			4 mos. +
No name	M	397	?	10/89	Iceland	Alive as of 1/90	Marineland, France (Sædyrasafnid, Iceland, until 1/90)			3 mos. +

NAME	SEX	SIZE length (cm.)	SIZE weight (kg.)	CAPTURE date	CAPTURE place	POD[2/3]	AQUARIUM[4]	STATUS	FINAL SIZE length (cm.)	FINAL SIZE weight (kg.)	TIME IN CAPTIVITY
No name	F	337	?	10/89	Iceland		Sædyrasafnid, Iceland (awaiting shipment)	Alive as of 1/90			3 mos. +
No name	F	310	?	10/89	Iceland		Sædyrasafnid, Iceland (awaiting shipment)	Alive as of 1/90			3 mos. +
No name	F	427	?	10/89	Iceland		Marineland France (Sædyrasafnid, Iceland, until 1/90)	Alive as of 1/90			3 mos. +

APPENDIX 7

INSTITUTIONS THAT HAVE KEPT KILLER WHALES CAPTIVE

AUSTRALIA

Marineland of Australia
Box 823
Southpost, Q 4215, Main Beach
Gold Coast, Queensland, Australia
*(Two orcas exhibited 1969-71;
none since)*

BRAZIL

Acuarama
Play Center Amusement Ride and
  Game Park
São Paulo, Brazil
*(Two orcas exhibited in the late 1980s; one
died, one sent to Sea World in U.S. in
1989; none since)*

CANADA

Marineland and Game Farm
7657 Portage Road
Niagara Falls, ON L2E 6X8
Telephone: 416-356-8250
Private company
*(Thirteen orcas exhibited; several later
shipped to Sea World in U.S. and
Kamogawa, Japan; five alive 11/89)*

Sealand of the Pacific Ltd.
1327 Beach Drive
Victoria, B.C. V8S 2N4
Telephone: 604-598-3366/73/74
Private company
(Ten orcas exhibited; three alive 11/89)

Vancouver Aquarium
Box 3232
Vancouver, B.C. V6B 3X8
Telephone: 604-685-3364
Owned by nonprofit society
*(Ten orcas exhibited, including Moby Doll,
several orcas at Pender Harbour and one
calf briefly in 1988; three alive 11/89)*

FRANCE

Marineland Côte D'Azur
avenue Mozart, 06600
Antibes, France

Telephone: 93-334949
Private company
*(Eight orcas exhibited since 1970; five alive
1/90)*

GREAT BRITAIN

Clacton Pier
Clacton-on-Sea, Essex
Great Britain
*(Three Icelandic orcas exhibited briefly
beginning 1981; two died soon after,
and one sent to Windsor Safari Park;
none since)*

Cleethorpes Zoo and Leisure Park
(closed 1978)
Kings Road
Cleethorpes, South Humberside
Great Britain
*(One orca exhibited for a few months in
1970; none since)*

Dudley Zoological Society Ltd.
(Dudley Zoo)
Castle Hill
Dudley, Worcester
Great Britain
Telephone: (0384) 52401
Owned by Zoological Society
(One orca exhibited 1971-74; none since)

Flamingo Land
(Flamingo Park Zoo)
Kirby Misperton
Malton, Yorkshire
Great Britain Y017 OUX
Telephone: (065386) 287
Private company
(One orca exhibited 1968-71; none since)

Windsor Safari Park
Winkfield Road
Windsor, Berkshire SL4 4AY
Great Britain
Telephone: (0753) 830886
*(Four orcas exhibited since 1970; one alive
1/90)*

HONG KONG

Ocean Park Ltd.
Wong Chuk Hang Road
Aberdeen, Hong Kong
Telephone: 5-555222
Nonprofit trust
*(One orca exhibited since 1979; another
obtained in 1989; two alive 11/89)*

ICELAND

Saedyrasafnid
(Hafnarfjord Marine Zoo)
Box 224
220 Hafnarfjordur
Island (Iceland)
Telephone: 50000/51020
*(Since 1979, this zoo/aquarium has kept
orcas that were captured around Iceland
for up to two years pending sales to
world aquariums)*

JAPAN

Enoshima Marineland
2-17-25 Katase-Kaigan
Fujisawa-Shi
Kanagawa-Prefecture
Japan
*(One orca exhibited 1982-84, plus one calf,
born in 1982, that lived seven days; none
since 1984)*

Izu-Mito Sea Paradise
Numazu-City
Shizuoka-Prefecture
Japan
*(One orca exhibited for 1½ years beginning
1986; none since)*

Kamogawa Sea World
1464-18 Higashichoh
Kamogawa-City
Chiba-Prefecture, 296

Japan
Telephone: 04709-3-3564
*(Three orcas exhibited 1970-74; two more
obtained in 1980, two in 1985 and four in
1988; four alive 10/89)*

Taiji Whale Museum
Taiji
Wakayama-Prefecture
Japan
*(Six orcas exhibited since 1979, plus others
held prior to shipment; one alive 10/89)*

World Safari Co., Ltd.
(Adventure World, Japan)
Shirahama-cho
Nishimuro-Gun
Wakayama-Prefecture
Japan
*(Seven orcas exhibited since 1978; two
alive 9/89)*

MEXICO

Aquarama on Parade
Isla Mujeres, Estado de Quintana Roo
México
*(In 1982, one orca became part of
Aquarama's travelling circus, performing
in Argentina at Mar del Plata and Buenos
Aires; it died in 1983)*

Reino Marino
México D.F., México
(One orca exhibited since 1985; alive 11/89)

NETHERLANDS

Dolfinarium Harderwijk b.v.
Strandboulevard-00ST1
3841 AB Harderwijk, Holland
Telephone: 03410-16041
Private company
*(One orca exhibited for a few months in
1968; two others obtained in 1976 and
1977; one died, and the other exported in
11/87; none since)*

SPAIN

Rioléon Safari
Tarragona, Spain
(One orca exhibited between 1980 and 1983; none since)

Zoo Barcelona
Parc Zoológic de Barcelona, S.A.
Parc de la Ciutadella
08003 Barcelona
Telephone: 309-25-00
(One orca exhibited since 1983)

SWITZERLAND

Connyland
CH 8557
Lipperswil (T.G.)
Switzerland
(One orca exhibited 1980 to 1982; exported 1982)

UNITED STATES

J & L Attractions, Inc.
dba Seven Seas
Box 777
Arlington, Texas 76010
(One orca exhibited in the early 1970s; none since)

Japanese Deer Park
Los Angeles, California
(One orca exhibited briefly in the early 1970s; none since)

Marineland of the Pacific
(closed 1987)
(Hanna-Barbera's Marineland, later
Marineland Amusement Corp.,
purchased by Sea World, Inc.)
Box 937
Rancho Palos Verdes, California 90274
Private company
(Eleven orcas exhibited, including one briefly in 1961 and four calves born between 1977 and 1985 — none of which lived longer than 46 days; two orcas moved to Sea World, San Diego, in 1/87; none exhibited since)

Marine World Africa U.S.A.
Marine World Parkway
Vallejo, California 94589
Telephone: 707-644-4000
Foundation
(Five orcas exhibited since 1968; two alive 11/89)

Miami Seaquarium
4400 Rickenbacker Causeway
Virginia Key
Miami, Florida 33149
Telephone: 304-361-5705
Corporation
(Two orcas exhibited since 1968; one alive 10/89)

Naval Ocean Systems Center
Box 997
Kailua, Oahu
Hawaii 96734
U.S. Government
(Two orcas in training beginning 1968; one escaped during a manoeuvre in 1971; the other died in 1974; none since)

New York Aquarium
New York Zoological Society
Boardwalk at West 8th Street
Seaside Park
Brooklyn, New York 11224
Telephone: 212-266-8500
(One orca exhibited briefly in 1968; none since)

Sea-Arama Marineworld
3507 91 Street and Seawall Boulevard
Galveston, Texas 77550
Telephone: 713-744-4501
(Two orcas exhibited from 1968 to 1974; none since)

Sea World, Inc.
1720 South Shores Road
Mission Bay
San Diego, California 92109
Telephone: 619-222-6363
Corporation
*(The first of Sea World's parks to keep
killer whales, in 1965. Exact counts at any
one park are difficult because the orcas are
moved around as needed. To date, at least
33 killer whales — many using the stage
names of Shamu, Kandu or Namu — have
been exhibited at the various Sea Worlds.
Ten have come from Iceland since 1977.
Six have been born in captivity, five
surviving through December 1989.
Including the calves, 15 were alive in
12/89, with each park housing from three
to six orcas.)*

Sea World of Florida
7007 Sea World Drive
Orlando, Florida 32821
Telephone: 305-351-3600

Sea World of Ohio
1100 Sea World Drive
Aurora, Ohio 44202
Telephone: 216-562-8101

Sea World of Texas
10500 Sea World Drive
San Antonio, Texas 78251
Telephone: 512-523-3611

Seattle Marine Aquarium
(closed 1977)
Pier 56
Seattle, Washington 90101
*(This private aquarium, originally called
the Seattle Public Aquarium, was initially
owned by Ted Griffin, who exhibited about
four orcas beginning with Namu in 1965.
In the late 1960s, the aquarium was bought
out by Sea World, and while it continued to
exhibit orcas, it was mostly used as a
temporary holding facility for recently
captured orcas bound for San Diego
or Florida.)*

WEST GERMANY

In the early 1970s, one orca was
exhibited briefly at Munich and another
at Bremen. Both were owned by Donald
Goldsberry, then of Seattle Marine
Aquarium, and were leased to James W.
Tiebor of the travelling "Florida Delphin
Show" (Leienfelsstrasze 26, 8000
München 60, West Germany). In 1979,
one orca was kept briefly at Lübeck
(Hansaland Park, Sierksdorf – also
owned by "Florida Delphin Show") and
later transferred to Kamogawa Sea
World, Japan. Also in 1979, one orca was
kept in storage at Mannheim before
being sent on to Switzerland in early
1980.

Hagenbecks Tierpark
Postfach 540930
D-2000 Hamburg 54
West Germany
*(One orca exhibited from 1981 to 1985;
none since)*

APPENDIX 8

A CONCISE HISTORY OF MAN AND ORCA

C. 100 B.C.   Nazca natives of Peru paint killer whale designs on their icons as symbols of power, warrior courage and fertility, and they build temples dedicated to killer whale deities.

C. 50 A.D.   Pliny the Elder watches the public slaughtering of a killer whale stranded in the harbour at Ostia near Rome and, in the earliest published reference to the species, calls orca "an enormous mass of flesh armed with savage teeth" and "the enemy of other whales [who does] charge and pierce them like warships ramming."

1758   Swedish botanist Carolus Linnaeus gives the name *Orcinus orca* to the species.

1792   Captain George Vancouver, the first white man to sail Johnstone Strait, finds "numerous [probably killer] whales, enjoying the season . . . playing about the ship."

1843   English writer/painter Sir Oswald Brierly visits Twofold Bay, Australia, and tells of orcas assisting whalers in the hunting of large baleen whales.

1862   Danish zoologist D.F. Eschricht reports finding pieces of 13 porpoises and 14 seals in the stomach of a male orca. His account, often misquoted, is a source of orca's bad reputation.

1874   Whaler Captain Charles Scammon tells of killers chasing large whales "like a pack of hounds," tearing out the lips and tongues of their victims.

1911   Twice on Captain Robert F. Scott's final Antarctic expedition, his men are suddenly stranded on moving ice floes and become terrified when curious orcas swim around them.

1930   "Old Tom" dies at Twofold Bay, Australia, ending almost a century of symbiotic hunting between man and orca.

1956   U.S. Navy airplanes destroy hundreds of killer whales near Iceland, where the whales were apparently damaging nets, cutting the fish catch in half.

1961   First killer whale captured at Newport Harbor (California) by Marineland collectors, dies the following day.

John C. Lilly captures public imagination with publication of *Man and Dolphin,* in which he speculates on the intelligence of dolphins, orcas and other whales and on the possibility of communicating with them.

1962   Marineland (California) collectors try to hoop-net a killer whale in Puget Sound. A female orca, caught by the tail, and her bull "escort" charge the boat. Collectors shoot both animals, killing the female.

1964   U.S. Air Force practises strafing runs on orcas in the North Atlantic.

First orca exhibited in captivity. Vancouver Aquarium collectors harpoon a killer whale off B.C. coast for sculptor's model, but Moby Doll survives and, for three months, becomes an international celebrity, moderating the species' killer reputation.

1965	Ted Griffin of Seattle Public Aquarium brings bull orca to Seattle while thousands cheer. Namu survives a year.
	Griffin and Don Goldsberry develop a netting technique for capturing orcas in Puget Sound, selling the animals mostly to Sea World.
1968	Canadian fishermen begin commercial netting in Pender Harbour to supply aquariums around the world.
	At Marine World Africa U.S.A. (California), two orcas impregnated in the wild deliver stillbirths.
1970	Peak year for orca captures in the Northwest. Of an estimated 90 caught off southern Vancouver Island and Puget Sound, 16 are either sent to aquariums or die in the nets.
	U.S. veterinarian Mark Keyes reveals that in some samples, as many as 25 percent of the Puget Sound killer whales examined after aquarium capture have bullet holes in their bodies.
	Sealand (Victoria, British Columbia) captures albino killer whale. Chimo brings international headlines and $1 million offer to Sealand from a U.S. aquarium.
	Three carcasses of young killer whales, slit open and weighted like victims of gangsters, are found floating near Penn Cove, Washington, site of a large Seattle Public Aquarium capture months earlier. Public controversy over orca captures follows.
	Canadian federal laws passed to prevent harassment, capture and killing of orcas except for restricted permits to Canadian captors.
1971	Washington State laws to regulate orca captures require a $1,000 permit per whale and presence of state officials after capture to ensure humane handling.
	U.S. Navy researchers call killer whales uncooperative after teaching them to retrieve objects from the ocean floor. An orca named Ishmael escapes on a training manoeuvre off Hawaii, never to be seen again, while Ahab takes researchers on a 50-mile 24-hour chase before being recaptured.
1972	U.S. Marine Mammal Protection Act extends federal protection to killer whales, further restricting permits to capture them.
	Killer whale attacks human. Eighteen-year-old surfer Hans Kretschmer "mouthed" by orca off Point Sur, California — probably a case of mistaken identity. He survives with 100 stitches and scars showing orca teeth.
1973	Canadian biologist Michael Bigg, with Ian MacAskie, initiates intensive photographic study and census of orcas in Johnstone Strait.
1976	Public outcry over Goldsberry orca capture pits State of Washington against Sea World, while whales wait in the nets. Washington wins. Sea World releases captives and agrees to stop catching in the Northwest. Puget Sound becomes, in effect, a killer whale sanctuary.
	Photographer Ken Balcomb and others begin intensive photographic study of "southern community" killer whale pods off San Juan Island, Washington.
	Goldsberry and Sea World move capture operations to Iceland.
1977	B.C. sports fisherman rescues sick bullet-wounded calf, Miracle, and gives it to Sealand in Victoria, where it is nursed back to health.

First killer whale to be conceived in captivity is born alive to Corky II and Orky II at Marineland (California) but dies after 16 days.

1978   Peak year for Icelandic captures. Of 10 captured for aquariums, 5 are sent to Sea World in California. Five others fall ill while waiting to be shipped from Icelandic aquarium; after two die, the other three are released.

1979   At U.S. Marine Mammal conference, Canadian biologist Michael Bigg describes the self-sufficiency of orca pods based on his seven-year study of B.C. orcas. With the long-term bonding Bigg observed in each pod, he also found a very low birth rate – at 4 to 5 percent, probably the lowest of all whales and dolphins.

U.S. biologist Deborah Duffield and veterinarian Lanny Cornell find chromosomal and biochemical evidence that killer whales live in incestuous groups with only limited exchanges with other pods.

Canadian biologist/acoustician John Ford identifies dialects in orca vocalizing.

First netting of killer whales in Japanese waters. Of five sent to Japanese aquariums, three die within three months.

1980   Russian whalers take 916 orcas in the Antarctic, from January through March. Possible effect of this intense exploitation subject of hot debate at International Whaling Commission meeting in June. Zero quota set for 1981.

Robson Bight proposed as ecological reserve to protect unique Vancouver Island bay where killer whales come to rest, play and rub. Large Canadian logging company wants to build logging port at the bight.

1982   B.C. government declares that no logs will be boomed in Robson Bight and designates it a marine ecological reserve.

Sealand (Victoria, British Columbia) proposes to return Haida, its performing veteran of 14 years, to the wild and to capture two new youngsters to be released, in turn, after four to six years. The permit is granted, but Haida dies before his release. Environmentalists block the capture of more B.C. whales; Sealand closes for six months, then reopens with three new orcas purchased from Iceland.

Fourth killer whale to be conceived at Marineland (California) lives longest to date: 46 days.

First orca born in Japanese aquarium (Enoshima Marineland) dies after seven days.

1983   Sea World granted a five-year permit from National Marine Fisheries Service to capture 100 Alaskan orcas – 10 for permanent display and 90 for research and later release. While environmentalists, concerned biologists and Alaskan residents contest the permit, Washington State Congressman Rod Chandler introduces a bill to prohibit the taking and importation of all killer whales for public display.

1984   Sea World arrives in Alaska to carry out basic photo-identification research on killer whales, preparatory to the captures. Northwest residents, including Alaska's governor and legislature, oppose the orca captures. Sea World eventually leaves Alaska empty-handed.

1985   Baby Shamu, born to an Icelandic mother and a Northwest Coast father (Ramu III or Winston), on September 26, at Sea World, Florida. The baby becomes the first to survive beyond 42 days. Still alive in 1989.

1986   In late December, Sea World's parent company, Harcourt Brace Jovanovich, buys Marineland of the Pacific near Los Angeles, closes it a few weeks later and moves

Orky II and Corky II to Sea World in San Diego. Orky breeds and fathers two calves.

1987   At Sea World in San Diego, Kandu V plays roughly with trainer JoAnne Webber and other trainers in a number of incidents over a two-year period. Webber later sues Sea World, contending that the stress on the whales from too much performing produces the aggression.

During a Sea World show in November, in an unfortunate accident after being miscued, Orky II lands on trainer John Sillick, seriously injuring him. Three executives are fired in the wake of bad publicity, and trainers, partly because of earlier incidents, are ordered to stay out of the water. New management returns trainers to the water seven months later.

1988   Eighteen months after Orky II's arrival at Sea World, the bull dies, having lost 4,000 pounds in the final two months (about one-third of his weight). His death comes only three days after a calf he sired, Baby Shamu III, was born to Kandu V while thousands watched at Shamu Stadium in San Diego.

First captive killer whale birth in Canada at the Vancouver Aquarium. Female calf dies 22 days later.

1989   On March 23, the tanker *Exxon Valdez* runs aground on a reef in Prince William Sound, Alaska, dumping crude oil that eventually covers an area of more than 1,000 square miles. The toll of birds and animals caught in the slick may be the worst ever from an oil spill. Hundreds, perhaps thousands, of sea otters die. Killer whales are seen swimming through the crude, and several grey whales are found dead, possibly from the oil.

Kandu V, mother of Baby Shamu III, born in captivity in 1988, rams Corky II, an older female formerly of Marineland, during a Sea World show in San Diego. Kandu spouts blood and dies 45 minutes later of a massive haemorrhage triggered by an upper-jaw fracture. Corky escapes with minor cuts, and Baby Shamu is left disoriented at the loss.

Sea World parks sold to Anheuser-Busch, the world's largest brewer, for $1.1 billion.

BIBLIOGRAPHY

AELIANUS, C. *On the Characteristics of Animals*. Vol. XII. Translated by A.F. Scholfield. Cambridge: Harvard University Press, 1958, pp. 205-209. Killer whales in the Middle Ages – "ram-fishes" – described as sea monsters and man-eaters who "even snatch men standing on the shore."

"A Field Report." *Vancouver Public Aquarium Newsletter*, Vol. XVIII, No. 5. Sept./Oct. 1974. Account of B.C. ferry accidentally hitting a young killer whale and adult whales coming to the youngster's aid, supporting him.

ALPERS, A. *Dolphins: The Myth and the Mammal*. Boston: Houghton Mifflin Co., 1961. Popular book about dolphins; killer whales on pp. 160-169.

ANDERSON, G.R.V. "A Re-examination of Pregnancy Rates and Calf Ratios in *Orcinus orca*." *Report*, International Whaling Commission, Vol. 32, 1982, pp. 629-631.

ANDERSON, P.K. AND R.I.T. PRINCE. "Predation on Dugongs: Attacks by Killer Whales." *Journal of Mammalogy*, Vol. 66, No. 3, 1985, pp. 554-556.

ANDERSON, S.S. AND A.D. HAWKINS. "Scaring Seals by Sound." *Mammal Review*, Vol. 8, 1978, pp. 19-24. Recorded killer whale sounds used to control seals.

ANDREWS, B. AND T. DESMOND. "Killer Whale Births." *Whalewatcher*, Vol. 15, No. 1, 1981, pp. 8-9. Former curator of mammals and orca trainer from Marineland, California, present their account of several live births to Corky and Orky.

ARISTOTLE. *Historia Animalium*. Books I-IX. Translated under editorship of W.D. Ross. Reprinted by arrangement with Oxford University Press for The Great Books, Vol. 9, *Works of Aristotle*. Chicago: Encyclopaedia Britannica, 1952, p. 156. "The gentle and kindly nature of the dolphin," according to Aristotle from the fourth century B.C.

ARNASON, U., M. HOGLUND AND B. WIDEGREN. "Conservation of Highly Repetitive DNA in Cetaceans." *Chromosoma*, Vol. 89, No. 3, 1984, pp. 238-242. DNA analysis of various species of whales and dolphins including killer whales, using Southern blot hybridization, shows a common ancestry for toothed and baleen whales.

ARNBOM, T., V. PAPASTAVROU, L.S. WEILGART AND H. WHITEHEAD. "Sperm Whales React to an Attack by Killer Whales." *Journal of Mammalogy*, Vol. 68, No. 2, 1987, pp. 450-453.

ASPER, E.D. AND L.H. CORNELL. "Live Capture Statistics for the Killer Whale (*Orcinus orca*) 1961-76 in California, Washington and British Columbia." *Aquatic Mammals*, Vol. 5, No. 1, Jan. 1977, pp. 21-26. Sea World's accounting of the number and fate of the orcas it and other aquariums removed from the Northwest (Puget Sound and B.C. waters).

AWBREY, F.T., J.A. THOMAS, W.E. EVANS AND S. LEATHERWOOD. "Ross Sea Killer Whale Vocalizations; Preliminary Description and Comparison With Those of Some Northern Hemisphere Killer Whales." *Report*, International Whaling Commission, Vol. 32, 1982, pp. 667-670.

AUBE, L.J. "Orca." *Sea Frontiers*, Vol. 34, 1988, pp. 320-325.

BACKUS, R.H. "Stranded Killer Whale in the Bahamas." *Journal of Mammalogy*, Vol. 42, 1961, pp. 418-419.

BAIRD, R.W. AND P.J. STACEY. "Variation in Saddle Patch Pigmentation in Populations of Killer Whales (*Orcinus orca*) from British Columbia, Alaska and Washington State." *Canadian Journal of Zoology*, Vol. 66, No. 11, 1988, pp. 2582-2585. Saddle-patch shapes differ substantially in unrelated or distantly related "communities" of Northwest Coast orcas. Differences in saddle patches might be used to establish stocks of killer whales in other areas of the world.

BALCOMB, K.C. Orca Survey 1977. Final report of a field photographic study conducted by the Moclips Cetological Society in collaboration with the U.S. National Marine Fisheries Service on killer whales (*Orcinus orca*) in Puget Sound. Unpublished report to Marine Mammal Division, NMFS, Seattle, Wash. 1978, 10 pp.

BALCOMB, K.C., III, J.R. BORAN AND S.L. HEIMLICH. "Killer Whales in Greater Puget Sound." *Report*, International Whaling Commission, Vol. 32, 1982, pp. 681-686.

BALCOMB, K.C., J.R. BORAN AND R.W. OSBORNE. Killer Whales (*Orcinus orca*) in Greater Puget Sound. Abstracts from presentations at the Third Biennial Conference on the Biology of Marine Mammals. Oct. 7-11, 1979. Seattle, Wash. Photographic study of J pod in Puget Sound; summary of findings 1976-79.

BALCOMB, K.C., J.R. BORAN, R.W. OSBORNE AND N.J. HAENEL. "Observations of Killer Whales (*Orcinus orca*) in Greater Puget Sound, State of Washington." NTIS PB80-224728, U.S. Dept. of Comm., Springfield, Va., 1980, pp. 1-42. The 79 resident orcas in the southern community are estimated to eat a yearly total of 725 to 1,350 tons of food species in the U.S. portion of their range. Even if the whales consumed just salmon, the total would only be equivalent to 3 to 7 percent of the U.S. salmon fishery's annual catch in the same area.

BALCOMB, K.C. AND C.A. GOEBEL. A Killer Whale Study in Puget Sound. Final report of a field photographic study conducted in 1976 under National Marine Fisheries Service contract NASO-6-35330. Unpublished report to Marine Mammal Division, NMFS, Seattle, Wash., 1976.

BALDRIDGE, A. "Killer Whales Attack and Eat a Gray Whale." *Journal of Mammalogy*, Vol. 53, No. 4, 1972, pp. 898-900.

BARR, N. AND L. BARR. "An Observation of Killer Whale Predation on a Dall Porpoise." *Canadian Field-Naturalist*, Vol. 86, 1972, pp. 170-171.

BARTLETT, D. AND J. BARTLETT. "Patagonia's Wild Shore: Where Two Worlds Meet." *National Geographic*, Vol. 149, No. 3, March 1976, pp. 314-317. Photographs of killer whales tossing young South American sea lions into the air.

BATESON, G. "Problems in Cetacean and Other Mammalian Communication." In *Whales, Porpoises and Dolphins* (K.S. Norris, ed.). Berkeley, Los Angeles: University of California Press, 1966, pp. 569-579. Psychiatrist/anthropologist Bateson's thoughts about communication and social systems after observing captive dolphins.

BECKEL, A.I. "Response of Sea Otters (*Enhydra lutris*) to Killer Whales (*Orcinus orca*) in Prince William Sound, Alaska, U.S.A." *Murrelet*, Vol. 61, No. 1, 1980, pp. 46-47. Sea otters are probably not a significant prey of orcas, although otters will flee or remain "alert and watchful" while orcas are in the vicinity.

BENIRSCHKE, K. AND L.H. CORNELL. "The Placenta of the Killer Whale, *Orcinus orca*." *Marine Mammal Science*, Vol. 3, No. 1, 1987, pp. 82-86.

BERZIN, A.A. AND V.L. VLADIMIROV. "A New Species of Killer Whale (Cetacea, Delphinidae) From the Antarctic Waters." *Zoologicheskii Zhurnal*, Vol. 62, No. 2, 1983, pp. 287-295. Possible new species (*Orcinus glacialis*), according to Russian scientists, based on morphological differences found in animals from the Indian Ocean sector of the Antarctic.

BEST, P.B., D.W. RICE AND A.A. WOLMAN. Age, Growth and Sexual Dimorphism in Killer Whales (*Orcinus orca*). International Conference on Determining Age of Odontocete Cetaceans, La Jolla, Calif. Sept. 5-7, 1978. Proceedings (Abstracts), p. 24.

BEST, R. AND C. ANGUS. "White Killer Whale Captured." *Vancouver Public Aquarium Newsletter*, Vol. 14, No. 2, 1970, pp. 6-7.

BIGG, M.A. Interaction Between Pods of Killer Whales off British Columbia and Washington. Abstracts from presentations at the Third Biennial Conference on the Biology of Marine Mammals. Oct. 7-11, 1979, Seattle, Wash. After seven years of intensive field photographic study in the Northwest, Bigg reports finding discrete long-term family groups of the same individuals. Large pods (more than 10 individuals) are the productive ones, and smaller pods, because of the discreteness, are destined to die out. Killer whale reproduction rate estimated at 4 to 5 percent new calves per year.

BIGG, M.A. "Assessment of Killer Whale (*Orcinus orca*) Stocks off Vancouver Island, British Columbia." *Report*, International Whaling Commission, Vol. 32, 1982, pp. 655-666. Complete census statistics and pod breakdown (bulls, cows and calves) for Vancouver Island killer whales. Low annual birth rates indicate an average calving interval of 8½ years in cropped pods and 12½ years in uncropped pods. The shortest interval between births was three years. "The large number of nonbreeding adult females in the population suggests that the species might be controlling its birth rate in a manner similar to that of wolves and African wild dogs."

BIGG, M.A., G.M. ELLIS AND K.C. BALCOMB. "The Photographic Identification of Individual Cetaceans." *Whalewatcher*, Vol. 20, No. 2, 1986, pp. 10-12.

BIGG, M.A., G.M. ELLIS, J.K.B. FORD AND K.C. BALCOMB. *Killer Whales: A Study of Their Identification, Genealogy & Natural History in British Columbia and Washington State.* Nanaimo, B.C.: Phantom Press & Publishers, 1987, pp. 1-79. Excellent story and photographs of pioneer killer whale research, including fascinating genealogies of each of the resident and transient pods.

BIGG, M.A., I.B. MACASKIE AND G. ELLIS. Abundance and Movements of Killer Whales off Eastern and Southern Vancouver Island With Comments on Management. Unpublished preliminary report to Arctic Biological Station, Ste. Anne de Bellevue, Quebec, 1976, pp. 1-20. Pioneer study of killer whales in their natural habitat, with detailed notes about pod groupings and movements off the B.C. coast.

BIGG, M.A., I.B. MACASKIE AND G. ELLIS. "Photo-identification of Individual Killer Whales." *Whalewatcher,* Vol. 17, No. 1, 1983, pp. 3-5.

BIGG, M.A. AND A.A. WOLMAN. "Live-Capture Killer Whale (*Orcinus orca*) Fishery, British Columbia and Washington, 1962-73." *Journal*, Fisheries Research Board of Canada, Vol. 32, No. 7, 1975, pp. 1213-1221. Report on the capture fishery in the Northwest, with management comments.

BORAN, J.R., F.L. FELLEMAN, S.L. HEIMLICH AND R.W. OSBORNE. Habitat Use of Puget Sound Killer Whales. Abstracts from presentations at the Fourth Biennial Conference on the Biology of Marine Mammals, Dec. 1981, San Francisco, Calif.

BOURNE, A.G. "Exploitation of Small Whales in the North Atlantic." *Oryx*, Vol. 8, 1965, pp. 185-193. North Atlantic killer whales shot on sight by fishermen who believe the whales scare the fish.

BOWERS, C.A. AND R.S. HENDERSON. *Project Deep Ops: Deep Object Recovery With Pilot and Killer Whales.* Naval Undersea Center. NUC TP 306, 1972, pp. 1-86. The U.S. Navy's work with pilot and killer whales that were trained to recover objects on the ocean floor.

BRADY, E.J. "The Law of the Tongue: Whaling by Compact at Twofold Bay." *Australia To-Day*, Dec. 1, 1909, pp. 37, 40, 42. Contemporary mention of symbiotic whaling with killer whales at Twofold Bay. For full accounts, see W.J. Dakin, T. Mead, C.E. Wellings and H.P. Wellings.

BRAHAM, H.W. AND M.E. DAHLHEIM. "Killer Whales in Alaska Documented in the Platforms of Opportunity Program." *Report*, International Whaling Commission, Vol. 32, 1982, pp. 643-646.

BRANSON, J. "Killer Whales Pursue Sea Lions in Bering Sea Drama." *Commercial Fisheries Review*, March 1971, pp. 39-40. Killer whale pod chasing Steller sea lions around a Soviet trawler. Two photographs.

BRENT, P. *Capt. Scott and the Antarctic Tragedy.* New York: Saturday Review Press, 1974, pp. 154-156. Fearful reactions of Captain Scott's men to curious Antarctic killer whales.

BROWN, D.H. AND K.S. NORRIS. "Observations on Captive and Wild Cetaceans." *Journal of Mammalogy*, Vol. 37, No. 3, 1956, pp. 325-326. Orcas seen feeding on common dolphins and dead basking shark off Baja California.

BUDYLENKO, G.A. "Distribution and Some Aspects of the Biology of Killer Whales in the South Atlantic." *Report*, International Whaling Commission, Vol. 31, 1981, pp. 523-525.

BULLEN, F.T. *The Cruise of the Cachalot.* New York: Dodd, 1948 (orig. edition 1899), pp. 1-301. Orcas seen feeding on bowhead whales in the North Pacific.

BURGESS, K. "The Behaviour and Training of a Killer Whale, *Orcinus orca*, at San Diego Sea World." *International Zoo Yearbook*, Vol. 8, 1968, pp. 202-205. Trainer's account of the original Shamu and her first days at Sea World.

BURRAGE, B.R. "An Observation Regarding Gray Whales and Killer Whales." *Transactions*, Kansas Academy of Science, Vol. 67, No. 3, Dec. 11, 1964, pp. 550-551. Grey whales fleeing from killer whales.

BUSNEL, R.G. "Information in the Human Whistled Language and Sea Mammal Whistling." *Whales, Porpoises and Dolphins* (K.S. Norris, ed.). Berkeley, Los Angeles: University of California Press, 1966, pp. 544-568. Discussion of human whistled language used in a small French village in the Pyrenees and the idea of teaching it to dolphins.

BUSNEL, R.G. "Symbiotic Relationships Between Man and Dolphins." *Transactions*, New York Academy of Sciences, Vol. 35, No. 2, 1973, pp. 112-131.

BYCHOV, V.A. "On Killers Attack of Fur Seals Offshore the Island Robben." *Zoologicheskii Zhurnal* (in Russian with English summary), Vol. 46, No. 1, 1967, pp. 149-150.

CALDWELL, D.K., J.N. LAYNE AND J.B. SIEBENALER. "Notes on a Killer Whale (*Orcinus orca*) From the Northeastern Gulf of Mexico." *Quarterly Journal*, Florida Academy of Sciences, Vol. 19, No. 4, 1956, pp. 189-196.

CALDWELL, D.K. AND D.H. BROWN. "Tooth Wear as a Correlate of Described Feeding Behavior by the Killer Whale, With Notes on a Captive Specimen." *Bulletin*, Southern California Academy of Sciences, Los Angeles, Vol. 63, Pt. 3, 1964, pp. 128-140. Account of the first killer whale taken captive, by Marineland of the Pacific in 1961; autopsy and tooth study.

CALDWELL, D.K. AND M.C. CALDWELL. "Addition of the Leatherback Sea Turtle to the Known Prey of the Killer Whale, *Orcinus orca*." *Journal of Mammalogy*, Vol. 50, No. 3, 1969, p. 636. First reptile found in killer whale stomach.

CALDWELL, M.C. AND D.K. CALDWELL. "Epimeletic (care-giving) Behavior in Cetacea." *Whales, Porpoises and Dolphins* (K.S. Norris, ed.). Berkeley, Los Angeles: University of California Press, 1966, pp. 755-789. Accounts of killer whales (on pp. 771-772) supporting injured pod members; reports of killer whale attacks.

CAMERON, W.M. "Killer Whales Stranded Near Masset." Fisheries Research Board of Canada, *Pacific Progress Report 49*. 1941, p. 17.

CAMPBELL, R.R., D.B. YURICK AND N.B. SNOW. "Predation on Narwhals, *Monodon monoceros*, by killer whales, *Orcinus orca*, in the eastern Canadian Arctic." *Canadian Field-Naturalist*, Vol. 102, No. 4, 1988, pp. 689-696. Killer whales prey on narwhals, and the narwhals seem to have evolved defensive strategies. Inuit hunters know these strategies and take advantage of them to hunt narwhals.

CARAS, R.A. *Dangerous to Man*. New York: Chilton Books, 1964, pp. 55-68. Discusses the alleged dangers of killer whales, as perceived before the captivity era.

CARL, G.C. "A School of Killer Whales Stranded at Estevan Point." *B.C. Provincial Museum of Natural History and Anthropology Report* (1945), 1946, pp. 21-28. Twenty killer whales stranded on Vancouver Island beach; story, detailed measurements, pod composition.

CARL, G.C. "Albinistic Killer Whales in British Columbia." *B.C. Provincial Museum of Natural History and Anthropology Report*, 1959, pp. 29-36. Sighting records of white killer whales off the B.C. coast from 1923 to 1959.

CASTELLO, H.P. "Food of a Killer Whale: Eagle Sting-Ray, *Myliobatis*, Found in the Stomach of Stranded *Orcinus orca*." *Scientific Reports*, Whales Research Institute (Tokyo), No. 29, 1977, pp. 107-111.

CHANDLER, R., C. GOEBEL AND K. BALCOMB. "Who Is That Killer Whale? A New Key to Whale Watching." *Pacific Search*, Vol. 11, No. 7, 1977, pp. 25-35. Puget Sound photographic study of killer whales. See also K.C. Balcomb.

CHRISTENSEN, I. "Preliminary Report on the Norwegian Fishery for Small Whales: Expansion of Norwegian Whaling to Arctic and Northwest Atlantic Waters and Norwegian Investigations of the Biology of Small Whales." *Journal*, Fisheries Research Board of Canada, Vol. 32, 1975, pp. 1083-1094.

CHRISTENSEN, I. "Spekkhoggeren (*Orcinus orca*) i det Nordostlige Atlanterhav. (The Killer Whale in the Northeast Atlantic.)" *Fisken og Havet* (in Norwegian with English summary), Vol. 1, 1978, pp. 23-31. General feeding notes, stomach studies (herring and octopus), Norwegian names for killer whales and explanations, tagging studies; killer whales able to distinguish between herring and whaling boats – the same except for gun mounted on the bow.

CHRISTENSEN, I., Å. JONSGÅRD AND C. RØRVIK. "Catch Statistics for Minke Whales (*Balaenoptera acutorostrata*) and Killer Whales (*Orcinus orca*) Caught by Norway in 1979." *Report*, International Whaling Commission, Vol. 31, 1981, pp. 635-637.

CHRISTENSEN, I. "Killer Whales in Norwegian Coastal Waters." *Report*, International Whaling Commission, Vol. 32, 1982, pp. 633-642.

CLARKE, J. *Man Is the Prey*. New York: Stein and Day, 1969, pp. 226-227. Calls orca "the biggest confirmed man-eater on earth" yet fails to cite a single convincing case.

CODERE, H. "The Kwakiutl." *Perspectives in American Indian Culture Change* (E.H. Spicer, ed.). Chicago: University of Chicago Press, 1961, pp. 431-516. Anthropologist's detailed account of how the Kwakiutl of Alert Bay and surrounding villages have adapted to the 20th century, with an excellent review of materials on the Kwakiutl.

COLLET, R. *Norges Pattedyr*. Kristiania: H. Aschehoug and Co. (W. Nygaard), 1912, pp. 1-744. Baleen whales and orcas observed feeding together on herring.

COLWELL, M. *Whaling Around Australia*. London: Angus and Robertson (U.K.) Ltd., 1970 (reprinted Adelaide: Seal Books, 1977), pp. 1-168. Killer whales in Australia plus Twofold Bay story.

CONDY, P.R., R.J. VAN AARDE AND M.N. BESTER. "The Seasonal Occurrence and Behaviour of Killer Whales, *Orcinus orca*, at Marian Island." *Journal of Zoology* (London), Vol. 184, 1978, pp. 449-464. Resting and rubbing behaviour of killer whales in the southwest Indian Ocean.

CORNELL, L.H. "Puget Sound Already Is a Killer Whale Sanctuary." *Pacific Search*, Vol. 9, No. 1, 1974, pp. 16-18. Sea World's defence of capturing killer whales in Puget Sound.

CORNELL, L.H., E.D. ASPER AND D.A. DUFFIELD. "Census Update: Captive Marine Mammals in North America." *International Zoo Yearbook*, Vol. 22, pp. 227-232.

CORNELL, L.H. AND S. LEATHERWOOD. "Killer Whale Birth at Sea World." *Whalewatcher*, Vol. 20, No. 1, 1986, pp. 8-10.

COTTON, B.C. "Killer Whales in South Australia." *South Australian Naturalist* (Adelaide), Vol. 22, No. 2, 1943, pp. 2-3. Blue whale cow and calf chased by killer whales.

"Cranky Killer Whales Put Trainers Through Their Paces." *The Province* (Vancouver), May 5, 1978, p. 1. Temperamental orcas at the Vancouver Aquarium.

CROMIE, W.J. "Killer Whale!" *Rod & Gun* (Canada), Sept. 1962. Condensed version in *Reader's Digest*, March 1963, pp. 176-180. Stories of killer whales in the Antarctic.

CUMMINGS, W.C. AND P.O. THOMPSON. "Gray Whales, *Eschrichtius robustus*, Avoid the Underwater Sounds of Killer Whales, *Orcinus orca*." *Fishery Bulletin* (U.S.), Vol. 69, No. 3, 1971, pp. 525-530. Recorded sounds of killer whales, transmitted underwater, caused grey whales migrating south to Baja California to swim away from the sound source, while pure tones and random noise had no effect.

CURIO, E. *Ethology of Predation*. Berlin, New York: Springer-Verlag, 1976, pp. 1-250. Explanation of predator-prey relationships.

CURTIS, E.S. *The Kwakiutl: The North American Indian*. Vol. 10, 1915 (reprinted New York: Johnson Reprint, 1970), pp. 37-38, 85, 91. Kwakiutl stories about killer whales.

DAHLHEIM, M.E. "A Review of the Biology and Exploitation of the Killer Whale, *Orcinus orca*, With Comments on Recent Sightings From Antarctica." *Report*, International Whaling Commission, Vol. 31, 1981, pp. 541-550. The average yield of oil for a killer whale is 4.88 barrels, or 170.8 gallons. It would take 21.9 killer whales to equal the oil production of one blue whale.

DAHLHEIM, M.E., S. LEATHERWOOD AND W.F. PERRIN. "Distribution of Killer Whales in the Warm Temperate and Tropical Eastern Pacific." *Report*, International Whaling Commission, Vol. 32, 1982, pp. 647-654.

DAKIN, W.J. *Whalemen Adventurers*. Sydney: Angus and Robertson, 1934, pp. 145-158. (Reprinted in other editions 1938, 1963 and 1977.) Sydney zoologist's account of the symbiotic hunting of large whales by whalers and killer whales at Twofold Bay. Killer whales named for distinctive marks on their dorsal fins, like Johnstone Strait whales. Lively, popular account; best introduction to this remarkable story.

DALTON, S. "Understanding Killer Whales: To Attack or Not to Attack." *Pacific Diver*, Vol. 3, No. 3, July/Aug. 1977, pp. 18-19, 33-34. Accounts of possible killer whale attacks; discussion of danger to divers.

DARLING, J.D. The Behaviour and Ecology of the Vancouver Island Grey Whales, *Eschrichtius glaucus* Cope. Unpublished master's thesis, University of Victoria, 1977. Peaceful killer whale/grey whale encounters off Vancouver Island's west coast.

DARLING, J.D. "Whales. An Era of Discovery." *National Geographic*, Vol. 174, No. 6, 1988, pp. 872-908.

DAVIS, R. "Sea Wolves of the Pacific Northwest." *B.C. Outdoors*, Pt. I, Vol. 31, No. 3. May/June 1975, pp. 6-10; Pt. II, Vol. 31, No. 4, July/Aug. 1975, pp. 20-25. Lengthy discussion of pros and cons of capturing and keeping killer whales.

DEARDON, J.C. "A Stranding of Killer Whales in Newfoundland." *Canadian Field-Naturalist*, Vol. 72, 1958, pp. 166-167.

DEMASTER, D.P. AND J.K. DREVENAK. "Survivorship Patterns in Three Species of Captive Cetaceans." *Marine Mammal Science*, Vol. 4, No. 4, 1988, pp. 297-311. Discussion of problems in determining the longevity of killer whales in captivity.

DERGERBÖEL, M. AND N.L. NIELSEN. "Biologiske Iagttagelser over og Maalinger af Hvidhvalen og dens Fostre." *Medd. Grönland*, Vol. 77, No. 3, 1930, pp. 117-144. Orcas attacking beluga whales off Greenland.

DEVINE, E. AND M. CLARK. *The Dolphin Smile: Twenty-nine Centuries of Dolphin Lore*. New York: Macmillan Co., 1967, pp. 1-370.

DI SCIARA, G.N. "A Killer Whale (*Orcinus orca* L.) Attacks and Sinks a Sailing Boat." *Natura* (Milano), Vol. 68, No. 3-4, 1977, pp. 218-220. Inconsistent with Levitt's account of the sinking of the *Guia III* but probably more authoritative. Yet there are errors in this report, and accounts of earlier "attacks" that are doubtful are repeated as fact.

DOLPHIN, W.F. "Observations of Humpback Whale, *Megaptera novaeangliae* and Killer Whale, *Orcinus orca*, Interactions in Alaska: Comparison with Terrestrial Predator-Prey Relationships." *Canadian Field-Naturalist*, Vol. 101, No. 1, 1987, pp. 70-75. Killer whales, like lions, often coexist with some of their prey species, such as humpback whales. Account of humpbacks joining killer whales to attack a sea lion.

DOUGLAS-HAMILTON, I. AND O. DOUGLAS-HAMILTON. *Among the Elephants*. New York: Viking, 1975, pp. 1-285. Comparative study of a social mammal group.

DUDOK VAN HEEL, W.H. "An Experiment in Two-Way Communication in *Orcinus orca* L." *Aquatic Mammals*, Vol. 9, No. 3, 1982, pp. 69-82. A captive orca in Holland was encouraged to attempt elementary communication with sounds of different frequencies used to represent words.

DUDOK VAN HEEL, W.H. "From the Ocean to the Pool." In *Research on Dolphins* (M.M. Bryden and R. Harrison, eds.). Oxford: Oxford Science Publications, pp. 163-182. Dudok van Heel's detailed chapter on captive orcas is a primer on how to catch, transport and keep orcas.

DUFFIELD, D. AND L. CORNELL. Observations on Population Structure and Dynamics in *Orcinus orca*. Abstracts from presentations at the Third Biennial Conference on the Biology of Marine Mammals. Oct. 7-11, 1979, Seattle, Wash. Chromosomal and biochemical evidence that killer whales live in incestuous groups and have only limited exchanges with other pods.

DUFFIELD, D.A. AND K.W. MILLER. "Demographic Features of Killer Whales in Oceanaria in the United States and Canada, 1965-1987." *Rit Fiskideildar*, Vol. 11, 1988, pp. 297-306. Annual mortality rate estimated from "animal years" in captivity was 8.9 percent. Females have a linear growth rate up to age 10-12 and males up to 12-16 − about the time they become sexually mature. Various females first gave birth at age 11, 12, 13 and 15. A 17-month gestation period based on serum and urine progesterone studies.

EASTON, N. "The Death of Marineland." *Los Angeles Times Magazine*, Aug. 9, 1987, pp. 6-10, 23-26.

ELLIS, G.E. "Killer Whales of Southern Alaska: A Catalogue of Individuals Photo-identified in 1984." Unpublished report, Hubbs-Sea World Research Institute Technical Report 84-176, 1984, pp. 1-73.

ELLIS, R. *Dolphins and Porpoises*. New York: Alfred A. Knopf, 1982, pp. 1-270. Good killer whale summary on pp. 167-189, 246-251.

EMERY, M. "Mystery of Von Donnop Lagoon." *Daily Colonist* (Victoria), Sept. 18, 1960, p. 6. Twin killer whales born while pod stranded in lagoon.

ERICKSON, A.W. Population Studies of Killer Whales, *Orcinus orca*, in the Pacific Northwest:

A Radio Marking and Tracking Study of Killer Whales. Preliminary report on Marine Mammal Commission Contract MM5A012, 1976, pp. 1-65. Report of 1976 University of Washington study to attach tracking devices to killer whales captured at Budd Inlet.

ESCHRICHT, D.F. "Om Spaekhuggeren (*Delphinus orca*, L.) Kongelige Danske Videnskabernes Selskabs Forhandlinger." 1862, pp. 65-91, 234-264. "On the Species of the Genus Orca Inhabiting the Northern Seas." In *Recent Memoirs on the Cetacea* (W.H. Flower, ed.). London: Ray Society, 1866, pp. 151-188. Fascinating account − often misquoted later − of classic autopsy of male killer whale whose stomach contained pieces of 13 porpoises and 14 seals.

EVANS, W.E. AND A.V. YABLOKOV. "Intraspecific Variation of the Color Pattern of the Killer Whale, *Orcinus orca*." *Izdatel'stvo Nauka* (*Advances in Pinniped and Cetacean Research*). Moscow: U.S.S.R. Academy of Sciences, 1978 (in Russian with English summary), pp. 102-115. Killer whales may have colour patterns unique to each geographical area.

EVANS, W.E., A.V. YABLOKOV AND A.E. BOWLES. "Geographic Variation in the Color of Killer Whales." *Report*, International Whaling Commission, Vol. 32, 1982, pp. 687-694.

FELLEMAN, F.L. AND J.R. HEIMLICH-BORAN. Movements and Behavior of Killer Whales and Salmon Relative to Oceanographic Conditions in Puget Sound, Wash. Abstracts from presentations at the Fifth Biennial Conference on the Biology of Marine Mammals, Nov. 1983, Boston, Mass.

FELLEMAN, F., J.R. HEIMLICH-BORAN AND R.W. OSBORNE. "Feeding Ecology of the Killer Whale (*Orcinus orca*)." In *Dolphin Societies and How We Study Them* (Pryor, K. and K.S. Norris, eds.). Berkeley: University of California Press, 1988.

FISH, J.F. AND J.S. VANIA. "Killer Whale, *Orcinus orca*, Sounds Repel White Whales, *Delphinapterus leucas*." *Fishery Bulletin* (U.S.), Vol. 69, No. 3, 1971, pp. 531-535. The underwater playback of killer whale sounds kept white whales, or belugas, from feeding on salmon smolt in the Kvichak River in Alaska.

FORD, J.K.B. "Acoustic Traditions of Killer Whales." *Whalewatcher*, Vol. 19, No. 3, 1985, pp. 3-6.

FORD, J.K.B. Call Traditions and Dialects of Killer Whales (*Orcinus orca*) in British Columbia. Unpublished Ph.D. thesis, University of British Columbia, Vancouver, B.C., 1984, pp. 1-435.

FORD, J.K.B. "A Catalogue of Underwater Calls Produced by Killer Whales (*Orcinus orca*) in British Columbia." *Canadian Fisheries and Aquatic Sciences*, Vol. 633, 1987, pp. 1-165.

FORD, J.K.B. Group-Specific Vocalizations of the Killer Whale (*Orcinus orca*). Abstracts from presentations at the 146th National Meeting of the AAAS (American Association for the Advancement of Science). Jan. 3-8, 1980, San Francisco, Calif., p. 40. Study of killer whale dialects off the B.C. coast reveals that pod sounds seem important in maintaining the cohesion and identity of social units and that they remain stable over long periods of time (15 years recorded).

FORD, J.K.B. Group-Specific Dialects of Killer Whales (*Orcinus orca*) in British Columbia. Abstracts from presentations at the Fifth Biennial Conference on the Biology of Marine Mammals, Nov. 1983, Boston, Mass. "Dialects . . . reveal patterns of relationships among pods . . . not always apparent from observed interactions and provide information on the nature and rate of pod formation."

FORD, J.K.B. AND H.D. FISHER. "Group Specific Dialects of Killer Whales (*Orcinus orca*) in British Columbia." In *Communication and Behavior of Whales* (Payne, R., ed.). Boulder, Colorado: Westview Press, 1983, pp. 129-162.

FORD, J.K.B. AND H.D. FISHER. "Killer Whale (*Orcinus orca*) Dialects as an Indicator of Stocks in British Columbia." *Report*, International Whaling Commission, Vol. 32, 1982, pp. 671-680. The study of killer whale dialects as a useful technique for identifying populations and determining their social organization.

FORD, J. AND D. FORD. "The Killer Whales of B.C." *Waters*, Vol. 5, No. 1, 1981, pp. 3-32. Excellent popular account of Vancouver Island killer whale research, focusing on discovery of sound dialects.

FORESTER, J.E. AND A.D. FORESTER. *Fishing: British Columbia's Commercial Fishing History*. Saanichton, B.C.: Hancock House, 1975, pp. 1-224. B.C. salmon and other commercial fishing, including whaling.

FRASER, F.C. "Report on Cetacea Stranded on the British Coasts." London: British Museum (Natural History), No. 11, 1934; No. 12, 1946; No. 13, 1953; No. 14, 1974. Reports of killer whale and other whale and dolphin strandings from 1927 to 1966.

FREUCHEN, P. AND F. SALOMONSEN. *The Arctic Year*. New York: G.P. Putnam's Sons, 1958, pp. 1-438. Orcas attack narwhals off Greenland.

FRIED, D.L. AND J. WILKENS. "Kandu Bled to Death After Fight." The *San Diego Union*, Aug. 23, 1989. See also Jahn, E.; Smith, G.; and McIntyre, M.

FROST, P.G.H., P.D. SHAUGHNESSY, A. SEMMELINK, M. SKETCH AND W.R. SIEGFRIED. "The Response of Jackass Penguins to Killer Whale Vocalizations." *South African Journal of Science*, Vol. 71, 1975, pp. 157-158. Study determined that killer whale sounds would keep penguins out of oil slicks.

GABE, S. AND R. WOODWARD. "Vancouver's Lovable Killers." *Pacific Search*, Vol. 8, No. 4, Feb. 1974, pp. 6-7. Observations of resting behaviour and sexual interactions among killer whales and dolphins at the Vancouver Aquarium.

GASKIN, D.E. *Whales, Dolphins and Seals: With Special Reference to the New Zealand Region*. Auckland: Heinemann Educational Books, 1972, pp. 118-121. Includes discussion of killer whales in the South Pacific and comments on Twofold Bay story of symbiotic hunting of orcas and whalers.

GILMORE, R.M. "Killer Whales in the San Diego Area, Del Mar to the Coronado Islands." *Newsletter of the American Cetacean Society* (San Diego), 1976, pp. 4-5.

GLADSTONE, W. "Killer Whale Feeding Observed Underwater." *Journal of Mammalogy*, Vol. 69, No. 3, 1988, pp. 629-630.

GOBLE, E.U. The Killer Whale (*Orcinus orca* Linné 1758): Its Biology, Distribution and Management. Unpublished thesis, University of British Columbia, 1978, pp. 1-27. Good literature survey.

GOLDSBERRY, D.G., E.D. ASPER AND L.H. CORNELL. "A Live-Capture Technique for the Killer Whale, *Orcinus orca*." *Aquatic Mammals*, Vol. 6, No. 3, 1978, pp. 91-96.

GOODALL, J.V.L. *In the Shadow of Man*. London: William Collins, 1971, pp. 1-297. Comparative study of a social mammal group.

GREENWOOD, A.G. AND D.C. TAYLOR. "Captive Killer Whales in Europe." *Aquatic Mammals*, Vol. 11, No. 1, 1985, pp. 10-12. Of 32 killer whales examined after dying in aquariums around the world, half had died of bacterial infections, one-quarter of pneumonia.

GRIEG, J.A. "Nogle Notiser Fra et Spækhuggerstæng ved Bildöströmmen i Januar 1904." *Arbok*, Bergens Museum (2), 1906, pp. 1-28. Herring found in orca stomachs off Norway coast.

GRIFFIN, E.I. "Making Friends With a Killer Whale." *National Geographic*, Vol. 129, No. 3, 1966, pp. 418-446. Story of the capture and early confinement of Namu at the Seattle Public Aquarium.

GRIFFIN, T. (E.I.). *Namu: Quest for the Killer Whale*. Seattle: Gryphon West, 1982, pp. 1-237.

GRIFFIN, E.I. AND D.G. GOLDSBERRY. "Notes on the Capture, Care and Feeding of the Killer Whale, *Orcinus orca*, at the Seattle Aquarium." *International Zoo Yearbook*, Vol. 8, 1968, pp. 206-208. Accounts of the first few Griffin-Goldsberry captures in Puget Sound.

HAHN, E. "Getting Through to the Others." *The New Yorker*, Pt. I, Apr. 17, 1978, pp. 38-103; Pt. II, Apr. 24, 1978, pp. 42-90. Attempts to teach animals to talk, from Clever Hans to John Lilly's dolphins to the recent work teaching American Sign Language to chimpanzees.

HALEY, D. "Views on the Killer Whale Dispute." *Pacific Search*, Vol. 5, No. 1, Oct. 1970, pp. 1-3. Interviews with scientists, conservationists, killer whale captors and aquarium owners involved in the controversy over capturing orcas in Puget Sound.

HALEY, D. "Albino Killer Whale." *Sea Frontiers*, Vol. 19, No. 2, Mar./Apr. 1973, pp. 66-71. The life and death of Chimo, the white whale captured in 1970 off Vancouver Island.

HALEY, D., ed. *Marine Mammals of Eastern North Pacific and Arctic Waters*. Seattle: Pacific Search Press, 1986 (2nd edition), pp. 1-295.

HALL, J.D. AND C.S. JOHNSON. "Auditory Thresholds of a Killer Whale, *Orcinus orca* Linnaeus." *Journal*, Acoustical Society of America, Vol. 51, No. 2, 1972, pp. 515-517. Using operant conditioning techniques, an audiogram was obtained for a captive orca, with frequencies between 500 Hz and 31 kHz. Greatest sensitivity was observed at 15 kHz, with upper limit of hearing at 32 kHz.

HANCOCK, D. "Killer Whales Kill and Eat a Minke Whale." *Journal of Mammalogy*, Vol. 46, No. 2, 1965, pp. 341-342.

HAND, D. "Keeping an Ear on Orcas." *Oceans*, Vol. 20, July/Aug. 1987, pp. 10-19.

HAWKINS, H.S. AND R.H. COOK. "Whaling at Eden: With Some 'Killer' Yarns." *The Lone Hand*, Vol. 3, 1908, pp. 265-273. Contemporary account of Twofold Bay story mentioning symbiotic relationship between whalers and killer whales.

HEALY, S.C., R.W. OSBORNE AND A.R. HOELZEL. Comparison of Call Use Among Three Socially Interacting Pods of Killer Whales (*Orcinus orca*). Abstracts from presentations at the Fifth Biennial Conference on the Biology of Marine Mammals, Nov. 1983, Boston, Mass.

HEEZEN, B.C. AND G.L. JOHNSON. "Alaskan Submarine Cables: A Struggle With a Harsh Environment." *Arctic*, Vol. 22, No. 4, 1969, pp. 413-424. Killer whale found tangled and drowned in submarine telegraph cable at 3,378 feet — the deepest recorded orca dive.

HEIMLICH, S.L. Social Organization of Puget Sound Killer Whales. Abstracts from presentations at the Fourth Biennial Conference on the Biology of Marine Mammals, Dec. 1981, San Francisco, Calif.

HEIMLICH-BORAN, J.R. "Behavioral Ecology of Killer Whales (*Orcinus orca*) in the Pacific Northwest." *Canadian Journal of Zoology*, Vol. 66, No. 3, 1988, pp. 565-578.

HEWLETT, K.G. "The Killer Whale: A Need for Perspective." *Pacific Search*, Vol. 9, No. 1, 1974, pp. 18-19. Vancouver Aquarium curator argues the importance of zoos and aquariums and of keeping killer whales captive.

HEWLETT, K.G. AND M.A. NEWMAN. "'Skana,' the Killer Whale." *International Zoo Yearbook*, Vol. 8, 1968, pp. 209-211. Skana's early training and veterinary remarks.

HOFFER, S. "Observations on the Whales." *Vancouver Public Aquarium Newsletter*, Vol. XVI, No. 5, Sept./Oct. 1972. Observations on resting behaviour and sexual interactions of captive Vancouver killer whales. See also S. Gabe and R. Woodward.

HOYT, E. "Singing With Killer Whales." *Pacific Discovery*, Vol. 28, No. 5, 1975, pp. 28-32. Mimicry and synthesizer exchanges with Johnstone Strait killer whales.

HOYT, E. "*Orcinus orca*: Separating Facts From Fantasies." *Oceans*, Vol. 10, No. 4, 1977, pp. 22-26. Killer whale studies in the Northwest; Canadian government census; orcas feeding peacefully beside minke whales and Dall's porpoises, common prey in other seas.

HOYT, E. "The Steller Sea Lion of the North Pacific." In *Wildlife '80. The World Conservation Yearbook* (N. Sitwell, ed.). Danbury, Conn.: Danbury Press (Grolier), 1980, pp. 36-45. Natural history of Steller sea lions plus interactions with killer whales. Also background of war with fishermen and comments about management.

HOYT, E. "Orca: The Sociable Whale." *Equinox*, Vol. 1, No. 2, Mar./Apr. 1982, pp. 20-39.

HOYT, E. "Great Winged Whales." *Equinox*, Vol. 2, No. 4, Jul./Aug. 1983, pp. 24-47. Humpback whale research off Maui, including photo-identification studies and analyses of the songs.

HOYT, E. *The Whale Watcher's Handbook*. Garden City, New York: Doubleday; and Toronto: Penguin/Madison Press Books, 1984, pp. 1-208. Illustrations by Pieter Folkens.

HOYT, E. "The Whales Called 'Killer.'" *National Geographic*, Vol. 166, No. 2, Aug. 1984, pp. 220-237.

HOYT, E. "A Conversation With Michael Bigg." [Interview.] *Cetus*, The Whale Museum (Friday Harbor, Wash.), Vol. 6, No. 1, Spring, 1985, pp. 1-4.

HOYT, E. "Saving Whales From Themselves." *Equinox*, Vol. 6, No. 36, Nov./Dec. 1987, p. 140. Story of pilot whales successfully returned to the wild after stranding and many months in captivity could provide a model for returning captive orcas to the wild.

HOYT, E. AND J. BORROWMAN. "Diving With Orcas." *Diver*, Vol. 5, No. 8, Nov./Dec. 1979, pp. 20-23. Attempts to photograph killer whales underwater.

HUI, C.A. AND S.H. RIDGWAY. "Survivorship Patterns in Captive Killer Whales (*Orcinus orca*)." *Bulletin*, Southern California Academy of Sciences, Los Angeles, Vol. 77, No. 2, 1978, pp. 45-51. Study of causes and rates of killer whale mortalities at established North American aquariums undertaken by the Biosciences Dept. of Naval Ocean Systems Center, San Diego, to answer a specific query by a congressional committee looking into the survival of captive killer whales.

HUME, M. "Tsitika Saga: The Disappearing Frontier." *Victoria Times*, Sept. 12, 1978, p. 9.

HUME, M. "Farewell to Tsitika." *B.C. Outdoors*, Vol. 35, No. 7, July 1979, pp. 36-37, 58-59. The final chapter in the unsuccessful bid to save the Tsitika, the last eastern Vancouver Island river valley to remain unlogged and untouched.

HUNTER, R. Bob Hunter (column). *The Vancouver Sun*, Oct. 25, 1974, p. 56. The argument against keeping killer whales captive. Temporary sentences — "putting them back" — as a lesson in conservation that aquariums could teach.

International Whaling Commission. "Report of the Workshop on Identity, Structure and Vital Rates of Killer Whale Populations – June 1981." *Report*, International Whaling Commission, Vol. 32, 1982, pp. 617-632.

IVANOVA, E.I. "O Tikhookeanskoi Kosatke (*Orcinus orca* L.) Akademiia Nauk SSSR." *Trudy Instituta Morfologii Zhivotngkh*, Vol. 34, 1961, pp. 205-215. Notes (in Russian) on the morphology of the killer whale in the North Pacific.

IVASHIN, M.V. AND L.M. VOTROGOV. "Killer Whales, *Orcinus orca*, Inhabiting Inshore Waters of the Chukotka Coast." *Report*, International Whaling Commission, Vol. 31, 1981, pp. 521-522.

IVASHIN, M.V. AND L.M. VOTROGOV. "Occurrence of Baleen and Killer Whales off Chukotka." *Report*, International Whaling Commission, Vol. 32, 1982, pp. 499-503.

IWASHITA, M. "Shachi higae taisaku no gutai-teki hosaku." *Waka Shio*. ("Concrete Plans on Measures Against Damage by *Orcinus*." *Youthful Current*.) 1958, pp. 15-18. Suggestions to Japanese fishermen to control orca predation on tuna.

IWASHITA, M., M. INOUE AND Y. IWASAKI. "Shachi no shokugai Hokoku ni yoru Taiheiyo Nan-Boku Sekido Kaiiki no shachi no bunpu ni tsuite." *Tokai Daigaku Suisan Kenkyusho Hokoku*. ("On the Distribution of *Orcinus* in the Northern and Southern Pacific Equatorial Waters as Observed From Reports on *Orcinus* Predation." *Report of Fisheries Research Laboratory of Tokai University*.) Vol. 1, No. 1, 1963, pp. 24-30. Tuna predation by killer whales spreads through the South Pacific and Indian Ocean almost as fast as new fishing areas are opened.

JAHN, E. "Questions Surface in Sea World Accident." The *San Diego Union*, Dec. 3, 1987, pp. A-1, A-14, A-15. See also Smith, G.; Fried, D.L.; and McIntyre, M.

JEHL, J.R., W.E. EVANS, F.T. AWBREY AND W.S. DRIESCHMANN. "Distribution and Geographic Variation in the Killer Whale (*Orcinus orca*) Populations of the Antarctic and Adjacent Waters." *Antarctic Journal of the United States*, Vol. 15, No. 5, 1980, pp. 161-163.

JEUNE, P. *Killer Whale: The Saga of Miracle*. Toronto: McClelland and Stewart, 1979, pp. 1-190. Journalist's account of the rescue of the bullet-wounded baby orca Miracle as well as his theories about how it was separated from its pod.

JONSGÅRD, Å. "A Note on the Attacking Behavior of the Killer Whale (*Orcinus orca*)." *Norsk Hvalfangst-tidende*, Vol. 57, No. 4, 1968, pp. 84-85. Killer whales attacking bottlenose whales, biting at the flippers and flukes.

JONSGÅRD, Å. "Another Note on the Attacking Behavior of the Killer Whale (*Orcinus orca*)." *Norsk Hvalfangst-tidende*, Vol. 57, No. 6, 1968, pp. 175-176. Whales and seals with missing flippers or scarred flukes escaped killer whale attack, indicating that it is probably difficult for orcas to catch them under normal circumstances.

JONSGÅRD, Å. AND P.B. LYSHOEL. "A Contribution to the Knowledge of the Biology of the Killer Whale *Orcinus orca* (L.)" *Norwegian Journal of Zoology* (*Nytt Magasin for Zoologi*), Vol. 18, No. 1, 1970, pp. 41-48. Biological data (sizes, sexes, distribution, stomach studies) from 1,413 killer whales caught by Norwegian whalers between 1938 and 1967.

JONSGÅRD, Å. AND P.ØYNES. "Om bottlenosen (*Hyperoodon rostratus*) og spekkhoggeren (*Orcinus orca*)." *Fauna* (Oslo), No. 1, 1952, pp. 1-18. (Killer whale section translated into English by O.A. Mathisen, College of Fisheries, University of Washington, Seattle, 1967.)

KAMIYA, T., T. TOBAYAMA AND M. NISHIWAKI. "Epidermal Cyst in the Neck of a Killer Whale." *Scientific Reports*, Whales Research Institute (Tokyo), No. 31, 1979, pp. 93-94.

KASTELEIN, R.A. AND N. VAUGHAN. "Food Consumption, Body Measurements and Weight Changes of a Female Killer Whale (*Orcinus orca*)." *Aquatic Mammals*, Vol. 15, No. 1, 1989, pp. 18-21.

KASUYA, T. "Consideration of Distribution and Migration of Toothed Whales off the Pacific Coast of Japan Based on Aerial Sighting Records." *Scientific Reports*, Whales Research Institute (Tokyo), No. 23, 1971, pp. 37-60.

KATONA, S.K., V. ROUGH AND D.T. RICHARDSON. *A Field Guide to the Whales, Porpoises and Seals of the Gulf of Maine and Eastern Canada: Cape Cod to Newfoundland*. New York: Charles Scribner's Sons, 1983, pp. 1-256. Good general guide to East Coast marine mammals with killer whale section on pp. 109-117.

KELLOGG, R. "Whales, Giants of the Sea." *National Geographic*, Vol. 77, No. 1, 1940, pp. 35-90. Orcas attacking various whales, including narwhals.

KELLOGG, W.N. *Porpoises and Sonar*. Chicago: University of Chicago Press, 1961, pp. 1-177.

Experimental psychologist, who demonstrated echolocation in porpoises with his experiments in the 1950s, explains porpoise sonar.

KENYON, K.W. *The Sea Otter in the Pacific Ocean.* New York: Dover, 1975, pp. 1-352. Orca/sea otter interactions.

"Killer Whales Destroyed. VP-7 Accomplishes Special Task." *Naval Aviation News*, Dec. 1956, p. 19. U.S. Navy planes destroy "hundreds of Icelandic killer whales with machine guns, rockets and depth charges."

"Killers in the Surf." *Audubon*, Vol. 77, No. 5, Sept. 1975, pp. 2-5. Orcas catch young South American sea lions off Patagonia and toss them in the air. Photographs by John Wilson.

"Killer Whale Grabs Surfer." *San Francisco Examiner*, Sept. 11, 1972, p. 16. Report of probable killer whale attack. See also C.R. Snorf, et al.

KIRKEVOLD, B.C. AND J.S. LOCKARD, eds. *Behavioral Biology of Killer Whales.* New York: Alan R. Liss, Inc., Zoo Biology Monographs, Vol. 1, 1986, pp. 1-457. Sixteen research papers on killer whales in the Northwest.

LANG, T.G. AND K.S. PRYOR. "Hydrodynamic Performance of Porpoises (*Stenella attenuata*)." *Science*, Vol. 152 (3721), 1966, pp. 531-533. Open-ocean speed runs of trained porpoises from which Scheffer estimated killer whale top speed at 30 miles per hour.

LEATHERWOOD, S., K.C. BALCOMB III, C.O. MATKIN AND G. ELLIS. "Killer Whales (*Orcinus orca*) off Southern Alaska: Results of Field Research 1984. A Preliminary Report." Unpublished report, Hubbs-Sea World Research Institute Technical Report 84-175, 1984, pp. 1-59.

LEATHERWOOD, S., K.C. BALCOMB III, C.O. MATKIN AND G. ELLIS. "Killer Whales (*Orcinus orca*) of Southern Alaska: Results of Field Research 1984. Preliminary Report." *Report*, International Whaling Commission. Vol. 36, 1986, pp. 504-505.

LEATHERWOOD, S., A.E. BOWLES, E. KRYGIER, J.D. HALL AND S. INGELL. "Killer Whales (*Orcinus orca*) of Shelikof Strait, Prince William Sound, Alaska and Southeast Alaska: A Review of Available Information." *Report*, International Whaling Commission, Vol. 34, 1982, pp. 521-530.

LEATHERWOOD, S. AND M.E. DAHLHEIM. "Worldwide Distribution of Pilot Whales and Killer Whales." Naval Ocean Systems Center, San Diego. N.O.S.C. Technical Report 295, 1978, pp. 24-39.

LEATHERWOOD, S., R.R. REEVES AND L. FOSTER. *The Sierra Club Handbook of Whales and Dolphins.* San Francisco: Sierra Club Books, 1983, pp. 1-302. Excellent general guide to whales and dolphins; killer whale section on pp. 167-170.

LEATHERWOOD, S., R.R. REEVES, W.F. PERRIN AND W.E. EVANS. *Whales, Dolphins and Porpoises of the Eastern North Pacific and Adjacent Arctic Waters: A Guide to Their Identification.* Seattle: NOAA, NMFS (NOAA Technical Report; NMFS Circular 444), 1982, pp. 1-246. Good field guide to identification of North Pacific whales and dolphins; killer whale section on pp. 113-117.

LEVITT, M. "Abandon Ship." *Motor Boating and Sailing.* June 1976, pp. 63, 90-92. Account of *Guia III*, claimed to have been sunk by a killer whale in the Atlantic.

LIEN, J., G.B. STENSON AND P.W. JONES. "Killer whales (*Orcinus orca*) in Waters off Newfoundland and Labrador, 1978-1986." *Rit Fiskideildar*, Vol. 11, 1988, pp. 194-201.

LILLY, J.C. *Man and Dolphin.* New York: Doubleday, 1961, pp. 1-240. Dolphin research up to 1961; the possibility of communicating with dolphins introduced.

LILLY, J.C. *The Mind of the Dolphin.* New York: Doubleday, 1967, pp. 1-310. Research to 1967; report of interspecies living arrangement between a dolphin and a human.

LILLY, J.C. *Lilly on Dolphins, Humans of the Sea.* New York: Anchor Press, 1975, pp. 1-500. Part of *Man and Dolphin* with *The Mind of the Dolphin*, *The Dolphin in History* and several short papers.

LILLY, J.C. *Communication Between Man and Dolphin.* New York: Crown, 1978, pp. 1-269. Summary of Lilly's dolphin work with emphasis on possibility of communication, plus annotated bibliography and useful appendices.

LJUNGBLAD, D.K. AND S.E. MOORE. "Killer Whales (*Orcinus orca*) Chasing Gray Whales (*Eschritius robustus*) in the Northern Bering Sea." *Arctic*, Vol. 36, No. 4, 1983, pp. 361-364. Killer whales pursuing grey whales made no underwater sounds.

LOPEZ, J.C. AND D. LOPEZ. "Killer Whales (*Orcinus orca*) of Patagonia and Their Behavior of Intentional Stranding While Hunting Nearshore." *Journal of Mammalogy*, Vol. 66, No. 1, 1985, pp. 181-183.

LORENZ, K. *On Aggression*. New York: Harcourt, Brace & World, 1966, pp. 1-306. Landmark treatise on the aggressive drive in animal and man.

LOWRY, L.F., R.R. NELSON AND K.J. FROST. "Observations of Killer Whales, *Orcinus orca*, in Western Alaska: Sighting, Strandings and Predation on Other Marine Mammals." *Canadian Field-Naturalist*, Vol. 101, No. 1, 1987, pp. 6-12. Killer whales eating grey whales, minke whales, walruses, beluga whales and seals.

LUBOW, A. "Riot in Fish Tank II." *New Times*, Oct. 14, 1977, pp. 36-53. The story of the freeing of two captive dolphins in Hawaii and a discussion of the rights of animals.

LYRHOLM, T., S. LEATHERWOOD AND J. SIGURJÓNSSON. "Photo-identification of Killer Whales (*Orcinus orca*) off Iceland, October 1985." *Cetology*, No. 52, 1987, pp. 1-14. Report of pilot photo-identification study of Icelandic killer whales.

MACASKIE, I. *The Long Beaches*. Victoria, B.C.: Sono Nis Press, 1979, pp. 1-136.

MACASKIE, I.B. "Unusual Example of Group Behavior by Killer Whales (*Orcinus rectipinna*)." *Murrelet*, Vol. 47, No. 2, 1966, p. 38.

MCINTYRE, J., ed. *Mind in the Waters*. New York: Charles Scribner's Sons, 1974, pp. 1-240. Stories, legends, research, illustrations "to celebrate the consciousness of whales and dolphins." Killer whale section by P. Spong, pp. 170-185.

MCINTYRE, M. "PR Campaign Order of Day at Sea World." The *San Diego Union*, Aug. 23, 1987, pp. A-6, A-7. See also Jahn, E.; Smith, G.; and Fried, D.L.

MACLEAN, H.I.C. "Four Observations of Killer Whales With an Account of the Mating of These Animals." *Scottish Naturalist*, Vol. 70, 1961, pp. 75-78.

MCNALLY, R. "Echolocation: Cetaceans' Sixth Sense." *Oceans*, Vol. 10, No. 4, 1977, pp. 27-33.

MART, J. "Cosmic Plot." *Oceans*, May 1976, pp. 56-59. Background of Budd Inlet capture, Sea World's final stand in the Northwest; some inaccuracies.

MARTINEZ, D.R. AND E. KLINGHAMMER. "The Behavior of the Whale, *Orcinus orca*: A Review of the Literature." *Zeitschrift für Tierpsychologie*, Vol. 27, 1970, pp. 828-839.

MATKIN, C. "Orca: Killer Whale." *Whalewatcher*, Vol. 15, No. 1, 1981, pp. 3-4.

MATTHEWS, A. "Air Transportation by Helicopter of Juvenile *Orcinus orca*." *Aquatic Mammals*, Vol. 6, No. 3, 1978, pp. 97-98.

MATTHEWS, L.H. *The Natural History of the Whale*. New York: Columbia University Press, 1978, pp. 1-219.

MAZZONE, W.S. "Walrus, *Odobenus rosmarus*, and Whale Interactions: An Eyewitness Account." *Canadian Field-Naturalist*, Vol. 101, No. 4, 1987, pp. 590-591. Killer whales attacking walruses off Alaska.

MEAD, T. *Killers of Eden*. London: Angus and Robertson, 1962, pp. 1-222. Journalist's novelized account of the symbiotic relationship between whalers and killer whales at Twofold Bay, Australia.

MECH, L.D. *The Wolf: The Ecology and Behavior of an Endangered Species*. Garden City, N.Y.: Natural History Press, 1970, pp. 1-384. Comparative study of a predator/social mammal.

MELVILLE, H. *Moby-Dick; or, The Whale*. New York: 1851, pp. 1-634. "Of [the killer] little is precisely known to the Nantucketer, and nothing at all to the professed naturalist. . . . He is very savage . . . takes the great . . . whales by the lip and hangs there like a leech till the mighty brute is worried to death. . . . Exception might be taken to [his] name . . . for we are all killers, on land and on sea; Bonapartes and sharks included."

MIKHALEV, Y.A., M.V. IVASHIN, V.P. SAVUSIN AND F.E. ZELENYA. "The Distribution and Biology of Killer Whales in the Southern Hemisphere. *Report*, International Whaling Commission, Vol. 31, 1981, pp. 551-565.

MINASIAN, S.M., K.C. BALCOMB AND L. FOSTER. *The World's Whales*. Washington, D.C.: Smithsonian Books, 1984.

MITCHELL, E. *Porpoise, Dolphin and Small Whale Fisheries of the World: Status and Problems*. Morges, Switzerland: International Union for Conservation of Nature and Natural Resources, Monograph No. 3, 1975, pp. 1-129. The whaling of killer whales by Japan, Norway, U.S.S.R., etc., on pp. 67-75; good bibliography.

MITCHELL, E. AND A.N. BAKER. "Age of Reputedly Old Killer Whale, *Orcinus orca*, 'Old Tom' from Eden, Twofold Bay, Australia." *Report*, International Whaling Commission (Special Issue No. 3), 1980, pp. 143-154. In-depth discussion of symbiotic relationship between whalers and killer whales, plus ageing of the legendary killer Old Tom at 35 years; good bibliography.

MITCHELL, E. AND R.R. REEVES. "Records of Killer Whales in the Western North Atlantic, with Emphasis on Eastern Canadian Waters." *Rit Fiskideildar*, Vol. 11, 1988, pp. 161-193.

MOHNEY, R. "Will the Killer Whales Be Driven Out of Puget Sound?" *Pacific Search*, Vol. 8, No. 9, July 1974, pp. 1-4. Argues against continued Sea World capture in Puget Sound.

MOREJOHN, G.V. "A Killer Whale/Gray Whale Encounter." *Journal of Mammalogy*, Vol. 49, No. 2, 1968, pp. 327-328. Unsuccessful killer whale attack on grey whales.

MORRIS, D. "Must We Have Zoos?" *Life*, Vol. 65, Nov. 8, 1968, pp. 78-86. Zoologist, author and onetime curator of animals at London's Regent's Park Zoo strongly criticizes the effects that life in captivity has on animals.

MORTON, A. "Into the World of Orcas." *International Wildlife*, Vol. 17, Sept./Oct. 1987, pp. 12-17. ·

MULVANEY, K. "Captive Whales." *Turning Point*, No. 8, Autumn 1987. The story of Nemo and Winnie, orcas kept captive in U.K. aquaria.

MURIE, A. *The Wolves of Mt. McKinley*. Washington: U.S. Gov't. Printing Office, 1944, pp. 1-238. Comparative study of a predator/social mammal by first biologist to debunk wolf myths.

MURIE, A. *A Naturalist in Alaska*. New York: The Devin-Adair Co., 1961, pp. 1-302. Comparative study of a predator/social mammal.

NEWBY, T. "Killer Whale Deaths Reported." *Pacific Search*, Jan. 1, 1971. Young orcas, bodies slashed and anchors tied to their tails, wash up on Washington State beach near site of recent aquarium capture.

NEWMAN, M.A. AND P.L. MCGEER. "A Killer Whale (*Orcinus orca*) at Vancouver Aquarium." *International Zoo Yearbook*, Vol. 6, 1966, pp. 257-259.

NEWMAN, M.A. AND P.L. MCGEER. "The Capture and Care of a Killer Whale, *Orcinus orca*, in British Columbia." *Zoologica*, Vol. 51, No. 2, 1966, pp. 59-69. The story of Moby Doll, the first killer whale displayed in captivity.

NIKOLAEV, A.M. "On the Feeding of the Kurile Sea Otter and Some Aspects of Their Behavior During the Period of Ice." *Marine Mammals* (E.N. Pavlovskii, B.A. Zenkovich et al., eds.), 1965. Translated by Nancy McRay, April 1966, p. 231. Orcas seen feeding on sea otters in the North Pacific.

NISHIWAKI, M. AND C. HANDA. "Killer Whales Caught in the Coastal Waters off Japan for Recent Ten Years." *Scientific Reports*, Whales Research Institute (Tokyo), Vol. 13, 1958, pp. 85-96. Stomach studies and biological data from 364 killer whales caught by Japanese whalers from 1948 to 1957. Fish and squid main food items, followed by dolphins, whales and seals; salmon in 1.6 percent of the stomachs.

NORDQUIST, C. AND M. HUTCHINS. "Killer Whale (*Orcinus orca*) Shares Food with Gulls (*Larus glaucescens*) at the Vancouver Public Aquarium." *Zoo Biology*, Vol. 4, No. 4, 1985, pp. 367-374. Thoughts on why a young female orca from Iceland shares food with gulls.

NORRIS, K.S. "Facts and Tales About Killer Whales." *Pacific Discovery*, Jan. 1958, pp. 24-27. One of the first modern articles to debunk the myths of the killer whale; account of orcas feeding on basking shark off California.

NORRIS, K.S. "The Echolocation of Marine Mammals." *The Biology of Marine Mammals* (H.T. Andersen, ed.). New York, London: Academy Press, 1969, pp. 391-423. Survey of echolocation in various marine mammals; good bibliography.

NORRIS, K.S. *The Porpoise Watcher*. New York: W.W. Norton, 1974, pp. 1-250. Popular book about Norris's studies of sound and behaviour in porpoises.

NORRIS, K.S. AND J.H. PRESCOTT. "Observations on Pacific Cetaceans of Californian and Mexican Waters." *Publications in Zoology*, University of California, Berkeley, Vol. 63, No. 4, 1961, pp. 330-334.

ODLUM, G.C. "An Instance of Killer Whales Feeding on Ducks." *Canadian Field-Naturalist*, Vol. 62, 1948, p. 42.

OHSUMI, S. "Catch of Marine Mammals, Mainly of Small Cetaceans, by Local Fisheries Along the Coast of Japan." *Bull. Fish. Res. Lab.* (Shimizu), Vol. 7, 1972, pp. 137-166.

OHSUMI, S. "Review of Japanese Small-Type Whaling." *Journal*, Fisheries Research Board of Canada, Vol. 32, No. 7, 1975, pp. 1111-1121. Includes whaling of killer whales in Japanese waters.

ONO, M., N. KANNAN, T. WAKIMOTO AND R. TATSUKAWA. "Dibenzofurans a Greater Global Pollutant than Dioxins? Evidence From Analyses of Open Ocean Killer Whales." *Marine Pollution Bulletin*, Vol. 18, No. 12, 1987, pp. 640-643. Analyses of toxic chemicals in killer whale tissues to give clues to long-range distribution patterns.

OSBORNE, R., J. CALAMBOKIDIS AND E.M. DORSEY. *A Guide to Marine Mammals of Greater Puget Sound.* Anacortes, Wash.: Island Publishers, 1988, pp. 1-191. Features a catalogue of individual orca and minke whales.

OSBORNE, R.J., F. FELLEMAN AND J. HEIMLICH-BORAN. "Review of Orca Natural History." *Cetus*, Vol. 6, No. 1, 1985, pp. 9-11.

OTTEN, T. "First Killer Whale (*Orcinus orca*) Ever Born in Captivity." *Whalewatcher*, Vol. 11, No. 3, 1977, pp. 13-14. Report of first live birth conceived in captivity at Marineland (California).

PAULIAN, P. "Pinnipèdes, Cétacés, Oiseaux des Iles Kerguélen et Amsterdam." *Mem. Inst. Sci. Madagascar*, A8, 1953, pp. 111-234. Orcas attacking southern elephant seals in the Indian Ocean.

PAULIAN, P. "Contribution à l'étude de l'Otarie de l'Ile Amsterdam." *Mammalia*, 28, Suppl. 1, 1964, pp. 1-146. Orcas attacking southern elephant seals and southern fur seals in the Indian Ocean.

PAYNE, R. "At Home With Right Whales." *National Geographic*, Vol. 149, No. 3, March 1976, pp. 322-339. Scientist's account of his family's study of right whales off the Patagonian coast of Argentina.

PAYNE, R. "Humpbacks: Their Mysterious Songs." *National Geographic*, Vol. 155, No. 1, January 1979, pp. 18-25. The study of the complex songs of humpback whales may be "a possible route in the future to assess the intelligence of whales."

PAYNE, R., ed. *Communication and Behavior of Whales.* New York: AAAS, Special Publication, 1983.

PERRIN, W.F., ed. "Report of the Workshop on Identity, Structure and Vital Rates of Killer Whale Populations." *Report*, International Whaling Commission, Vol. 32, 1982, pp. 617-631.

PERRIN, W.F. AND S.B. REILLY. "Reproductive Parameters of Dolphins and Small Whales of the Family Delphinidae." *Report*, International Whaling Commission (Special Issue 6), 1984, pp. 97-133.

"Phantom Killer Whales." *South African Shipping News and Fishing Industry Review*, Vol. 30, No. 7, 1975, pp. 50-53. South African SPCA project to overcome seal problem to seine fishery by playing orca sounds.

PIKE, G.C. AND I.B. MACASKIE. "Marine Mammals of British Columbia." *Bulletin*, Fisheries Research Board of Canada, No. 171, 1969, pp. 19-23. Predatory activity, strandings and sightings of orcas off the B.C. coast.

"Playful Whale Grabs Bikini-Clad Woman." *The Province* (Vancouver), April 21, 1971, p. 2. Sea World's Annette Eckis bitten by Shamu after trying to ride the whale.

PLINIUS SECUNDUS (Pliny the Elder). *Natural History.* Book IX. Translated by H. Rackham. London: William Heinemann, 1947, pp. 171-172, 177-187. Orcas described as savage killers of large whales in first century A.D.; dolphins, as friendly to man.

PLUTARCH. *Moralia.* Vol. 12. Translated by H. Cherniss and W.C. Helmbold. London: William Heinemann, 1957, pp. 469-477. The dolphin as friend to man (early second century A.D.).

PREVOST, J. "Ecologie du Manchot Empereur." *Actualités Scientifiques et Industrielles 1291*, 1961, pp. 1-204. Emperor penguins found in orca stomachs in the Antarctic.

PRYOR, K. *Lads Before the Wind. Adventures in Porpoise Training.* New York: Harper & Row, 1976, pp. 1-278. Good account of porpoises and porpoise training at Hawaiian aquarium.

REEKIE, K. "Fishermen Shoot Whale in Skirmish." *The Bellingham Herald*, Sept. 16, 1962, pp. 1, 5. Account of 1962 Marineland collecting expedition in which two orcas charged the boat after one was captured with hoop net.

REEVES, R.R. AND E. MITCHELL. "Killer Whale Sightings and Takes by American Pelagic Whalers in the North Atlantic." *Rit Fiskideildar*, Vol. 11, 1988, pp. 7-23.

REEVES, R.R. AND E. MITCHELL. "Distribution and Seasonality of Killer Whales in the Eastern Canadian Arctic." *Rit Fiskideildar*, Vol. 11, 1988, pp. 136-160.

REINHOLD, R. "At Sea World, Stress Tests Whale and Man." *The New York Times*, April 4, 1988, pp. 1, A-19.

RICCIUTI, E.R. *Killers of the Seas.* New York: Walker and Co., 1973, pp. 223-232. Discussion of dangers of wild and especially captive orcas, with several detailed incidents at Sea World and other aquariums.

RICE, D.W. "Stomach Contents and Feeding Behavior of Killer Whales in the Eastern North Pacific." *Norsk Hvalfangst-tidende*, No. 2, 1968, pp. 35-38.

276

RICE, D.W. AND A.A. WOLMAN. "The Life History and Ecology of the Gray Whale (*Eschrichtius robustus*)." *Special Publication*, American Society of Mammalogists, Vol. 3, 1971, pp. 1-142. Eighteen percent of grey whales examined in North Pacific had orca scars — but probably few successful attacks.

RICE, F.H. AND G.S. SAAYMAN. "Distribution and Behavior of Killer Whales (*Orcinus orca*) off the Coasts of Southern Africa." *Investigations of Cetacea*, Vol. 20, 1987, pp. 231-250. Killer whales seen catching seals, dolphins, penguins and cormorants.

RICE, H. "Puget Sounders Cheer as Whales Go Free." *Pacific Search*, May 1976, p. 30. Background of Sea World's final whale capture in Puget Sound.

RIDGWAY, S.H. *Mammals of the Sea: Biology and Medicine*. Springfield, Illinois: C.C. Thomas, 1972, pp. 1-812. Detailed information about marine mammal husbandry; general information about killer whales on pp. 129-132; section on dolphins' sexual behaviour on pp. 423-429.

RIDGWAY, S.H. "Reported Causes of Death of Captive Killer Whales." *Journal of Wildlife Diseases*, Vol. 15, Jan. 1979, pp. 99-104. Navy veterinarian discusses causes of captive killer whale deaths.

RIDOUX, V. "Feeding Association Between Seabirds and Killer Whales, *Orcinus orca*, Around Subantarctic Crozet Islands [France]." *Canadian Journal of Zoology*, Vol. 65, No. 8, 1987, pp. 2113-2115. Some bird species off Possession Island follow feeding pods while others, mainly pelagic, follow orcas and wait for floating offal.

RIEDMAN, S.R. AND E.T. GUSTAFSON. *Home Is the Sea: For Whales*. Chicago: Rand, 1966, pp. 1-264. Popular account of whales with sections on orcas, especially in captivity.

ROBERTSON, D. *Survive the Savage Sea*. New York: Praeger, 1973, pp. 14-20, 245-249. Controversial claimed attack of killer whales on sailboat in mid-Pacific.

ROHNER, R.P. AND E.C. ROHNER. *The Kwakiutl Indians of B.C.* New York: Holt, Rinehart and Winston, 1970, pp. 1-111. Modern account of Kwakiutls around Alert Bay, B.C.

SAMARAS, W.E. AND S. LEATHERWOOD. "Killer Whale Attack on Elephant Seal." Washington: Smithsonian Institution Center for Short-Lived Phenomena, Jan. 8, 1974.

SATO, H. AND E. HOYT. "Whale Watcher/Whale Hunters: Reflections on Whaling in Japan." *Whalewatcher* (American Cetacean Society), Vol. 20, No. 2, Summer 1986, pp. 16-18 (also published in *Pacific* magazine of *The Seattle Times* and in *Reader's Digest* international editions). Story of "oikomi-ryo" drive fisheries for small whales and dolphins at Taiji, Japan. This method has also been used to capture killer whales live for aquaria in Japan.

SCAMMON, C.M. "The Orca." *Overland Monthly*, Vol. 9, No. 1, 1872, pp. 52-57.

SCAMMON, C.M. *The Marine Mammals of the North-Western Coast of North America, Described and Illustrated: Together With an Account of the American Whale-Fishery*. San Francisco: Carmany and Co., 1874 (reprint New York: Dover Publications, 1968), pp. 88-92. Whaler/naturalist Scammon reports orcas tearing lips and tongues from large baleen whales in the North Pacific.

SCHALLER, G.B. *The Year of the Gorilla*. Chicago: University of Chicago Press, 1964, pp. 1-260. Comparative study of a social mammal group.

SCHALLER, G.B. *The Serengeti Lion*. Chicago: University of Chicago Press, 1972, pp. 1-480. Comparative study of a social mammal group.

SCHEFFER, V.B. "The Killer Whale." *Pacific Search*, Vol. 1, No. 7, 1967, pp. 3-4.

SCHEFFER, V.B. "Marks on the Skin of a Killer Whale." *Journal of Mammalogy*, Vol. 50, Pt. 1, 1969, pp. 151-152.

SCHEFFER, V.B. "The Cliché of the Killer." *Natural History*, Oct. 1970, pp. 26-28, 76-77.

SCHEFFER, V.B. "Exploring the Lives of Whales." *National Geographic*, Vol. 150, No. 6, Dec. 1976, pp. 752-766.

SCHEFFER, V.B. "Killer Whale." *Marine Mammals of Eastern North Pacific and Arctic Waters* (D. Haley, ed.). Seattle: Pacific Search Press, 1978, pp. 120-127.

SCHEFFER, V.B. "Conservation of Marine Mammals." *Marine Mammals of Eastern North Pacific and Arctic Waters* (D. Haley, ed.). Seattle: Pacific Search Press, 1978, pp. 243-244.

SCHEFFER, V.B. "Alaska's Whales." *Alaska Geographic*, Vol. 5, No. 4, 1978, pp. 5-14. Scheffer's articles on the killer whale, full of information about the animals' natural history, were among the first to debunk the myths. As a federal biologist for some 40 years in Washington State and later as a writer and conservationist, he has made an eloquent plea for the life and "right to be" of all whales.

SCHEFFER, V.B. AND J.W. SLIPP. "The Whales and Dolphins of Washington State With a Key to the Cetaceans of the West Coast of North America." *The American Midland Naturalist*, Vol. 39, No. 2, 1948, pp. 257-337. General information about whales, with some good anecdotes about killer whales.

SCHEVILL, W.E. *The Whale Problem*. Cambridge, Mass.: Harvard University Press, 1974, pp. 1-419. The problems of whaling and whale management.

SCHEVILL, W.E. AND W.A. WATKINS. "Sound Structure and Directionality in *Orcinus* (Killer Whale)." *Zoologica*, Vol. 51, 1966, pp. 70-76. First analysis of killer whale sounds (on Moby Doll at the Vancouver Aquarium). Comparison with other whale sounds.

SCHWARZ, A.L. AND G.L. GREER. "Responses of Pacific Herring, *Clupea harengus pallasi*, to Some Underwater Sounds." *Canadian Journal of Fisheries and Aquatic Science*, Vol. 41, No. 8, 1984, pp. 1182-1183. Herring did not respond to killer whale or other sounds made by their predators. They did move away from ship and some small boat sounds.

SERGEANT, D.E. "Age Determination in Odontocete Whales From Dentinal Growth Layers." *Norsk Hvalfangst-tidende*, Vol. 48, No. 6, 1959, pp. 273-288. Hypothetical method of ageing orcas by counting rings in their teeth.

SHEPHERD, G.S. "Killer Whale in Slough at Portland, Oregon." *Journal of Mammalogy*, Vol. 13, 1932, pp. 171-172. Account of female orca that swam 110 miles up the Columbia River and fed on carp from the drainage of a packing plant before being killed by residents.

SHEVCHENKO, V.I. "Kharakter vzaimootnoshenii kasatok i drugikh kitoobraznykh." *Morskie mlekopitayushchie. Chast' 2*. ("The Nature of the Interrelationships Between Killer Whales and Other Cetaceans." *Marine Mammals, Part 2*.) Kiev: Naukova Dumka, 1975, pp. 173-175. Killer whales feeding on baleen whales, according to stomach studies by Soviet whalers. Possible case of cannibalism in which remains of a killer whale were found in the stomachs of two males.

SIGURJÓNSSON, J. AND S. LEATHERWOOD (eds.) *North Atlantic Killer Whales*. (Special Issue of *Rit Fiskideildar*, Vol. 11). Reykjavík, Iceland: Marine Research Institute, 1988, pp. 1-316. Twenty-one papers on killer whales in the North Atlantic based on a 1987 workshop held in Provincetown, Mass. Some individual articles are listed and annotated elsewhere in this bibliography. This was the first concentrated attempt to evaluate the species in the North Atlantic, particularly around Iceland, where they continue to be caught for the world's aquariums.

SIGURJÓNSSON, J. AND S. LEATHERWOOD. "The Icelandic Live-Capture Fishery for Killer Whales, 1976-1988." *Rit Fiskideildar*, Vol. 11, 1988, pp. 307-316. Long overdue detailed report of the Icelandic killer whale captures.

SINGER, P. *Animal Liberation: A New Ethics for Our Treatment of Animals*. New York: Avon, 1977, pp. 1-297. The manifesto for people who believe animals are victims of "speciesism" and deserve rights themselves.

SINIFF, D.B. AND J.L. BENGTSON. "Observations and Hypotheses Concerning the Interaction Among Crabeater Seals, Leopard Seals and Killer Whales." *Journal of Mammalogy*, Vol. 58, No. 3, 1977, pp. 414-416. Orcas feeding on leopard seals; scars on crabeater seals probably came more from leopard seals than killer whales.

SIVASUBRAMANIAM, K. "Predation of Tuna Longline Catches in the Indian Ocean by Killer Whales and Sharks." *Bulletin*, Fisheries Research Station, Colombo, Ceylon, Vol. 17, No. 2, 1964, pp. 221-236. Increasing problem of killer whale predation on tuna in the Indian Ocean.

SKINNER, B.F. "How to Teach Animals." *Scientific American*, Vol. 185, Dec. 1951, pp. 26-30. Theory used to train captive killer whales and dolphins.

SLIJPER, E.J. *Die Cetaceen. Vergleichend — Anatomisch und Systematisch . . . Capita Zoologica*. Vols. 6 and 7, 1936, pp. 1-590.

SLIJPER, E.J. *Walvissen*. Amsterdam: D.B. Centen: Uilgeversmaatschappij, 1958, p. 1-524. Translated as *Whales*. London: Hutchinson and Co., 1962, pp. 1-475. Dutch cetologist's classic accounts of general biology and anatomy of whales and dolphins, with pp. 200-202 and 272-275 about killer whale predation, including a misrendering of Eschricht's "parts of 13 seals and 14 porpoises in 1 orca stomach." Slijper showed an illustration and reported them as *whole* seals and porpoises, and his mistake has been often copied.

SMITH, G. "Baby Whale Is Expected to Survive Mother's Death." The *San Diego Tribune*, Aug. 23, 1989, pp. C-1, C-6. See also Jahn, E.; Fried, D.L.; and McIntyre, M.

SMITH, T.G., D.B. SINIFF, R. REICHLE AND S. STONE. "Coordinated Behavior of Killer Whales,

Orcinus orca, Hunting a Crabeater Seal, *Lobodon carcinophagus.*" *Canadian Journal of Zoology*, Vol. 59, 1981, pp. 1185-1189.

SNORF, C.R., T. HATTORI AND J. HUGHES. "Killer Whale Attack on Surfer. A Case Report." *Journal of Bone and Joint Surgery* (U.S.), Vol. 57, No. 1, 1975, p. 138. Documented case of probable orca attack off California, summer 1972.

SPALDING, D.J. "Comparative Feeding Habits of the Fur Seal, Sea Lion and Harbour Seal on the Coast of British Columbia." *Bulletin*, Fisheries Research Board of Canada, Vol. 146, 1964, pp. 1-52.

SPENCER, R.F. *The North Alaskan Eskimo: A Study in Ecology and Society*. Bull. 171. Washington: Smithsonian Institution Press, 1969, pp. 275-276. The Eskimos' fear of the killer whale's revenge documented in modern stories.

SPONG, P. AND D. WHITE. Cetacean research at the Vancouver Aquarium 1967-69. University of British Columbia Division of Neurological Sciences, Cetacean Research Lab., 1969, pp. 1-49, mimeographed.

SPRADLEY, J. *Guests Never Leave Hungry. The Autobiography of James Sewid, a Kwakiutl Indian*. New Haven, Conn.: Yale University Press, 1969, pp. 1-310. Story of Jimmy Sewid, fisherman and elected chief of Kwakiutls at Alert Bay.

STEINER, W.W., J.H. HAIN, H.E. WINN AND P.J. PERKINS. "Vocalizations and Feeding Behavior of the Killer Whale (*Orcinus orca*)." *Journal of Mammalogy*, Vol. 60, No. 4, 1979, pp. 823-827. Whistles or pure tones (as in dolphins) found in sounds of Atlantic orcas.

STELTNER, H., S. STELTNER AND D.E. SERGEANT. "Killer Whales, *Orcinus orca*, Prey on Narwhals, *Monodon monoceros*: An Eyewitness Account." *Canadian Field-Naturalist*, Vol. 98, No. 4, 1984, pp. 458-462. Killer whales systematically attacking several hundred narwhals in Eclipse Sound, Northwest Territories, Canada.

STENUIT, R. *The Dolphin, Cousin to Man*. New York: Sterling, 1968, pp. 147-150. Belgian diver-oceanographer discusses possible dangers of swimming with orcas.

STRANECK, R., B.C. LIVEZEY AND P.S. HUMPHREY. "Predation on Steamer-Ducks by Killer Whale." *The Condor*, Vol. 85, No. 2, 1983, pp. 255-256.

STRANGE, I.J. "Penguins of the Falklands." *Pacific Discovery*, Vol. 26, 1973, pp. 16-24. Killer whales taking sub-antarctic penguins.

SUGARMAN, P. *Field Guide to the Orca Whales of Greater Puget Sound and Southern British Columbia*. Friday Harbor, Wash.: The Whale Museum, 1984, pp. 1-27.

TARPY, C. "Killer Whale Attack." *National Geographic*, Vol. 155, No. 4, April 1979, pp. 542-545. Photographically documented account of orcas eating large cavity in the back of a fleeing 60-foot-long blue whale; organized feeding behaviour with distinct divisions of labour.

TAYLOR, D.C. "Killer Whales, *Orcinus orca*, at Flamingo Park Zoo and Cleethorpes Marineland and Zoo." *International Zoo Yearbook*, Vol. 11, 1971, pp. 205-206. Veterinarian's account of captive killer whales in England.

TAYLOR, R.J.F. "An Unusual Record of Three Species of Whale Being Restricted to Pools in Antarctic Sea Ice." *Proceedings*, Zoological Society of London, Vol. 129, 1957, pp. 325-332. Rare opportunity for studying living Antarctic whales in oceanarium conditions. Orcas stuck with many baleen whales for months showed "lack of ferocity" toward other whales and toward scientists who hit them on their snouts with ski poles. Good photographic documentation.

THOMAS, J.A., S. LEATHERWOOD, W.E. EVANS, J.R. JEHL JR. AND F.T. AWBREY. "Ross Sea Killer Whale (*Orcinus orca*) Distribution, Behavior, Color Pattern and Vocalizations." *Antarctic Journal of the United States*, Vol. 16, No. 5, 1981, pp. 157-158.

TILLEY, K. "Beaten by Killer Whales." *The Mercury* (Hobart, Tasmania), Oct. 10, 1979, p. 1. Orcas robbing Tasmanian trevalla fishermen of their catch.

TOMLIN, A.G. "O povedenii i zvukovoi signalatsii kitoobraznykh." *Trudy Instituta Okeanologii Akad Nauk SSSR*, Vol. 18, 1955, pp. 28-47. Translated by A. De-Vreeze and D.E. Sergeant. On the behaviour and sonic signalling of whales. Fisheries Research Board of Canada. Translation Series No. 377, Montreal, pp. 1-41. General whale behaviour and sonic signalling: probable evolutionary development.

TOMLIN, A.G. *Zveri SSSR i prilezhashchikh stran. Kitoobraznye*. Moskva: Izdatel'stvo Akademi Nauk SSSR, Vol. 9, 1957, pp. 643-667. Translated by Israel Program for Scientific Translations, *Mammals of the U.S.S.R. and Adjacent Countries. Cetacea*, Vol. 9, Jerusalem, 1967, pp. 605-626. Russian scientist's detailed notes on physical appearance, measurements, teeth, geographical distribution, feeding, social behaviour and whaling of orcas.

Tsitika Planning Committee. *Tsitika Watershed Integrated Resource Plan*. Summary Report. Vol. II. Province of B.C. Ministry of Forests, Victoria, 1978, pp. 1-52. The official plan to log the Tsitika River Valley on Vancouver Island.

ULMER, F.A. "Notes on a Killer Whale (*Grampus orca*) From the Coast of New Jersey." *Notulae Naturae*, Vol. 83, 1941, pp. 1-5.

"Um háhyrningsveidar á vegum Sædýrasafnsins." *Sædýrasafnid* (Box 224, Hafnarfirdi, Iceland), May 1979, pp. 27-31. Capture of Icelandic killer whales by local aquarium Sædýrasafnid for sale to world market; 14 black-and-white photographs.

VANCOUVER, G. *Voyage of Discovery to the North Pacific Ocean and Round the World* (J. Vancouver, ed.). Vol. 1. London: G.G. and J. Robinson, 1978. Facsim. reprint, 1967. Amsterdam Israel Bibliotera Australiana, pp. 329, 336-341.

VOISIN, J.F. "Notes on the Behaviour of the Killer Whale, *Orcinus orca* (L.)." *Norwegian Journal of Zoology*, Vol. 20, 1972, pp. 93-96. Feeding and playing behaviour of killer whales at Possession Island in the south Indian Ocean; playing with kelp; copulation (or attempt) witnessed.

VOISIN, J.F. "On the Behaviour of the Killer Whale, *Orcinus orca* (L.)." *Norwegian Journal of Zoology*, Vol. 24, 1976, pp. 69-71. Feeding and lack of playing behaviour noted among killer whales at Hog Island in the south Indian Ocean; orcas were mostly males that patrolled the coast, staying out from shore.

VON ZIEGESAR, O., G. ELLIS, C. MATKIN AND B. GOODWIN. "Repeated Sightings of Identifiable Killer Whales (*Orcinus orca*) in Prince William Sound, Alaska, 1977-1983." *Cetus*, Vol. 6, No. 2, 1986, pp. 9-13.

WADA, S. "Japanese Whaling and Whale Sighting in the North Pacific 1979 Season." *Report*, International Whaling Commission, Vol. 31, 1981, pp. 783-786.

WALKER, L.A., L. CORNELL, K.D. DAHL, N.M. CZEKALA, C.M. DARGEN, B. JOSEPH, A.J.W. HSUEH AND B.L. LASLEY. "Urinary Concentrations of Ovarian Steroid Hormone Metabolites and Bioactive in Killer Whales (*Orcinus orca*) During Ovarian Cycles and Pregnancy." *Biological Reproduction*, Vol. 39, No. 5, 1988, pp. 1013-1020. Reproductive hormone profiles from six captive killer whales studied over a two-year period. Based on serum and urine progesterone studies, the gestation period is about 17 months long.

WARHOL, P. "The Calf With No Name." *Whalewatcher*, Vol. 16, No. 4, 1982, pp. 16-18. Account of the fourth captive-orca birth, to Corky and Orky, and the 46-day life of the "calf with no name."

WATSON, E. "Maritime Mystery." *Seattle Post-Intelligencer*, Nov. 24, 1970, Sec. 2, p. 13. Gangster-type killing of newborn or fetal orcas near site of aquarium capture in Puget Sound.

WELLINGS, C.E. "The Killer Whales of Twofold Bay, N.S.W., Australia, *Grampus orca*." *The Australian Zoologist*, Vol. 10, Pt. 3, 1944, pp. 291-293. Whaler's account of symbiotic relationship between whalers and killer whales.

WELLINGS, H.P. "The Brothers Imlay." *Royal Australian Historical Society: Journal and Proceedings*, Vol. 17, Pt. 4, 1931, pp. 209-214. Background of Twofold Bay whaling by brother of one of the whalers.

WELLINGS, H.P. *Benjamin Boyd in Australia (1842-1849) Shipping Magnate, Merchant, Banker, Pastoralist and Station Owner, Member of the Legislative Council, Town Planner, Whaler*. Sydney: D.S. Ford, 1936. Background of Twofold Bay whaling by brother of one of the whalers.

WELLINGS, H.P. *Shore Whaling at Twofold Bay: Assisted by the Renowned Killer Whales*. Printed at the office of *The Magnet-Voice* (Eden, Australia), 1964, pp. 1-15. Account of symbiotic relationship between whalers and killer whales by brother of one of the whalers.

"Whale's Victim Bears No Grudge." *The Vancouver Sun*, May 5, 1978, p. A-12. Report of the near drowning of Marineland (Calif.) trainer by Orky.

"Whale Talk: Song and Dialect." *Science News*, Vol. 117, No. 2, Jan. 12, 1980, p. 21. Short report about John Ford's study of orca dialects off B.C. coast. See also Ford, J.K.B.

"Whaling at Twofold Bay." *The Illustrated Sydney News*, Sept. 30, 1871, pp. 160, 162. Contemporary account of whaling at Twofold Bay. See also Dakin, W.J.; Mead, T.; Wellings, C.E.; Wellings, H.P.

WENZEL, F. AND R. SEARS. "A Note on Killer Whales in the Gulf of St. Lawrence, Including an Account of an Attack on a Minke Whale." *Rit Fiskideildar*, Vol. 11, 1988, pp. 202-204.

WHITE, D. "Let's Not Lose Our Remaining Killer Whales." *The Vancouver Sun*, April 12, 1975, p. 6. Discussion of killer whale captures in the Northwest.

WHITE, D., N. CAMERON, P. SPONG AND J. BRADFORD. "Visual Acuity in the Killer Whale (*Orcinus orca*)." *Experimental Neurology*, Vol. 32, 1971, pp. 230-236. Study at Vancouver Aquarium showed that an orca could see about as well underwater as a cat in air.

WHITE, D., P. SPONG, N. CAMERON AND J. BRADFORD. "Visual Discrimination Learning in the Killer Whale (*Orcinus orca*)." *Behavior Research Methods and Instrumentation*, Vol. 3, 1971, pp. 187-188.

WHITEHEAD, H. AND C. GLASS. "Orcas (killer whales) Attack Humpback Whales." *Journal of Mammalogy*, Vol. 66, No. 1, 1985, pp. 183-185.

WILSON, J.P.F. AND T.J. PITCHER. "Feeding and Behaviour of a Killer Whale, *Orcinus orca*, in the Foyle Estuary, Ireland." *Irish Naturalists' Journal*, Vol. 19, No. 10, 1979, pp. 352-354.

WOOD, F.G. *Marine Mammals and Man: The Navy's Porpoises and Sea Lions*. Washington, New York: Robert Luce, Inc., 1973, pp. 1-264. Detailed guide to the United States Navy's unclassified work with marine mammals; good annotated bibliography. Written by a Navy senior scientist, a former curator of the original Marineland in Florida.

WÜRSIG, B. AND M. WÜRSIG. "Day and Night of the Dolphin." *Natural History*, Vol. 88, No. 3, March 1979, pp. 60-67. Social behaviour of dusky dolphins of Patagonia, South America, with mention of killer whale predation.

YABLOKOV, A.V., V.M. BEL'KOVICH AND V.I. BORISOV. *Whales and Dolphins*. Arlington, Va.: Joint Publications Research Service, 1974 (distr. by NTIS, National Technical Information Service, U.S. Dept. of Commerce, Springfield, Va.), Part I, JPRS-62150-1, pp. 1-244. Part II, JPRS-62150-2, pp. 245-402. Russian scientists report on many aspects of whale behaviour and biology.

YUKHOV, V.L., E.K. VINOGRADOVA AND L.P. MEDVEDEV. "Ob'ekty pitaniya kosatok (*Orcinus orca* L.) v Antarktike i sopredel'nykh vodakh." *Morskie mlekopitayushchie. Chast'2.* ("The Diet of Killer Whales in the Antarctic and Adjacent Waters." *Marine Mammals, Part 2.*) Kiev: Naukova dumka, 1975, pp. 183-185. Whales and dolphins in orca-stomach-study examinations by Russian scientists.

ZENKOVICH, B.A. "O kosatke ili kite ubiitse, *Grampus orca* Lin." ("On the Grampus or Killer Whale, *Grampus orca* Lin.") *Priroda* (4), 1938, pp. 109-112. Orcas feeding together with fin whales on herring schools. Orcas attacking walruses; orca-stomach studies show young walruses and bearded seals.

ZENKOVICH. B.A. *Vokrug sveta za kitami.* (Round the World After Whales.) Moskva: Izdatel'stvo Geografichceskoi Literatury, 1954, pp. 1-408. Parts of grey whale found in orca stomach from western Bering Sea.

INDEX